FamilyFun

VACATION GUIDE

Southwest

By Kathryn Hopper,
and the experts at **FamilyFun** Magazine

EDITIONS
New York

FamilyFun
VACATION GUIDE
Southwest

Editorial Director
Lois Spritzer

Design & Production
IMPRESS, INC.
Hans Teensma
Pam Glaven
Katie Craig
Lisa Newman
James McDonald
Katie Winger

Disney Editions and *FamilyFun*

Book Editors
Alexandra Kennedy
Wendy Lefkon
Lisa Stiepock

Research Editor
Beth Honeyman

Contributing Editors
Jon Adolph
Rani Arbo
Duryan Bhagat
Jodi Butler
Jaqueline Cappuccio
Deanna Cook
Tony Cuen
Ann Hallock
Jessica Hinds
Martha Jenkins
Heather Johnson
Rich Mintzer
Jody Revenson
David Sokol
Deborah Way

Copy Editors
Diane Hodges
Jenny Langsam
Monica Mayper
Jill Newman

Editorial Assistants
Laura Gomes
Jean Graham

Production
Janet Castiglione
Sue Cole

This book is dedicated to our *FamilyFun* readers, and contributors, and to traveling families everywhere.

Kathryn Hopper is the mother of four boys—James, Henry, Will, and Andrew—who lives in Southlake, Texas. Her work has appeared in *FamilyFun* magazine, as well as *The New York Times*, *The Washington Post*, *Dallas Morning News*, and *Fort Worth Star-Telegram*.

Illustrations by **Kandy Littrell**

IMAX® IMAX Corporation

NASCAR is a trademark of the National Association for Stock Car Auto Racing, Inc. All rights reserved.

SeaWorld is a registered trademark of the Busch Entertainment Corporation, a division of Anheuser-Busch Companies, Inc.

For information, address Disney Editions, 114 Fifth Avenue, New York, New York 10011-5690.

Printed in the United States of America

First Edition
1 3 5 7 9 10 8 6 4 2
Library of Congress Catalog Card Number 2001017482
ISBN 0-7868-5300-X

Visit www.disneyeditions.com

CONTENTS

Dear Parents,

A FRIEND OF MINE—a dad—said something recently that rang true to me. "A great childhood," he said, thinking aloud, "is really made up of a thousand small good moments." His comment prompted me to step back and take stock of what those moments might be for my own two young sons. What will be their happiest memories? Topping the list in my mind are the simple but extraordinary pleasures we've had traveling together: the hermit crabs we discovered at a Maine beach, the afternoon spent playing catch on the Mall in Washington, the thrill of a first flight, a first train ride, a first hike to a mountaintop.

As parents, we all work incredibly hard to find the time and money to take our children on vacation. We want to show them the remarkably varied American landscape and introduce them to its many cultures and histories. We want to get away from jobs, homework, and household chores long enough to enjoy one another's company uninterrupted. And most of all, we want to have fun.

The editors at *FamilyFun* and I take great pride in this book and others in the series. They are a culmination of ten years' worth of gathering for our readers' the best vacation advice out there. Traveling with children is an art—and our charge is to help with your decisions every step of the way so that you can make the most of every minute of your time away.

Alexandra Kennedy

Alexandra Kennedy
Editorial Director

How to Use This Guide

WELCOME TO THE world of *FamilyFun* magazine's new travel guide series. In our effort to present you with the finest in vacation options, we called on the best experts we know: our hardy group of writers. All are parents who travel with their kids, and all live and work in the area(s) about which they're writing. These are the people who can tell you where to find that teddy bear shop that isn't in the main mall, which restaurant has the best milk shakes, which museum will invite your toddler to roll up his sleeves and create art, and which theme park will give your preteen a good return on the price of admission. With all their recommendations comes the endorsement of their kids: our traveling children have been our best critics.

Since all of the guides in this series cover more than one state, we have divided them into easy-to-use sections. So here's a guide to the guide.

READY, SET, GO!—is a mini-encyclopedia of handy facts, practical advice, what to do/where to go/when to go/how to travel: in other words, all you need to know about planning a successful family vacation.

INTRODUCTION—will give you an overview of the states being covered in this guidebook. Read it—it will whet your appetite, and perhaps give you some new ideas for family activities.

CHAPTERS—States and chapters are presented in geographical order. Chapters represent the regions we think your family will enjoy most. We have omitted those places that we feel would not be family-friendly or are too expensive for what you get in return. We also make note of attractions that appeal only to a certain age range.

FamilyFun has given each entry a rating—stars (★) that range from one to four—to guide you to our favorites. Remember, however, that this guidebook contains nothing that we do not recommend—it's just that we liked some things better than others. We've also assigned a dollar sign rating (**$**)—in high season for a family of four, also ranging from one to four. Check the price range at the start of each chapter as the key changes. We hope that this will help you to decide whether a hotel, restaurant, or attraction will fit in with your budget.

Typically, we start each chapter with an introduction, followed by *FamilyFun*'s Must-See List of up to ten things to try to do while visiting. We've divided attractions into two categories: "Cultural Attractions" (museums, historic sites, and so on) and "Just for Fun" (water parks, zoos, aquariums, roller coasters, and the like). Wherever possible, we've included Website information.

What more can we say? We hope that this guide helps you to fashion the best possible vacation for your family, one that is a pleasure in the planning, a delight in the doing, and one that will leave every member of your clan with memories that will last a lifetime—or at least until ninth grade.

Bon Voyage!

Southwest

PLANNING A TRIP to one or more Southwestern states—Arizona, Colorado, Nevada, New Mexico, Texas, and Utah—can seem as daunting as climbing Pikes Peak or trekking down the Grand Canyon. True, there's lots for your family to see and do, but we've tried to make your planning easier. This book highlights ways to pack many of the region's vast vistas into a week, weekend, or even a quick day trip, and describes family-friendly resorts that can thrill toddlers and teens.

Most families come here for the incredible natural beauty—the snowcapped mountaintops of Rocky Mountain National Park, and wind-carved sculptures of Utah's Bryce Canyon. Sure, the Grand Canyon is a must-see, but your kids will also love sliding down the dunes of White Sands National Monument and playing house in the ancient Anasazi ruins at Mesa Verde National Park. The photo ops are good, too—snap your child grinning, with toes planted in four different states at Four Corners, for instance.

You'll find great active family vacations in the Southwest, too—

from hiking in the summer to skiing in the winter. Water lovers can go tubing down the Guadalupe River through the Texas Hill Country. In winter, take a break from the slopes and hitch a ride on a horse-drawn sleigh or hop aboard a dogsled.

Some of the nation's top theme parks are here: you'll find plunging roller coasters to thrill your preteen and carousels and bumper cars that will please any preschooler. You can also cool down and splash around in any of the region's huge water parks that spout up even in the deserts of Arizona. The Southwest is also home to one of the most distinctive—if not the most cultural with a capital C—attractions around: Las Vegas. We'll give you some tips for finding the kid-friendly activities within this adult-oriented sin city.

Some of the best museums in the nation are in the Southwest—you can easily spend a day taking in the exhibits, big-screen movies, and planetariums. Living history ranches and farms give kids hands-on lessons from costumed pioneers who demonstrate the arts of churning butter and shoeing a horse.

When you're ready to bunk down for the night, you'll find plenty of family-oriented lodging choices, from plush resorts to cozy cabins. Many of the area's top resorts and lodges offer supervised children's activities where kids can experiment with Native American sandpainting or take a nature hike. If you prefer to sleep under the stars, you'll find campsites with some of nature's top amenities, including bubbling streams and natural springs. Or consider spending time at a dude ranch, where you can hit the trail on horseback and enjoy breakfast cooked over a campfire.

The local food specialties are as distinctive as the landscape. When it's time to rustle up some grub, your family can sample the Southwest's unique culinary treats—from *kolaches* in Texas to sopaipillas in New Mexico.

The American Southwest's magic has lured artists, adventurers, and visitors for generations. Your family is sure to make special memories in the region's red-rock deserts, soaring mountaintops, and gentle plains. So get ready for lots of wide-open spaces—and wide grins, too.

Let the family fun begin!

**Pack up and get going.
You're on vacation!**

Ready, Set, Go!

Just ten years ago, *FamilyFun* was a fledgling magazine, and the family travel "industry"—now a booming, $100 billion annual trade—was as much a newcomer as we were. In a way, you could say we have grown up together.

FamilyFun was one of the first national magazines to actively research and publicize travel ideas for families with school-age children (a fun job, we must add). Over the last decade, as the numbers of traveling families increased, so did the business of family travel. These days, there are more resources, opportunities, and means for the vacationing family than ever before —which, in turn, gives *FamilyFun* the chance to be an even more valuable clearinghouse of ideas for you.

Through the years, we have been privileged to work with veteran travel writers and editors who have gone around the world with their kids. We've also taken time to listen to our readers—insightful, creative families from across the United States—and to note (and sometimes publish) their stories, recommendations, and tips on traveling as a family. A combination of those two wisdoms is what awaits you on the following pages.

Although it may not be readily apparent, a lot of trial and error underlies these pages. Each destination, before it reaches this book, undergoes a rigorous investigation, and not all make the grade.

We know that family vacations are a big investment, and we know that's why you're here. You're hoping to sidestep the pitfalls of experimentation and to locate destinations that will be a real hit with your family. Congratulations! You've come to the right place.

FIRST STEPS

At the outset, organizing a family vacation can seem as daunting as landing a probe on Mars. Better to stay home and watch the Discovery Channel, you think—maybe toast a few marshmallows in the fireplace.

The truth is that planning an adventurous vacation can be fun, especially if you prepare for it in advance and involve your kids. The onerous part is remembering all the things you have to think about.

That's where we come in. This introductory chapter covers family travel from A to Z, from deciding where to go, to getting there and making the most of your vacation. Some of this may seem like old news to you, but we want to make sure you don't forget a thing.

How much do we spend?

Chances are, you already know approximately what you have to spend on a vacation—and you've already got a modus operandi when it comes to money matters. Maybe you're a family that carefully figures a budget, then finds a vacation to fit it. Or maybe you're the type to set your heart on a once-in-a-lifetime trip, then scrimp and save until you can make it happen.

For information on how to research and book **travel plans on the Web**, turn to page 31.

Determine the type of trip you will take. Before you even start your planning, take a moment to consider: what kind of trip are you taking? Are you splurging on a dream vacation, or conserving on a semi-annual getaway? What aspects of this trip are most important to you?

Budget carefully. Once you know what those broad parameters are, the next step is to think through your vacation budget in detail—if not at the outset of planning, then at an opportune point along the way. When you know what you have to spend, you'll make quicker and less stressful decisions en route and you'll be able to pay the bills without a grimace once you get home. You'll find lots of budget-saving tips in this introductory chapter.

When can we go?

Scheduling your vacation well can make a big difference in everyone's experience of the trip.

Consider each individual. Most likely, tight school and work schedules will decide when you travel — but if possible, aim for a time slot that allows everyone to relax. For instance, an action-packed road trip sounds exciting, but it might be just the wrong medicine for a parent who's squeezing it into a packed work schedule. End-of-summer trips may be tough for kids with back-to-school anxieties, and midyear trips that snatch kids from school sometimes cause more trouble than they're worth.

Where do we go?

In this book (and the others in this travel series), you'll find scores of winning family destinations. By all means, though, don't stop here. Doing your own research is half the fun, and these days, you have a wealth of resources at your disposal.

Make a list of destinations. What hot spots intrigue your clan? What adventures would you like to try? Draw up a big list, and don't worry about coming up with too many ideas—you can return to this list year after year. Here are a few trails you can follow: relatives, friends, and coworkers (who love to report on their own successful trips), a professional travel agent, local chambers of commerce and state tourism boards, and magazines, the Internet (see page 34 for some good family travel sites), and local hotels and outfitters in the geographic areas you're interested in.

Evaluate your family. A good vacation has to accommodate *everyone* in the family, no matter what their ages, limitations, or interests. While no destination will make everyone happy all the time, you should search vigilantly for those that offer a niche for each family member.

Involve your kids. The more involved your kids are in planning—especially during these early, brainstorming stages — the more likely they are to work to make the trip a success.

Experiment wisely. While experimentation can add spice to a trip, too much may overwhelm your kids (and you). If your child has her heart set on horseback riding, for example, make sure she tries it out at home before you put down a deposit on a dude ranch vacation.

Check the season. Be informed about travel conditions for the time of your trip and make sure you're not heading for trouble (hurricane season in Florida, for example, or black-fly season in the Adirondacks). This is especially important if you're cashing in on off-season deals.

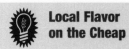

Local Flavor on the Cheap

Don't wait till you arrive at your destination to investigate opportunities for local fun—research a few in advance:

♦ Check out a regional festival or agricultural fair. For fairs in the western U.S., visit www.fairs net.org and for festivals nationwide, visit www.festivals.com

♦ Explore a college campus (which may offer green space, bike paths, museums, observatories, and more). To find a list, go to a general Internet search engine like www.yahoo.com, click on education, and search for colleges by state. Then, call the school's information office for a map and a roster of special events.

♦ Visit a farmers' market. For a list of markets around the U.S., log on to www.ams.usda.gov/farmersmarkets/

♦ Take in an air show (they're usually free at military bases). For a list of air shows by region, see www.airshows.org

♦ Find a local nature center or Audubon preserve.

Schedule appropriately. How much time do you need to give this particular destination its due? You don't want to feel like you're rushing through things—but neither do you want to run out of activities that will interest your kids.

Should we have an itinerary?

Drawing up a travel itinerary, whether it's rough or detailed, will ensure that you travel wisely, hit the hot spots, and give everyone in your group a say in what you'll see.

Include something for everyone. No doubt, each member of your family will have his or her own list of must-sees. If a unanimous vote on itinerary stops is out of the question, ask everyone to write down top choices, then create a schedule that guarantees each person at least one or two favorites. If your children span a wide age range, remind them that there will be some patient standing by while siblings (and Mom and Dad) have their moments in the sun.

Involve the kids (again). Once you've got the basic stops down, kids can help research destinations, plan driving routes, locate pit stops, and help plan rainy-day alternatives.

Make a plan, then break it. Don't let your preplanned schedule get in the way of spontaneous delights. What if your kids want to ride that water slide for an extra three hours? One fun moment in hand is usually worth at least two on the itinerary.

Beat the crowds. Remember to head for popular attractions first thing in the morning or in late afternoon and early evening. Save the middle of the day for poolside fun or activities that take you off the beaten path and away from crowds.

Travel in tune with your family's natural rhythms. Preschoolers tend to be at their best early in the day—a good time for structured activities. Many teens, on the other hand, are pictures of grogginess before noon. Adapt your itinerary to suit ingrained family habits—including your usual meal and nap times—and you'll have smoother sailing. When visiting very popular destinations, take the time to find out in advance when their slowest periods are.

Train Your Own Tour Guides

Guided tours at historic sites and museums are often a snooze (or too sophisticated) for young kids. Instead, create your own tour—have each family member study up on a different attraction by writing or calling for brochures, surfing the Web, and visiting the library. Then, when you arrive, you'll have an expert guide on board.

GETTING THERE

As we all know, the experience of taking kids from point A to point B runs the gamut from uneventful (read: bliss) to miserable. Knowing the ins and outs of your travel options will speed you toward a sane trip.

FamilyFun **READER'S TIP** -

Hire Some Junior Travel Agents

When we were planning a summer trip to Louisiana, I overheard one of my kids tell another that they were going to have to do everything Mom and Dad wanted to do. That's when I decided that each family member would get to plan a full day of our trip. I purchased a regional travel guide and told everyone they had $200 for one day's activities, meals, and accommodations, so they would have to budget (a useful exercise for my 10- and 12-year olds). Every night, any money left over from that day was given to the next planner. I am proud to say that everything went well, and the kids proclaimed it the best vacation ever!

Cindy Long, Spring, Texas

By Plane

PROS: It's fast. And if you land a good deal, air travel can actually be affordable.

CONS: If you don't land a good deal, air travel can be prohibitively expensive, especially for a big family. Other pitfalls include flight delays, mounting claustrophobia on long trips, and strict baggage restrictions.

Look for deals. Traveling in off-peak season and taking off-peak flights (very early or very late in the day) may save you money; flying midweek and staying over Saturday night almost always will. You may also wish to research deals at different airports (for instance, T. F. Green Airport in Providence, Rhode Island, often offers cheaper fares than Boston's Logan Airport 45 minutes away). Also, remember that most sale tickets have a cutoff date—you'll have to book two, three, or four weeks ahead of your departure date to get the deal.

Consider using an agent. Booking your own airline reservations on the Web is a cinch these days (see pages 35 and 36), but there are still advantages to using a professional travel agent who knows your family's needs. First of all, for the $10 or $20 per-ticket surcharge you may pay, you'll save Web-surfing time, and you'll be spared the stress of baby-sitting the fickle airline market. Also,

an agent may be able to suggest a Plan B (such as using a smaller airport to get a better deal)—something the Web search engines can't do for you. Try to get a good agent recommendation through friends, coworkers, or relatives; if you need further help, the American Society of Travel Agents (703-739-2782, www.astanet.com) provides a list of members, as well as brochures on travel topics (including one on how to choose a travel agent).

By Car

PROS: Road trips are the cheapest way to get from here to there, and they can also be real adventures. In addition, the car is familiar territory for your kids, so they'll feel right at home (for better or worse) during the trip. And, of course, a road trip affords you priceless flexibility.

CONS: You're in for major advance planning, from making sure your car is in good condition to scheduling regular rest stops and having a dependable cache of road snacks, games, and other diversions. Even with those, the hours of close confinement may quickly erode your family's wanderlust.

Get a good map. If you belong to AAA, request a free "TripTik" map. Otherwise, you can map your route and download printed driving directions on Websites like www.map quest.com, www.freetrip.com, and www.mapsonus.com

Flying with Kids

WHEN YOU BOOK

♦ Try first for a nonstop flight. If that's not available, fly "direct," which means you'll stop at least once but won't switch planes.

♦ Book flights that depart early in the day, if possible. If your flight is delayed, you—and the airline—will have time to make other arrangements.

♦ Specify your ticketing preferences, whether paper or electronic.

♦ Check to see if a meal will be served in flight. If so, order meals your kids like. Many airlines offer kids' meals or a vegetarian choice that may be pasta. If not, plan accordingly.

♦ Ask for the seats you'd like, whether they're a window, an aisle, or the bulkhead for legroom.

PACKING TIPS

♦ Stuff your carry-on for every contingency. Pack all medications, extra clothes for little kids, diapers, baby food, formula, wet wipes, and snacks (they'll also help kids swallow to relieve ear pressure).

♦ Have each child carry a small backpack with travel toys, a light sweatshirt, and a pair of socks for the flight.

ON THE DAY OF YOUR TRIP

♦ Call ahead to check for delays.

♦ Have all photo IDs within easy reach (not necessary for kids under age 18 traveling with their parents on domestic flights; on most international flights, even infants will need a passport).

♦ If you have heavy bags, check your luggage first and then park.

♦ If you are early for the flight or run into long delays, don't go straight to the gate. Instead, meander through the airport's diversions: windows onto the runways, children's play areas (many major airports now have these), Web access computers, and, of course, stores where kids can find a treat to tide them over.

♦ Carry on extra bottled water. It's easy to get dehydrated on a plane, and the drink service may be slow in reaching you.

ON THE PLANE

♦ Ask if your child can view the cockpit (the best time may be after the flight is over).

♦ Secure pillows and blankets for family members who may want to nap.

♦ Take breaks from sitting; occasionally walk the aisles and switch seats.

FLYING FEARS

Most children are fearless fliers—and those who are afraid often can trace their concerns to adults who unintentionally transmit their own fears. If you need help answering your children's questions, you can ask them on-line at www.wic-kid.com

FamilyFun TIP

Bookworms

When you're on the road, there's nothing like a good story to pass the time. For night drives, audio books can be a lifesaver. Try borrowing or renting one from your local library, or visit www.storytapes.com, the Website for Village StoryTapes (800-238-8273). You can either rent or purchase from their excellent selection; three- to four-week tape rentals cost $6 to $17 (for *Harry Potter IV*); to buy, tapes cost $12 to $60.

Be prepared for emergencies, large and small. It goes without saying that your car should be in prime working order before you depart. You should have supplies for road emergencies on board, as well as a good first-aid kit (see page 33 for a list of what to include), and, if you have one, bring a cell phone.

Keep things orderly. We all know what happens to our cars within minutes of the time the kids buckle in; on long road trips, expect the chaos to rise by a factor of ten. In an effort to keep things in check, bring containers to hold trash and toys; pack the children's luggage so it's easiest to reach; divvy up the back-seat space so kids know where their boundaries are; and go over basic behavior rules before you leave.

Drive in time with your family's rhythm. Night driving offers less traffic and a chance that young kids will sleep (you can let them ride in their pj's). Alternatively, an early start may avoid late-afternoon, kid-cranky hours. When possible, go with your family's natural flow.

Help prevent motion sickness. Have frequent, small meals during your trip (symptoms are more likely to occur on an empty stomach). Over-the-counter medications such as Dramamine, as well as ginger ale, ginger tea, or ginger candy also can help, but once symptoms begin, it's usually too late for oral medications. Make sure the car is well ventilated, and have sickness-prone travelers take a window seat, which offers

WEATHER WATCHERS Before you leave, assign forecaster duties to one of your kids. Using the Internet, he or she can research and predict the type of weather you'll encounter (and advise everyone on what to pack). Try www.weather.com

fresh air and a view of the road. If a child feels nauseated, have him look straight in front of the car or focus attention on the horizon. If your child becomes carsick, stop the car to give him a break from the motion; having him lie down with his head perfectly still also may help.

By Train

PROS: First of all, trains are just plain cool, for kids and adults alike. Second, there's room to explore, and everyone can kick back and enjoy the view. And third, if you are headed to a major metropolitan area with a good public transit system, you'll avoid the expenses and hassles of city driving and parking.

CONS: There's only one national passenger rail service, Amtrak, and at press time its future was in question. Also, Amtrak's limited network may not be convenient to your destination (ask about connector trains and rental car agencies when you call). In some regions of the United States, Amtrak's city-to-city service rivals car, bus, and plane travel for efficiency; on cross-country hauls, this is not the case. If you're investing in a long train trip, you're in it more for the experience of train travel.

Inquire about special deals. Children ages 2 to 15 usually ride for half fare when accompanied by an adult who pays full fare. Each adult can bring two children at this discounted rate. Amtrak also offers

A Road Trip Survival Kit

A BAG OF TRICKS

♦ mini-puzzles with a backboard
♦ video games, cassette or CD player (with headphones)
♦ paper, pens, pencils, markers
♦ travel versions of board games
♦ stuffed animals
♦ Etch A Sketch
♦ colored pipe cleaners
♦ deck of cards
♦ cookie sheet (a good lap tray)
♦ word puzzles
♦ small action figures or dolls
♦ stickers
♦ Trivial Pursuit cards
♦ cotton string (for cat's cradle games)

A COOLER OF SNACKS

Bring lots of drinks and a cache of snacks like granola bars, trail mix, grapes, carrot sticks, roll-up sandwiches, fruit leather, and popcorn.

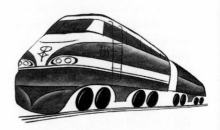

Keeping 'Em Busy: 60-Second Solutions

SQUABBLE SOLUTIONS

Give your kids 25 cents in pennies at the start of the trip. Each time they fight or whine, charge them a penny. Offer a reward, such as doubling or tripling their money, if they haven't lost a cent during the ride.

WAGER AND WIN

Kids are natural wagerers—they love to bet how much, how long, how far, how many. If you're in a bind for a moment's entertainment, ask them to guess the number of French fries on your plate or to estimate how many steps it will take to walk to your airport gate. The key here is to be able to verify the guesses—you'll need to wear a watch with a second hand and carry a calculator.

CREATIVE COMPETITION

Kids love challenges. Need to get rid of the trash in the car? See who can smash the trash into the smallest paper ball, then toss it in the wastepaper bag. Want quiet time? Hold a five-minute silence contest. Need to get through errands in a hurry? Challenge your kids to a race against time. You may feel that your motives are transparent, but your kids won't care.

special seasonal rates, other family deals, and Web-only deals.

How to find them. Amtrak's Website, www.amtrak.com, provides information on fares, schedules, reservations, routes and services, station locations, and special offers. You can also call Amtrak at 800-872-7245 for information and reservations. When you book, ask if there is a full-service dining car and ask whether you can reserve a block of seats for your family.

Consider a sleeper car. For overnight trips, sleep-in-your-seat fares are the cheapest, but first-class bedrooms are much more comfortable.

Arrive early. If your train seats are unassigned, get to the station early for the best chance of eveyone's sitting together. You can even have one parent run ahead to grab a group of seats while the other shepherds children and luggage to the platform.

By RV

PROS: It's a home away from home, which means you can eat, sleep, and use the indoor plumbing (as everyone will agree, one of the finest features of RV travel) whenever you want. In an RV, you are free to explore with independence, self-sufficiency, and freedom—three assets that can be priceless when you're traveling with kids.

CONS: It's a home away from home,

FamilyFun **READER'S TIP** --

Patchwork Pillows

I am 10 years old, and every year my family goes camping. I collect patches from each place we visit, including the Grand Canyon, Yellowstone and Yosemite National Parks; San Francisco; Las Vegas; and, most recently, Santa Fe, New Mexico. I put all the patches I've collected during each year on separate pillows. I keep the pillows on my bed to remind me of our great trips.

Alex Smythe, Tucson, Arizona

which means you face dishes, cooking, and maintenance (generators, water pumps, waste tanks, and the engine, for starters). In addition, RV rentals are not cheap, although they can compare favorably to the cost of a week's lodging, food, and travel (especially for big families).

What they cost. Expect to pay rental fees between $500 and $1,500 per week, depending on location, model, and time of year you'll be traveling, and the luxury factor (RVs can get pretty posh). Gasoline costs will be high, but you'll save considerably on food and accommodations (campground fees average $20 to $40 per night).

How to find them. Rental information is available through auto clubs and through Go RVing (888-GO-RVING, ask for the free video and literature; www.gorving.com). Cruise America (800- 327-7799) offers 150 rental centers across the United States and Canada. The RV America Website (www.rvamerica.

com) has listings of dealers, clubs, and resources.

Be a savvy renter. Choose an RV that's big enough for your family, but know that many campgrounds only permit vehicles less than 30 feet long. Before you rent, ask how many people fit comfortably in the RV, what powers the appliances, how much insurance is required, and whether supplies such as linens and kitchen utensils are included in the rental price. Get a demonstration of how to work everything in the vehicle, read the manual, practice a little ahead of time, and you'll be ready to take the plunge.

By Bus

PROS: The major advantages of bus travel are that it's cheap, that it spares you the stress of driving, and that tickets usually can be purchased on the day of your trip, at the station. **CONS:** Unfortunately, traveling by bus often takes longer than by car. What's more, bus travel offers little opportunity for diversion for your

Thinking of Skipping School?

If you are, then according to a recent Travel Industry Association of America poll, you're in lots of company. The TIA survey found that one in five parents allows a child to miss school to gain travel experience (of these, 72 percent, however, missed only one or two days). If you're planning to play hooky on vacation, start by keeping the school well informed of your plans. Discuss with the teachers what work your kids will have to keep up with, and create a regular routine during your vacation when they can do so. To help kids stay in touch with their classmates and to broaden their learning experience, establish a way for them to share their travel adventures with the class, either while they're en route (by e-mailing or posting letters) or once they return to school.

children. And since you're sitting close to other passengers, many lively family games are off-limits (some buses offer a TV movie; ask when you call).

How to find them: Greyhound Lines (800-229-9424) offers service across the United States. In the Northeast, between New Hampshire and Washington, D.C., Peter Pan Bus Lines (800-237-8747) is another option. Both have Websites, www.greyhound.com and www.peterpanbus.com, complete with fare and schedule information. To locate smaller local or regional bus lines, try the local Yellow Pages or the department of travel and tourism in the region you'll be visiting.

By Rental Car

PROS: This isn't exactly a pro, but if you've flown or trained into an area without a safe and dependable public transport system, you'll need a rental to get around. Plus, a rental car is cost-efficient for families (as opposed to solo travelers). Best of all, you won't be putting miles on your own car—and if you rent a minivan, you can have drink-cup slots and elbowroom for every single kid.

CONS: None, really, save the expense and a list of rental and insurance decisions that can be as daunting as a Starbucks menu.

How to find them: Your travel agent can book a car for you, but if you want to do it yourself, you'll find all the major agencies in the 800 directory.

Compare costs. Whether you shop on-line or over the phone, compare costs for as many companies as you can (no one company has the best deals in every city or state). In general, weeklong and weekend rentals are a better deal than per-day rentals. In your research, you may wish to inquire about companies' service records, especially if you're going with a local budget chain.

Ask about discounts. Membership in AAA or other associations, credit cards, entertainment book coupons, and package-deal reservations may net you bargains: ask about potential discounts when you make your reservation.

Ask about services and charges. Rental car companies put a lot of information in fine print. So, before you pay (and before you drive away), ask lots of questions. What are the mileage and one-way drop fees? Is there a fee for early or late car returns? Should you bring the car back with an empty gas tank or a full one to get the best refueling price? Does the company offer 24-hour breakdown service? Do the cars have air-conditioning, a jack, and a spare tire? Is there a fee for extra drivers (married couples are often exempt,

FamilyFun TIP

Compare Quotes

When you book a room at a major hotel chain, call both the hotel's local number as well as the toll-free reservation number; the rates you'll be quoted may differ.

but you should check). Are car seats available at no extra charge? (Even if the answer is yes, your own car seat may be cleaner, and, because it's familiar, more comfortable for your child.)

Pay only for the insurance you need. The car, and any damage to it, will be your responsibility for the duration of your trip. Before you purchase insurance from the rental agency, check to see whether your own auto or liability insurance provides adequate coverage. Some credit card agreements may also include rental protection; call the customer service

FamilyFun READER'S TIP

Tabletop Scrapbook

Here's a fun project my family has long enjoyed while traveling. After we have mapped out our vacation, my kids, and now grandchildren, use a laundry pen to draw our route on a cotton tablecloth. We pack up the cloth along with colored markers, and while on the road, family members take turns marking the name of towns and rivers and noting funny signs. When we stop for picnic lunches, we not only use the cloth but also continue adding drawings of sights we've seen and things we've done. After the trip is over, we have a memory-filled tablecloth to use for years to come.

Janet Askew, Adair, Iowa

number on the back of your card to inquire.

WHERE TO STAY

Where you tuck your kids in at night depends entirely on your family's traveling style and budget—and, of course, on what's available in the area to which you're traveling. There are so many options—hotels, motels, inns, cottages, cabins, condominiums, resorts, time-shares, campgrounds—it can be hard to know where to start.

Lists of local accommodations can be found through tourism boards, the Web, travel books, and the 800 numbers or published directories of major franchises. However, finding the places that really go the extra mile for families isn't easy. This book—and other family travel publications—will be your best bets, as will the time-tested recommendations of friends and acquaintances. Always, always ask your own questions as well: see our checklist on page 25 for some basics.

Hotels, Motels & Lodges

From generic chains, to mom-and-pop operations bursting with character, to ritzy palaces, this category really runs the gamut. If you don't have a dependable recommendation (from a friend, trusted travel agent, or guidebook like this one), you may wish to place your trust in the major chains (budget or no) where you at least know what you're getting.

How to find them: Most major chains can be found in the 800 directory (as well as on the Web) and can provide a list of property locations. Alternatively, you can contact regional travel bureaus or consult a national rating system, such as those in Mobil Travel Guides (available in bookstores or the on-line store at www.mobil.com) or the Automobile Association of America (call your local AAA office to order regional TourBook guides).

PICKY EATERS? If you have picky eaters in the family (or if you suspect a child may not enjoy the food at a certain restaurant), feed them ahead of time—and let them enjoy an appetizer or dessert during your meal.

Inns, B&Bs, and Farm Stays

These have traditionally been the domain of honeymooning couples and retirees. Increasingly, though, they are accommodating a growing family travel market. There are certainly gems out there for your discovery—but do your research rigorously (speak with the owner, if possible) to find out whether kids are *truly* welcome at the destination of your choice. The last thing you want to be doing on vacation is shushing your kids and shooing them away from pricey antiques. Look for inns and B&Bs attached to a working farm—these tend to be more kid-friendly, with animals to watch and feed and plenty of outdoor play space.

How to find them: Try travel magazines, regional chambers of commerce, and two excellent Websites, www.bedandbreakfeast.com and www.bbgetaways.com

Condos and Cottages

These are ideal if your group is staying put for the length of your vacation, since they offer room to spread out and cook your own meals. When you book, ask about amenities: does the condo come with linens, pots and pans, a television, phone, dishwasher, and washer/dryer? Are there extra tax and/or booking fees? If you rent directly from the owner, be even more rigorous in your questioning. Is there

WHAT TO ASK BEFORE YOU BOOK

1 ACCOMMODATIONS: What rooms (or condos or cabins) are available? How many beds are there and what size are they? Are the rooms nonsmoking? What amenities are included (laundry, phone, cable TV, refrigerator, balcony, coffee service, cots, cribs, minibar)? Are the rooms located in the main building? What specific views are available? Is there a charge for kids staying in the same room with parents? Are there family packages? Can guests upgrade rooms upon arrival?

2 DINING: Are there dining facilities on the property? If so, are there restrictions for kids? What are some menu items, and what does the average meal cost? Is there a kids' menu? Is there a complimentary breakfast offered? Are there snack and/or drink machines? If there are no dining facilities on-site, is there a family restaurant nearby?

3 RECREATION: What recreational facilities are available (game rooms, pool, tennis courts, equipment rental, and so on)? At what hours are they available? Are there additional charges for their use? Are there age or time restrictions for any recreation? What recreational options are available in the nearby community (movie theater, minigolf, bowling, and the like)?

a cancellation policy if the place is not up to your standards?

How to find them: The Internet has made it easy to connect potential renters with homeowners and rental brokers. Unfortunately, that means there are literally thousands of sites to sift through. Luckily, most sites offer very detailed information on properties, so you can actually make an informed decision on-line to pursue a place.

For starters, here are the Website addresses for a number of national and international vacation rental clearinghouses: www.eLeisure Link.com (888-801-8808); Barclay

----

Family Hostels

A CHEAP SLEEP

If you think hostels are the exclusive domain of students and backpackers, think again: many of the neatest have private family rooms that can be reserved in advance. Some also offer special programs, such as historic walking tours, natural history programs, and sports activities. Hostels in the Hostelling International/ American Youth Hostels system are as varied as their locations and include registered historic buildings, lighthouses, and a former dude ranch. For the latest edition of *Hostelling Experience North America*, call *202-783-6161* or visit www.hiayh.org

International Group (800-845-6636; www.bar clayweb.com); and 10,000 Vacation Rentals, Inc. (888-369-7245; www. 10kvacationrentals.com).

To rent directly from a property owner, try Vacation Rentals by Owner at www.vrbo.com. You also can locate condos and cottages by inquiring at local tourism bureaus, local realtors (especially for seaside properties), and major resorts, which often keep lists of rentals on property or nearby.

Campgrounds

These range from the extremely rustic—grassy knolls with fabulous views to the luxurious—complexes with video games, sports areas, and fax and modem hookups.

Depending on where and how you prefer to camp, you'll have your pick of sites in state or national parks, national forests, or private campgrounds. (See "Happy Campers," pages 38-39.)

When you book a site, inquire: What are the nightly fees? Does the campground accept reservations? If no, how early should you arrive in order to claim a site? Is there a pool or lake? Lifeguards? Equipment rentals? Laundry facilities, rest rooms, and hot showers? A grocery store nearby? Remember that campgrounds near major tourist attractions fill up early, so make reservations in advance (choice spots in some national parks, for example, fill up months ahead).

How to find them: In addition to the campgrounds recommended in this book, you can find lists of campgrounds on the Internet: check out About.com's camping section at www.camping.about.com, www.camping-usa.com, and the National Association of RV Parks & Campgrounds at www.gocampingamerica.com. For campgrounds in national parks, visit www.nps.gov and state. For a national directory of KOA campgrounds, visit www.koa kamp grounds.com

Resorts

A resort vacation is a big investment, and up-front research is essential to ensure you get your money's worth. When you are making inquiries, don't be shy about taking up the resort staff's time with questions. Be sure to grill them with the entire housing quiz on page 25. Ask, too, about programming for kids and families. If there is a children's pro-

> ## FamilyFun TIP
>
> ### Walk it through
>
> When you're booking a room or condo over the phone, ask the reservation specialist to "walk" you through the place, virtually, from the front door to the balcony view (if there is one!). They may think you're going overboard — but you'll really know what you're getting.

gram, what days and times does it run? Is it canceled if not enough kids sign up? What is the ratio of counselors to children? What are the age divisions? What activities does the program offer? What are the facilities? What, if any, is the additional cost? Are there games, programs, or organized recreation especially for families? Baby-sitting services? Assistance for kids who get sick? What are the terms for these? If the resort is "all-inclusive," find out

---

FamilyFun READER'S TIP

Invent a Travel Kit

When our family flies, I make travel kits for my two sons, Noah, 8, and Paul, 4. I fill old wipes boxes with a variety of treats: chocolate kisses, fruit snacks, a sealed envelope with a love note inside, stickers, and a small wrapped package such as a pencil sharpener, pencils, and a blank book (I staple together scratch paper). I write the boys' names on the front with a permanent marker, and then, in flight, they decorate the boxes with stickers. The trick is not to give them the travel kits until we're on the plane. After they exhaust their supply of goodies inside, they can refill it with things they collect during the trip.

Kathy Detzer, White River Junction, Vermont

Travel Insurance

It's not for everyone, but some travelers like to invest in this just-in-case insurance. Cancellation policies cover losses if you can't make your trip due to illness or a death in the family (you may wish to consider this if you have to put down a hefty deposit or prepay for your vacation in full). Medical policies provide for some emergency procedures. You can buy travel insurance from a specialty broker (see below), from your travel agent, or directly from an insurance company. Do not buy insurance from the tour operator or cruise line you will be traveling with.

Travel Guard International
(800-826-1300; www.travel-guard.com)

CSA Travel Protection
(www.csatravelprotection.com)

Travel Assistance International (800-821-2828; www.travelassistance.com)

Access America (866-807-3982; www.accessamerica.com)

exactly what is covered. If you will be taking advantage of the services included in the price, it may mean a good deal for your family; if not, you might be better off elsewhere.

How to find them: Travel magazines, travel agents, and family travel Websites (see page 34) will all be able to offer recommendations on family resorts. Also, the Globe Pequot Press (www.globepequot. com) has two good resource books: *100 Best Family Resorts in North America* and *100 Best All-Inclusive Resorts of the World.*

SAVING MONEY

A great vacation balances moments of extravagance with activities that are as enjoyable as they are affordable. The key, then, is to find painless ways to cut costs so that you can feel good about indulging. Here's a host of secrets from budget-savvy travelers.

Stock up at home. Specialty items, such as sunscreen, film, batteries, over-the-counter medications, and first-aid supplies can be outrageously expensive in vacation spots. Buy them in bulk at home and bring them with you.

Travel off-peak. Whether it's a ski resort town in the summertime, or Yosemite National Park in the spring, or the Adirondacks in the winter, off-peak travel is one of the best ways to save, as long as you're primed to enjoy the unique flavor of an off-season trip. Rates for travel and lodging are often slashed considerably—and you can enjoy a different perspective (and fewer crowds) at the destination of your choice.

Don't delay. The sooner you begin planning and booking your vacation (six months to a year or more in advance is not too early), the more deals will be available to you.

Shop around. This is the cardinal rule of vacation planning. Take time to compare prices for every service that you'll be buying, from airfares, hotels, and rental cars to tickets for attractions.

Ask for discounts. Don't be shy about asking for discounts. Call ahead to the attractions that you plan to visit and ask where one finds discount coupons. When making

Guided Tours

WHEN DO YOU NEED ONE?

For certain types of specialty travel (technically-challenging outdoor adventures for example), an expert guide is a necessary aid for a safe and enjoyable trip. In addition, using a local guide for day trips (say, fishing or snowmobiling) can be a wonderful way to connect with local lore and culture in the region you're visiting. In general, however, guided tours (especially group tours that include full itineraries and meals) tend to be pricey, tightly scheduled, and lacking the freedom most families value highly.

hotel reservations, ask if discounts are available—if not on the room alone, then on a package that may include the room and tickets to a nearby attraction. Coupons are also available on-line: a good place to start is the coupon link at www.about.com

STRAP A SHOE BAG to the back of the front seat and stuff it with your small kid-entertainment supplies: crayons and coloring books; kids' magazines; craft supplies, such as pipe cleaners, markers, glue sticks, and construction paper; songbooks; paper doll kits; a deck of cards; and a cassette player with story tapes. And don't forget a Frisbee, jump rope, and chalk (to draw hopscotch grids) for rest stops.

Make Your Own Postcards

While traveling by car or plane, my kids entertain themselves by creating their own postcards. Before the trip, I buy blank, prestamped postcards from the post office. Once we are under way, the kids draw pictures on the cards — usually of things they have done on vacation or are looking forward to doing. We address the cards to relatives and friends and drop them in the mail, making sure we send a few home for our own travel journal. This activity has been so successful, we now give friends travel kits of the prestamped cards and crayons as a bon voyage gift.

Lynette Smith, Lake Mills, Wisconsin

Look at package deals. At first blush, packages can seem outrageously expensive. But before you pass them up, compare them carefully to what you'd pay if you bought all the pieces of your vacation separately. Rates for airfare, lodging, and car rentals can be substantially lower when purchased together, especially for popular destinations. Contact your travel agent for information or research deals from travel clubs like AAA (call your local chapter or visit www.aaa.com), American Express Travel Services (800-346-3607; www.americanexpress.com), and from tour agencies affiliated with major airlines.

Use member benefits. Membership in an auto club, professional organization, or Entertainment book club may score you discounts on travel bills—ask before you book. Your credit card company, as well, may offer free services, such as collision-damage and travel-accident insurance, if you use the card to pay for travel expenses (call to request a copy of the company's travel benefits policy). If you travel regularly, the savings you'd garner from Web-saver clubs like www.bestfares.com can be well worth the $50 to $70 annual fee.

Tickets to attractions. Buying tickets to attractions in advance through an association or organization or at the hotel desk often will save you money. Equally important, you'll avoid the ticket line itself. On-line, try www.citypass.com for discount tickets in major metropolitan areas.

Keep your distance. Unless on-site housing offers necessary convenience for your family, consider lodging that's outside the major tourist area or city you're visiting. An extra 15 minutes of travel can considerably reduce lodging expenses, especially if you're staying more than a few days.

Check out kids' deals. Look for hotel deals where kids eat and/or stay free with their parents.

Consider cooking. Dining out is certainly part of the vacation experience, but three meals per person, per day add up quickly. Cooking your own meals can save you lots of money, even if you factor in the expense of a room with a kitchenette. In a regular hotel room, you can probably manage breakfast and/or lunch with a well-stocked cooler.

Pack your own minibar. Those high-priced hotel mini-bars are magnets for kids. Make a list of your kids' favorite treats, then purchase them in bulk as individually wrapped items. Pack a selection in a separate box or bag that can double as the designated minibar once you arrive at the hotel.

Let's do lunch. If you have a yen to try a particular fancy restaurant, head there during lunch. The atmosphere will be the same, and the menu will be similar, but smaller lunchtime portions will be accompanied by lower prices.

Revel in free fun. Remember the birthday when your child spent more time playing with the wrapping paper than with the actual toy? Vacations are filled with similar, low-cost but memorable moments, including hours at the beach, hiking trails, parks, and playgrounds. If you're in a new area, scan the local paper for listings, or call a local travel bureau or chamber of commerce for ideas.

Be savvy about souvenirs. Decide ahead of time how much you're willing to spend on souvenirs. Depending on the age of your kids, give each child his or her own spending money (they'll be stingier with their own funds than they are with yours). As an added incentive, let them keep a portion of any money they don't spend.

USING THE WEB

With the advent of the World Wide Web, individuals now have access to all the tools that travel agents use (and then some). The trick is to know how to use them well.

PROS: Researching travel ideas on the Web may draw in your kids more readily than a guidebook would.

31

Packing With—And For—Kids

Like so much of your family vacation, packing is a balancing act—in this case between including everything you need and making sure you can actually lift your bags. No matter where you're headed, this checklist should cover most of the essentials.

Give the kids a role. Every child has favorite outfits as well as clothing that he or she won't wear (and that you shouldn't bother packing). Young children can select the clothes they'd like to bring and set them aside for you. Older kids can do much of their own packing, especially if you help them write up a checklist of their own.

Don't worry about wrinkles. Like aging, this happens even with the best of precautions. Suggest some folding methods, but don't insist on your kids' finessing this. One surprisingly effective technique for kids is simply to roll everything up.

Make each child responsible for his or her own luggage. A backpack and a soft-sided suitcase for each child will do the trick. Let your kids decorate their bags with stencils and stickers — and remember to attach a name tag.

Separate toiletries in sealed, waterproof bags. Lids on toiletries often pop off or open during travel.

Take precautions in case of lost luggage. If you're flying to your vacation destination, pack at least one complete outfit for each family member in each suitcase. That way, if a piece of luggage is lost, everyone still has a change of clothes. Also, pack medications, eyeglasses, and contact lens solution in carry-ons.

Clothing

Include an outfit for each day of the week, plus extra shirts or blouses in case of spills. If your children are younger, encourage them to choose brightly colored outfits that will make them easier to spot in the crowd.

- Comfortable shoes or sneakers
- Socks and undergarments
- Sleepwear
- Light jackets, sweaters,or sweat-shirts for cool weather
- Bathing suits
- Sandals or slip-on shoes for the pool
- Hats or sun visors
- Rain gear, including umbrellas

Toiletries

- Toothbrushes, toothpaste, dental floss, and mouthwash
- Deodorant
- Combs, brushes, hair accessories, blow-dryer
- Soap
- Shampoo and conditioner
- Shaving gear
- Feminine-hygiene items

- Lotions
- Cosmetics
- Nail care kit
- Tweezers
- Cotton balls and/or swabs
- Antibacterial gel for hand washing
- Sunscreens and lip balm
- Insect repellent

Miscellaneous "must-haves"

- Essential papers: identification for adults, health insurance cards, tickets, traveler's checks
- Wallet and/or purse, including cash and credit cards
- Car and house keys (with duplicate set packed in a different bag)
- Eyeglasses and/or contact lenses, plus lens cleaner
- Medications
- Watch
- Camera and film (pack film in your carry-on bag)
- Tote bag or book bag for day use
- Books and magazines for kids and adults
- Toys, playing cards, small games
- Flashlight
- Extra batteries
- Large plastic bags for laundry
- Small plastic bags
- Disposable wipes
- First-aid kit
- Travel alarm
- Sewing kit

Keep Your First-Aid Kit Handy

There's no such thing as a vacation from minor injuries and ailments, so a well-stocked first-aid kit is essential to have on hand. You can buy a pre-packaged kit or make your own by packing the following items in an old lunch box:

- Adhesive bandages in various sizes, adhesive tape, and gauze pads
- Antacid
- Antibacterial gel for washing hands without water
- Antibacterial ointment
- Antidiarrheal medicine
- Antihistamine or allergy medicine
- Antiseptic
- Antiseptic soap
- Pain relief medicine—for children and adults
- Cotton balls and/or swabs
- Cough medicine and/or throat lozenges
- Motion sickness medicine
- Fingernail clippers
- First-aid book or manual
- Ipecac
- Moleskin for blisters
- Ointment for insect bites and sunburn
- Premoistened towelettes
- Thermometer
- Tissues
- Tweezers and needle

FamilyFun TIP

The Internet Travel Bible

If you're serious about researching (and especially booking) travel plans yourself, consult *Online Travel* by Ed Perkins (Microsoft Press, $19.95). This paperback tome is an invaluable resource on getting the best deals available and navigating the benefits and pitfalls of today's travel market, both on- and off-line.

Plus, when it comes time to book reservations, the Web can be a treasure trove of bargains—if you know how to hunt for them (see "The Internet Travel Bible" above). Why is that so? In essence, the Internet allows travel service providers to change their bargain pricing structures and unload unsold seats and rooms at a moment's notice. Of course, agents are still out to make as much money as they can—but you often can reap the benefits of their last-minute sales. In fact, many of these sales are available only on-line.

CONS: Keeping tabs on the travel market on-line can be extremely time-consuming if you are determined to find the best deal possible. In addition, since Web search engines can't read your mind and ask you questions, they can't ferret out all your options—just the ones that fall within the parameters you specify. So if you aren't a savvy searcher, you might miss the best deals (or the best destinations) even after hours of research.

Family travel Websites. It's a challenge to locate truly family-friendly sites among the hundreds available. For researching travel ideas and gathering travel tips, here are some of the best sites. Try our own website too—www.familyfun.com—it too has a lot of travel ideas.

♦ www.vacationtogether.com is a searchable database of family vacation ideas, reprinted from various publications (including *FamilyFun* magazine). You'll also find packing checklists and links to reservation sites here.

♦ www.travelwithkids.about.com is a terrific clearinghouse for family vacation ideas, package deals, current bargains, lists of accommodations, packing checklists, travel tips and games, downloadable maps, and more.

♦ www.thefamilytravelfiles.com is a well-organized family travel Website that showcases a range of trip ideas and offers a free travel e-zine.

♦ www.familytravelforum.com is a monthly on-line newsletter specializing in well-screened links to family-friendly accommodations, airfare deals, seasonal events, and more.

General travel sites. In addition to family-specific sites such as the ones listed above, there are literally thousands of useful Websites that can help you plan and book your vacation. They are too numerous to list here! We have included many of our favorites throughout this chapter; in addition to those, here are a few you may find useful.

♦ www.officialtravelinfo.com lists contacts for travel and tourism bureaus worldwide (you can search the United States by state).

♦ www.fodors.com, www.frommers.com, and www.nationalgeographic.com are sites related to travel magazines. Often, they'll post selections from current issues, as well as other travel-related articles.

♦ www.travel-library.com (a wide range of travel topics, travelogues, and destination information) and www.about.com (a general site with good travel links) are sites that can lead you to travel information that you may (or may not!) be looking for.

Book your own airline reservations. Using the same databases as travel agents use, the leading travel sites have made booking your own flight as simple as typing in when you'd like to leave, when you'd like to return, your origin and destination, and airline choice. They kick back a list of flights that most closely match

Broker a Hotel Deal

Great deals at major hotels usually turn up off-season or at the last minute, but here's another tactic families can try: work with a hotel consolidator (also called a hotel broker or discounter).

Consolidators work by securing blocks of hotel rooms at wholesale prices, then reselling them at rates that are—in theory, at least—lower than the published "rack" rate. Some consolidators will only reserve your room; you pay the hotel directly. Others require a prepaid voucher that you present to the hotel upon arrival. Many consolidators claim savings of 10 to 50 percent (some even more), but as with any bargain, it pays to know what you're getting into.

SOME TIPS:
- Ask about service charges. Is there a user fee for the consolidator?
- Are there financial penalties for trip cancellation or rescheduling?
- Compare rates. The consolidator may not beat a hotel's special offers.

With those caveats, try:
Quikbook: Good selection and easy to use, with hotels in 33 cities. Call 800-789-9887 or see www.quikbook.com
Central Reservation Service: Lists hotel deals in ten major cities. Call 800-555-7555 or visit www.roomconnection.com

Gumshoe Games

The detectives in your group will just love these tests of their sleuthing ability.

Secret highway messages: Pass out the pencils and paper, and keep your eyes peeled for official road signs. Each time you spot one, write down the first letter. When you've passed five to seven signs—and have five to seven letters— you're ready to crack the code. Here's how: each letter stands for a word. So the letters D, S, C, S, and A could stand for the secret message "Drive slowly, construction starts ahead." Of course, others in your family may interpret it as "Dad, stop, candy store ahead."

Two truths and one lie: The first person makes three statements about himself or herself. Two are true; the other is a lie. For example, you could say, "I had a dog named Puddles. My sister cut off my hair once when I was asleep. I won the school spelling bee when I was in third grade." Everybody then holds up one, two, or three fingers to show which statement they think is the lie. Reveal the answer and let the next person fib away.

your specifications and then let you choose the flights you want. After confirming your choices, you pay with a credit card, print your itinerary, and either receive your paper tickets in the mail or, more likely, pick up your tickets when you check in at the airport. **N O T E :** Some people prefer paper tickets because if a flight is missed or cancelled an e-ticket may not be exchangable at a different airline's counter.

Our favorite flight sites are Expedia (www.expedia.com), Travelocity (www.travelocity.com), and Trip. com (www.trip.com). Don't assume that all offer the same flights or the same prices; the important thing is to shop around, even among these sites.

Before you pay for your tickets, you should double-check with two other sources. First, look at your chosen airline's home site to see if they offer extra miles for booking flights on-line, or special, unadvertised Web deals. And call your travel agent, tell her the flight you're interested in, and see if she can beat the price. Lastly, be sure you're aware of the taxes, airport surcharges, and possible site use fees that may be added to your ticket price.

For more information about airlines, airports, and online reservations, go to www.iecc.com/airline/. Also, check out Ed Perkins' *Online Travel* (Microsoft Press, $19.95). To find out more about frequent flier mile programs, visit www.frequent flier.com

Book hotel and rental car reservations. In general, hotel and rental car reservations work the same way that airfare reservations do. The Web is an excellent source of hotel deals (especially for vacation packages, if you're a savvy shopper); rental car companies, on the other hand, generally offer little in the way of discounts above what you can get at the desk.

Best Western offers free road atlases with Best Western sites: call 800-528-1234.

Sign up for e-mail newsletters. If you find a good travel Website that offers a free newsletter, it doesn't hurt to sign up—you may receive timely notice of travel deals that you otherwise would miss. Just be sure that you save any information on how to cancel the subscription in case you want to opt out.

Are Internet travel arrangements foolproof? No, unfortunately. The Internet is prime territory for scams, although you can guard against most of them with a few protective strategies. First, deal with major sites (like the ones listed in this book) or directly with brand-name company sites (like Avis or Holiday Inn) whenever possible. When you're transmitting your credit card information, make sure your connection is secure (your browser should tell you when one has been established). Also, you should double-check to see that the service provider's Website has a secure server. (Look for a locked padlock in the corner of your browser's window or "https"—the "s" stands for "secure"—in the URL.) If a site doesn't seem completely aboveboard, it may not be. Finally, when in doubt, back out. As long as you don't give a company your credit card number, they can't charge you anything.

FamilyFun **READER'S TIP** ---

A Colorful Road Game

This homemade road game is a big hit with my 4-year-old son, Tommy. I clip cards out of colored construction paper and print a different letter of the alphabet on each. During a car ride, each of us picks a card and searches for an object or a structure that matches the color and begins with the letter on our card. For example, a player with a *B* on a yellow card might spot a school bus. Since we began playing this game, my son tends to remember many more details about our travels. Instead of hearing, "Are we there yet?" we hear, "Oh no, I haven't found mine yet!"

Susan Robins, Cottage Grove, Oregon

If your family's idea of a vacation involves nightly campfires, sleeping bags, and potential wildlife sightings near (or in!) your living space, check out these great resources for tent and RV camping.

The Trailer Life Directory provides travelers with a list of several thousand campgrounds and RV parks throughout the United States and Canada. Each location is rated on a three-step scale that assesses the park's facilities, cleanliness, and overall appeal; ratings are updated on an annual basis. You can register at www.tl directory.com to search the directory for free or order your own copy for the road on-line or at bookstores.

Woodall's campground directories also rate a large number of parks— more than 14,000 locations throughout the United States and Canada are scored on their facilities and recreation. You can purchase a directory which covers the entire area, or shorter versions of the guide are available for the western and eastern regions. Woodall's also publishes a directory exclusively for tent campers. Again, you can register to access campground listings for free at www. woodalls.com, but the on-line directory does not include Woodall's convenient rating system. The complete directories can be purchased at Woodall's Website or bookstores.

There's no centralized reservation system for every campsite within the **National Park system**, so your best bet is to contact each individual park. Campground reservations here usually must be made several months in advance since the sites are so popular, so don't count on finding a space unless you've planned ahead. Contact information for the National Parks can be found at their Website, www. nps.gov. Policies for state parks also vary from place to place, so you'll have to contact individual campgrounds for camping information.

Veteran car campers recognize **KOA Kampgrounds** by their familiar yellow, red, and black signs. KOAs allow your family to rough it while enjoying many of the amenities of home. Novice campers will be thrilled to have access to hot showers, flush toilets, laundry facilities, and convenience stores. All KOA locations have both tent and RV sites, and some even have cabins that your family can rent. If you plan to stay multiple nights at one or more KOA Kampgrounds, consider purchasing a Value Kard. You'll get a 10 percent discount on your registration fees and a free copy of the KOA directory (you'll still pay for shipping). You can also research KOA locations for free at www.koakampgrounds.com or purchase your own directory on-line or by calling 406-248-7444.

If you're looking for campgrounds where your family can pitch a tent in peace and quiet, check out *The Best in Tent Camping* series (published by Menasha Ridge Press). The books detail the best in scenic, tent-only sites without all of the bells and whistles.

One key to a great camping trip is remembering all of your supplies. If your family is RV or car camping, you can usually purchase any forgotten items on the road. However, if you're traveling far off the beaten path, you'll need to be careful to double-check your belongings.

Here's a checklist of supplies to make your camping experience go smoothly. If you're renting an RV, be aware that you may be able to rent your bedding and cooking supplies for an additional fee and save the trouble of bringing your own.

♦ Tent(s) and tent stakes
♦ Plastic ground cloth/tarp
♦ Sleeping bags (or bedding, for an RV)
♦ Sleeping pads
♦ Camp stove (with extra fuel)
♦ Pots, plastic dishes, mugs, and utensils
♦ Water bottle or canteen
♦ Lantern and/or candles
♦ Bottle and/or can openers
♦ Sharp knife (parents should hold on to this)
♦ Plethora of plastic/trash bags
♦ Dish soap (preferably biodegradable)
♦ Stocked coolers
♦ Water (or a portable filter or purifying tablets)
♦ Waterproof matches or lighter(s)
♦ Flashlights (and extra batteries)
♦ Bandanna (for use as a head covering, pot holder, and napkin)
♦ Trowel
♦ Folding saw
♦ First-aid kit, medications
♦ Sunscreen
♦ Insect repellent
♦ Toilet paper
♦ Day packs
♦ Child carriers (for little ones)
♦ Compass and area map
♦ Clothing (make sure to pack many layers)
♦ Two pairs of shoes (in case one gets wet)
♦ A hat
♦ Sunglasses
♦ Toiletries (try to take only necessary items)
♦ Camera
♦ Binoculars
♦ Kid supplies (toys, books, favorite stuffed animal)

Texas

TEXAS IS FAMOUS for its wide-open spaces, which include the sandy shores of the Gulf Coast, the pine forests of East Texas, the desert vistas of Big Bend National Park, and the bluebonnet prairies of the Hill Country. Outdoorsy types can go hiking, fishing, swimming, and—of course—horseback riding. The beaches of the Texas Gulf offer everything from the bustling shores of South Padre Island to the remote reaches of Mustang Island.

In and around the cities, you'll encounter top-notch museums, zoos, and theme

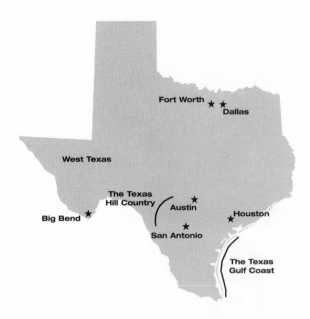

Fort Worth ★ ★ Dallas

West Texas

The Texas Hill Country

Austin ★

Big Bend ★

★ Houston

★ San Antonio

The Texas Gulf Coast

parks. Your little astronauts will have a blast at Houston's Johnson Space Center, and for the sports fans, major league sports teams. Preteens will love the Texas-size malls and incredible theme parks like SeaWorld and Six Flags Over Texas.

The state's famous cowboy past comes alive in places like Fort Worth's Stockyards, where you can wander past longhorn steers on brick streets little changed in the last hundred years. You'll even get a taste of Mexico in San Antonio, where mariachi bands play on the famous River Walk.

Whether your family stops in one place or roams all the way across Texas, you'll find this state is a special place that lives up to its larger-than-life image.

ATTRACTIONS
$	under $5
$$	$5 - $10
$$$	$10 - $20
$$$$	$20 +

HOTELS/MOTELS/CAMPGROUNDS
$	under $50
$$	$50 - $100
$$$	$100 - $200
$$$$	$200 +

RESTAURANTS
$	under $10
$$	$10 - $20
$$$	$20 - $30
$$$$	$30 +

FAMILYFUN RATED
★	Fine
★★	Good
★★★	Very Good
★★★★	FamilyFun Recommended

Bandera is called the cowboy capital of the world. You and your kids can saddle up at a local dude ranch.

Austin and the Texas Hill Country

THE HILL COUNTRY is home to Austin (the state capital, which sits at the Hill Country's eastern edge), meadows bursting with wildflowers (including those famous bluebonnets—see "Bluebonnets" on page 49), and lazy rivers perfect for tubing on sunny summer days. People here are down-home friendly and laid-back. Hill Country is, after all, home to Luckenbach, Texas, the small town (population: 25) just east of Fredericksburg, made famous in the Willie Nelson–Waylon Jennings song by the same name where "ain't nobody feelin' no pain." Austin filmmaker Richard Linklater spotlighted the casual lifestyle in his film *Slacker*, shot in and around his alma mater, the University of Texas at Austin. Be ready to slow down during your stay in the Hill Country. The more leisurely pace is a welcome

THE **FamilyFun** LIST

MUST-SEE
MUST-SEE

Austin Children's Museum (page 46)

Austin Nature and Science Center (page 48)

The Bats of the Congress Avenue Bridge (page 48)

Bob Bullock Texas State History Museum (page 46)

Enchanted Rock State Park (page 60)

Lady Bird Johnson Wildflower Center (page 50)

Schlitterbahn (page 64)

Texas Capitol Complex (page 47)

Zilker Park and Barton Springs Pool (page 52)

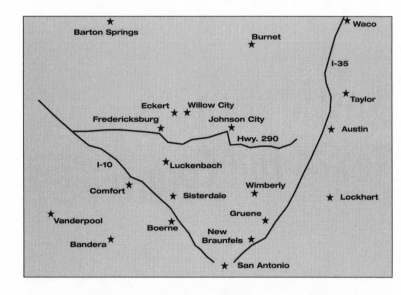

relief from most families' stressful schedules. Relax and enjoy doing nothing but watching the sun set over Lake Travis or savoring the view after helping your kids climb Enchanted Rock.

Home to five universities, the city has a wealth of cultural events and loads of outdoor activities—something for every member of the family. On sunny days, it seems as though everyone is outside jogging or mountain biking. (Here even the trails by Town Lake suffer some gridlock from all the spandex-clad bikers and in-line skaters.) Sunsets are lovely, but from March through October, the real show happens at

In addition to the usual **state symbols** like the flower (bluebonnet) and motto ("Friendship"), Texas also has a state pepper (jalapeño) and state sport (rodeo).

dusk when thousands of Mexican free-tailed bats take to the sky, leaving their home under the Congress Avenue Bridge.

Although Houston and Dallas like to think they have the best dining establishments in the state, Austin and the Hill Country have their share of fine eateries; what's more, these tend to be less stuffy (and more family-friendly) than the five-star spots in those towns.

The Hill Country was settled in part by Germans, and their heritage lives on in places like Fredericksburg, where local restaurants serve up Wiener schnitzel, and New Braunfels, where the local newspaper is called *Die Zeit*. The area's Czech settlers brought with them recipes for *kolache*, a thick roll filled with fruit jelly that is sold in the region's Czech bakeries. (Some stores offer them frozen in plastic bags to go if you want them for breakfast the next day.) Perhaps the most outstanding culinary treat of the Hill Country is its barbecued beef. If your family likes to eat, we mean *really* eat, then plan a day trip sampling the fare at a few of the state's best barbecue joints near Austin (for more information, see "'Cue It Up, Texas Style" on page 60).

Austin doesn't necessarily make a good base for exploring the region. Hotel rooms are typically more expensive here than in other, more picturesque Hill Country towns. For example, at press time, a room at Austin's Four Seasons runs $175 or more per night and even Motel 6 rooms start at $65. Both your travel experience—and your budget—would benefit far more

from a stay in the smaller towns of New Braunfels or Fredericksburg; both are a short distance from Austin and offer interesting alternatives to the standard hotel chains. In New Braunfels, your family can spend the night in a one-room schoolhouse at the Kuebler-Waltrip Haus, and in Fredericksburg you can stay in a renovated stone barn.

The Hill Country is also a wonderful place to get a taste of the Old West. Bandera, southwest of Austin, is called the Cowboy Capital of the World and is home to a slew of dude ranches where your family can book a weekend or weeklong stay (see "Hill Country Dude Ranches" on page 54). Even if ranches aren't your thing, consider a trip on the Hill Country Flyer excursion train that travels from Cedar Point, just north of Austin, to the town of Burnet, where you may be able to witness a staged Wild West shoot-out.

If you're coming here in the summer, be sure to pack swimsuits.

FamilyFun **READER'S TIP** -

It's in the Cards

My family loves to travel, and I have found a wonderful way to preserve our vacation memories. First, we buy postcards at all the different locations we visit. On the back, I jot down the highlights of the trip or funny things that happened while we were there. After we have returned home, I laminate all the postcards, punch holes in the top left corners, and put them all on a ring clip. It's exciting to see all of the places we have been, and the cards are inexpensive souvenirs of our travels.

Stefanie Wirths, Camdenton, Missouri

Schlitterbahn water park has welcomed generations of Texas families with cool waters fed by a natural spring. The best place to cool off in Austin is Barton Springs, but it gets crowded fast, so get there early. The area's many rivers, including the Frio, the Comal, and the Guadalupe, are filled with tubers on warm days. It's smart to call one of the many outfitters, who will set up your family with tubes and handle all the transportation needs (like how to get back upriver where your car is parked). They also know the water conditions and will call off trips if the river is too high to be safely navigated or too low to cause a rocky (and bumpy) ride.

Whether your family wants to head out on a trail ride or float down the river, in Austin and the Hill Country, you won't have to work hard to have a good time. Just sit back and let us get you to places where you'll want to stay a spell.

Austin

CULTURAL ADVENTURES

Austin Art Museum ★★/$-$$
Exhibits change, so check listings to see what's going on during your visit. The museum offers children's programs during the summer and on weekends. The gift shop has plenty of items for your aspiring Picasso. *823 Congress Ave., Austin; (512) 495-9224; www.amoa.org*

★MUST-SEE★ FamilyFun Austin Children's Museum ★★★/$
This hands-on museum is a great place to start the day. Kids can get a few bat facts at the Bat Hangout, where they learn about bat dining habits (such as the fact that bats eat mosquitoes, so they can't be that bad). The Weather Gallery has an outstanding exhibition on tornadoes that explains what they are and how they're formed; you can also watch one being created by a machine that kids can actually touch. *201 Colorado St., Austin; (512) 472-2499; www.austinkids.org*

★MUST-SEE★ FamilyFun Bob Bullock Texas State History Museum ★★★★/Free-$
Kids get in free to this museum celebrating the unique history and spirit of Texas. A large-screen IMAX theater shows rotating films and the Texas Spirit Theater shows a film highlighting the history of the Lone Star State with rumbling oil gushers and a rocket takeoff from

Mission Control at the Johnson Space Center. Exhibits depict the first encounters between Native Americans and European explorers and show how oil changed the state. There are plenty of interactive displays so kids won't get bored. The third floor houses exhibits that change every six months or so; check out the museum's Website (*see below*) to see what will be offered during your trip. The gift shop stocks unique items such as bluebonnet seeds and broomstick ponies. *Corner of Martin Luther King, Jr., Blvd. and N. Congress Ave., Austin; (512) 936-8746;* wwwthestoryoftexas.com

Governor's Mansion
★★/Free

This elegant, white-columned home was built for a mere $14,500 back in 1856. Over the years it has been home to such luminaries as Sam Houston, Ann Richards, and George W. Bush. Visitors get to tour the first floor and the garden (the governor's family quarters are off-limits). Tours run every 20 minutes Monday through Thursday from 10 to 11:40 A.M. It's first come, first served, so get here early (by 9:45 A.M. at the latest). It's also wise to call ahead to make sure the mansion isn't hosting a major event or large tour group that day. Also, call ahead if you or someone traveling with you is in a wheelchair so that a special tour can be arranged. *1010 Colorado Ave., Austin; (512) 463-5516.*

Texas Capitol Complex
FamilyFun ★★/Free

Dubbed The Pink Lady for its unique colored granite, the Texas statehouse underwent a recent renovation that added to its splendor. Free tours, which last about 45 minutes, are available when the state legislature isn't in session (state lawmakers typically meet during odd-numbered years). Tell your kids to stand in the star on the floor of the capitol's rotunda and whisper. Their hushed voices will echo through the massive space. Youngsters get a hands-on civics lesson as they tour the elaborate house and senate chambers and can see how elected officials cast their votes. If nothing else, stop for a photo (head a few blocks north for a nice vantage point) or enjoy a picnic lunch on the capitol's parklike grounds. Two-hour free parking is available at 15th and Congress. *The Capitol Complex visitors' center is located at 112 E.*

FamilyFun SNACK

Bag o' Bugs

Place a few graham crackers in a plastic bag, seal it shut, and crush the crackers into a fine sand, using a large spoon. Add a few raisins and let your kids dig for bugs in the sand. Experiment with other tasty critters: dried cranberry ladybugs, chocolate or carob-chip ants, even gummy worms.

11th St., Austin; (512) 305-8400; www.house.state.tx.us/common/capinfo.htm

JUST FOR FUN

Austin Duck Adventures
★★★/$-$$

If your family has only a day in Austin and wants to see the city's highlights, consider this innovative tour that leaves from the Austin visitors' center, Wednesdays through Fridays at 11 A.M. and 2 P.M., and on weekends a third tour is also available at 4 P.M. The 90-minute tour takes place aboard an amphibious bus that gives you a "duck's-eye view" of Austin. It takes you first on the city's streets past the State Capitol and along Congress Avenue, and then floats you into the waters of Town Lake. Travelers are given duck calls to quack all through town. *Buy tickets inside the visitors' center at 201 E. 2nd Ave., or better yet, call ahead to 512-4-SPLASH; the tours have become quite popular and are filling up several days or weeks in advance.* www.austinducks.com

 ### Austin Nature and Science Center
★★★/Free

Located in busy Zilker Park, this 80-acre outdoor museum is home to more than 40 animals that have been orphaned or injured in the wild, including an albino raccoon, barn owls, and snakes. The trails and pond provide a welcome break from the city's crowded scene. There's no charge, but donations are encouraged. *301 Nature Center Dr., Austin; (512) 327-8181;* www.ci.austin.tx.us/nature-science

Austin Zoo ★★★/$

Not as large or diverse as the state's major zoos in San Antonio, Fort Worth, and Houston, this one still has its charms. Most of the 300 or so animals here were mistreated, abandoned, or confiscated after being illegally imported. The zoo's intimate setting gives kids and keepers the chance to get closer to the animals. For example, two recently added Siberian tigers were declawed, making it possible for the zookeepers to pet and play with them. There is a miniature train you can hop aboard for a one-and-a-half-mile loop. *10807 Rawhide Trail, Austin; (512) 288-1490;* www.austinzoo.org

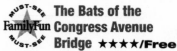 ### The Bats of the Congress Avenue Bridge ★★★★/Free

Just like the swallows that return each year to Capistrano, the bats migrate in early March from central Mexico to various parts of the Southwest, including Carlsbad Caverns, New Mexico, and this bridge, which alone draws some 750,000 female bats each spring. (For more on this must-see event, see "Going Batty In and Around Austin" on page 51.)

Central Park ★★/Free

Located just behind Central Market, the city's grocery shopping mecca, this 39-acre green space is a tranquil setting with ponds and a smooth 5.8-mile trail. There are lots of ducks, a picnic area, and a playground that's accessible to the disabled. Enter from the Guadalupe parking lot or the retail stores on the Lamar side. *Corner of 38th St. and Lamar, Austin.*

Disc Golf Courses ★★/Free

Disc golf, which involves throwing a Frisbee toward a pole that acts much like the hole in golf, has become popular in Austin. Your family can give it a whirl, too. And don't worry about paying any greens fees: it's free. Courses are located in Pease Park, Zilker Park, Bartholomew Park, and Slaughter Creek. *For more information, call the city's Parks and Recreation Department at (512) 974-6700.*

Hill Country Flyer Steam Train ★★★/$$$$

Hop aboard this train operated by the Austin and Texas Central Railroad for a leisurely two-hour, 33-mile trip to the small town of Burnet, where you can eat lunch and watch a staged gunfight by the station during the two-hour layover before returning. If weather permits, sit in one of the open-air cars (on 100-plus-degree days, the air-conditioned parlor cars are more appealing). At press time, the railroad's 1916 Southern Pacific locomotive was down for repairs, but the line continued operating with a 1950s-era diesel. *The train leaves Cedar Park City Hall (near U.S. 183 and R.M., or Road to Market, 1431)*

Bluebonnets

Spring is one of the best times to visit Austin and the Hill Country because the weather is crisp without being too chilly and, if you're lucky, the bluebonnets are blooming. Just when and where the blue carpet will emerge is difficult to predict. It can depend on when and if fall and winter rains penetrated the seeds and whether enough sunshine followed. Dry winters can mean dull meadows, but too much rain can wash away seeds. Given the huge numbers of *Lupinus texensis*, the proper scientific name for the state flower, you'll probably find more than enough for a nice roadside photo.

One word of etiquette: it's considered rude (and detrimental to future generations of bluebonnets) to plop your youngsters on top of a stand of bluebonnets, because the children's weight can destroy the flowers. Instead, put the kids in front of the flowers. This also reduces the risk of having them seated on top of a mound of fire ants (a less pleasant Texas tradition).

just north of Austin and is one of several train excursions offered. Call ahead for reservations during spring break and summer; (512) 477-8468; www.austinsteamtrain.org

Jourdan Bachman Pioneer Farm
★★★/$

Step back in time, about 100 years or so, at this well-preserved homestead. Tour the homes of three families who lived here back in the 1800s: frontier homesteaders, wealthy cotton merchants, and slaves turned sharecroppers. Kids can experience farm life firsthand, including milking cows and making sausage, by participating in the frequent weekend demonstrations. Docents dressed in period costumes answer youngsters' questions about what life was like before Nintendo. *11418 Sprinkle Cut Off Rd., Austin; (512) 837-1215; www.pioneerfarm.org*

Lady Bird Johnson Wildflower Center
★★★★/$

In Texas, the former First Lady is known for her grace, grit—and wildflowers. She donated these 60 acres to showcase the state's bounty of blooms and other native trees and shrubs. Kids can scamper along the many paths, and the casually landscaped meadows/gardens make a perfect backdrop for memorable family photos. The best time of year to visit is during spring flowering season (March through May). *4801*

La Crosse Ave., Austin; (512) 292-4200; www.wildflower.org

Millennium Youth Complex
★★/$$

Perfect for a rainy day, or simply to escape the Texas summer sun, this facility has something for everyone. Young kids can frolic in the soft play area dubbed Kids Kingdom and older ones can take their pick of bowling, roller-skating, or hanging out in the video arcade. There's also a movie theater and a food court. *1156 Hargrave, on the corner of Rosewood and Hargrave, Austin; (512) 472-6932; www.myec.net*

Vanishing River Cruise
★★★/$$$

A relaxing way to commune with nature (and learn something too), these two-and-a-half-hour cruises on Lake Buchanan are narrated by naturalists who point out seasonal flora and fauna, such as bald eagles (which nest in the area from November through March) and wild deer and turkey (which can be spotted during spring and summer months). There's a snack bar on board that serves munchies, or you can save a few bucks and bring your own. Make a day of it by bringing a picnic and swimsuit to enjoy the lake's beaches. Sunset cruises—which include a full dinner served on board—are offered on Saturday nights in the summer. *From Burnet, drive three miles west on U.S. 29. Take*

GOING BATTY
In and Around Austin

WHO KNEW back in 1980 that a deck renovation to the Congress Avenue Bridge would lead to a city discovering its battiness?

Austin is the seasonal home to thousands of Mexican free-tailed bats—and the city markets its wing-flapping night creatures well. In October, Austin celebrates Bat Days with bat-themed exhibits and a street festival in Zilker Park. Every evening at dusk, the bats emerge from under the bridge for their nightly feeding, which includes consuming from 10,000 to 30,000 pounds of insects per night for the whole colony.

One of the coolest ways to enjoy the nightly flight is to take one of the "bat-viewing cruises" on Town Lake offered by Capital Cruises (512/480-9264), whose dock is located by the Hyatt Regency Town Lake. Reservations are required; get to the dock at least 30 minutes before departure. At press time, tickets ranged from $8 for adults to $5 for kids ages 4 to 12.

You can also see the bats free—simply park near the bridge and walk over to the entrance of the Austin American-Statesman, where you can learn more about bats and their ways at the information kiosks: for example, bats aren't blind, aren't related to rats, and, best of all, don't want to fly into your hair. (The stop is worthwhile even if you aren't here during bat-viewing times.) Then, armed with your newfound bat info, walk under the bridge, where you can hear their high-pitched squawks. Watch your head under the bridge: this spot is also a popular pigeon stoop. Keep walking west and pick a spot to watch the bats' nightly trip out for dinner. Remind your kids that a single bat can eat as many as 600 mosquitoes! And remind yourself to wear bug repellent anyway because they don't get all of them.

If the Austin scene is too crowded for you, try another bat hangout (or is it hang-up?). South of Fredericksburg, the Hygieostatic Bat Roost near Comfort is home to a bat colony that's even larger than the one in Austin. Here, in an abandoned railroad tunnel, bats also set out for dinner around dusk during the season. Some days, there are naturalists on hand to give lectures and answer questions. *To get here from Comfort, take Highway 473 north about four miles toward Sisterdale, then keep going straight on Highway 9. After another nine miles, you should see the parking lot and a large mound of rocks on a hill.* For more information on the Hygieostatic Bat Roost, call (830) 238-4487.

Ranch Road 2341, then turn right and go about 17 miles; (800) 4-RIVER-4; (512) 756-6986; www.vtrc.com

Zilker Park and Barton Springs Pool
★★★★/Free-$

Zilker Park is where Austin families (and most everyone else, it seems) invariably wind up on a sunny day. The soccer fields are packed, parking is at a premium, and mountain bikers and joggers jostle for space on the trails. The park's crown jewel is Barton Springs Pool (fee), which measures 1,000 feet by 125 feet (its depth fluctuates but is generally three to four feet in the summer). Fed by a natural spring that pumps approximately 32 gallons of water from the underground Edwards aquifer, the pool is a constant 68 degrees year-round. That's chilly enough to make it a great spot for cooling off on sweltering days. Lifeguards are on duty during the warmer months and on most weekends. You'll be able to change clothes in the large bathhouse, and there's a gift shop where you can get snacks. *2101 Barton Springs Rd. For information, call (512) 476-9044; www.ci.austin.tx.us/zilker/*

Give your kids a geology and ecology lesson at **Splash**, a mini museum next to Barton Springs; here they can learn how aquifers work and the importance of caring for our water sources. There are several interactive exhibits, including one that lets your kids operate a miniature submarine through the aquifer to discover the source of water contamination. Another one allows kids to test the water quality of area creeks and provides sound effects and flashing lights to alert them when something's in the water. They will be so mesmerized they may forget to go back to the pool. *The museum is at the bathhouse; (512) 481-1466.*

And don't forget to begin or end your day with a ride on the **Zilker Zephyr** miniature train. Little ones (and Moms and Dads) love this relaxing two-mile trip through the park's fields and forests. The train leaves the station, located just across

Kolache: Czech it Out

Kolache, a Czech pastry, is sold at bakeries operated by descendants of Czech settlers who came here in the 1870s and 1880s. The thick rolls come with apple, peach, cherry, prune, or cream cheese stuffed in the middle. If you're driving down Interstate 35, you can pull off at the exit for the city of West, about 20 miles north of Waco, and hit the *kolache* capital. There are half a dozen *kolache* bakeries on Main and Oak streets alone. Our favorite is the Village Bakery (*108 E. Oak St.; 254/826-5151*), which dates back to 1952. There are a few tables and plenty of juices available.

the street from Barton Springs Pool, every hour on the hour on weekdays and every half hour on weekends, weather permitting. *2100 Barton Springs Rd., Austin; (512) 478-8286.*

BUNKING DOWN

Canyon of the Eagles Lodge
★★★★/$$$

If your family wants to get away from it all, this remote lodge not too far from President George W. Bush's ranch in Crawford is a perfect place to escape. The 64-room lodge is spread over 940 acres on Lake Buchanan, northwest of Austin. You can unwind in rocking chairs on the huge porch and glimpse deer passing nearby. Tent and RV facilities are available, too, and you can rent kayaks and canoes. There's a full-service restaurant, so you won't have to rough it. During summer and holiday periods, the lodge offers kid-friendly programs, ranging from reptile shows to singing cowboys. Stargazing parties are held year-round at the lodge's Eagle Eye Observatory. *The lodge is located at the end of RR2341, about 18 miles west of Burnet. Get complete directions and a calendar of upcoming events at www.canyonofthe eagles.com (800) 977-0081; (512) 756-8787.*

> The armadillo, the state mammal of Texas, is only born in fours. The quadruplets are always identical, so all four offspring are the same sex.

Four Seasons Austin
★★★/$$$$

Yes, it's pricey, but this upscale hotel pampers you and your kids, making it worth the splurge. Special kid treatment includes a snack package—a tin bucket filled with cookies and milk with your youngster's name inscribed on the outside in chocolate; be sure to request it when making reservations. Also, upon request, the housekeeper will stock your room with a video game or old-fashioned board game—and even kid-size bathrobes. The luxury of the place will appeal to Mom and Dad; the pool and all the other kid-friendly goodies will keep the youngsters content. The hotel affords a nice view of Town Lake and is within walking distance of the bats at the Congress Avenue Bridge. You can also rent bikes through the concierge and hit the Town Lake Trail. Two restaurants can be found for family dining. *98 San Jacinto Blvd., Austin; (800) 332-3442; (512) 478-4500;* www.four seasons.com

Habitat Suites ★★★/$$

This place bills itself as an "ecotel," meaning it embraces ecological practices, such as not replacing your room towels as often as other hotels might, for water and energy conservation. The hotel also embraces Eastern religious and New

HILL COUNTRY DUDE RANCHES

I F YOU WANT a unique family vacation, saddle up your clan and play cowboy at a Texas dude ranch. Unlike many of the larger dude ranches in the West, few Texas establishments offer "working vacations" that force you to round up strays for your supper. The emphasis here is on having fun—and maybe getting just a bit saddle sore (another excuse to get in the hot tub). **NOTE:** Many times, children under age 6 are not allowed on trail rides, so call ahead to avoid any disappointment; also, generally, no one over 240 pounds is allowed to ride.

If you have little or no riding experience, don't worry: many ranches offer lessons and promise to give you a slow horse. Bring your own cowboy duds, but don't get too fancy. Simple jeans and T-shirts are fine. It's worth bringing a pair of heeled boots (if you have them) to help keep your feet in the stirrups, but sneakers will do.

The Hill Country is home to 20-plus dude ranches, from upscale, corporate retreats to game-hunting havens to down-home and casual, family-oriented resorts.

Here are our picks for the best places to wrangle your young cowpokes:

Dixie Dude Ranch ★★/$$

Popular with families looking for hayrides and kitschy cowboy entertainment, this ranch also offers guests beginning riding lessons. There's no organized children's program, but baby-sitting can be arranged and kids under age 6 can ride with an adult as long as they don't exceed the 250-pound weight limit. All rides are guided, and go no faster than a trot. Fishing (catch-and-release) and nature hikes are also available. All meals are provided in a central mess hall, and evening entertainment includes two-stepping hoedowns. Be sure to bring your own towels for the pool and hot tub. *FM 1077, Bandera; (830) 796-4481;* www.dixiedude ranch.com

Flying L Guest Ranch ★★★/$$

During summer, spring break, and other school holidays, the Flying L offers a children's program, including storytelling, fishing, and crafts. Kids ages 6 and older can enjoy trail rides. There's a Texas-size pool, plus Medina Lake and San Julian Creek are on the property. Meals are often served creekside, and entertainment includes a rodeo, marshmallow roasts, and sing-alongs by the campfire. *Off Hwy. 16 and Hwy. 173, 40 miles outside San Antonio on Flying L Drive, Bandera; (800) 292-5134; (830) 460-3001;* www. flyingL.com

Guadalupe River Ranch
★★★★/$$$-$$$$

Once home to actress Olivia de Haviland (Melanie in *Gone with the Wind*), this ranch offers upscale digs with a down-home feel. In the summer, it offers children's programs that include crafts and nature hikes. In the evening, hayrides and fireside sing-alongs are on the schedule. Hike or horseback ride on the ranch's trails—or simply sit on the porch swing and take in the view. *605 FM 474 in Boerne; (800) 460-2005;* www. guadaluperiverranch.com

Mayan Dude Ranch
★★★/$$$

Another family-friendly place, the Mayan Ranch offers stone cottages and a central lodge nestled on the banks of the Medina River. Guests here can get two trail rides a day, or ride once and take the afternoon to go tubing in the river. The children's programs—offered two hours in the morning and two hours in the afternoon—are geared to kids ages 6 and older, with arts and crafts, games, and outings. Don't sleep in or you might miss the ranch's famous Cowboy Breakfast, which includes flapjacks and bacon by the campfire. Book early: the ranch gets plenty of repeat customers. *301 Mayan Ranch Rd., Bandera; (830) 796-3312;* www.mayanranch.com

Age principles. There's a book containing many of Buddha's teachings in the bedside drawer, and macrobiotic and vegan options are offered at breakfast. To add to the Zen-like experience, there's a small but well-tended garden and afternoon servings of Kukicha twig tea. Good karma for your kids? Maybe—it's worth a try. Kids will appreciate the playground; Mom and Dad will really appreciate the large, two-bedroom suites and convenient laundry facilities. *500 E. Highland Mall Blvd., Austin; (800) 535-4663; (512) 467-6000;* www.habitatsuites.com

GOOD EATS

Amy's Ice Cream ★★/$

At last count, this popular parlor could be found at three Austin locations: *10000 Research Blvd., (512) 345-1006; 1012B W. 6th St., (512) 480-0673; 3500 Guadalupe St.; (512) 458-6895;* www.amysicecreams.com

Crescent City ★★★/$-$$

So, New Orleans is a few hundred miles east; that doesn't mean you can't have some muffaletta sandwiches and beignets. Kids (and parents) love these sugar-dusted, deep-fried golden pillows of dough, which are easily the best beignets in town (okay, they're also the *only* ones in town). Try to eat just two, or three, or four. *1211 W. 6th St., Austin; (512) 472-9622.*

Hang Town Grill
★★★/$-$$

Inexpensive, informal, and delicious—who could ask for anything more? Kids' meals—pizza, soft tacos, burgers, salads—are just as tasty as the adult-size ones; in fact, they're just scaled-down versions. Upbeat music (reggae to rock), vibrant decor, and jars of crayons at every table make this place a winner for the whole family. *701 N. Capital of Texas Hwy., Austin; (512) 347-1039.*

Pet Savvy

It's easier than ever to bring your pet along on vacation. A number of hotels now accept pets, and some even offer exercise areas and pet room service. (A few go so far as to bring dog biscuits and bottled water to your room on a silver tray!)

Ready Buddy for travel by making sure his ID tags are complete and by taking him on short trips close to home (so he doesn't think getting in the car means going to the vet). Try calling these hotel and motel chains to find out their pet policies: Best Western (800-528-1234); Four Seasons (800-332-3442); Holiday Inn (800-465-4329); Loews (800-235-6397); and Motel 6 (800-466-8356).

Katz's ★★★/$-$$

This is a Texas-style New York deli, which means it's a place you can get a Reuben with jalapeños on the side. The creative kids' menu includes a peanut-butter-and-banana sandwich, which is a Southern thing. *618 6th St., Austin; (512) 472-2037.*

Kerbey Lane Café
★★★/$-$$

Stop here for breakfast (it's served 24 hours a day) and seriously consider the incredible gingerbread pancakes. *3704 Kerbey Lane, Austin; (512) 451-1436.*

Kreutz Market ★★★★/$

You have to earn your meal here. There's generally a line, and getting to the counter requires walking by the fiery hot pit (be sure to keep young children away from the coals; better yet, consider letting one parent wait in the air-conditioned dining room while the other endures the inferno). It's all worth it. The ribs are especially outstanding. *Hwy. 183, Lockhart; (512) 398-2361.*

Louis Mueller Barbecue ★★★/$

This famous pit has brown-tinged walls and windows from all the smokin' going on. Be aware that the sausage links are spiced with jalapeños. *206 W. 2nd St., Taylor; (512) 352-6206.*

The Salt Lick ★★★★/$$-$$$

Located just outside Austin, this barbecue joint encourages you to belly up to the picnic tables and enjoy family-size helpings of BBQ and side dishes in a country setting under live oak trees. Save room for the blackberry (or peach) cobbler. *18300 FM 1826, Austin; (512) 858-4959.*

Threadgills ★★★★/$$-$$$

This Austin restaurant is an institution (the qualification being any place where both Janis Joplin and Willie Nelson have eaten). Kids like the miniature menus, and who can resist the chocolate pie? *Located close to Zilker Park and the bats. 6416 N. Lamar Blvd., Austin; (512) 451-5440;* www.threadgills.com

SOUVENIR HUNTING

Boggy Creek Farm

A real farm in the heart of the city, Boggy Creek has chickens and tractors and friendly farmers, and although you can go only on Wednesdays and Saturdays from 9 A.M. until 2 P.M., there's no charge—other than the produce you buy; after you see and taste it, you'll know this was a great deal. *3414 Lyons Rd., Austin; 926-4650;* www.boggy creekfarm.com

Central Market

This is a mecca for food lovers—including those under age 12—and a perfect place to restock your picnic hamper. You can get gourmet sand-wiches, salads, and cookies packed to go, but after walking around the store snarfing down all the free samples, you may not be hungry for a while. *Two locations: 4477 S. Lamar Blvd., Austin; (512) 899-4300; and 4001 N. Lamar Blvd., Austin; (512) 206-1000.*

Kid Genius

This store sells old-fashioned toys, not just stuff that's a marketing extension of kids' TV shows. Every day Kid Genius also hosts myriad activities for children—from weekly infant play dates to preschool art sessions, story hours, and live music. Most events are free (or very cheap), making this an economical destination as well. *3663 Bee Caves Rd., Austin; (512) 327-0273.*

Party Pig

Are you or your kids party animals? Then indulge yourself at this shop, which celebrates any and all parties and is the place to go for unique costumes, invitations, and decorations. *Three Austin locations: 2900 W. Anderson, (512) 454-2518; 1000 E. 41st, (512) 450-1115; and 5601 Brodie Rd., (512) 892-2721.*

Wild Child

It's a bit pricey, but if you want an outfit you won't find among the chain store offerings, then shop here. Girls have their pick of animal prints, tulle, organza, maribou, velvet, and vintage-inspired outfits. *1601 W. 38th St., Austin; (512) 451-0455.*

Bandera

Located in the heart of the Hill Country, this small town (population: 11,000) will make your family feel as though they have stepped back in time. And even if you don't plan on staying at a ranch (see "Hill Country Dude Ranches" on page 54), it's worth making the trip to Bandera to check out its colorful downtown—it looks like something right out of a Western film set.

CULTURAL ADVENTURES

Frontier Times Museum ★★/$
What you'll find here is an eclectic collection that includes more than 500 bells, a stuffed two-headed goat, and a South American shrunken head. *510 13th St., Bandera; (830) 796-3864.*

JUST FOR FUN

Lost Maples State Park ★★★★/$
Some of the best fall foliage in the state can be found in this state park located west of Bandera in Vanderpool. The name "lost" given to these big-tooth maple trees refers to a prehistoric phenomenon that gave the area perfect soil conditions for the trees, which are usually not found

in this region. The park combines rugged limestone canyons, plateau grasslands, wooded slopes, and clear streams. Peak colors (and crowds) tend to occur in November. Camping and hiking are the park's most popular activities. Call ahead to book a campsite. *(830) 966-3413;* www.tpwd.state.tx.us/park/lostmap/lostmap.htm

BUNKING DOWN

Dixie Dude Ranch ★★/$$
It may be hokey, but as dude ranches go, this place gets a thumbs-up from us (for more information, see "Hill Country Dude Ranches" on page 54).

Flying L Guest Ranch ★★★/$$
This ranch caters to corporate types (it's the only dude ranch in the state with its own golf course), but families are welcome, too (for more information, see "Hill Country Dude Ranches" on page 54).

Fox Fire Log Cabins ★★★/$-$$
Just a mile from Lost Maples State Park, this place offers two-bedroom cabins with kitchens and fireplaces. Children under 14 stay free. There's a volleyball court, a basketball court, a barbecue pit, and laundry facilities. *Hwy. 187, one mile south of Lost Maples State Park, Vanderpool; (830)*

966-2200; (877) 966-8200; www.tex
ashillcountrymall.com/fox/fire.htm

Mayan Dude Ranch ★★★/$$$

Another family-friendly place, the
Mayan Ranch offers stone cottages
and a central lodge nestled on the
banks of the Medina River (for more
information, see "Hill Country Dude
Ranches" on page 54).

GOOD EATS

Cabaret Café and Dance Hall
★★★★/$$-$$$

This is where the cowboys come to
party. Popular with locals and dude-
ranch guests, the Cabaret offers a
variety of kids' meals, including
chicken fingers shaped like dinosaurs;
for Mom and Dad, there is great
gourmet cuisine including steaks,
catfish, chicken, and Mexican dishes.
But the real appeal is the adjacent
dance hall where old and young come
to two-step to Western swing music.
Lessons from the locals are available,
or you can simply wing it. *801 Main
St., Bandera; (830) 796-8166; www.
thecabaretcafe.com*

O.S.T. Restaurant
★★★/$$-$$$

Named for the Old Spanish Trail,
which runs through town, this place
serves up chicken-fried steak and
Tex-Mex fare, but kids will be tick-
led by the dinosaur-shaped chicken
fingers; it's quite appropriate since
a real dinosaur footprint was discovered about 20 miles south of
Bandera. *305 Main, Bandera; (830)
796-3836.*

Fredericksburg

Fredericksburg's well-preserved
downtown looks movie-set perfect,
with shops best described as Bavaria
meets the Wild West. The city tends
to draw well-heeled city folk who are
into antiquing, but there are a few
points of interest for kids.

There's the perfectly kid-named
Enchanted Rock State Park, for
starters (see page 60), the Admiral
Nimitz State Park (at right), and the
Pioneer Museum (see page 60).
www.fredericksburg-texas.com

CULTURAL ADVENTURES

Admiral Nimitz State Park
★★/$

This park showcases the military
craft and weapons used in WWII.
The grounds also include a Japanese
Garden of Peace. This attraction will
be of interest to older children who
have studied the war in school, or

those with an interest in war arti-facts. *340 E. Main St., Fredericksburg; (830) 997-4379;* www.tpwd.state.tx.us/park/nimitz/nimitz.htm

Pioneer Museum ★★/$

The historical structures here give children a glimpse into 19th-century life; there's a barn, a smokehouse, a log cabin, a schoolhouse, and a "Sunday House"—one of the many

tiny houses in town that were used by area farmers when they would come to the city to shop on Saturday and attend church on Sunday. *309 W. Main St., Fredericksburg; (830) 997-2835;* www.pioneermuseum.com

JUST FOR FUN

Enchanted Rock State Park ★★★★/$

Enchanted Rock rises 600 feet in the air, and this domed, gran-ite hilltop looks like a Martian land-scape—except that it's in the heart of the Hill Country. The peak offers spec-tacular views, but be ready for a stren-uous 20-minute hike on sheer rock.

Kids over age 6 or so should be able to handle it, but preschoolers

'CUE IT UP, TEXAS STYLE

FORGET POLITICS. The *real* thing Texans debate is who has the best barbecue. The consensus comes down to several joints located in small towns about 30 miles outside of Austin—a kind of barbecue loop. Any and even all of these places are worth a detour or—in the case of one personal expedition—a whole day, multiple-taste-test dining marathon.

The entire scene is an experience: Finding the places, standing in line,

and then eating meat served on butcher paper, with silverware kept to a minimum. (Bring wipes.)

We know it can be hard to lure kids away from fast-food chains (no bar-becue place we've heard of gives out kids' meal prizes), but tell them they can eat with their fingers and see a big fire pit and maybe you'll pique their curiosity.

First a few pointers: these are infor-mal places. You line up at a counter, may need some help (many parents carry toddlers in backpacks as they ascend). Make sure everyone wears appropriate shoes and attends to all needs before starting the hike up (there are no rest rooms at the top). There's a shaded playground near the rest rooms, and there are campsites at the base of the rock. All park campsites are tent only, no RVs. **NOTE:** Get here early. Due to erosion problems, the park limits the number of guests that can enter each day, so if you arrive after 3 P.M. on a busy day, you may not be allowed in. The afternoon heat can also be oppressive, as it radiates off the rock. Because of the high temperatures, no one will accuse you of wimping out if you only hike up a small part of the rock and forgo the climb to the top.

If you come in the summer, be forewarned that at night the huge rock makes loud creaking and moaning sounds as it cools off. (Comanche Indians said the eerie sounds were the spirits of the dead.) There's a small entry fee ($5 per person, under 13 are free at press time). *The park is located 18 miles north of Fredericksburg on Ranch Road 965; (915) 247-3903;* www.tpwd.state.tx. us/park/enchantd/enchantd.htm

BUNKING DOWN

Schmidt Barn ★★★★/$$
One of Fredericksburg's many small *gastehauses*, this one is actually set in an old stone barn with timber beams and a cozy sleeping loft. Don't

place your order by the pound or half pound (the choices are typically pork ribs, pork chops, beef brisket, and sausage links). Sometimes the meat is served on butcher paper instead of plates. Asking for sauce is considered rude (and very touristy). The meat is so succulent and flavorful that sauce isn't needed. To blend in with the locals, order a Big Red (a cherry-cola drink). Ask for bread and you'll get the old-fashioned white-loaf stuff. Side dishes vary, but potato salad and beans are standard offerings. Our favorite 'cue spots are **Louis Mueller Barbecue** in Taylor and **Kreutz Market** in Lockhart (see Good Eats on page 56 for both).

Even if you aren't 'cue crazy, a trip to these 'cue shrines takes you through scenic small towns and farmland that have provided perfect locations for Hollywood films, including *What's Eating Gilbert Grape* and *The Great Waldo Pepper* (both filmed in Lockhart).

Thanks, I'll Pass

When driving on the rural two-lane roads of Texas, you may notice that a slow-moving car ahead of you begins to pull over and then drives on the shoulder of the highway. The driver probably isn't distracted; he or she is simply letting you pass. Give a wave of thanks as you drive by.

worry: it also has modern amenities, including a microwave and a coffeemaker. Book through Gastehaus Schmidt. *231 W. Main, Fredericksburg; (830) 997-5612;* www.schmidt barn.com

Good Eats

Hilltop Café ★★★★/$$-$$$

After a hard day hiking at Enchanted Rock, refuel at this popular restaurant, about 11 miles north of Fredericksburg on Highway 87. The cuisine is a curious mix of Cajun and Greek, though the kids' menu includes macaroni and cheese, fried shrimp, chicken fingers, and, yes, peanut-butter-and-jelly sandwiches. There's a pinball machine in the back. Reservations are advised on weekends. *312 W. Main St., Fredericksburg; (830) 997-8922.*

Souvenir Hunting

Texas Jack

This Western store has outfitted several movie and television productions, including *Lonesome Dove* and *Gunsmoke.* Your kids will get a kick out of the long johns. *117 Adams St., Fredericksburg; (830) 997-3213.*

Wildseed Farms

Here's a place where picking something out means literally *picking* it. This working wildflower farm (yes, wildflowers take work) lets you pick your own flowers (whatever's blooming) for $3 a bucket. *Located seven miles east of Fredericksburg on Hwy. 290; (830) 990-1393;* www.wild seed farms.com

New Braunfels

New Braunfels, founded in 1845 by a German prince and about 200 settlers, is located between Austin and San Antonio along Interstate 35. The town retains much of the feel of the Old Country, with German restaurants, architecture, and festivities such as the annual Wurstfest, typically held the last week of September and the first week of October, where you can hear top yodelers and accordion players. (*For a detailed schedule of events, check out the city's Website,* www.nbcham.org) Thanks to its proximity to larger cities and its own unique attractions, such as the Schlitterbahn water park and resort, New Braunfels makes a great base for your Hill Country vacation.

Nearby, the small city of Gruene (pronounced Green) is a great place to spend a day or afternoon checking out its famous weekend flea markets and its dance hall, said to be the oldest in Texas. It's a true taste of the Lone Star State your family is sure to enjoy.

JUST FOR FUN

Gruene Market Days ★★★/Free

On Saturdays from April through December, more than a hundred vendors set up their wares in the small community of Gruene, just north of New Braunfels on the Guadalupe River. You can buy handmade toys and other trinkets here. After your shopping spree, stop by Gruene Hall, which claims to be the state's oldest dance hall; it certainly feels about as Texas as you can get. Lone Star state legends from Willie Nelson to George Srait have performed here. It's worth a visit just to watch the locals two-step—you may even want to try a few steps with your kids. *To get to Gruene, take Loop 337 from New Braunfels to Gruene Road.*

Guadalupe River ★★★★/Free

The Guadalupe River is a favorite place for rafting and riding inner tubes. However, while it often looks lazy enough, be aware that the river can turn treacherous after a heavy rain; it can also get very low in the

FamilyFun READER'S TIP -

Travel Trivia

My husband and I wanted our family trip to be both educational and fun for our 9- and 11-year-old boys. To engage their interest, we devised a game to play while sight-seeing. Every morning I would give my sons three questions pertaining to the places we would visit that day. If they answered all three, they could order the dessert of their choice at dinner. They could use any resource, including a plaque at the site, a tour guide, brochures, and the like. They thought it was great fun to win a dessert off Mom and Dad, and they were so successful that we bought a round every night. Websites and guidebooks were our sources for the questions. With that little bit of preparation, our kids ended up not only having a great time but learning a lot, too.

Kathy Davis, Charlotte, North Carolina

FamilyFun GAME

A Is for Armadillo

This is a terrific game to play with preschoolers. More populated areas yield more interesting results. The leader picks a letter and announces it to the other players, who then join the leader in competing to find three things (both in and out of the car) that start with the designated letter. Choose A, for example, and you might spot an armadillo, an automobile, and an apple. The first person to succeed gets to choose the next letter.

summer months, making for a rocky raft ride. If you prefer to stay on land, you can still enjoy a view of the river at Guadalupe State Park, which has a mile of river frontage. The park also has camping areas and, if you do decide to get wet, places to put your canoe or tube in the river or simply go for a swim. *The park is located off Highway 46, about 37 miles west of New Braunfels.* If you need to rent equipment or feel too inexperienced to tackle the river without a guide, call an outfitter. One of our favorites is the **Gruene River Rafting Co.***; (830) 625-2800.*

Schlitterbahn
FamilyFun ★★★/$$$$
In case you're curious, *schlitterbahn* means slippery road in German, and that's what your family will find at this fun-filled,

all-purpose amusement park complex—lots of slippery roads, including the Master Blaster, a water coaster that takes you to a height of six stories before dropping you into a pool (gulp!). It's located on the banks of the spring-fed Comal River, and the park uses cool spring water in some of its rides. In fact, some of the tube chutes actually sweep you into the river, where you can float alongside fish and turtles.

The park is split into two separate sections, which are located about three blocks apart but connected by free trams and buses. The original site is probably a better bet for families with younger children. Rides include Sand Castle Cove, a five-story water fun house with four water slides. The other side of the park has more thrill rides. The Black Knight is a good bet if you don't want to wait in a long line. If you're traveling here from Austin or San Antonio, get the half-day ticket—it's cheaper and still gives the kids plenty of exercise. Some families build their whole vacation around this place, even staying at one of the park's riverside motel rooms, cottages, or condominiums. Room rates are reasonable, starting at about $100 a night at press time (for more information, see page 65). Parking is free and families are welcome to bring in coolers and picnics—glass containers and anything alcoholic are prohibited. The park opens for the season in late April, operating on weekends only until Memorial Day weekend, and generally closes for the season in September. *New Braunfels; (830) 625-2351;* www.schlitterbahn.com

BUNKING DOWN

Guadalupe River Ranch
★★★★/$$$-$$$$
Play wild west at a dude ranch that welcomes young cowpokes with nature hikes, crafts, hayrides, fireside sing-alongs, and more (for more information, see "Hill Country Dude Ranches" on page 54).

Kuebler-Waldrip Haus
★★★★/$-$$$
Stay in a former one-room school-house at this bed-and-breakfast located between New Braunfels and Greune. Situated on 43 acres, the inn feels more like a farm (cows, goats, deer, and three cats wander the grounds). Try to get one of the two rooms in the lower level of the Danville Schoolhouse, both of which

accommodate four. Also, the two rooms share an extra whirlpool bath, making them a good arrangement for larger families who need more space; they also have refrigerators and microwaves. **NOTE:** The inn charges $30 per night for adults and $20 per night (at press time) for children ages 3 to 18. Rates include breakfast. *1620 Hueco Springs Loop, New Braunfels; (800) 299-8372; (830) 625-8300.*

Schlitterbahn Resorts
★★★/$$-$$$$
If your family expects to spend a day or two at the famous New Braunfels water park, plan on staying on-site at one of the resort's many homes, inns, or motels. Considering the convenience and the fact that resort guests get a 20 percent discount on park admission, it's a great deal. Accommodations include town homes, hot tub suites, and two- and three-bedroom duplexes with kitchens, as well as basic motel rooms. *New Braunfels. Call (830) 625-2351 for reservations;* www. schlitterbahn.com/resort.htm

COUNTING COWS Play as individuals or teams. First, decide on a destination where you will stop counting. Then, count the cows on your side of the road. The goal is to have the highest number when the destination is reached. Pass a cemetery on your side and you have to start over again. You also can count red cars, mailboxes, or phone booths.

Wimberley

If you're looking for a relaxing place that seems worlds away from the bustling cities of Austin and San Antonio but is really only an hour's drive from either, then consider this town nestled on the banks of the Blanco River. Wimberley is famous for an enclave of artisans who sell their wares in shops along the town's square. If shopping isn't your bag, then relax and enjoy the city's chill-out attractions, which in the summer include a unique outdoor movie theater and a swimming hole. If you want to downshift to a slower pace, Wimberley is the place to be.

JUST FOR FUN

Blue Hole
★★★/$
This old-fashioned swimming hole in Wimberley has been cooling off Texas kids for decades. Get here early and pack a picnic to enjoy under the canopy of cypress trees by the 13-foot-deep, spring-fed creek. There's music on weekends. The property's owners charge $5 per person for a one-time entry to the hole (locals or long-term visitors can buy a $50 family membership, good for a year). There's also an adjacent campground with 50 campsites. *Located a quarter of a mile from downtown Wimberly. From Ranch Road 12 on the square, take the Old Kyle Road at the Texaco station; make a left after the cemetery. On Blue Hole Lane, Wimberly;* (512) 847-9127.

Corral Theater
★★★/$
While Mom and Dad reminisce, the whole family can enjoy the latest movies and the twinkling fireflies at the same time at this vintage outdoor movie theater, which dates back to the 1940s and retains its old-time charm with cheap ticket prices ($3 and under). Most films shown are not rated above a PG-13. Families are welcome to bring quilts and lawn chairs or sit on the wooden bleachers. *Flite Acres Rd., Wimberley;* (512) 847-2513. Open from Memorial Day through Labor Day only.

SOUVENIR HUNTING

Wimberley Pie Co.
Walk into this bakery and you'll be overwhelmed by the aroma of freshly baked pies. Selections vary daily: on a recent trip they included peach crumb and pecan. There are a few tables if you choose to eat in, or you can pack up your pies to go. *Ranch Rd. 12, Wimberley;* (512) 847-9462; www.wimberleypie.com

SCENIC HILL COUNTRY DRIVES

T HE HILL COUNTRY is full of scenic, two-lane blacktops, perfect for a short drive and perhaps a picnic. Here are a few suggestions:

Peach Pit Stops

Take U.S. 290 from Fredericksburg to Johnson City for a scenic drive through some of the state's prime peach orchards. In the summer, there are many roadside stands selling peaches and other fruits in season. Stonewall, a town between Fredericksburg and Johnson City, is the home of many stands and the heart of peach country. There are more than 25 varieties of peaches, all with different ripening dates. Some stands also sell cantaloupes, tomatoes, squash, watermelon, and okra. In the spring, U.S. 290 from Fredericksburg to Austin offers one of the state's best bluebonnet displays.

The Willow City Loop

From Fredericksburg, take Highway 16 north to Eckert, then head east on Farm Road 1323. Go about three miles to Willow City, then watch for a small wooden sign pointing out the Willow City Loop. You will drive on the side of a ridge for about 13 miles, then swoop down into Coal Creek Valley, also called Devil's Kitchen or the Dungeon. Centuries ago, meteors crashed here, leaving a large earthen gash and mounds of rocks. In the spring, you'll enjoy great views of bluebonnets in the valleys below. The road leads through Cedar Mountain, home to the state's only serpentine quarry. Be careful to watch the road for wandering cattle and deer.

Wimberley and the Devil's Backbone

From San Marcus, take Ranch Road 12 about 15 miles to the town of Wimberley. Stop and enjoy a walk around the scenic town square and pick up a pie at the Wimberley Pie Co. on Ranch Road 12 just south of the square. Take a right on Ranch Road 32 for a ride on the twisting road, dubbed the Devil's Backbone for its sharp switchbacks. **NOTE:** The road's sharp turns have actually made some passengers carsick, so think about administering motion sickness meds before making this drive.

After the hustle and bustle of Dallas, kick back in casual Fort Worth. Check out the daily cattle drives in the historic district.

Dallas and Fort Worth

DALLAS—famous for being home to the Dallas Cowboys and the popular '70s television show *Dallas*—and Fort Worth, its neighbor to the west, together are home to almost five million people. Known locally as the Metroplex, the region sprawls across the north Texas prairie from Plano to the north to Waxahachie in the south, with everything conveniently connected by fast-moving freeways. Although it's often hard to tell when you leave one city and enter another, the individual towns and neighborhoods vary widely in their cultural histories and attitudes.

For example, Dallas and Fort Worth are only 25 miles apart on Interstate 30, but worlds apart in many ways. Dallas, with its glittering skyline and world-class shopping malls, is dressier and faster

THE **FamilyFun** LIST

MUST-SEE · MUST-SEE

The Ballpark in Arlington
(page 74)

Cowgirl Hall of Fame (page 72)

Dallas Arboretum and Botanical Garden (page 74)

Fort Worth Museum of Science and History (page 72)

Fort Worth Stockyards
(page 77)

Fort Worth Zoo (page 78)

The Science Place (page 72)

Six Flags Over Texas
(page 79)

Texas Stadium (page 80)

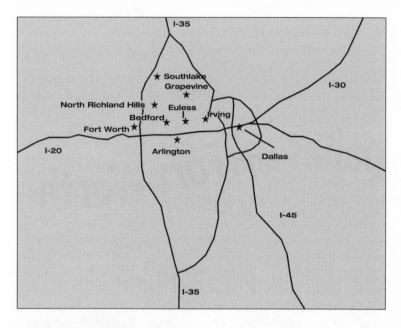

paced. In Fort Worth, a laid-back and casual attitude prevails. Once the start of the Chisholm Trail, Fort Worth offers visitors an authentic taste of the Old West, plus nationally renowned museums and arts events. Arlington, located between Dallas and Fort Worth, is a popular family destination because it is home to the Six Flags Over Texas theme park and the Texas Rangers professional baseball team. And in nearby Irving, sports fans can walk the hallowed grounds of Texas Stadium, home of the five-time NFL champions the Dallas Cowboys. To learn more about this sports-crazy city's all-star hangouts, see "From Punts to Pucks" on page 83.

Many families arrive in the area via the huge Dallas/Fort Worth International Airport; it's not a bad idea to base your stay at one of the hotels near the airport since it's located in the middle of the Metroplex—30 minutes' drive to either Dallas or Fort Worth. But if you only have a weekend, it may be wiser to focus on one city rather than spending all your time on the highway driving back and forth. By the way, you probably will have to rent a car if you aren't planning to drive one to the area. While Dallas has a new rail-transit system known as DART and a few trains run between Dallas and Fort Worth, it's still a very car-driven (pardon the pun) society. (Some tourists have given up attempts to walk across busy highways and exchanges that separate major attractions, and will hail a cab even to go a mile or less!) Also, be advised that in image-conscious Dallas valet parking rules, even at the occasional barbecue joint, so be prepared to cough up the standard $1 to $2 tip.

Although the region is home to glittering new skyscrapers and shiny, state-of-the-art mega-malls, it has several interesting historical sites. Many Americans remember Dallas as the place where former president John F. Kennedy was assassinated, and today the Sixth Floor Museum recounts that tragic episode in our nation's history. While it isn't appropriate for preschoolers, older children can see where history was made—even checking out the view from the spot where Lee Harvey Oswald allegedly shot President Kennedy—and at the same time learn about other theories on what might have happened. At the historic Fort Worth Stockyards, younger kids can get a chance to view the nation's only city-operated cattle drive, along the Trinity River, and to take a trip on the Tarantula Steam Train. In Dallas, Old City Park recreates what the town looked liked around 1887 and families can take a leisurely carriage ride—horse-drawn evidence of how much more slowly time must have moved in the 19th century.

The 212-foot-tall Texas Star **Ferris wheel** at Fair Park is the tallest Ferris wheel in North America.

North Texas is home to several kid-friendly museums—including the Fort Worth Science and History Museum, where your children can splash around in the water play area or see educational films at the IMAX theater. The Fort Worth Zoo just completed a major expansion that added a large native-animal habitat—including a prairie-dog town—called Texas Lives. The museum at the Ballpark in Arlington, accessible from the south side of the stadium, has an impressive collection of baseball memorabilia and lets kids record their own voices calling part of a famous game. And when hunger strikes, you can have lunch or din-

Clap, Tickle, Tug

It's the sitting—and sitting and sitting—that gets to kids on the road. Get their belted-in bodies moving with this game of competitive copycat. The first player makes an expression or a movement, such as a hand clap; the next player repeats that movement and adds another; and so on. Kids will be pulling on their ears, sticking out their tongues, tipping back their heads, holding their elbows—and smiling! When a player forgets a movement, he's out. When everyone's out, start over.

ner in the company of an army of alligators at the Rainforest Café in Grapevine Mills. Awesome!

Its "Big D" image aside, it's possible for you and your family to pack in a lot of fun in Dallas/Fort Worth without spending like someone who just struck oil. We'll help you create and organize a fun—and budget-minded—trip to the area that combines the best of city living with a taste of the Old West. Valet park or saddle up—you can go either way in this diverse Metroplex.

CULTURAL ADVENTURES

Cowgirl Hall of Fame
FamilyFun ★★★★/$$$$

This new museum celebrates the can-do spirit of women ranchers and cowgirls with interactive displays and mini-biographies. It's a must-stop for any horse crazy girl in your crew, but boys will find plenty to do too and everyone in the family will have fun seeing if they have what it takes to be a true cowgirl. There's a talking horse and nice photo opportunity aboard a bronco with a rodeo backdrop. The museum's honorees include famous cowgirls like Annie Oakley, but also a few you might not expect, like Supreme Court Justice Sandra Day O'Connor, who grew up on an Arizona ranch, and Wilma Mankiller,

a leader of the Cherokee nation. The museum is located just west of downtown Fort Worth in the cultural district and can easily be paired with nearby museums such as the Fort Worth Museum of Science and History for a great day trip. The museum is closed Mondays. *1720 Gendy St., Fort Worth; (817) 336-4475;* www.cowgirl.net

Fort Worth Museum of
FamilyFun **Science and History**
★★★/$-$$

This museum is popular with families because it has something for everyone. Teens and older kids will want to check out the Nobel Planetarium's laser-light and astronomy shows. There's also an IMAX theater that shows science- and history-related films. Downstairs at the Kidspace, there's a waterworks section and a play area for even the smallest crawlers. Outside, kids can dig for dinosaur bones at the DinoDig exhibit. *1501 Montgomery St., Fort Worth; (817) 732-1631;* www.fortworthmuseum.org

The Science Place
FamilyFun ★★★/$

Physics actually seems like fun at this museum, with hands-on experiments and do-it-yourself displays, including an area where your kids can play with lasers (safely, of course). At the Kids' Place area, younger children 6 and under can wander through the Number Forest, a room filled with giant numbers that reach from floor to ceiling, and spend a good part of the afternoon tinkering with boats and waterwheels at the Waterworks station. The museum also has an IMAX theater and a planetarium (recent shows have included a Cowboy Astronomer who tells funny stories and tall tales based on the constellations). *1318 Second Ave., in Fair Park, Dallas; (214) 428-5555;* www.scienceplace.org

The Sixth Floor Museum
★★★/Free-$$

History often marks tragic events, and this museum, housed on the sixth floor of the old Texas School Book Depository, recounts the events leading up to and following President John F. Kennedy's assassination in Dallas in 1963. The exhibit includes photographs and film newsreels that present vivid images of that time; there's even a re-creation of the corner from which Lee Harvey Oswald allegedly shot the president, just as it appeared then. Given the grim subject matter and powerful presentation, the museum is appropriate only for older elementary school students who appreciate hands-on history. They can actually write in a memory book that's provided to record what visitors think about the assassination—how it changed the country and/or affected their family. *411 Elm St., Dallas; (214) 747-6660;* www.jfk.org

The Women's Museum
★★★★/$

Opened in 2000, this museum celebrates the triumphs and tribulations of American women, where you can learn just how much they have contributed to our history and heritage (as if you didn't already know). Your young ladies (and men) will learn the stories of more than 3,000 women, including Blanche Stuart Smith, the first woman to fly an airplane back in 1910. There's not much here for preschoolers, but kids ages 7 and up will enjoy the interactive exhibits that include touch screens, computer stations, and video and audio footage of, among others, athletes such as soccer star Mia Hamm and great comediennes such as Lucille Ball. Daughters (and sons) can use the Career Scoreboard to figure out what they want to be when they grow up. *3800 Parry Ave., Dallas; (214) 915-0861;* www.thewomensmuseum.org

FamilyFun TIP

Call Ahead

Besides scouting resources at your library, call or write to city chambers of commerce and state tourism boards for information about your destination. Let your kids make lists of the things they hope to see and let each child pick one activity to do each day (parents have veto power over monster truck rallies, of course).

JUST FOR FUN

American Airlines Center
★★★/$$

This new arena just west of Downtown Dallas is home to the NHL's Dallas Stars and the NBA's Dallas Mavericks. Parents will appreciate the 20 family rest rooms located throughout the facility; there's also a lost child program that lets you register your children through guest services where they are given a wristband with information on how to find their parents. The concession stands stock Texas barbecue and bratwurst along with standard pizza and hot dogs. *2500 Victory Ave., Dallas; (214) 665-4700; www.americanairlinescenter.com*

 The Ballpark in Arlington
★★★★/$$-$$$$

Sports fans alert: these stadiums offer surefire scores. For more information, see "From Punts to Pucks" on page 83.

Dallas Arboretum and Botanical Garden
★★★/$-$$

Only about 15 minutes north of downtown Dallas, this park is spread over 66 acres along the shores of White Rock Lake. Its annual Dallas Blooms festival, typically held in late March through mid-April, showcases thousands of daffodils, tulips, and iris bulbs, as well as scores of azaleas. The park frequently has child-friendly exhibits and boasts the city's best picnicking spot—a grassy meadow that trails

Fort Worth
Where the West Begins

9 A.M. Begin your tour of Cowtown with breakfast downtown at **Le Madeleine** (see page 81); its menu is so diverse that there's something to satisfy everyone in the family. The cafeteria-style line also means little or no wait for your food.

10 A.M. Head up to the **Fort Worth Stockyards**; it's a short drive, two miles north of downtown on Main Street. Take in some of the retail shops selling all types of Western apparel and paraphernalia, including kid-size chaps and cowboy hats. (For more information about the Stockyards, see page 77.)

11:30 A.M. Fort Worth folks eat lunch early, so beat the lunch rush and head to **Joe T. Garcia's** (see page 81), the city's famous Tex-Mex mecca. If it's sunny, and it typically is, then take a seat in the restaurant's beautiful patio area. The menu here is limited to two items: enchiladas and fajitas. If your childown to the lake. In 2000, the Texas Pioneer Adventure was added. Here, youngsters can explore the exhibit's sod house, log cabin, and covered wagon and get a hands-on look at life a hundred years ago. The arboretum frequently has special weekend events geared to families, including children's music concerts, hay bale mazes, and lectures on plants and flowers. *8525 Garland Rd., Dallas; (214) 327-8263; www.dallasarboretum.org*

Dallas World Aquarium
★★★/$$$

Located in the popular West End section of downtown Dallas, this aquarium has thirteen 2,000-gallons tanks filled with water life from all over the world. Children love walking through the entrance tunnel where they are surrounded by brightly colored tropical fish. In 1999, the facility added two manatee sisters from Venezuela; both were rescued after being entangled in fishing nets and separated from their mother. The aquarium staff hopes to one day return the manatees to the sea and plans to continue to be a home for other orphaned marine mammals. Other exhibits showcase giant humphead wrasses, stingrays, and endangered green sea turtles. There's also an exhibit that simulates the South American rain forest, with exotic plants, monkeys, and soft-billed toucans. *1801 N. Griffin St., Dallas; (214) 720-2224; www.dwazoo.com*

Dallas Zoo ★★★★/$$
The newly opened Lacerte Family Children's Zoo is nirvana for families looking for an interactive zoo experience. The two-acre facility (it's

dren aren't accustomed to such fare, then take the safer choice of the fajitas. Even the most finicky eater will likely devour these homemade tortillas. The restaurant doesn't serve dessert, so save room for ice cream later.

1 P.M. Head southwest on Riverside Drive to the city's Museum District. The **Fort Worth Museum of Science and History** (see page 72) has a great play area downstairs where younger children can watch the fascinating waterworks. They won't even get too wet—thanks to the museum's supply of raincoats.

3 P.M. If you're raring for some more action, take University Drive south to the entrance of the **Fort Worth Zoo** (see page 78). Be sure to see the gorillas, cheetahs, penguins, and the koala exhibit. Grab some ice cream at Milwaukee Joe's shop next to the petting zoo. At day's end, hop on the **Forest Park Train** (it's located across the street from the zoo) for the 45-minute ride along Forest Park on the Trinity River.

Cheer the Steers

Fort Worth lives up to its Cowtown nickname by being the only city in the country that holds daily cattle drives. The town actually owns a herd of a dozen or so longhorn steers and drives them each day from the historic Fort Worth Stockyards to a grassy area on the west fork of the Trinity River just north of downtown—an easy, flat spot that's less than a mile away. The city spends about $300,000 a year for the cattle drives, which are designed to highlight Fort Worth's cowboy heritage dating back to 1866, the first time longhorn cattle passed through town on the way to Kansas markets. Admission is free for the daily drive and times may vary, depending on the season. *For more information, call the Fort Worth Convention and Visitors Bureau at (817) 336-8791; www.fortworth.com*

inside the main zoo) gives kids plenty—the kid-sized "mongoose burrow," which they can crawl in and out of and where they delight in popping up from holes located right inside the mongoose habitat. At the Wallaby Walkabout, your youngsters can scamper around the small Australian marsupials as they roam freely across the walkways. Parents of preschoolers will love the Tot Spot, a playground with a sandbox and small jungle gym. The zoo also features an endangered-tiger habitat and Primate Place, the home of the zoo's monkeys and gibbons. On Saturdays and Sundays, zookeepers give lectures and answer kids' questions. Check the schedule at the entrance for times and locations. If you get hungry, there's a Subway restaurant and Ndebele Café, which sounds exotic but really offers standard kid favorites like hot dogs, cheeseburgers, cotton candy, and a variety of frozen treats, including the great Texas delicacy, Blue Bell ice cream. *650 South R.L. Thornton Fwy., Dallas; (214) 670-5656; www.dallas-zoo.org*

Fair Park ★★★/Free-$$

Built in the 1930s to house two international expositions, Fair Park is a gem of Art Deco architecture that is home to Cotton Bowl Stadium, which is where the area's major league soccer franchise, the Dallas Burn, practices and plays its home games. The stadium also hosts the annual football showdown between the University of Texas Longhorns and University of Oklahoma Sooners and, of course, the annual Cotton Bowl. Fair Park is also home to most of Dallas's major museums, including **The Science Place** (see page 72) and the new **Women's Museum** (see page 73). Other museums located here include the **Dallas Aquarium** (which is fair but not as impressive as the Dallas World Aquarium—confusingly enough, not the same place), and the **Age of Steam Museum**, an outdoor collection of refurbished trains and related memorabilia. The **Fair Park Music Hall** hosts performances by touring companies of Broadway musicals, and the **Smirnoff Amphitheater** often holds major rock and pop concerts.

In addition, Fair Park is home to the **State Fair of Texas**, a huge event held during the last week of September through the third week of October. The fair is a family tradition for many Texans, and any visit to the state fair has to include Big Tex, the 52-foot-tall, jeans-clad cowboy who welcomes everyone with his booming "Howdy Partner!" The food groups found at any self-respecting state fair are here—corn dogs, funnel cakes, and candied apples. *1300 Robert B. Cullum Blvd., Dallas; (214) 670-8400;* www.bigtex.com

Fort Worth Stockyards
FamilyFun ★★★/Free

When tourists come to Texas to see the Old West, they head to this historic district, once home to the area's cattle slaughterhouses. (Fort Worth was also once on the great longhorn cattle drive toward the Chisholm Trail, which technically started at the Red River.) The meatpackers are gone and the 100 acres of stock pens have been reduced to a mere 15 acres. But that's enough to get a feel for what used to be. Don't worry about getting caught in a roundup or a stampede. There are really not many cattle still around, just a handful used for photo opportunities and the small herd of about a dozen or so owned by the city of Fort Worth (see "Cheer the Steers" on page 76).

The Stockyards delight most kids—they love the small kiddie rides that operate most weekends, and the shops filled with plenty of pint-size cowboy and cowgirl gear. For information about tours or brochures for a self-guided exploration of the area, go to the **Livestock Exchange Building** *(131 E. Exchange Ave.),* a Spanish-style building that houses the Stockyards Museum. Stockyards Station is a western-themed retail center where the Tarantula Steam Train makes its runs to and from Grapevine (see page 80). *130 Exchange Ave., Fort Worth; (817) 625-9715;* www.fortworthstockyards.org

BILLBOARD POETRY Take turns picking out four words from road signs. Give the words to the other players who have one minute to use the words in a four-line, rhyming poem, using one word in each line.

Fort Worth Zoo
FamilyFun ★★★/$-$$

Opened in 1901, this zoo has expanded through the years and now houses more than 4,000 animals on 58 acres. Among the new residents in recent years are penguins and koalas, living in their natural habitats. The World of Primates exhibit lets you view gorillas in a simulated rain forest. There's also a section called Texas Wild, featuring animals of Texas—including a herd of buffalo and a prairie dog village—and an adjacent farm and petting zoo with lots of hungry goats (you can buy feed from small machines located inside the petting area). Don't miss the incredible ice cream served up at the shop next to the farm. And save time for a trip on the Forest Park Train, across from the zoo entrance; the 45-minute ride on this miniature steam train is the perfect way to unwind and rest tired feet. *1989 Colonial Pkwy., Fort Worth; (817) 871-7050; www.fortworthzoo.com*

Grapevine Mills ★★/Free
Located just north of DFW International Airport, this large mall—it has more than 200 shops, movie theaters, and restaurants—is an attraction in itself; it's not uncommon to see shoppers wheeling shopping carts alongside their luggage as they seek out bargains while on a layover. The mall marries outlet shops with entertainment offerings, including a 30-screen megaplex and a Gameworks video arcade. Kids love the Rainforest Café, where they can eat dinner (the usual stuff: burgers, PB&J, chicken fingers) surrounded by "animatronically correct" jungle wildlife. *3000 Grapevine Mills Pkwy., Grapevine; (972) 724-4910.*

NRH2O ★★★/$$$
If you're visiting in the summer and need a place to cool off, head for this water park owned and operated by the city of North Richland Hills, located about 15 miles northeast of downtown Fort Worth on Texas Highway 26. The park has a splash area that's perfect for preschoolers who want to frolic next to a kid-size, water-spouting train. Older kids can enjoy the more thrilling water slides and the giant wave pool. There's also a lazy river for relaxing. Be sure to get there when it opens (typically 10 A.M.) because all the tables and lounge chairs in the few shaded areas go fast. *9001 Grapevine Hwy., North Richland Hills; (817) 656-6500; www.nrh2o.com*

FamilyFun TIP

Layover Plans

If you get stuck with a long layover, give your children a portable tape recorder so they can interview family members or fellow travelers about their destinations. Also, make sure favorite travel games, toys, and books are packed in their carry-on luggage.

Old City Park ★★★/Free-$

Nestled next to modern downtown Dallas is a 19th-century version of downtown. At this park, located on 13 acres, your family can meander through the village, checking out a log cabin, Victorian-era homes, a bank, a train depot, the General Store (which carries old-fashioned toys such as dolls and cap guns), and a blacksmith shop where you can watch the smithy at work; if your kids are curious, he'll explain what he's doing. Take a family ride in a horse-drawn carriage and enjoy the slower pace of yesteryear. *1717 Gano St., Dallas; (214) 421-5141; www.oldcitypark.org*

Pioneer Plaza ★★/Free

This 4.2-acre park features what's billed as "the world's largest bronze monument," a bronze version of a herd of 47 longhorn steer being driven by three cowboys on horseback. The park also has native plants and a small stream, providing great photo opportunities if you can steer your kids in the right direction. *Corner of Young and Griffin Sts., downtown Dallas.*

Six Flags Over Texas

FamilyFun ★★★/$$$$

Each section of this theme park reflects a different piece of the history of the state of Texas—there's a Mexican village, a frontier town, even an area that re-creates the 1950s. Roller coaster fans from all over consider the Texas Giant to be one of the best wooden coasters in the country. Ride it, but only if you can take the 14-story drop! If you really want a giant roller coaster, you can also check out the new Titan, which will take you up to 85 mph. There's a special area for little kids, too, and family favorites such as bumper cars and a carousel. *2201 Road to Six Flags, Arlington; (817) 640-8900; www.sixflags.com/texas*

The Studios at Las Colinas ★★/$$

Your kids can check out the place where popular shows such as *Barney* and *Gerbert* are filmed, but don't expect to run into the PBS stars. Their sets are typically closed, but you can tour other parts of the studio and see lots of famous movie memorabilia, including the dress Judy Garland wore as Dorothy in *The Wizard of Oz* and the bench where Tom Hanks contemplated the box of chocolates in *Forrest Gump*. Tours last around an hour. *6301 N. O'Connor Rd., Irving; (972) 869-FILM; www.studiosatlas colinas.com/*

Tarantula Steam Train
★★★/$$$-$$$$

A historic steam train built in 1896 or a diesel locomotive (if the steam train is in the shop) runs from Grapevine to Fort Worth twice daily, providing a unique link between Grapevine's historic Main Street and the Fort Worth Stockyards. It's a great excursion for budding train buffs. The train is actually owned by the city of Grapevine, which is located just north of Dallas Fort Worth International Airport, about 25 miles northeast of Fort Worth. Board the train at the historic depot near the intersection of Dallas Road and Main Street at 10 A.M. and enjoy a leisurely hour-and-a-quarter ride into the Stockyards and then back again. Be advised this is an all-day affair, so you may want to pack extra snacks and diversions. Special themed trips and promotions are held regularly, including the "Bluegrass Train" and "Ugly Hat Day," so check the Website for details. If you want a shorter ride, simply catch the train southbound at the Stockyards and ride it to Eighth Avenue and back to the Stockyards, about an hour and a half round-trip. *(817) 625-RAIL;* www.tarantulatrain.com

Don't bother looking under your seats for spiders if you ride on the **Tarantula Steam Train**. Back in the late 1800s, someone mentioned that the proposed train routes out of Fort Worth looked like a tarantula, and the word was forever associated with the Texas train.

Texas Stadium
★★★★/$$-$$$$

MUST-SEE FamilyFun **MUST-SEE**

This stadium is home to the five-time NFL champion Dallas Cowboys. For more information, see "From Punts to Pucks" on page 83.

BUNKING DOWN

Blackstone Courtyard by Marriott in Fort Worth ★★★/$$

Housed in the renovated Blackstone Hotel (originally built around 1920), this Courtyard by Marriott isn't typical of the chain because cars are "parked" on the third floor where they are taken by elevator. While most of the rooms offer standard, bland furniture and design, there are a few—including two with huge windows overlooking Main Street on the second floor—that retain the building's historic style. The downtown location is convenient and right next door to the delicious Corner Bakery restaurant. *601 N. Main St., Fort Worth; (817)885-8700;* www.courtyard.com

Embassy Suites ★★/$$

This hotel is just north of DFW International Airport and within walking distance of Grapevine Mills. The chain's suite setup is ideal for families, allowing Mom and Dad to sleep in the bedroom while kids share the pullout bed in the living room. There's also a small kitchen. A huge breakfast buffet is included in the price. *2401 Bass Pro Dr., Grapevine; (972) 724-2600;* www.embassy suites.com

The Four Seasons in Las Colinas ★★★★/$$$$

If your family wants a relaxing spa vacation, head to this ultraluxe resort located just east of DFW Airport. There's a golf course and an amazing pool where kids can spend hours floating along a lazy river and sliding down slides. Moms and Dads will enjoy getting spritzed with Evian by the ever-attentive staff. Children also like playing the in-room video games (check with the concierge for old-fashioned board games). Your family can opt for room service or the resort's breakfast buffet. The Sunday brunch buffet includes everything from muffins to chocolate mousse. *4150 N. MacArthur Blvd., Irving;(972)717-0700;* www.fourseasons.com

GOOD EATS

Buckaroo's Soda Shop ★★★/$

This small restaurant harkens back to those drugstore diners, but adds a Western-themed edge by including mechanical pony rides and plenty of stick horses to occupy your kids until

the dinner bell rings. Burgers are the specialty, but you can opt for a salad or corn dog. Save room for some ice cream for dessert. This makes a great stop if you are doing the Tarantula train ride and need a quick lunch in Stockyards Station. *140 E. Exchange Ave., Fort Worth; (817) 624-6631.*

Joe T. Garcia's ★★★/$$

Patrons of this Cowtown establishment don't just come here for the food: they come for the experience. Dining on the beautifully landscaped patio is indeed divine, but the Tex-Mex cuisine is pretty good, too. While the fajitas are gaining in popularity, enchiladas rule with longtime devotees. There are children's dishes, but no American standards like burgers. Young diners love running around the brick sidewalks that wander through the huge, lush garden-and-patio area, with its plentiful fountains and small pool—just don't let them get too close to the pool. *2201 N. Commerce St., Fort Worth; (817)626-4356;* www.joets.com

La Madeleine ★★★/$-$$

This taste of France deep in the heart of Texas is a local favorite thanks to its addictive French-roast coffee and tomato basil soup. The cafeteria-style line moves quickly, so hungry kids can grab their croissants and go. There's no kids' menu, but most children can find something they like. If they aren't in the mood for a big breakfast, just let them enjoy the restaurant's free supplies of bread and jam while you enjoy your coffee. *Various locations throughout the region, including one in Sundance Square at 305 N. Main St., Fort Worth; (817) 332-3639; www.lamadeleine.com*

Milwaukee Joe's ★★/$

The flavors at this homemade-ice-cream shop change daily but are always imaginative. Kids like Snickerdoodle Crunch and Triple Chocolate Chip. *1417 Main St., Southlake in Town Square, (817) 251-1667; and 201 Harwood Rd., Bedford, (817) 581-1953;* www.milwaukee joes.com

The Purple Cow ★★★/$$

The average age of the diners at this hip Dallas restaurant is probably about 6. Kids love it because it's fun—and who can resist an all-beef hot dog and an Oreo shake. Though it's probably not a great testament to the cuisine, parents can be comforted by the fact that the restaurant sells individually wrapped Alka-Seltzer tablets for 50¢ each. *110 Preston Royal Shopping Center, Dallas; (214) 373-0037. Also at 4601 West Fwy., Fort Worth; (817) 737-7177, and 2051 W. Airport Fwy., Euless; (817) 858-9000.*

Rainforest Café ★★★/$$$

Roaring tigers, trumpeting elephants, grunting gorillas. Eating at the Rainforest Café isn't anyone's idea of an intimate restaurant, but kids love it. Every 30 minutes or so, a thunder-storm erupts, sending animatronic wildlife—and your kids—into a tizzy. The scene delights 5-year-olds and up, but may be a bit overwhelming for some preschoolers. Youngsters can select from menu items such as Gorilla Grilled Cheese, pasta, and cheeseburgers. The more laid-back mushroom bar offers a quieter alternative to the main seating area. *3000 Grapevine Mills Pkwy., in Grapevine Mills Mall, Grapevine; (972) 539-5001; www.rainforestcafe.com*

SOUVENIR HUNTING

Build-a-Bear Workshop

Kids can create their own bear (or other stuffed animal) from scratch at this innovative toy shop. *The Parks in Arlington Mall (lower level), Interstate 20 and Cooper St., Arlington; (817) 465-0800;* www.buildabear.com

Cowgirl Hall of Fame

Who says heroes have to always be cowboys? This museum/gift shop highlights the hard-riding heroines of the West. *Located in Sundance Square at 1720 Gendy St., Fort Worth; (817) 336-4475.*

The Modern at Sundance Square

This outpost of Fort Worth's Museum of Modern Art stocks innovative board games, T-shirts, and toys for parents and kids alike. *410 Houston St., Fort Worth; (817) 335-9215; www.themodern.org*

FROM PUNTS TO PUCKS
Hanging out with Dallas's (and America's) teams

THE DALLAS-FORT WORTH Metroplex has wonderful museums, fabulous zoos, and more retail space per person than anywhere in America, but many visitors come here for one reason and one reason only: the Dallas Cowboys.

Fans new to town have been known to pull off Airport Freeway to simply gawk at **Texas Stadium**, the 65,000-seat shrine that's home to the consistently award-winning Cowboys. Unless the team is having an 0-and-15 season, game tickets can be difficult—often impossible— to come by, but fans can still get an up-close look at the team's digs. During the 45-minute tour, fans can check out the locker rooms (and have their photo taken in front of a favorite player's locker), see the view from the press box, and even make a touchdown dash on the field. The tour can also include special parties for kids (you need to arrange these in advance), including a cake and visit from the team mascot, a character dressed in a Cowboys uniform. Tours are not offered on game days or when concerts or special events such as high school games are going on; call ahead to check availability. *2401 E. Airport Fwy., Irving; (972) 785-4780.*

The Texas Rangers are also popular, but tickets to their games are generally available at the gates on game day. Kids can watch the team taking batting practice for free generally two hours before a game's scheduled start. *For more information, call the team office at (817) 273-5222.* Even in the off-season, fans enjoy a trip to **The Ballpark in Arlington** where they can eat lunch overlooking the stadium at Friday's Front Row Grill. *(817) 265-5191.*

The Ballpark's **Legends of the Game Museum** is home to one of the nation's best collections of baseball memorabilia. The museum traces the evolution of balls, bats, and gloves, and has a display of special uniforms, including an all-black one worn by the New York Giants in the 1911 World Series. *1000 Ballpark Way, Arlington; (817) 273-5222;* www.museum.texasrangers.com

NOTE: Sports fans alert: the Dallas Mavericks (NBA) and the Dallas Stars (NHL) are now playing at the new American Airlines Center (just west of downtown Dallas). *2500 Victory Ave.; (214) 665-4797.*

The Martian Matrix at Space Center Houston is a five-story fun house.

Houston

F AMOUS FOR being the nation's largest city without zoning regulations, Houston is a massive, metropolitan area that's home to four million people and is spread over 600 square miles. The size and scope of the city can be a bit overwhelming for families who come here to enjoy its world-class museums, shopping, and amusement parks. Rather than trying to see Houston all in one whirlwind weekend (which would mean spending a lot of time driving the city's miles of 12-lane freeways), we suggest focusing on one or two areas and a handful of attractions per trip. Even if you have a week or more to explore, it will be nearly impossible to take in everything. By the time you drive Loop 610, the freeway that circles the core of the city, you can be sure someone will have added something new.

THE FamilyFun LIST

Blue Bell Creamery
  (page 91)

Children's Museum of Houston
  (page 88)

George Ranch Historical Park
  (page 88)

**Houston Museum of Natural
  Science** (page 89)

Houston Zoological Gardens
  (page 92)

Kemah Boardwalk (page 93)

Minute Maid Park (page 93)

**Six Flags AstroWorld and
  WaterWorld** (page 96)

Space Center Houston (page 91)

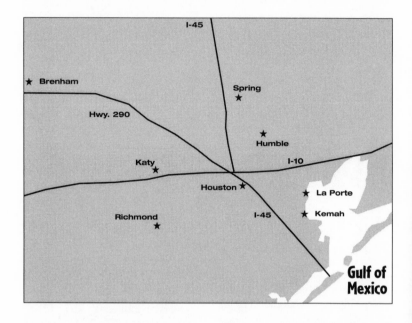

Only a few years ago, Houston's downtown was dead after 6 P.M., but it's now home to a vibrant shopping and restaurant scene and the city's latest jewel, Minute Maid Park—the state-of-the art ballpark with retractable roof that is home to the Houston Astros (for more information see "Minute Maid Park: Batter Up—and Other Home Run Treats" on page 94).

There are other great places where you can enjoy Houston's lush, green outdoors. Herman Park, down the street from Rice University and the city's medical complex, is a 402-acre green space that is home to the city's zoo, an outdoor theater, playgrounds accessible to disabled persons, and the Museum of Natural Science.

After a busy day seeing those sites, take a break riding the park's small train, or feed the ducks at the lake.

If your kids love rides, they'll want to get over to Six Flags AstroWorld, and its water park neighbor, Water-World. For a nostalgic trip, go by the nearby Astrodome, once dubbed the eighth wonder of the world, and home to that indestructible grass called AstroTurf. If shopping is your family's thing, be sure to go to the Galleria, home to no less than 300 stores and restaurants, and Katy Mills, the new megamall where you can hit the outlet shops; then walk over to the NASCAR Silicon Speedway (at entry 8 of the mall), where you can buckle up in a ride that simulates the high speeds of a NASCAR race.

Located 25 miles south of Houston, the Clear Lake area—home to the Space Center Houston and NASA's Johnson Space Center—is another big family destination, as is the nearby Kemah Boardwalk, a 40-acre theme park—with a Ferris wheel, a carousel, and fountains.

Whatever you plan for your visit, we'll help you navigate those wide Houston highways and find the right places for you to park your family for great vacation memories.

CULTURAL ADVENTURES

Art Car Museum ★★★/Free

This avant-garde art museum celebrates designs from Houston's famous Art Car Show, where artists decorate cars with everything from steer heads to a giant bunny. The exhibits change and sometimes the subject matter includes hot political issues such as the death penalty, but it can make for a thought-provoking outing for older kids. Open Wednesdays through Sundays. *140 Heights Blvd., Houston; (713) 861-5526;* www.artcarmuseum.com

Battleship Texas ★★/$

Roam the crew's quarters, the engine rooms, and the decks of this circa 1914 ship, billed as the Navy's oldest surviving battleship. Kids can check out the hand-cranked guns.

Self-guided tours are also available. *3527 Battleground Rd., La Porte; (281) 479-2431.*

Bayou Bend ★★★/$-$$

Built in the 1920s, this mansion was once home to Will, Mike, and Ima Hogg (yes, that was her real name), children of former Texas governor Jim Hogg. Older children can appreciate the museum's collection of fine silver and ceramics, among the top decorative arts collections in the world. Guided 90-minute tours are given from 10 A.M. to 2:45 P.M., and reservations are required. Given the large number of breakable objects here, this place is best for non-bull-in-a-china-shop kids, over age 10, but on special Family Days, generally the third Sunday of most months, there are special, free kid-friendly music and drama performances and hands-on arts-and-crafts workshops that can also entertain younger children. *One Westcott St., Houston; (713) 639-7750;* www.bayoubend.uh.edu

FamilyFun TIP

Do the Twist

Pipe cleaners and twist ties have saved many a parent's sanity on long car trips. Kids can quietly fashion these building tools into an endless array of designs — from stick figures and animals to houses with furniture.

Children's Museum of Houston ★★★/$

Kids can run around on a rainy (or steamy) day here as they explore science and technology, archaeology, agriculture, and the environment. Instead of watching television, your youngsters can create it at the KID-TV studio, which has real sound-and-video equipment. The museum's courtyard is a great place for a snack or lunch and features a pirate ship and a Victorian playhouse where your little ones will want to stay for hours. **NOTE:** You can save the $5 admission charge by planning your visit for a Thursday between 5 and 8 P.M., when admission is free. The museum is closed Monday except in the summer months when it is open seven days a week. *1500 Binz St., Houston; (713) 522-1138;* www.cmhouston.org

George Ranch Historical Park ★★★★/$$

Get a taste of Texas pioneer days at this 740-acre living history museum that features costumed guides who discuss what life was like around nearby Fort Bend from 1824 to 1939. Your family can tour the period homes and watch demonstrations of blacksmithing and farming methods. Throughout the year, the park schedules a variety of outstanding special events. The Dry Creek General Store, located at the visitors' center, sells Native American handmade jewelry, Texas history books, traditional Victorian toys and games, cowboy hats, and rock candy. If you get hungry, head to the Dinner Belle Café; kids can order grilled cheese or peanut-butter-and-jelly sandwiches, and adults can opt for hamburgers or chili pies—tortilla chips topped with cheese sauce, chili, and jalapeños. *10215 FM Rd. 762, Richmond; (281) 545-9212;* www.georgeranch.org

Holocaust Museum ★★★/Free

The nation's third-largest museum of its kind, it includes exhibits, photos, and an interactive learning center that documents one of history's most horrific crimes against humanity. Best for kids ages 8 and older (young tots won't understand and may be frightened), the museum is especially meaningful for children who have studied the Holocaust in school and are ready for a more in-depth history lesson. *5401 Caroline St., Houston; (713) 942-8000;* www.hmh.org

Houston Fire Museum ★★/Free

Your little fireman (or firewoman) can see hats, uniforms, axes, and badges from all over the world at this small museum. There's also a 19th-century steam engine with a water-tower truck on display. The museum is closed Sunday and Monday. *2403 Milam St., Houston; (713) 524-2526;* www.houstonfire museum.org

Houston Maritime Museum
★★/Free

This small museum operated by retired naval architect James Manzolillo reflects his life's work collection treasures of maritime history. The collection includes an 1812 diving helmet, a piece of coal from the *Titanic* and the petrified tooth of a prehistoric shark. *2204 Dorrington St., Houston; (713) 666-1910.*

 **Houston Museum of Natural Science**
★★★★/$-$$

Home to a planetarium, an IMAX theater, and a tropical-butterfly forest, this museum can take all day to fully enjoy. The three floors of permanent exhibits include roaring dinosaurs, rare gems, and wildlife displays that detail such creatures as the Texas horned lizard. Kids can check out the enormous Foucault pendulum, watching it knock down the wooden pins on the perimeter circle as the earth turns on its axis. Don't miss the Weather Center, where your kids can appear on television forecasting the weather. The Weiss Energy Hall, another must-do, celebrates Houston's title of Energy Capital of the World with interactive displays detailing drilling methods and refining processes used for oil and natural gas. Kids love the Neon Refinery that uses different colored neon lights to show how gasoline is made. *In Herman Park, One Herman Circle Dr., Houston; (713) 639-4600;* www.hmns.org

Museums and More

H OUSTON is home to some terrific kids' museums. Here's how to see a couple and give your family plenty of playtime, too:

9 A.M. Breakfast at **Buffalo Grille** *(1017 Bissonnet St.)*; try the apple-smoked bacon and the blueberry pancakes.

10 A.M. Children's Museum of Houston (see page 88). Lunch at the snack bar (sandwiches and burgers), then let the kids play in the pirate house and Victorian playhouse areas of the museum's shaded courtyard.

1:30 P.M. Either the **Houston Zoological Gardens** (see page 92) or the **Museum of Natural Science** (at left)—kids' choice.

3:30-4 P.M. Relax and people-watch on a bench, or rent a paddleboat at **Herman Park** (see page 92).

Houston Police Museum
★★/Free

If you have a child who's crazy for the boys and girls in blue, then check out this small museum near Bush Intercontinental Airport. Exhibits include a full-size helicopter, motorcycles, and underwater gear used by search-and-rescue teams. Among the memorabilia is a pocket watch that saved the life of a 1927 detective by deflecting a bullet, and a collection of police uniforms from around the world. *17000 Aldine-Westfield Rd., Houston; (281) 230-2361.*

Houston Ship Channel Tour
★★/Free

Houston is actually the second-busiest port in the nation and eighth busiest in the world. What's being shipped? Find out on a narrated, 90-minute tour aboard the MV *Sam Houston,* an inspection vessel operated by the city's port authority. **NOTE:** It is essential to call ahead

for reservations. Tours fill up quickly; in fact, tour operators discourage walk-up customers by not divulging the tour's starting point until a reservation has been made. Don't be put off by this: the ride is worth it. *(713) 670-2416.*

Museum of Fine Arts
★★★/$-$$

Opened in 1900, this museum is now home to more than 100,000 works of art and an art-history research center. Try to visit on a Sunday, when the museum typically hosts kid-oriented events, including story times that combine reading aloud and hands-on arts-and-crafts workshops. Be sure to check out the unique tunnel between the main building and a new addition; designed by artist James Turell, it's guaranteed to get a "way cool" from your kids. Youngsters also enjoy the sculpture garden across the street *(5101 Montrose)*, which

---

FamilyFun READER'S TIP -

T Squares

My son, Jason, age ten-and-a-half, has a number of T-shirts from sports teams he's played on, camps he's gone to, and places we've visited. Jason's aunt, Linda, came up with a creative way to preserve those memories after he has outgrown the shirts. She cuts a section from the front and back of each shirt, sews them together, and lightly stuffs them to make mini-pillows. She then sews the pillows together to make a soft and comfortable quilt. It's a great keepsake, and as Jason gets older and taller, the quilt just grows with him.

Debbie Emery, Northboro, Massachusetts

features works by Rodin and Matisse. *1001 Bissonett St., Houston; (713) 639-7300;* www.mfah.org

⭐ Space Center Houston
FamilyFun ★★★★/$$$

Space Center Houston, the visitors' center at NASA's Johnson Space Center, is an awesome interactive experience with behind-the-scenes tours. Kids can use a computer simulator to pretend they're retrieving a satellite and can actually touch a moon rock; there's also an IMAX theater that details the history of space travel. Occasionally, astronauts and NASA scientists and engineers are available to give demonstrations and answer questions. **NOTE:** If you have younger children (or are short on time), skip the tram tour at Johnson Space Center, which can be miserable on a hot, humid day. *1601 NASA Rd. 1, Houston; (281) 244-2101; (281) 244-2100;* www.spacecenter.org

In September 1992, Mark Lee and N. Jan Davis became the **first American married couple to fly in space** when they took part in the 50th space shuttle mission.

JUST FOR FUN

Armand Bayou Nature Center
★★★/Free

An excellent place to defrost from all the air-conditioned space in town, this center near Clear Lake City offers interactive events such as farm life demonstrations on weekends. Events vary with the season, so call ahead to see what's going on during your visit. *8500 Bay Area Blvd., Houston; (281) 474-2551;* www.abnc.org

⭐ Blue Bell Creamery
FamilyFun ★★★★/$$

Looking for a fun day trip? Head west of Houston to the small town of Brenham and "the little creamery," where 20 million gallons of ice cream are produced annually and sold throughout Texas and neighboring states. The factory tour includes a short film on the history of the company. Afterward, kids can watch production of such popular flavors as Banana Split and Triple Chocolate from an observation deck. **NOTE:** The 45-minute tours are given on weekdays only and are limited to only 1,000 people a day, so it's imperative to call ahead for information, especially if you are visiting during popular vacation times such as spring break and Easter. The nominal admission fee of $2 for kids ages 6 to 12 and $2.50 for adults includes a serving of ice cream. After the tour, check out the gift shop, where you can buy Blue Bell–emblazoned T-shirts, aprons, and key chains. The shop is closed on Sunday. The 70-mile trip from Houston is a very scenic drive on Highway 290 that takes you past family dairy farms. *Farm Road 577,* *two miles southeast of Brenham; (979) 836-7977; (800) 327-8135; www. bluebell.com/*

The Galleria ★★★/Free

If the phrase "I shop, therefore I am" applies to you or your kids—especially your preteens—this is your retail nirvana. Home to 300 stores and restaurants, an ice rink, and two hotels, this mall is where Houston shops, or at least pretends to, just to get out of the heat. *5075 Westheimer Ave., Houston; (713) 621-1907;* www.galleriahouston.com

Herman Park ★★★/Free

Located next to Rice University and the huge Texas Medical Center complex, this 402-acre park is a lush escape from city streets. It's home to the city zoo, the Houston Museum of Natural Science, an outdoor theater, and lots of outdoor activities, including a miniature-golf course, a lake with paddleboats, several playgrounds, and a miniature train. *6201-A Golfcourse Dr., Houston; (713) 524-5876.*

Houston Arboretum and Nature Center ★★★/Free

If your family wants to take a quiet walk, or your kids want to commune with nature, this is the place to be. The 155-acre forest sanctuary has children's programs most weekends, including ones called Naturalist Explorers that target kids ages 5 to 12. Past areas of study have included

night bugs and butterflies. There are also classes for kids ages 3 to 5 called Tadpole Troopers, which tackle topics such as backyard birds. *4501 Woodway Dr., Houston; (713) 681-8433;* www.houstonnaturecenter.org

Houston Zoological Gardens ★★★/$

The zoo's gorillas have their own huge jungle habitat here, and a new tropical birdhouse features more than 200 feathered friends. There's also a hippo dome, a tiger habitat, a huge collection of reptiles, and a colony of vampire bats (don't worry—they won't suck your blood). A special favorite with younger kids is the petting zoo at the Discovery Center. There's no admission to the zoo on city holidays. *In Herman Park at 1513 N. MacGregor St., Houston; (713) 523-5888;* www.houstonzoo.org

Katy Mills ★★★/Free

The latest challenge to the Galleria as Houston's favorite place to shop, this huge mall blends outlet stores, restaurants, movies, and interactive games to offer what its operators call shoppertainment. Attractions include a 20-foot climbing wall and the Nascar Silicon Motor Speedway, where racing simulators put you behind the wheel of a Winston Cup race car. Your kids can see what it's like to drive at 200 miles per hour—the family minivan will never seem the same. *5000 Katy Mills Circle, Katy; (281) 644-5000;* www.katymills.com

Kemah Boardwalk
FamilyFun ★★★★/Free

Want to go to a place where the carnival never leaves town because it is the town? Then bring your family to this 40-acre entertainment complex that includes a slew of restaurants and rides. Located between Houston and Galveston, this park each year attracts more than three million people who are hungry for cotton candy and Ferris wheel rides. Be sure to bring your camera for shots of the kids on the beautiful 36-foot-high carousel, with its carved creatures including a dragon, a pig, a rooster, and a bear. Pack a change of clothes, too, in case your kids (or their parents) give in to the temptation to splash around in the Dancing Waters fountain. **NOTE:** Weekends here are packed, so try to come during the week to avoid the crowds. Also, plan to have dinner here early, because after 6 P.M. the wait for a table can stretch to an hour or more.

Mercer Arboretum and Botanic Gardens ★★/Free

This 214-acre preserve located in northeast Houston offers miles of walking trails and showcases plants from around the world, including carnivorous varieties as well as Texas wildflowers. There's also a butterfly nursery, a koi pond, and plenty of picnic tables. *22306 Aldine-Westfield Rd., Humble; (281) 443-8731;* www.cp4.hctx.net/mercer

Top Air Travel Tips

♦ Book early for good seats.
♦ Order kids' meals when you make your reservation.
♦ Stuff your carry-on for every contingency: pack medications, extra kids' clothes, diapers, baby food, and formula. And be sure the kids' toys are in their carry-ons.
♦ Make each child who is old enough responsible for his own luggage.
♦ Check luggage curbside.
♦ Let kids work off energy in the lounge — save sleepy moments for the plane.
♦ To quell plane fears, explain each step of the flight to first-time fliers so they understand that sudden noises and shaking do not signal an imminent crash.
♦ Locate pillows and blankets as soon as you board.

Minute Maid Park
FamilyFun ★★★★/$-$$$

The Houston Astros baseball team moved to this plush stadium (formerly known as Enron Field) in 2000, leaving behind the famous Astrodome. For more information, see "Minute Maid Park" on page 94.

MINUTE MAID PARK

Batter Up—and Other Home Run Treats

SINCE IT OPENED—on March 30, 2000—as Enron Field (yes, *that* Enron), this has been the place to be in Houston. Your family will have so much fun wandering around the ballpark, you may miss much of the game. The stadium offers incredible views of the city skyline, plus a retractable roof. If you're planning to go to a game during your visit, you may want to stay at a downtown hotel to avoid the parking hassles. Otherwise, consider one of the Shortstop Shuttles, which pick people up at various points in the city, including Bayou Place and the Theater District. The parking garage One City Center, at Fannin and McKinney streets, is about eight blocks from the ballpark; it charges $5 to park and offers a $2 shuttle.

When buying tickets, consider Conoco Home Run Alley, located along the left and left-center field wall, and Conoco Home Run Porch, overlooking left-center field. Bring your gloves to the game. If you want a bargain, the outfield deck in the far upper reaches of left field has 1,700 seats priced at $5 for adults and $1 for kids 14 and under.

Once there, check out the clock tower that anchors the Hamilton side of the field. The tower's electronic carillon has a repertoire of 60 songs, including "Take Me Out to the Ball Game" and Baylor University's fight song (a request by Astros owner and Baylor alumnus Drayton McLane, Jr.). Your family may also want to stop by Union Station, which anchors the Crawford Street side of the park and provides options for pregame shopping including the Shed, the Astros' official gift shop.

Be aware that the team does not permit food or beverage to be brought into the ballpark; never fear though—there are plenty of offerings inside the park. On the main concourse, you'll want to check out Squeeze Play, an area of kid-oriented attractions next to Section 134 that includes a small water play area and batting cages. During the regular season, your kids can play interactive games and pose for their own "personal" baseball card section. Squeeze Play also offers special concession areas for kids featuring Little League–size meals that include a hot dog, juice, and a cookie. The nearby picnic tables and large-screen televisions are a perfect place for a family picnic. There also are 17 family rest rooms throughout the ballpark (they're unisex).

Even if your kids aren't into baseball, they'll enjoy watching the electronic-light train chug across the outfield scoreboard. The train makes its journey when the gates first open, when the Astros take the field at the start of the game, and whenever they score a home run (which is happening so often that the park's nickname is Home Run Field). Kids can also clown around with Junction Jack, the team's jackrabbit mascot. If you can't get to a game, consider taking a tour of the facility, offered year-round from the lobby of Union Station. You might also want to visit the official Astros team store called "The Shed," also located in Union Station. Astros apparel for kids and adults is plentiful. For **The Shed**, call *(800) ASTROS-4.* If you go on the tour, be sure to wear comfortable shoes because you will be walking more than a mile. *For tour information, call (713) 259-TOUR. For tickets, call (800) ASTROS-2, or go to the team's Internet site at* www.astros.com

The Orange Show ★★/Free

Kids get a kick out of seeing this folk-art creation that pays tribute to orange—both the fruit and the color. In fact, orange is the *only* color you'll see here. The show's creator, the late Jeff McKissick, spent 25 years making his citrus-inspired wonderland that's a patchwork of wagon wheels and whirligigs. It's weird, it's funky, it's bizarre—and, best of all, it's fun. It's generally open Wednesdays through Fridays during the summer from 10 A.M. to 1 P.M. and Saturdays and Sundays noon to 5 P.M. year-round. The Orange Show closes for several weeks between mid-December and early March. *2401 Munger St., Houston; (713) 926-6368;* www.orangeshow.org

The Reef ★★★/Free

For some laid-back fun, head for this popular swimming hole—actually a 20-acre, spring-fed lake. There's a children's activity beach with mushroom-shaped fountains and a family beach where you can rent a boat, kayak, or tube. Weekday rental charges for adults (at press time) were $6.50 for a half hour; no charge for kids 5 and under. *4800 Schurmier Rd., Houston; (713) 991-3483;* www.atthereef.com

Reliant Astrodome ★★/$

Consider it a history lesson when you take the family to this Texas landmark (even if you don't go into the stadium, it's worth a drive by).

Dubbed the eighth wonder of the world when it was built in 1965, it was revolutionary at the time, allowing fans to sit through football and baseball games in air-conditioned comfort. The stadium, now part of Reliant Park, was also the birthplace of AstroTurf. Times change; now the mammoth structure hosts the occasional gun show, rodeo, or circus. Tours are offered. Call for details, or just drive by and get a glimpse of this famous structure. *8400 Kirby Dr., Loop 610 S., Houston; (713) 661-3220.*

Six Flags AstroWorld and WaterWorld
★★★/$$$$

AstroWorld is a roller-coaster lover's paradise, with ten "screamers" at last count, including the Texas Tornado. There are more rides here than at any other theme park in the state, including several rides for younger kids in Looney Tunes Land. Height is everything here: kids 48 inches or shorter get to ride at a discounted

---

FamilyFun TIP

Tour Guides on Tape

Ride With Me tapes *(800-752-3195)* are cassettes keyed to common roadways. Put in a tape at the prescribed mile marker, and it's like having a guide versed in history, geography, and trivia along as you drive through a state. (But you won't have to give up an extra seat or share your lunch.)

---

rate, and kids under 3 ride free. WaterWorld, a 15-acre water park located next door, offers a white-water-rafting simulation ride called Thunder River, plus plenty of chutes and slides to glide down. You can float down the man-made, 900-foot-long lazy river, or let your kids scamper around the water play area. *Loop 610 at Kirby Dr., Houston; (713) 799-1234;* www.sixflags.com/houston *or* www.sixflags.com/astroworld

Splashtown ★★★/$$$
One of the biggest water parks in the country, Splashtown boasts 35 rides and attractions, including Tree House Island, a five-story, interactive play area with water guns, hose pipes, geysers, water curtains, and water slides. Don't come here unless you want to get wet! *21300 Interstate 45 North at Spring; (281) 355-3300;* www.sixflags.com

Williams Tower Water Wall
★★★/Free
Kids are fascinated by this huge water fountain, where thousands of gallons of water cascade down the inner and outer arch of a dramatic 64-foot, U-shaped wall. You may see a dog or two playing around in it, but think twice before letting your kids do more than dip in a big toe. The force of all that water is actually pretty strong (and can be dangerous); be ready to get wet from the mist alone. *2800 S. Post Oak Blvd., Houston.*

Bunking Down

Boardwalk Inn ★★★★/$$

If you're planning to hit Space Center Houston and Kemah Boardwalk, this is the place to stay. Located by the Boardwalk, its 52 rooms and four suites go fast, so book early. The hotel lobby has a jar of cookies placed by the check-in desk. *8 Kemah Boardwalk, Kemah; (281) 334-9880;* www.kemahboardwalk.com

Doubletree Guest Suites ★★★/$$$

Located by the Galleria, this all-suites hotel is popular with families who like to make their own meals. The rooms are larger than most and kids like the on-site convenience store and Olympic-size pool. *5353 Westheimer Rd., Houston; (800) 222-TREE; (713) 961-9000;* www.doubletreehotels.com

Four Seasons Hotel Houston ★★★/$$$$

It's expensive, but the location near Minute Maid Park and the free shuttles that go in and around downtown are wonderful when your kids get tired of walking. The outdoor pool is heated so it can still be enjoyed on those cooler Houston days, and the television offerings include two all-Arabic stations (this is, after all, a town with many foreign visitors), which our kids found fascinating. Call in advance and the concierge can arrange to have a Sony PlayStation installed in your room, plus several games as well. *1300 Lamar St., Houston; (800) 332-3442; (713) 650-1300;* www.fourseasons.com

Good Eats

Empire Café ★★★/$$

Head here for breakfast. The gingerbread waffles topped with strawberries, bananas, and cream will give you and your kids the carbohydrates you need to power your sight-seeing. *1732 Westheimer Rd., Houston; (713) 528-5282.*

Goode Co. Barbecue ★★★/$$

If your family wants some Texas barbecue, this restaurant is considered one of the state's best. Be advised that they don't serve French fries here, nor do they have a special kids' menu, but the side dishes—baked potatoes, dirty rice, and jalapeño beans—are delicious. *5109 Kirby St., Houston; (713) 522-2530.*

Lupe Tortillas ★★★★/$$

Don't tell your kids you're going to a restaurant; tell them you're going to a sandbox. That's one of the main attractions at this Mexican eatery. There's also a rocking horse, a playhouse, and plenty of toys. Kids can order a Mexican grilled cheese, made with Monterey Jack. Oh, yeah, the food is good enough that childless couples come here, too. *Two Houston locations: 2414 Southwest Fwy., (713) 522-4420; and 318 Stafford St., (281) 496-7580.*

Oscar's Creamery ★★★/$

Houston's hot weather provides plenty of excuses to consume ice cream, and this chain offers the city's best. There's a nostalgic feel here, with vintage stools and counter, and wild and wacky flavors that push the limits of creativity. If you don't have the energy to troop to the shop, don't worry—Oscar's delivers. *Three Houston locations: 5104 West FM 1960, (281) 440-1020; 5326 Kirby, (713) 520-1414; 1201-C Westheimer Rd., (713) 521-1808.*

Souvenir Hunting

Build-a-Bear Workshop

At this unique store, your kids can actually design, stuff, fluff, dress, and name their own special stuffed bear or other animal. *Second floor of the Galleria, 5085 Westheimer Rd., Houston; (713) 355-3388.*

Discovery Channel Store

This shop in the Galleria reflects the cable channel's focus on science, nature, and adventure. Kids like the bug capture kits, animal-print T-shirts, and stuffed animals. *5015 Westheimer Rd., Houston; (713) 840-9501;* www.discovery.com

Fine Toon Gallery

Located in Rice Village, this place elevates cartoons to fine art. Collectors alert: it's also an authorized gallery of all the major studios, including Disney and Warner Bros. *804 W. Gray, Houston; (713) 522-6499;* www.cartoonanimatedart.com

Palace Boot Store

Your little urban cowboy and cowgirl can get their kicks at this boot store where presidents—and even the Pope—have come for custom-crafted cowboy boots. *1212 Prairie St., Houston; (713) 224-1411.*

Tuesday Morning

This deep-discount store got its name because it originally opened its doors for special sales on Tuesdays. The chain sells toys and household trinkets for a fraction of their retail price, but be prepared for a grab bag of offerings that can include toy trains one month and Lego sets the next. There are several locations in the city, but the one inside *Loop 610 is located at 14438 Bellaire Blvd., Houston; (281) 568-2231.*

Variety Fair 5 & 10

Remember those old five-and-dime stores that sold notions? If your kids have never been to one, check out this one in Rice Village. There's a great selection of candies here. *2415 Rice Blvd., Houston; (713) 522-0561.*

CONVERSATION STARTERS

IME ON THE ROAD offers families the perfect opportunity to reconnect by having conversations that don't revolve around car pools, chores, or eating all your vegetables. If you have trouble switching conversational gears, try asking your kids these questions or similar variations. You can have them take charge sometimes, too, letting them ask you probing queries! Or you can turn this less-than-idle chat into a game by writing questions on slips of paper, placing them in a hat, and passing the hat—the question you pick out is the one you must answer, honestly. Make your queries silly or serious, but be sure they cannot be answered by just saying yes or no.

◆ If you could make up a holiday, what would it be and how would you celebrate it?

◆ What is the first thing you would do if you became president?

◆ Would you rather be a butterfly or a fish? Why?

◆ Do you think dogs are smarter than cats? Are dogs smarter than horses?

◆ What did settlers on the prairie have for breakfast 100 years ago? What will we be eating for breakfast in 100 years?

◆ If you had to lose one of your five senses, which would it be? Which one sense would you choose if you could only have one? Why?

◆ Would you like to have sonar like a bat, or be able to run as fast as a gazelle? Why?

◆ If you could choose five animal qualities for yourself from the animal kingdom, what would they be?

◆ What is the best book you've read recently, and why did you like it?

◆ What's the silliest thing you ever did?

◆ What will you do this summer?

◆ What's your earliest memory?

◆ What do you think the surface of the moon looks like?

◆ If you were going to write a book, what would it be about?

◆ What will you be doing in ten years?

◆ If you discovered a new island what do you imagine would be on it?

◆ What one thing would you change about school?

◆ Who is your hero and why?

◆ What should we surprise Mom with for her birthday this year?

◆ What is the best—and the worst—thing you have ever eaten?

◆ What is an item of international news that you have heard or read about in the past few months?

Families can get off their feet on a boat cruise down the San Antonio River.

San Antonio

NESTLED BETWEEN the Hill Country to the north and the coastal plain to the south, San Antonio is one of the nation's fastest-growing major cities. Home to more than two million people, the city has a strong Mexican identity, mixed with flourishes of German and Czech, brought by Hill Country settlers more than a century ago. The cultures come together in the region's Tejano music, which combines Latin rhythms with accordions sounding out a polka-like beat.

The area is one of the nation's top family vacation spots thanks to its unique culture, warm climate, and collection of kid-friendly attractions, including SeaWorld and Six Flags Fiesta Texas. Spring and summer are the most popular times to visit, particularly mid-March to mid-April, when the region's

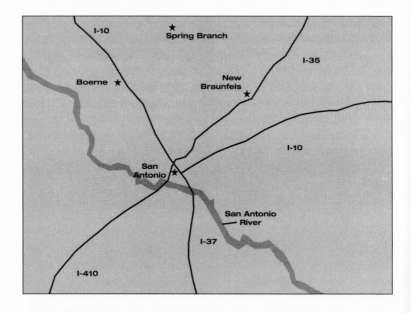

bluebonnets spread a blanket of color alongside highways and provide a perfect photo opportunity. April also brings Fiesta, the city's biggest party—with some of its largest crowds. San Antonio is much less crowded in the fall and winter and offers lodging bargains. The city twinkles during the holidays, when the River Walk is decorated with thousands of colorful lights.

To experience San Antonio's diverse offerings at your own pace, it will be necessary to rent a car or drive your own (outside the immediate downtown, San Antonio has limited public transportation). That said, parking in downtown San Antonio near the River Walk can be a nightmare, so try to go early in the day for the best shot at finding a space in a city garage or on the street.

If you're traveling with children under 7, consider staying at a hotel northwest of town near SeaWorld and Six Flags Fiesta Texas to minimize driving time and avoid rush-hour snarls. Older children may want to be in the middle of the action downtown on the River Walk, home to popular restaurants like Planet Hollywood and Dick's Last Resort, near the city's museums and IMAX theater, and, of course, close to the Alamo.

To beat the crowds, visit the Alamo in the morning, then eat lunch on the River Walk (plan to be in line for a waterside table by 11:30 A.M.). Skip the hokey Texas Adventure multimedia show and instead see the furnished log cabins and science tree house at the nearby Witte Museum. If you're going to Sea World or Fiesta Texas, buy tickets ahead of time from your hotel or the Convention and Visitors Bureau and arrive shortly before the gates open to avoid long waits for shows and rides. To save a few dollars, check to see what local promotions and ticket coupons are being offered. Last, don't try to do it all: there's so much to do in San Antonio and the surrounding Hill Country, it is hard to get to everything. That's why so many families keep coming back year after year.

CULTURAL ADVENTURES

The Alamo ★★★/Free

FamilyFun The first thing to remember about the Alamo is that it's actually a church, also called Mission San Antonio de Valero. The second thing is that it's a shrine, at least to many Texans, since 189 people died defending it from Mexican troops on March 6, 1836. Understandably, this is not a place for shrieks and giggles. You're expected to remove your hat or cap before entering, and you should expect docents to scold anyone talking much above a whisper (docents will also admonish anyone they spot touching the walls, so you may want to walk on the outside of your child

as you make your way through this often crowded landmark).

There really isn't a lot for small kids to interact with here, so you may consider just seeing it from the outside with kids under age 5. Inside, older kids can look at antique guns, swords, and other memorabilia enshrined in glass cases. (Another plus for the 10-and-older crowd: for a quick history lesson, they can learn more about the importance of the Alamo by viewing the film at the **IMAX theater** *located at Rivercenter Mall, 849 E. Commerce St.; 210/225-4620.* The 45-minute docudrama—which, on a six-story-high screen, records the attack on, and the defense of, the Alamo—is considered by many historians to be the most accurate dramatization of the event.) There's no charge to walk through the building, but donations are accepted. Next to the Alamo is a small store that sells plastic Alamo soldiers and Bowie knives and, of course, Davy Crockett coonskin caps. In addition, you'll find glass cases with small displays that use

FamilyFun TIP

A Tougher Tic-tac-toe

Make the classic game of tic-tac-toe a little more lively and a bit tougher with this one basic change: with each turn, a player can fill in the empty space of his choice with either an X or an O.

miniature soldiers to re-create the battle. Behind the Alamo is a lovely landscaped garden filled with benches that makes a great resting stop. (For more information about including this amazing place in a San Antonio day trip, see "One Day in San Antonio" on page 106.) *300 Alamo Plaza, San Antonio; (210) 225-1391; www.thealamo.org*

Buckhorn Saloon and Museum ★★★/$$

Located across the street from the San Antonio Children's Museum, one block from the River Walk, this museum celebrates all things western—including one of the world's most extensive collections of antlers. There's also a wax museum—originally created for the 1968 World's Fair—that spotlights events which shaped Texas history, and an old-fashioned arcade that has nickelodeons and penny presses. *318 E. Houston St., San Antonio; (210) 247-4000; www.buckhornmuseum.com*

 Magik Children's Theatre of San Antonio ★★★/$

This professional theater company puts on shows for kids and their families. Past productions have included *When Dinosaurs Rocked the World* and *The Grinch.* To add to the experience, actors often play games with kids before the show and interact with them afterward while still in costume. Inexpensive

(tickets were $8 for adults, $6 for children 3 through 17, and $2 for children 2 and under at press time), shows are typically an hour in length. Beethoven Hall, inside HemisFair Park. *420 S. Alamo St., San Antonio; (210) 227-2751; www.magiktheatre.org*

San Antonio Children's Museum ★★★/$

A great place to take the kids when it's rainy or you simply want to hang out in air-conditioning for a while, this museum is filled with hands-on displays targeting toddlers up to third and fourth graders. Kids can open a bank account or shop in a kids' market, climb in a giant bubble, or take a pretend airplane flight in this fun and educational environment. The under-5 crowd will enjoy giant building blocks and other activities in the tot spot. *A block from the River Walk, 305 E. Houston, San Antonio; (210) 212-4453.*

The Texas Adventure ★★/$$

This multimedia show includes the sounds of erupting gun- and cannon-fire, and several other special effects to keep kids awake during a retelling of the Battle of the Alamo. **NOTE:** Small children may be scared by the loud noises and ghostlike holographic images. *Located across the street from the Alamo at 307 Alamo Plaza, San Antonio; (210) 227-8224.*

Witte Museum
FamilyFun ★★★★/$$

MUST-SEE
MUST-SEE

If you don't tell your kids this is a museum, they may never know they're getting an education; they'll be too busy with the fun, interactive displays that explain the area's natural history and plant and animal life. The grounds include four homes and a log cabin, which show what early settlers' life was like here 150 years ago, and the science tree house, a four-story structure on the banks of the San Antonio River. The museum also has a Texas Wild exhibit featuring the animals of Texas, and an outdoor hummingbird-and-butterfly garden. **NOTE:** There's no admission charge Tuesdays from 3 to 9 P.M. *The museum is a short drive north of downtown San Antonio at 3801 Broadway St., San Antonio; (210) 357-1900;* www.wittemuseum.org

JUST FOR FUN

The Alamodome ★★/$
This sports-and-entertainment venue has little in common with its more historic namesake—other than the fact that it's seen its own share of battles, including the 1998 NCAA basketball Final Four games, and an NBA Championship series won by the San Antonio Spurs in 1999. Given its huge size (the stadium can seat up to 77,000 people), tickets are generally available for most games and

events held here. There's a 45-minute tour on Thursdays and Fridays, but skip it unless you enjoy climbing lots of stairs and wandering through huge locker rooms. *100 Montana St., San Antonio; (210) 207-3663;* www. alamodome.com

Bandera Bowl Funplex ★★/$
Come to this indoor recreation complex for its 56 bowling lanes, bumper cars, and video arcade. For the preschool set, there's a small, soft play area. *6700 Huebner Rd., at Bandera Rd., San Antonio; (210) 523-1716.*

Brackenridge Park
FamilyFun ★★★★/Free

MUST-SEE
MUST-SEE

At 343 acres, this park is a prime picnic, paddleboat, and playground spot. Hop aboard the Brackenridge Eagle, a small-scale train that takes you through the park with stops at the **Japanese Sunken Gardens**, with their wonderful ponds filled with goldfish, and the **Witte Museum** (for more information, see above). There's also an innovative playground, featuring a maze made from an old public shower house. **NOTE:** Some of the park's gravel paths are difficult for strollers. Be sure to leave time for a stop at **Kiddie Park** (*see below*). *3500 N. St. Mary's St., San Antonio;* www.alamocity.com/brackenridge/

HemisFair Park
FamilyFun ★★★/Free
MUST-SEE   Built for the 1968 World's Fair, this park has a shaded picnic area and a nice playground with a series of wooden jungle gyms and swings. On hot days, kids like to wade in the fountains, which are chlorinated. The park also is home to the Institute of Texan Cultures, which details the history of 27 ethnic groups that have settled in the state. *210 S. Alamo St., San Antonio;* www.sanantonio.gov/sapar

Kiddie Park ★★★/$
Some things never change, and we're very grateful that this park is one of them. One of the oldest children's amusement parks still in operation in the country (it was built in 1925), Kiddie Park has nine rides aimed at the 9-and-under set. The rides are classics—like a vintage carousel and a mini, kid-size Ferris wheel. There are also moving cars, planes, and helicopter rides. Parents can ride on a couple, but most are just for kids. Pay 80¢ per ride, or $6.45 per child for unlimited rides (a great deal when you consider all the smiles you'll get). The park is next door to Brackenridge Park, making it a treat after your family's trip to the San Antonio Zoo. *3015 Broadway St., San Antonio; (210) 824-4351;* www.kiddiepark.com

Lone Star Trolley Tours
★★/$-$$
An easy way to see downtown San Antonio without taking River Walk, these narrated, one-hour tours aboard air-conditioned trolleys are

ONE DAY IN SAN ANTONIO

9 A.M. Park in the Midcity Garage at the corner of Navarro and College or the municipal garage at St. Mary's and Travis. Begin the day at the **Alamo** (see page 103). Be sure to get the required photo in front of the famous structure, which served as a mission during the time of the battle. Remind kids that the site is considered sacred and that they need to be respectful by removing their caps

and speaking quietly. Hit the gift shop for Alamo-emblazoned snow globes or faux coonskin caps. The shop also has an array of children's books that spotlight Texas history.

10 A.M. Go to the **San Antonio Children's Museum** (see page 104). Then, if you have kids over age 8, make sure to stop at the **Witte Museum** (see page 105).

better suited to older kids. If you want to ride a trolley, but don't need the narration, take one of the city-run streetcars. How do you tell the difference? Lone Star Trolleys are red and green, and the city trolleys are plain green. *Lone Star Trolley tickets are sold at 301 Alamo Plaza, San Antonio; (210) 224-9299.*

Market Square
★★★/Free

Market Square is the place to buy souvenirs on your trip to San Antonio and get a real feel for the city's Hispanic heritage. Whether you're making your way through the open-air shops of El Mercado or the 80 specialty stores at Farmers Market Plaza, you'll find that the strolling mariachi bands add to the atmosphere. Two restaurants and a variety of food stalls sell everything from burritos to funnel cakes. Don't

leave without buying a colorful piñata for your child's next birthday. *514 W. Commerce St., San Antonio; (210) 207-8600.*

Natural Bridge Caverns and Wildlife Ranch ★★★/$$

This is the crème de la crème of caves. For the lowdown, see "Spelunking in Texas" on page 114.

River Walk (Paseo del Rio) ★★★★/Free

For most travelers, a trip to San Antonio means a stroll down the 2.8-mile River Walk, the beautifully landscaped—and heavily tourist-populated—stretch that frames the jade-green San Antonio River. The river originates from springs located on the grounds of the Incarnate Word College and winds through the city's downtown,

Noon Head over to the **River Walk** (see above), one block west of the Children's Museum on Houston Street. If you need an elevator, there is one located by the Hard Rock Café on Soledad. Most of the restaurants located on the River Walk are theme chains that welcome families: one of the best choices is **Joe's Crab Shack**, a casual seafood restaurant with a good kids' menu that includes the usual cheeseburgers, pizza, and fish and shrimp platters (see page 113).

It's located on the east side of the River Walk between Travis and Houston Streets.

1:30 P.M. After lunch, hop aboard one of the **Yanaguana River Cruises** (see page 110) on the San Antonio River. You can relax while listening to guides detail the city's interesting history and colorful characters. After the cruise, head back to your hotel for a nap or take in the IMAX show *Alamo, The Price of Freedom*.

one level below its busy streets. Older kids can appreciate the River Walk's unique beauty and/or its growing collection of theme restaurants, from the Hard Rock Café to Joe's Crab Shack (see page 113). But be prepared if your preschooler gets a bit tired of the scene after half an hour or so. **NOTE:** The River Walk isn't exactly stroller-friendly. It's hard to find a working elevator to take you down to the walk and, once there, the sidewalks are thin, bumpy, and often congested. A fun alternative to walking is taking the 30-minute boat cruise up and down the San Antonio River that is offered by Yanaguana River Cruises on one of their 40-seat boats (see page 110); www.hotx.com/rb

San Antonio Zoo
FamilyFun ★★★/$$

With so many other big attractions, the city's zoo often gets bypassed by families. Believe us: it's worth spending an afternoon to see some of this wildlife sanctuary's exotic creatures. The zoo boasts two snow leopards; one of the world's most extensive collections of African antelopes; an Australian Outback section that spotlights koala bears and kangaroos; and a breeding facility for the endangered cassowary bird. Your kids will ooh and aah over the petting zoo and the special children's zoo, populated with miniature animals from around the world. And, as an added treat, they'll love the tropical

boat tour that takes them through the habitats via water. There's also a playground and an educational center. *3903 N. St. Mary's, San Antonio; (210) 734-7183;* www.sazoo.org

SeaWorld
FamilyFun ★★★/$$$-$$$$

Billed as the world's largest marine-life park, Sea World has enough shows, rides, and education exhibits to keep your family busy for a day or two. Get here when the gates open to have the shortest lines at popular rides such as the Texas Splashdown log flume ride and the Rio Loco river-rapids ride. Preschoolers can go on the carnival-like rides at Shamu's Happy Harbor, while preteens can test their fortitude on the Steel Eel roller coaster that plummets 15 stories down.

After hitting the rides, take in one of the shows. See the Shamu show first—arrive about 15 minutes before the scheduled start time to get good seats, and check out the huge "Shamuvision" video screen. If you want to get wet, sit in one of the first 12 rows; otherwise, seek higher ground. The seal and walrus show—a hoot for everyone from toddlers to grandparents—has the sea mammals trying to help a hapless handyman. **NOTE:** The Rockin' Ski Party water stunt show is best for kids over age 7. The shark tank draws huge crowds, but we prefer the dolphin tank, where your child can dip his or her hand in and actually touch a dolphin. To increase the odds of getting up close and personal for this one, line up to buy fish about 30 minutes before the scheduled feeding times. **ANOTHER NOTE:** Food options are limited in the park and lines are often long at the few restaurants available. Consider snacking on food offered at the small stands instead or resolving to eat a hearty breakfast, then getting dinner at the McDonald's just outside the park. If you're coming in late spring or summer, be sure to pack a swimsuit and towel so you can enjoy Sea World's water park areas. Lost Lagoon features a wave pool and water slides for older kids, while those under age 8 will enjoy the Lil' Gators Lagoon water play area. For an extra charge, visitors ages 10 and older can participate in a two-hour program where they interact with beluga whales or sea lions. *Westover Hills Blvd., San Antonio; (210) 523-3900; www.seaworld.com*

Six Flags Fiesta Texas
FamilyFun ★★★/$$$-$$$$
Located in a former stone quarry, this theme park is like Sea World without the fish. Instead of Shamu, Looney Tunes characters Bugs Bunny, Daffy Duck, and others provide family photo opportunities. For thrill seekers, there's a new floorless roller coaster called Superman Krypton Coaster that's supposedly faster than a speeding bullet. Young kids will want to hang out in the Spassburg section of the park, a replica of a German Hill Country town, with a carousel, train, and collection of small rides. For those craving watery excitement, there's an extensive water park that includes 75 slides and a Texas-shaped wave pool, so bring a swimsuit. After sunset you can take a well-deserved break and watch the fireworks and laser show. **NOTE:** Most of the park's shows—including

FamilyFun **READER'S TIP** -

Window Shopping

I am always trying to make car travel more fun for my kids and easier on me. One idea that has worked very well is a picture scavenger hunt. I cut pictures out of old picture books, magazines, and catalogs and paste them on a piece of poster board. Then I punch holes in the two top corners of the poster, tie a piece of elastic between them, and hang the poster from the back of the front seat. Each time my kids see one of the items—an airplane, tractor, bicycle, or horse, for example—they place a sticker on that picture. My kids love this game so much that it entertained them throughout a recent 13-hour trip.

Lisa Reynolds, San Antonio, Texas

the revue of 1950s-era music and the collection of celebrity impersonators—will bore your younger kids. *Located 15 minutes north of downtown off I-10 West at exit 555; (210) 697-5050;* www.sixflags.com/ SanAntonio

Splashtown
★★/$$–$$$

Yet another water park, this one offers everything from a relaxing inner tube ride down a lazy river to the outer space-inspired StarFlight thrill ride. Admission prices drop after 5 P.M. *Located north of downtown off Interstate 35; (210) 227-1400;* www.splashtownsa.com

Yanaguana Cruises
★★★★/$–$$

The easiest and most fun way to see the River Walk is from the river on one of these compressed-gas cruise boats. Tours last 35 to 40 minutes and children are welcome; all they have to do is keep their hands and feet inside the boat. Guides point out historical sites and tell local folklore tales during the tour. Fares are reduced Tuesday and Wednesday mornings. Tickets can be purchased at the Rivercenter Mall and across the street from the Hilton at 200 S. Alamo St. If you'll be visiting during peak travel time or want to cruise during the evening or on a weekend, consider booking well before you get to town. *(800) 417-4139; (210) 244-5700.*

BUNKING DOWN

Guadalupe State Park ★★/$

Located along four miles of the Guadalupe River, this park 30 miles north of San Antonio is a great place if your family enjoys water activities such as canoeing, fishing, hiking and tubing (a favorite pursuit in central Texas rivers). On Saturday mornings, a naturalist leads a two-hour tour detailing plant and animal life. There are campsites for RVs with water and electrical hookups and an area for tent campers with water in the area. *3350 Park Rd. 31, Spring Branch; (830) 438-2656;* http:// www.tpwd.state.tx.us/park/guadalup/ guadalup.htm

Gunther Hotel ★★★/$$$

Renovated several years ago, this former Sheraton has regained some of its luster. Not surprisingly, it's the place where wealthy cattle ranchers stay when they come to town (in its heyday, it welcomed such western legends as John Wayne and Will Rogers). As for your family, it's a place where you can spread out in a suite with adjoining bedrooms—some have bunk beds for kids. And despite its historic facade, the hotel has Nintendo on the room television for a small fee. There's also an outdoor pool for cooling off when it gets hot in the summer months. *205 E. Houston, San Antonio; (210) 227-3241.*

Homewood Suites
★★★/$$-$$$

Looking for a room with a river view and a dishwasher and a microwave? This all-suites hotel is located on a quiet part of the River Walk and is within easy walking distance of Market Square and the Alamo. There's a free continental breakfast and an afternoon reception with soft drinks and snacks, and kids can play in the rooftop pool. If that's not enough to make this your home away from home, each room has two televisions and VCRs and there are laundry facilities. Ask for one of the two rooms with river views. *432 Market St., San Antonio; (800) CALL-HOME; (210) 222-1515;* www.homewood-suites.com

Hyatt Hill Country
★★★★/$$$-$$$$

This luxury resort is so incredible, you may not want to venture from its plush, manicured confines. Amenities include a 950-foot-long Ramblin' River water feature where you grab an inner tube and float away the day or stop at the shallow swimming area with its small, sandy beach, a favorite among preschoolers. The resort also has a playground and free bikes to take a relaxing ride, with training-wheel models and tricycles available, too. You can travel light and take advantage of the free laundry machines (you do have to buy the soap). The rooms are pricey during the spring and summer, but rates can be much lower in November and December.

During spring break (in mid-March) and throughout the summer, the busy activities schedule includes water-balloon races and sand-castle-building contests during the day and hayrides and marshmallow roasting at night. The Camp Hyatt program offers child care for kids ages 3 to 12 and includes nature

Teaching Your Kids How to Pack

Encourage your kids to think of mix-and-match outfits for various activities, just as they do when dressing paper dolls. (You even can have them practice by packing a doll wardrobe — trying out the different outfits — while they pack for themselves.) For example, ask a preschooler, "We're going hiking. Which of your comfortable pants do you want to wear?" After he lays these out, ask him to match them with two T-shirts (for two outfits), a sweatshirt in case it is cold, and appropriate shoes. Then, consider another vacation activity. Ask him to find two bathing suits, with a sun cover-up and a hat. Next, ask him to think about nighttime, laying out toothbrush and toothpaste, pajamas, a beloved but small stuffed animal, a bathrobe, and slippers.

111

hikes and storytelling. The hotel is located across the street from SeaWorld and offers a special rate in conjunction with the park's interactive whale and sea lion adventures. *9800 Hyatt Resort Dr., San Antonio; (800) 233-1234; (210) 647-1234;* www.hyatt.com *or* www.hill country.hyatt.com

San Antonio KOA ★★/$

Set up at one of this campground's 300 campsites or 22 cabins and enjoy amenities such as a year-round pool, hot tub, and fishing. The schedule of events includes nightly movies, ice cream socials, and a Sunday morning church service. The campground also offers holiday happenings, including a Halloween Hay Ride, Easter Egg Hunt, and July 4th picnic. The two-room cabins sleep up to six, but bring bedding and cooking utensils. *602 Gembler Rd., San Antonio; (800) 562-7783 or (210) 224-9296;* www.koakampgrounds.com

Westin La Cantera ★★★★/$$$-$$$$

San Antonio's newest entry in the luxury resort category caters to families who are willing to shell out big bucks in return for some pampering. Unlike the Hyatt Hill Country's lush landscaped grounds, this place is located on top of a hill and affords views of downtown San Antonio, the fireworks displays at Fiesta Texas (located only a mile or two away), and a rock quarry that is mined

FamilyFun GAME

Raindrop Race

Each player traces the course of a raindrop down the window. The first drop to reach the bottom wins.

much of the day. The hotel works to make families feel welcome; at check-in, kids are given bags filled with a baseball cap, crayons, cups, and a small toy. The large pool area includes a curving water slide and kiddie pool with bubbling fountains.

The hotel's Enchanted Rock Kids Club is available for kids ages 4 to 12 during spring break and May through September. On a recent trip, the ratio of kids to caregivers was about two to one, and the four-hour session included water games, making beaded key chains, and a short nature hike. Families can rent a suite, which has a pullout sleep sofa, or to really spread out, opt for a casita, which includes a full kitchen and separate bedrooms. The casitas are located several hundred yards from the main resort building, and families are given golf carts (for a fee) to get around the resort. Unless you have lined up babysitting through the concierge, skip the gourmet restaurant, Francesca's, and head to Brannon's Café, which offers buffets, including a small child-sized one during dinner, or choices from the regular menu. Your vacation budget will benefit if you have youngsters under 7, as they eat free. During spring break and through most of the summer, the café hosts Looney Tunes breakfasts most weekends with Six Flags Fiesta's Bugs Bunny, Daffy Duck, Elmer Fudd, and company on hand for photo opportunities. Make reservations in advance. *16641 La Cantera Pkwy., San Antonio; (800) WESTIN-1; (210) 558-6500;* www.westin.com

GOOD EATS

EZ's Brick Oven and Grill ★★/$$
Fashioned to look like a 1950s drive-in, this chain has above-average burgers and pizzas. Kids eat for free on Wednesday nights if they're with a paying adult. The kids' menu includes the standard chicken fingers, cheese pizza, and burgers with curly fries. *Five locations around San Antonio. 6493 N. New Braunfels Ave., San Antonio; (210) 828-1111.*

Hard Rock Café ★★★/$$
There's typically a wait at this outpost of the popular chain, and larger parties of five or more should consider splitting up because almost all the tables accommodate only four people. Kids (and adults) love the chain's juicy burger-and-fries plate. Youngsters also get a kick out of the 23-foot Cadillac hearse suspended upside down over the main floor. Be forewarned, the staff sometimes makes birthday celebrants perform

the famous "YMCA" song by the Village People. *111 W. Crockett St., San Antonio; (210) 224-7625;* www.hardrockcafe.com

Joe's Crab Shack ★★★/$$
Kids fit right in at this noisy River Walk restaurant. We loved the fact that they bring Saltines to the table while you wait for your meal. The kids' menu includes popcorn shrimp with fries, pizza, and macaroni and cheese. Adults can choose from the menu's extensive seafood offerings. Save room for Key lime pie or the chocolate overdose, a triple-level chocolate cake topped with fudge sauce. *212 College St., San Antonio; (210) 271-9981.*

La Fogata ★★★★/$$
This Mexican restaurant has a fiesta feel year-round thanks to the mariachi band that plays on the patio most evenings. There's also an air-conditioned indoor dining room that's more subdued. Most kids love the music and the small fountain located at the entrance (bring your pennies). The kids' specials include enchiladas, tacos, and quesadillas (the Tex-Mex version of grilled cheese). Go early, just before 6 P.M., to avoid a wait for a table. *2427 Vance Jackson Rd., San Antonio; (210) 340-0636;* www.lafogata.com

Luby's ★★★/$
Born in San Antonio, this cafeteria chain is a Texas institution and is

113

usually packed most Sunday afternoons after church services let out. The kids' menu includes corn dogs and chicken fingers that will tempt most adults; there's also Jell-O (kids can pick the color) and the choice of a vegetable (yes, French fries count). Older kids with bigger appetites, and most parents, are happy with the LuAnn Platter: your choice of entrée, two vegetables, and bread. *There are 22 locations in the San Antonio area, including one downtown at 911 Main St; (210) 223-1911;* www.lubys.com

The Magic Time Machine ★★/$$

How would your kids like to be served their lunch by Batman or

Spelunking in Texas

TEXAS IS HOME to many natural caves, most located in the limestone-rich Hill Country region in and around San Antonio. Here are a few of our picks for a cool, dark way to spend a day or just an afternoon:

Cascade Caverns ★★/$-$$

The highlight of this cave is the 90-foot waterfall, which is viewed near the end of the one-hour guided tour. The tour may be too tedious for kids under age 5, but older children will enjoy seeing the cave's expansive rooms and the flowing crystal river. *Located 14 miles northwest of San Antonio. Take exit 543 off I-10; (830) 755-8080.*

Cave Without a Name ★★/$

This small cave offers great caverns without the crowds. It's worth trying to navigate to its out-of-the-way location. *To get there from Boerne, take Scenic Highway 474 about six miles, then turn right on Kreutzberg Road and drive about five miles to the cave's entrance. Boerne; (830) 537-4212;* www.cavewithoutaname.com

Natural Bridge Caverns and Wildlife Ranch ★★★/$$

The biggest and best stop on the Texas caverns tour, these caves are estimated to be 140 million years old and contain a 60-foot-long limestone bridge. Tours last an hour and 15 minutes. Above ground, there's a shaded park and small museum. Make a day of it by also taking in the adjacent Wildlife Ranch, where native, exotic, and endangered species, including rhinos, roam its 200 acres. You can drive your car through the ranch and challenge your kids to entice some of the animals with the complimentary feed. *26495 Natural Bridge Caverns Rd., located eight miles off Interstate 35 between San Antonio and New Braunfels; (210) 651-6101;* www.naturalbridgecaverns.com

Kermit the Frog? Find out at this wacky restaurant where the waiters and waitresses dress up as cartoon characters and historical folk, like medieval knights and ladies. In case you think this is a new gimmick, the restaurant has been doing this since 1973. If you're really hungry, order the Roman Orgy, which includes barbecue brisket, ribs, and chicken with vegetables, salad, and bread. The price at press time was $17.99 for adults, $5.99 for kids. *902 N.E. Loop 410, San Antonio; (210) 828-1470; www.magictime machine.com*

Schilo's ★★★/$

A longtime local favorite, Schilo's serves the best wurst in town. Just tell the kids that bratwurst is German for hot dog and they'll eat it. If they balk, never fear—the restaurant also offers Oscar Mayer dogs, too. The large, bustling, open-room restaurant welcomes oompah bands on most Friday and Saturday evenings. *424 E. Commerce St., San Antonio; (210) 223-6692.*

Willie's Grill and Icehouse ★★★/$$

One of the least expensive, child-friendly spots in town, Willie's serves up great burgers and chicken fingers and has a huge outdoor sandbox and video room to keep the kids busy before and after eating. *15801 San Pedro Ave., San Antonio; (210) 490-9220.*

SOUVENIR HUNTING

Bambinos

If you didn't pack enough clothes for your kids, take them over to this upscale children's apparel shop, which also carries toys and some furniture. *5934 Broadway, San Antonio; (210) 822-9595.*

Central Market

If you're heading out for a picnic, make this upscale grocery store your first stop. You can get gourmet sandwiches, salads, and cookies packed to go to fill your hamper. On Saturday and Sunday, they set out free samples at every turn—you may not need to eat again all day! *4821 Broadway, San Antonio; (210) 368-8600.*

Monarch Collectibles

A mecca for doll collectors, this store is packed with more than 3,000 or so models, with one room devoted entirely to Barbies. There's also an elaborate collection of doll furniture housed in a mini mansion. *2012 N.W. Military Hwy., San Antonio; (210) 341-3655.*

Playworks

The place to shop for toys you won't find at Target or Toys "R" Us, this innovative store has elaborate Playmobil displays and a wide variety of hands-on science kits for sale, including ant farms and butterfly gardens. *1931 N.W. Military Hwy.; (210) 340-2328.*

Long beaches and gentle waves make a Texas Gulf Coast vacation terrific for families.

The Texas Gulf Coast

GREAT FAMILY beach communities should have long strands of sand, gentle waves, ample fishing opportunities, inexpensive cottages, and abundant wildlife. There also should be fun entertainment available for rainy afternoons, and plenty of seafood restaurants ready to serve up hearty platters. Texas's Gulf Coast towns—including Galveston, Port Aransas, Corpus Christi, and South Padre Island—have it all.

Along the 624 miles of Lone Star beaches, your family can search for shells on a desolate stretch of sand or ride horses in the surf. If the weather is cool or cloudy, you can head over to Galveston's Moody Gardens, where your kids can walk through an indoor rain forest filled with birds and butterflies or view a 3-D IMAX "ride film" that's so

THE **FamilyFun** LIST

Bayfront Arts and Science Park
(page 122)

Galveston Island State Park
(page 120)

Gladys Porter Zoo (page 128)

Moody Gardens (page 120)

Padre Island National Seashore
(page 123)

Port Isabel Lighthouse State Historic Park (page 129)

Schlitterbahn Beach Waterpark
(page 123)

Sea Turtle Inc. (page 129)

South Padre Island
(page 127)

Texas State Aquarium
(page 122)

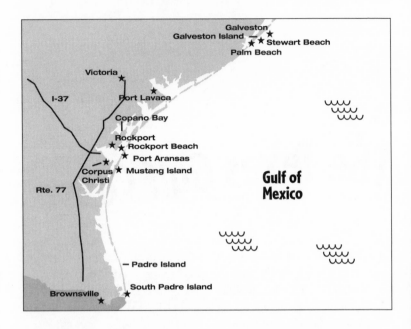

realistic, the images jump right off the screen. As for those seafood platters, never fear: family-friendly restaurants are on almost every corner. Fishing piers welcome families, too; just make sure you have a state fishing license. Kids can go on nature-watching boat cruises that take them up so close to dolphins they can actually give them a hug. In short, the beaches of Texas offer something for almost any family.

There's a downside to the beach scene, however: while these beaches offer many rewards, they aren't all perfect. Texas's Gulf Coast is home to many petrochemical plants, and the view (and the breezes) sometimes suffers. Also, on some of the beaches, debris may

wash up on the sand, so keep a close eye on what your kids scoop up. Mosquitoes can be a problem too, so be sure to bring (and wear) plenty of bug repellent. And don't come to this beach area expecting chichi resorts and lots of Starbuckses and Pottery Barns. Many of these Gulf Coast towns seem frozen in time and are still dominated by mom-and-pop establishments that serve basic needs—but therein lies this region's charm. It's a place that lacks the pretension (and prices) of better known coastal resorts (for more information about Texas Coast beaches, see "Best Texas Beaches for Families" on page 124).

Most families get here by car, driving along gorgeous coastal stretches such as Texas Highway 35, a scenic two-lane blacktop road that takes you through fishing villages and past farms. And at many of the state's beaches, you're allowed to drive your car right onto the sand. If you're traveling from Kingsville to Harlingen on your way to South Padre Island, fill up before you drive the desolate stretch of U.S. 77.

Galveston

Galveston was an economic hub of Texas until 1900, when a devastating hurricane blew through and left more than 6,000 dead; it was the worst natural disaster in the nation's history. The construction of a huge seawall and much-improved weather forecasting now prevent similar devastation. Today, families flock here to enjoy the island's 32 miles of beaches and to get a taste of history during such popular events as Dickens on the Strand, held the first week of December, when the island is transformed into Queen Victoria's London.

CULTURAL ADVENTURES

Ocean Star ★★/$

Kids can get an up-close look at what it takes to get oil out of the ground at this drilling site. Tour the refurbished oil rig and watch a video that explains the ways oil drillers search for oil, how they pipe it nationwide, and what environmental precautions they take. The presentation is sponsored by the oil industry, so expect it to be a bit one-sided. *Pier 19, Galveston; (409) 766-STAR.*

Treasure Island Tour Train
★★/$-$$

This 90-minute train tour includes a recorded narration covering the history of the island. Great for youngsters over 6. *2106 Seawall Blvd., Galveston Island; (409) 765-9564.*

JUST FOR FUN

The Colonel
★★★/$$

Board this three-story paddle wheeler for an hour-long tour of Galveston Bay. The captain narrates the tour, telling tales of Galveston's colorful history and pointing out sea life. *One Hope Blvd., Galveston; (409) 740-7797.*

Galveston Duck Tours
★★★/$$$

Sit back and enjoy a 90-minute tour of Galveston aboard World War II

119

amphibious vehicles. The tour covers the Seawall, Silk Stocking District, and the Strand and ends with a cruise to Offats Bayou. *Tours meet at 21st St. and the Seawall in Galveston; (409) 621-4771.*

⭐ᵐᵘˢᵗ⁻ˢᵉᵉ Galveston Island State
FamilyFun Park ★★★/Free
⭐ᵐᵘˢᵗ⁻ˢᵉᵉ Big—2,000 acres big!—this park offers places for swimming, camping, picnicking, beach-combing, and bird-watching. There are four miles of walking trails, and an amphitheater where musicals are performed during the summer. *Farm Rd. 3005, Galveston; (409) 737-1222.*

⭐ᵐᵘˢᵗ⁻ˢᵉᵉ Moody Gardens
FamilyFun ★★★★/$$-$$$
⭐ᵐᵘˢᵗ⁻ˢᵉᵉ Seeing everything at this huge, 156-acre attraction takes at least a day—and more like a weekend. Start off at the Rainforest Pyramid, a 10-story, 40,000-square-foot glass structure that houses a tropical rain forest complete with waterfalls, butterflies, birds, and fish; a recent addition is the Southwest's largest bat exhibit. Move on to the Discovery Pyramid, a trip into outer space. The journey starts with an IMAX "ride film," where the seats actually shift to simulate a blastoff and touchdown.

Spend the afternoon at the 1.5-million-gallon aquarium where penguins and harbor seals live. Then head over to Palm Beach, a white-sand beach and man-made blue lagoon swim area for kids. If you're still up for more, ride the Colonel paddle-wheel boat around Galveston Bay. Tickets for Moody Gardens are sold either as a day pass ($29.95 at press time) or per attraction. If you have young children who give out after a couple of hours, the à la carte menu may work better. *Two Hope Blvd., Galveston Island; (800) 582-4673; www.moodygardens.com*

BUNKING DOWN

Gaido's Seaside Inn
★★★/$-$$
Nothing fancy here, but clean comfortable digs and convenience makes this a family favorite. There's a beachfront pool, and most rooms offer Gulf views. When it's time to eat, simply head over to one of the adjacent restaurants—Casey's—which offers fresh seafood and baked breads, or the more fancy Gaido's, which is an 85-year-old Galveston seafood dining institution where as hotel guests you get priority seating. *3800 Seawall Blvd., Galveston; (800) 525-0064; (409) 762-9625.*

Moody Gardens Hotel
★★★★/$$$
If your kids are having so much fun at Moody Gardens that they don't want to leave, then don't: this new luxury hotel offers an indoor/outdoor pool and a child-care facility with a play area and video viewings.

This place is growing in popularity, so book your room a month or more in advance. *One Hope Blvd., Galveston; (800) 582-4673; (409) 744-4673; www.moodygardens.com*

GOOD EATS

Benno's on the Beach
★★★/$$

Wear flip-flops to this very casual beachside restaurant that serves Cajun and Creole-inspired seafood dishes, including shrimp po-boys and crayfish etouffée. *1200 Seawall Blvd., Galveston; (409) 672-4621.*

Mario's
★★/$-$$

If you're looking for a family-friendly spot to grab pizza and pasta, then this is the place. There's gourmet wood-fired pizza as well as basic cheese and pepperoni. Seafood pastas are a house specialty. *628 Seawall Blvd., Galveston; (409) 763-1693.*

SOUVENIR HUNTING

Colonel Bubbie's Strand Surplus Center

This store is packed with military surplus clothing and paraphernalia from around the world. Keep your curious kids occupied here sorting through canteens and camouflage clothes for hours. *2202 Strand Blvd., Galveston; (409) 762-7397.*

Vacations for the Birds

The Texas Gulf is a fabulous place for bird-watching. Some 500 species of birds have been sighted on and around the state's beaches, including the rare masked duck and the endangered whooping crane. Why do they come here? Because South Texas lies along what's called the **Central Flyway** where, during their seasonal migrations, birds traveling up the Mississippi River or the eastern United States converge with those heading west to the Rockies. In the summer, the area also gets some Central and South American birds.

As you drive the coast, you may see signs and observation areas that are part of what's called the **Great Texas Coastal Birding Trail**, an evolving route with more than 200 sites where birds have been spotted. If your kids want to try their hand at bird-watching, grab a copy of the Texas Parks and Wildlife Department's birding trail map *(800/792-1112)*, or simply pick up one of the many local guides available—the Corpus Christi Guides Association offers brochures and a bird hot line.

Corpus Christi, Port Aransas, and Victoria

Although Corpus Christi and Victoria have special appeal of their own, Port Aransas has been a popular family seaside vacation spot for generations. The island town has grown in recent years and now has high-rise condos nestled between older motels. Thankfully, growth hasn't affected Port Aransas's laid-back atmosphere; it's still an ideal place for long walks looking for shells, and bodysurfing in the waves. Kids love the five-minute ferry ride from Aransas Pass to the island, gleefully crowding the boat rails looking for sea life and birds. The other way to Port Aransas is via the highway from Corpus Christi, but that's nowhere near as much fun.

CULTURAL ADVENTURES

 **Bayfront Arts and Science Park ★★★/$-$$**

Located in downtown Corpus Christi, this complex includes the Art Museum of South Texas's Harbor Playhouse, a children's theater, and Heritage Park, a collection of eight homes dating from around 1900 with displays on the city's history. The real attraction for families is the Corpus Christi Museum of Science and History, where kids can board a miniature shrimp boat and don bird costumes in the children's play area, and get an up-close look at South Texas alligators. *1900 Shoreline Dr., Corpus Christi; (361) 883-2862.*

Texas State Aquarium ★★★★/$-$$

Kids love this museum, where they can touch a shark in the special touch tank and watch an otter family cavort on the riverbank. The 350,000-gallon main tank shows kids what sea life looks like in the Gulf of Mexico; there's even a coral reef created by an oil derrick. The popular Turtle Bend area showcases rare and endangered sea turtles. *2710 N.*

FamilyFun TIP

Cool It

Here's how to keep snacks cool in containers without having to deal with melting ice: add frozen juice boxes; make sandwiches on frozen bread; pack some frozen grapes; include a smoothie frozen in a tightly sealed container; use sealed ice packs.

nature walks at its station on Malaquite Beach. *Take Highway 358 (South Padre Island Dr.) from Corpus Christi. After crossing the JFK Causeway and the bridge onto Padre Island, continue 10 miles south on Park Road 22;* www.nps.gov/pais

Shoreline Dr., Corpus Christi; (800) 477-4853; (361) 881-1200; www.texas stateaquarium.org

JUST FOR FUN

Dolphin Connection ★★★★/$$$

This company offers hour-long tours that give you the opportunity to feed and even pet dolphins. Each boat normally attracts a dozen or so dolphins who will take turns doing big flips out of the water to get your attention—and perhaps to get some fish to eat. The operators can even introduce you to the dolphins they've come to know; they've actually named a lot of them. In Ingleside between Corpus Christi and Port Aransas. Reservations are required. *(361) 776-2887;* www. dolphinconnectiontexas.com

MUST-SEE FamilyFun MUST-SEE Padre Island National Seashore ★★★/$$

Just south of Corpus Christi, this 113-mile-long island is a prime spot for birding and shelling. In the summer, the National Park Service offers daily ranger-led programs on the island's ecology, plus

MUST-SEE FamilyFun MUST-SEE Schlitterbahn Beach Waterpark ★★★★/$$

This new beach version of the famous Hill Country water park is drawing raves from happily soggy families. Get there early to claim a prime lounging and picnic spot, then spend the day taking in attractions such as the Boogie Bahn, where hot-doggers can catch a never-ending wave in one of the world's largest surfing rides or the 571-foot-long Storm Chaser uphill water coaster. Younger kids will love Sand Castle Cove, which has a five-story water fun house and four water slides. Be sure to bring life vests for any weak swimmers in your family and pack swim diapers for tots. Lockers are available to rent so you can store keys, cash, and other valuables. The park also welcomes picnic hampers and coolers as long as you don't bring in any glass or alcohol. Saturdays during the summer can be packed, so come midweek to avoid the biggest crowds. *90 Park Road Hwy. 100, South Padre Island; (956) 772-SURF;* www. schlitterbahn.com

Texas Zoo ★★/$

The focus of this small zoo is on native Texas wildlife—with more

BEST TEXAS BEACHES FOR FAMILIES

WITH ITS MILES of white sands, Texas's Gulf Coast is a beach lover's paradise. Here are our favorite strands. All you have to do is apply sunscreen, lie back, and enjoy.

Galveston's Stewart Beach ★★★/Free

Located at Seawall Boulevard and Broadway at the north end of the island, this beach is alcohol free and has a water slide, go-carts, miniature golf, and bumper boats. **NOTE:** Be aware that the island's East Beach area is now the official "party beach," where bars serve beer and mixed drinks on the beach. www.galveston.com/beachparks/stewartbeach.shtml

Matagorda Island State Park ★★★/$$

If you want to escape the crowds, this is the place to go. To get here, you have to travel by boat (a ferry operates from South 16th Street at Maple Avenue in Port Aransas). It's a great place for fishing and bird-watching. In the winter, it's home to whooping cranes; and migratory birds flock here during the spring and fall. **NOTE:** This is a place for families who don't mind roughing it: there are no lifeguards, no drinking water, no rest room facilities, no electricity, and no food here, so plan accordingly.

Camping facilities are available, but call ahead to reserve a spot. *(361) 983-2215;* www.tpwd.state.tx.us/

Mustang Island State Park ★★★★/$

This park can get crowded on weekends and some summer days, but it offers clean sand, gentle surf, campsites, and rest rooms with showers. Bring your own picnic, since food is not available. Enjoy a horseback ride on the beach by booking through Mustang Riding Stables, which also can organize a hayride or beach party. *To reach the park, travel southeast from Corpus Christi on State Highway 358 to Padre Island; cross the JFK Causeway and continue one mile to the traffic light; turn left on State Highway 361 and go five minutes north to park headquarters; (361) 749-5246;* www.tpwd.state.tx.us/

Palm Beach at Moody Gardens ★★★★/$$

You have to pay to come here ($7.95 per adult and $5.95 ages 4 to 12), but it's worth it for the fun extras like the Octopus Slippery Slides and the 30-foot Yellow Submarine complete with periscope and water gun. Little kids can safely splash around in the cool, blue lagoon or build sand castles with the sugarlike sands that are actually barged over from Florida. Plenty of snack bars, beach chairs, and umbrellas are available. *1 Hope Blvd., Galveston; (800) 582-4673; (409) 744-4673.*

Rockport Beach Park
★★★/Free
This small park offers a white-sand beach, plenty of picnic tables, a fishing pier, a playground, and a saltwater pool. The parking lot is located at *210 Navigation Street in Rockport, north of Corpus Christi.*

South Padre's Isla Blanca Park **★★★/Free**
Located at the southernmost tip of the island, this park offers a white-sand beach with picnic and play-ground areas. There's also a full-service marina, restaurants, and a 1,000-foot sea walk that's great for biking or in-line skating. www.sopadre.com

than 200 creatures, including bears, armadillos, eagles, and wolves. *110 Memorial Dr., Victoria; (361) 573-7681;* www.texaszoo.org

USS *Lexington* **★★/$$**
This carrier took part in all the major Pacific battles during World War II. Now your kids can wander its decks and explore the huge hangar that once housed fighter planes. Volunteer guides (including many who served in the U.S. Navy) are available to answer questions. *2914 N. Shoreline Blvd., Corpus Christi; (361) 888-4873;* www.uslexington.com

BUNKING DOWN

Holiday Inn Emerald Beach
★★★/$$-$$$
This hotel has a great beach right out-side its back door, and many of its 368 rooms have bay views. For kids, there's a huge pool, Ping-Pong tables, and an indoor play area. There's also a full-service restaurant where youngsters 12 and under eat free when dining with an adult. *1102 Shoreline Blvd., Corpus Christi; (800) 465-4329; (361) 883-5731;* www.holiday-inn.com

Holiday Inn Sunspree
★★★/$$-$$$
Kids love the lobby here, with its aquariums, and walls decorated with sea life. Each room comes with a microwave and refrigerator (handy for making breakfast and light

Go Fish

Even if you've never cast a rod, you and your kids can have fun fishing the Gulf waters, where flounder, trout, redfish, tuna, snapper, and even shark are among the most common catches. To fish in Texas waters, adults ages 17 and over must have a Texas fishing license (younger folk do not need one), available for a small fee ($12 for a three-day permit at press time) at most fishing tackle shops and many convenience stores.

Fish off the rocks or seawalls or in the surf without any additional charge, or go to a public pier where you'll have to pay a small fee of $2 or so. Among the best piers in the area are the **Port Lavaca State Fishing Pier** in Port Lavaca and the **Copano Bay State Fishing Pier** on Texas Highway 35, which is more than a mile and half long and is the longest lighted fishing pier in the world.

If you catch something, be ready to either release it or clean it and cook it for dinner. Bring your camera and have your kids strike a classic fisherman pose, even if they only reel in a tiny minnow.

lunches), and amenities include playgrounds, a shuffleboard court, a swimming pool equipped for water basketball and volleyball, and a bike-rental service. *15202 Winward Dr., Padre Island; (800) 465-4329; (361) 949-8041;* www.holiday-inn.com/corpuschristi

Laguna Reef Hotel
★★★/$$-$$$

This hotel looks over Aransas Bay and offers suites with fully equipped kitchens, queen-size beds, and sofa beds. It also offers free continental breakfast, a picnic and barbecue area, a putting green, and access to a 1,000-foot lighted fishing pier. *1021 Water St., Rockport; (800) 248-1057; (361) 729-1742;* www.lagunareef.com

Port Royal Resort Condominium
★★★/$$$-$$$$

The pool here, supposedly the state's largest (with both a water slide and a swim-up bar) is so much fun your kids may never want to go back to the room. But the accommodations won't disappoint, either. All 210 units have full-size kitchens and a washer/dryer, and the three-bedroom units have a built-in hot tub on the balcony. The condos are in a gated community on Mustang Island, and privacy is part of the pricey package: you can take a stroll down the boardwalk and have the beach largely to yourself. *6317 Texas Hwy. 361, Port Aransas; (361) 749-5011;* www.port-royal.com

Good Eats

The Crazy Cajun ★★★/$$

The food is served on butcher paper at this ultracasual spot specializing in Cajun seafood; kids' like the peel-and-eat shrimp. *303 Beach Ave., Port Aransas; (361) 749-5069.*

Hofbrau Steaks ★★★/$$-$$$$

This Texas-based chain is famous for its juicy steaks and burgers and that Texas classic, chicken-fried steak. No kids' menu but they make pint-size burgers, corn dogs, chicken fingers, or other kid-friendly favorites and serve them with a huge helping of fries. *1214 N. Chaparral St., Corpus Christi; (361) 881-8722.*

Snoopy's Pier ★★★/$$

Dine on excellent seafood at this popular waterside place. The kids' menu has cheeseburgers, hamburgers, or fried-shrimp with fries. Save room for the ice cream at the shop next door. *13313 South Padre Island Dr., Corpus Christi; (361) 949-8815.*

Souvenir Hunting

Fly It

As the name promises, this shop sells kites, wind socks, toy airplanes, and other lofty creations. *405 Cutoff Rd., Port Aransas; (361) 749-4190.*

Souvenir City

You can buy shells, T-shirts, plastic crabs, and postcards here. Mail cards in the store, which also serves as a post office. *100 E. White St., Port Aransas; (361) 749-6424.*

South Padre Island

South Padre Island is famous as a spring-break party mecca, but the real wild life here is the wildlife. The island is a great place to catch a nature-oriented boat cruise and watch dolphins leap from the sea. The Island Equestrian Center welcomes children—kids ages 5 and under get pony rides; those 6 and older can ride horses on the beach. South Padre Island is also one of the best places in the world for bird-watching, so grab some binoculars and a naturalist guide and see how many species your kids can identify.

Just for Fun

Breakaway Cruises ★★★★/$$-$$$

This nature-tour company offers a variety of ecocruises and tours including a Dolphin Watch, where you cruise with a school of dolphins that the guides know so well they have named each one. The outfitter also offers trips on the Aqua Dog, an amphibious jeep that turns into a boat. *Sea Ranch Marina, Padre Blvd., South Padre Island; (956) 761-2212; www.breakawaycruises.com*

Fin to Feather Tours
★★★★/$$$-$$$$
Operated by a naturalist couple, this tour-guide service specializes in dolphin and birding tours. Kids love to watch the dolphins jump in the boat's wake. If you're lucky, you can see dolphins and birds actually interacting when a dolphin tosses a fish up to a hovering tern. At press time, a two- to three-hour tour cost $17.50 to $22.50 per person. *South Padre Island; (956) 943-BIRD;* www.fin2feather.com

Gladys Porter Zoo
FamilyFun ★★★★/$
Located in nearby Browns-ville, this zoo boasts 1,500 birds, mammals, and reptiles from all over the world, including rare lowland gorillas and a white rhinoceros. The zoo uses waterways to separate the animals, so there's a surprisingly open feel with no cages or bars in sight. Little kids love the Small World Nursery and Petting Zoo. The zoo is open 365 days a year from 9 A.M. to 5:30 P.M. weekdays and until 6 P.M. on weekends. The Zoofari Train offers tours on Sunday afternoons. *500 Ringgold St., Brownsville; (956) 546-2177;* www.gpz.org

Island Equestrian Center
★★★★/$$$$
The center offers horseback rides on the beach for kids ages 6 and older; younger members of the family can hop on the pony rides. The center's horses are specially trained to deal with inexperienced riders, so don't worry about your children getting thrown. Riders get to trot and lope a bit on the hour-and-a-

---

FamilyFun **READER'S TIP** -

She Shows Seashells

My family loves to spend our vacations at the beach. We always collect many seashells that we think are pretty enough to frame—so we make them part of our annual summer photo collage. Once we get home, Danielle, 9, and Tiffany and Stephanie, 7-year-old twins, pick out their favorite shells and glue them on the edge of an 8- by 10-inch frame. We cut up vacation photos and assemble the collage, then attach labels to caption the pictures. We hang the pictures proudly every year.

Lorene Hall, Starke, Florida

half ride. The hour-long ride is a bit slower, with more walking. This is not a trail ride in the traditional sense: guides are available to help riders, but you're largely left on your own to amble up and down the beach as you (and your horse) choose. The early—9 A.M.—ride is less crowded, and typically cooler. Reservations are highly recommended. *Located on South Padre Island, about 1 mile north of the Convention Center; (956) 761-HOSS; www.horsesonthebeach.com*

Laguna Madre Nature Trail
★★★/Free

Called the Birding Boardwalk, this 1,500-foot boardwalk runs across four acres of wetlands, making it a perfect spot for your family (especially kids in elementary school and older) to go bird-watching. Bring your binoculars; you'll probably spot kingfishers, herons, egrets—and lots of other flying folk. **NOTE:** Keep a tight grip on younger children since the boardwalk's sides are not secured. *7355 Padre Blvd., South Padre Island; (956) 761-3000.*

Port Isabel Lighthouse
FamilyFun State Historic Park
★★★/Free-$

This is the only lighthouse in Texas that's open to the public, and one of only a few remaining in the state. If you and the kids are up for the 70-step climb to the top, you'll be rewarded with a great view of South

Corpus Christi
Discovering the Gulf's Sea Life

10 A.M. Bayfront Arts and Science Park (see page 122).

1 P.M. Lunch at Hofbrau Steaks (see page 127).

2 P.M. The Texas State Aquarium (see page 122).

Padre Island and the Gulf. Admission to the lighthouse is free; there's a small charge for the tour ($3 for adults, $1 for kids 5 through 21, and kids under 4 are free). *Queen Isabella Blvd., South Padre Island; (956) 943-2262.*

Sea Turtle Inc.
FamilyFun ★★★★/Free

The late Ila Loetscher earned the nickname The Turtle Lady by adopting the cause of the endangered Kemp's ridley sea turtle as her own. Her passion lives on through this foundation that spotlights the species. The turtle shows here are a treat, staged Tuesday through Sunday (call for times). *6617 Padre Blvd., South Padre Island; (956) 761-4511; seaturtleinc.com*

Families can raft the Rio Grande during a visit to Big Bend National Park.

West Texas and Big Bend

AROUND THE WORLD, Texas is known as a place with wide-open spaces, and nowhere is that more true than in West Texas and Big Bend National Park. This is the Wild West, a place made famous in films like *Giant*—shot here in Marfa—for being larger than life. It's also a place that seems desolate, but which makes you feel alive. Maybe it's seeing the power of the Rio Grande and the incredible limestone walls it has worn away over the centuries. Or it could be catching a glimpse of a roadrunner or hearing a coyote howl. In a nation of chain stores and restaurants where every city somehow feels the same, West Texas remains amazingly different.

It will take a while for this place, with its vast vistas and Technicolor sunsets, to work its magic on your

THE **FamilyFun** LIST

Big Bend National Park
(page 135)

Big Bend Ranch State Park
(page 135)

El Camino del Rio (page 136)

Fort Davis National Historic Site
(page 133)

Marfa Lights (page 137)

McDonald Observatory
(page 134)

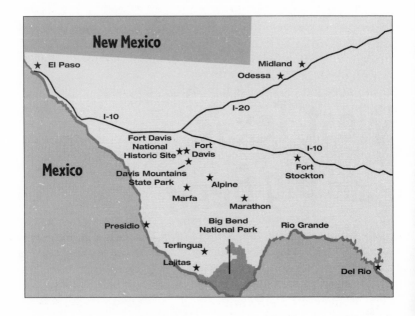

family, so plan on devoting at least four or five days here. It will also take time to get here. Most visitors fly into El Paso or Midland/Odessa airport, then rent a car and drive the 200 or so miles to reach this remote American treasure. Be aware that gas stations and restaurants are few and far between along the way, so make sure to carry some provisions in your car. The good news is that once you get here, crowds, even in the high seasons of spring and fall, are rare. That doesn't mean you shouldn't plan ahead. Because the number of hotels is relatively small, you need to be sure and make reservations to avoid being left out in the cold (and it does get pretty cold here at night, even in the summer). We'll

help you find the fun places that your kids won't soon forget.

Life in West Texas has never been easy; the people who settled here and survived its harsh climate and desolation are justifiably proud of their heritage. Kids can get firsthand experience with the region's history at Fort Davis National Historic Site, once home to 800 cavalry troops in the 1850s. The stone-and-adobe buildings have been restored to give your children a feel for what life in the Old West was really like. The site also was home to African American troops (dubbed buffalo soldiers) from the mid-19th century until 1891; a museum here details their contributions to settling the West.

Kids will get a natural-history lesson at Big Bend National Park. Over the years, it has been one of the least-visited national parks, but that is changing as more tourists make the lengthy trek here to raft the Rio Grande and explore the park's awe-inspiring rock statues carved by water and wind. Most families see the park from their car, but if your kids are seasoned mountain bikers or hikers, you may opt for one of the marked trails. A number of outfitters offer jeep tours, birding expeditions, and horseback riding through the park's vast 800,000 acres. Your family may also want to head into one of the sleepy Mexican villages across the border. **NOTE:** Although there are no official border crossings here, be sure to carry identification—such as a driver's license and/or birth certificate—in case you are stopped by the Border Patrol. Big Bend encompasses a vast landscape—far from the theme-park and miniature-golf scene—but it's a fascinating place we think you'll agree is well worth exploring.

FamilyFun SNACK

Good for You

Make some rocket fuel for your kids with a mix of dried apples, pineapples, cranberries, mangoes, and cherries, as well as banana chips and raisins. (1 cup of this will fulfill 2 of the recommended 5 minimum daily servings of fruits and vegetables.)

CULTURAL ADVENTURES

Alpine ★★★/Free

This small town is home to the Museum of the Big Bend, a great introduction to the region's history, located at Sul Ross University. The museum's collection includes artifacts from Spanish explorers and Native Americans, photos of ranchers and cavalry soldiers, and a stagecoach riddled with bullet holes (one of the things kids seem to remember). *Take Highway 90 east to Sul Ross University; the museum is in Lawrence Hall, Alpine; (915) 837-8143; www.sulross.edu*

Annie Riggs Memorial Museum ★★/$

Located in a converted 1899 hotel fashioned from adobe brick and wood with a veranda and heavy gingerbread trim, this small (15-room) museum will give your kids a unique view of pioneer relics from ranches and farms. *301 S. Main St., Fort Stockton; (915) 336-2167.*

Fort Davis National FamilyFun Historic Site ★★★★/$

Your kids can see what it was like to live on the fringe of the frontier between 1854 and 1891 at this fort, which once housed 12 cavalry and infantry companies. The renovated stone-and-adobe fort

133

buildings are located in a scenic canyon, sheltered by towering cliffs to the west. This fort was also home to black cavalry troops, called buffalo soldiers by enemy Comanche and Apache tribes who admired their toughness. In the summer, costumed participants stage a living-history program and demonstrate what pioneer and fort life was like. A museum in the main building highlights the history of the West. *Texas Hwy. 17; (915) 426-3225;* www.nps.gov/foda

The **Hotel Paisano** in Marfa served as the headquarters for the filmmakers of *Giant*. Ruins of the movie's sets are still visible in the area.

Globe Theater ★★★/$$-$$$

If your little ones are up for a bit of the Bard, check out this replica of Shakespeare's Globe Theater. There are also reproductions of Shakespeare's library and the cottage of his wife, Anne Hathaway. During the summer, various plays of Shakespeare are staged, but the theater is also used for other plays and musical revues. *2308 Shakespeare Rd., Odessa; (915) 332-1586;* www.globesw.org

McDonald Observatory
FamilyFun ★★★★/$

Perched atop 6,800-foot Mount Locke, this observatory features a 107-inch telescope and provides tours for visitors to see its 160 tons of moving parts. Programs include solar viewings, and star par-ties staged Tuesday, Friday, and Saturday evenings. For a real heavenly experience, try to reserve a spot on a night when the observatory lets visitors peer through the telescope. Viewings with the 107-inch telescope typically happen monthly on the Wednesday nights closest to a full moon; there are also special viewing nights for the 82-inch telescope. Both programs are extremely popular, and getting a coveted spot means making a reservation months in advance, particularly in the spring and summer.

If you can't make the viewing parties, enjoy a tour of the Public Observatory—offered every Tuesday, Friday, and Saturday at sunset—where your kids can view the moon, planets, some stars, and other galaxies through large telescopes. No reservations are needed. The observatory's store sells lots of games and toys that will blast off your kids' interest in space. There's also the Stardate Café for grabbing a quick bite to eat. *Spur 78 at Texas 118, Fort Davis; (915) 426-3640;* www.mcdonaldobservatory.org

Museum of the Southwest ★★★/Free

This large museum includes an art gallery that showcases artists inspired by the area's beauty. There's also a planetarium, but the real focus of your visit will likely be the Fredda Turner Durham Children's Museum, which has interactive exhibits, including My Town, a child-size city where kids can role-play at a bank, store, TV station, and magic shop. *1705 W. Missouri Ave., Midland; (915) 683-2882;* www.museumsw.org

Permian Basic Petroleum Museum ★★★/$

Your family will see more than a few oil-field derricks on your drives through West Texas. If your kids are curious to know how they operate, stop at this Midland museum. Here they can learn all about how oil was created (and the creatures that created it) 230 million years ago. There's a reproduction of a boomtown, where you can feel the force of an oil strike as it gushes from the ground. Kids also like the interactive oil-drilling game that lets them see whether they will strike it rich or go bust. *1500 Interstate 20 West; (915) 683-4403;* www.petroleum museum.org

Presidential Museum ★★/$

Don't try to figure out why Odessa is home to a museum dedicated to U.S. presidents—just enjoy it. Kids can see campaign posters through history and check out replicas of inaugural gowns worn by various First Ladies. *622 N. Lee St., Odessa; (915) 332-7123;* www. presidentialmuseum.org

JUST FOR FUN

Big Bend National Park FamilyFun ★★★★/$$
A park for lovers of rugged scenery and outdoor adventure, Big Bend National Park offers families white-water rafting, hiking, biking, and more (see page 140).

Big Bend Ranch FamilyFun **State Park** ★★/$$
Texas's largest park (265,000 acres), Big Bend Ranch Park is home to scenic canyons, Native American pictographs, Texas longhorns, and a waterfall; there are also

A Hiking Hand

Get your child geared up for a family hike with a walking stick she can design herself. All she'll need is a dry (not green) fallen branch from a hardwood tree (such as maple, ash, or hickory), acrylic paints, and twine. Generally, a stick should be about the same height as a ski pole—a little higher than the waist—and easy to grip. Once you've got the right one, peel away the bark. If it still feels rough, smooth it with some fine sandpaper. Then, your child can paint on bold patterns—or, try putting different colors on paper plates and rolling the stick in them to create a swirled effect. Use twine to tie on feathers and pinecones, or other treasures found along the trail.

primitive camping areas and hiking trails. Get a permit, drive around, and take in the magnificent setting. Stop at the park entrance to see the Barton Warnock Environmental Education Center, a museum with fossils, dinosaur bones, and a desert garden. *One mile east of Lajitas on Farm Rd. 170; (915) 424-3327;* www.tpwd.state. tx.us/park/bigbend/bigbend.htm

Davis Mountains State Park ★★★/$

Located six miles west of Fort Davis on Texas 118, this park offers numerous hiking trails and gorgeous views from Skyline Drive. One of the most scenic parks in Texas, it is home to grassland plains and juniper and oak mountain forests as the elevation changes, rising 1,000 feet. During the spring and fall migratory seasons, the park is a great bird-watching area. Bring some binoculars, and you and the whole family can check out the flights from the birding station at Limpia Creek. Scrub jays, white-wing doves, and curve-billed thrashers are among the most common species sighted. Camp in the

Limpia Canyon Primitive Area or book a room at the cozy Indian Lodge (see Bunking Down on page 139). *Texas 118 NW; (915) 426-3337;* www.tpwd.state.tx.us/

El Camino del Rio
MUST-SEE FamilyFun ★★★★/Free
MUST-SEE One of America's most scenic drives begins as Ranch Road 170 in Lajitas and heads west to become El Camino del Rio, or the River Road. Stretching 55 miles from Study Butte to Presidio, the River Road follows the Rio Grande with dips, climbs, and twists, marked most dramatically by Big Hill, a mile-high climb with an average grade of 14 percent. Be sure to stop at the top and take a photo of the kids—it'll be a breathtaking souvenir.

Langtry ★★/Free
This Rio Grande outpost was founded in 1881 with the arrival of the railroad. Romantics say that Judge Roy Bean named the town for his favorite actress, Lillie Langtry; more pragmatic types claim it was the last name of a train official at the time. The Judge Roy Bean Visitor Center is on the site, now restored, where the infamous judge claimed to be the "Law West of the Pecos" back in the 1880s. Kids can explore Bean's saloon, courtroom, and pool hall while parents peruse the free brochures, maps, and guides. A cactus garden is outside. *Located on U.S. Hwy. 90, northwest of Del Rio; (915) 291-3340.*

Marfa Lights
FamilyFun ★★★/Free

After dark, head west from Marfa on U.S. 90/67 and look for a sign indicating you are entering the official viewing area of the mysterious Marfa Lights (about nine miles out of town). Pull over and look southwest toward the Chinati Mountains and wait. Look closely and see if your family can spot the small, white balls of light. Several stories and theories circulate about the Marfa Lights' origin. Some say the lights belong to an Indian chief's spirit, lighting signal fires to guide his lost tribe home; or it could be that bats' wings are carrying radioactive dust; or maybe it's just a reflection of car lights. If you come on Labor Day weekend, you can celebrate at the Marfa Lights Festival (held in downtown Marfa), where they have crafts and food booths. *(915) 729-4942;* www.marfa lights.com

Paisano Pete
★★★/Free

A pure bit of Texas kitsch, this creation is billed as the largest roadrunner in the world, standing 11 feet tall and 22 feet long. It's a definite photo opportunity, along with the world's largest jackrabbit (see page 138). *The statue is on Main Street immediately south of U.S. 290 at Farm Road 1053 in Fort Stockton;* www.texastwisted.com /attr/paisanopete

A Travel Scrapbook

This suitcase-style scrapbook is just right for your child to pack with mementos of his vacation adventures— and it's a cinch to make.

Start with two cardboard report covers. Use one for the suitcase itself and one to cut out two U-shaped handles and two $1^{1}/_{2}$- by 18-inch straps.

Attach one handle to the front of the suitcase by gluing the ends to the inside of the upper edge. Match up the second handle with the first one and glue it to the back side. Now close the suitcase and glue on the straps. Position the strap tops on the front of the suitcase 1 inch down from the upper edge, then wrap the straps around the back of the suitcase. Finally, fold down the strap ends so that they overlap the tops and attach stick-on Velcro-type fasteners.

For a handy photo pocket, glue a large open envelope to the inner cover. Then, fill the suitcase with manila folders for storing ticket stubs, brochures, and other souvenirs.

Terlingua ★★/Free

This former ghost town is alive and well—it even hosts the World Champion Chili Cook-offs in November. Great photo ops await in the town's ruined houses, jail, and at the rocky cemetery. There are a few restaurants and shops; stop at the Terlingua Trading Company or visit the Starlight Theater to grab a bite. *Located on Hwy. 170, just west of Big Bend National Park; (915) 371-3205); for some panoramic photos, visit the Website at* www.terlin guatx.com

Woodward Agate Ranch ★★★/$

If your kids love to play with rocks, take them to this ranch where they can search a few of its 4,000 acres for red plume, pompom agates, amethysts, and opals. The ranch's store will polish your stones for a small fee, or sell you a few if you don't find any (the best stones cost 35¢ per gram). *The ranch is located*

16 miles south of Alpine on Texas 118, and is open from dawn until dusk; (915) 364-2271; www.woodward ranch.net

World's Largest Jackrabbit ★/Free

What is West Texas's fascination with huge animal statues? Just go with it and grab a photo of the kids with this 8-foot-tall, 40-plus-year-old bunny named Jack Ben Rabbit. *802 N. Sam Houston Ave., Odessa.*

BUNKING DOWN

Gage Hotel ★★★★/$$-$$$$

Built in 1927, this hotel looks and feels like the Old West, simple and charming in a rustic way. Watch sunsets with your family from a front-porch rocker, or enjoy a posthike dip in the heated pool. Families can also book adjoining rooms with a connecting bathroom. The hotel's Café Cenizo has the best breakfasts

---

FamilyFun READER'S TIP -

Fledgling Photographers

Last summer, I put an extra flash in our vacation. Instead of having grown-ups be the only photographers, I bought each of our five children, whose ages range from 7 to 19, a 24-exposure disposable camera and let them snap their own pictures. The kids loved it, and we were able to see our vacation through their eyes. Plus, since they were inexpensive cameras, I didn't worry about them being dropped or lost. For very little money, these simple cameras brought our family a lot of smiles.

Kathi Kanuk, Chardon, Ohio

WEST TEXAS AND BIG BEND

and dinners in town. *101 Hwy. 90 West, Marathon; (800) 884-GAGE; (915) 386-4205;* www.gagehotel.com

Hotel Paisano ★★★/$-$$
This 1927 hotel—now on the National Register of Historic Places—has hosted such luminaries as Franklin D. Roosevelt, Harry S. Truman, and John F. Kennedy. Some rooms include a full kitchen and separate living room. *North Highland St. at West Texas St., Marfa; (866) 729-7669;* www.hotelpaisano.com

Indian Lodge ★★★/$$
This pueblo-style motel inside Davis Mountains State Park was built by Civilian Conservation Corps workers in the 1930s. It's a great place for a family base camp, near many hiking trails and historic Fort Davis. The lodge also has a pool and restaurant. Reserve early—sometimes this place can be booked up a year in advance. *In Davis Mountains State Park; (915) 426-3254.*

Lajitas on the Rio Grande ★★★★/$$$
This Wild West town (at least it looks like one) is a great family resort with bunkhouse, hotel, and condos all outfitted with period reproduction furniture—but with modern amenities, including laundry facilities. There's a bakery and restaurant, a saloon, and a boardwalk with some shops. The town looks so authentic that it's been used as a movie set.

One portion of the resort is built on an old cavalry post, where troops were stationed while they searched for Pancho Villa. *Hwy. 70, Lajitas; (877) 525-4827; (915) 424-3471;* www.lajitas.com

Limpia Hotel ★★/$-$$
Built in 1912 by the Union Trading Company, this hotel is a National Historic Site. The upstairs balcony and enclosed veranda are great places to sit in rocking chairs and take in the sunset. The gift shop and bookshop offer children's items, and kids with green thumbs can check out the inn's herb garden. *On the town square, Fort Davis; (915) 426-3237;* www.hotellimpia.com

Prude Ranch ★★★/$$$
Choose from bunkhouse or motel-style lodging at this working ranch that welcomes visitors—including families. The ranch offers horseback riding, a tennis court, swimming, and ranch-style meals. *Located north of Fort Davis on Texas Hwy. 118N; (800) 458-6232;* www.prude ranch.com

BIG BEND NATIONAL PARK

For years, this beautiful, rugged park has drawn adventure travelers who want to raft the white waters of the Rio Grande or bike or hike along the park's treacherous peaks. Now many families are coming here too, looking for an easy (and safe) way to enjoy its spectacular offerings. If your family only has a day here, then you'll probably want to drive the roads and see the sights that way. Be sure to stop at **Panther Junction,** the park's headquarters, to collect maps of the roads and hiking trails, as well as pamphlets and brochures for camping, lodging, and ranger-led activities. There's also a quarter-mile hiking trail here that showcases plants found in the park.

At Big Bend's center, amid the mile-high Chisos Mountains, lies the Chisos basin, which is the only place inside the park with lodging and dining. It's typically 10 to 15 degrees cooler here, so be prepared with a light sweater or jacket in the summer.

Chisos Mountain Lodge (★★★/ $$–$$$; *915/477-2291*) has comfortable rooms and spectacular views, but it's usually booked months in advance. There's also a restaurant and an adjacent store, where you can pick up candy, drinks,

postcards, and stamps. Horseback rides are offered nearby and cover the basin's 7,200-foot-high South Rim. If you'd like to hike, consider the popular Lost Mine Trail, a three- to four-hour trek that offers breathtaking views. Be sure to carry an ample supply of water.

On the park's southeastern edge, you can visit Hot Springs, an abandoned resort about two miles off the main road, where natural springs provide a hot tub heated to about 108 degrees.

Consider signing up for a rafting trip on the Rio Grande. Many outfitters offer short, half-day trips along the more peaceful parts of the river that are perfect for families. Outfitters include **Texas River Expeditions** *(915/371-2633);* **Far Flung Adventures** in Terlingua *(915/371-2489);* and **Big Bend River Tours** in Lajitas *(915/424-3219).*

GOOD EATS

Fort Davis Drugstore
★★★/$-$$
Step back in time and take in this soda shop that makes fountain drinks the old-fashioned way. *Fort Davis; (915) 426-3118.*

La Kiva ★★★/$$
Tell your kids that you're going to eat in—in a cave, that is. This restaurant was built underground, and actually has a tree growing through it. The food is pretty standard fare, barbecue and steaks. If you get claustrophobic, there's an outdoor patio. *At Terlingua Creek on Farm Rd. 170, Terlingua; (915) 371-2250.*

Reata ★★★★/$$$-$$$$
This acclaimed restaurant serves up what's dubbed cowboy cuisine, or what a cowboy who has spent some time at a culinary institute would dream up. The results are heavenly, particularly the pecan biscuits and jalapeño cream soup. Families are welcome here, and blue jeans are always appropriate. There's no special kids' menu, but steak fingers and chicken fingers are offered as kids' specials. *204 Texas Hwy. 118, Marfa; (915) 837-9232.*

Starlight Theater and Restaurant ★★★/$$
A former movie house, this place is now home to one of the area's best restaurants. On weekends, there's generally entertainment, including singing cowboys. Though there is no kids' menu, the kitchen will prepare quesadillas on request. *Downtown Terlingua; (915) 371-2326.*

SOUVENIR HUNTING

Apache Trading Post
Located on the outskirts of Alpine on U.S. 90, this log cabin stocks all sorts of Native American and Old West paraphernalia—from beads to bolo ties. Kids will want to check out the moccasins, arrowheads, and geodes. It's a good place to get a few books on the area's geology, natural history, and folklore. *(915) 837-5506; www.apachetradingpost.com*

El Paso Saddleblanket Co.
Big—like everything else in Texas—this 36,000-square-foot store has a little bit of everything, including cowboy and Native American duds for your kids. Just be sure they steer clear of the bullwhips. *601 N. Oregon Ave., El Paso; (915) 544-1000; www.elpasosaddleblanket.com*

Lajitas Trading Post
This store has been here for generations and offers a real flavor of the area. Kids can meet Clay Henry, Jr., a goat who has served as the town's mayor and whose claim to fame is his thirst for cold beer. *Downtown Lajitas; (915) 424-3234.*

141

New Mexico

I T'S CALLED the Land of Enchantment, and your family will discover why as you explore this state's gorgeous mountains, serene desert vistas, and charming cities and towns. Most families already plan to visit the capital, Santa Fe, and the state's largest city, Albuquerque, but your itinerary also can include checking out Smokey Bear Historical State Park, rafting on the Rio Grande, hiking the trails around the picturesque town of Ruidoso, and tasting Frito pie and sopaipillas.

The state is also famous for its close encounters with extraterrestrials and records the his-

Taos ★
★ Santa Fe
★
Albuquerque

Ruidoso ★   Roswell ★

Southern New Mexico

tory of those "events" at the International UFO Museum in Roswell. Your kids will get a kick out of our government's attempts to detect evidence of life beyond our universe. Preschoolers will enjoy the strange, lunarlike landscape of White Sands National Monument where they can pretend they're walking on the moon.

New Mexico also offers lots of history and art thanks to its unique blend of Native American, Hispanic, and Anglo cultures. Don't miss the International Folk Art Museum in Santa Fe or the Indian Pueblo Cultural Center in Albuquerque.

Whether you want a simple family getaway or have an interest in southwestern cultures, New Mexico will fill the bill.

ATTRACTIONS
$	under $5
$$	$5 - $10
$$$	$10 - $20
$$$$	$20 +

HOTELS/MOTELS/CAMPGROUNDS
$	under $50
$$	$50 - $100
$$$	$100 - $200
$$$$	$200 +

RESTAURANTS
$	under $10
$$	$10 - $20
$$$	$20 - $30
$$$$	$30 +

FAMILYFUN RATED
★	Fine
★★	Good
★★★	Very Good
★★★★	FamilyFun Recommended

Try to visit the famous Taos Pueblo on a ceremonial dance or feast day.

Albuquerque, Santa Fe, and Taos

NORTHERN New Mexico is a land of converging cultures: Native American, Hispanic, and Anglo attitudes blend, giving the area a unique personality that can seem exotic to visitors. Great museums and art galleries are a prime reason many adults come here—but don't tell your kids they're going on an educational trip. Tell them they'll climb mountains, hike forests, and dip their toes in the Rio Grande. Once you're here, let them sample some of the child-friendly cultural offerings, such as Santa Fe's Museum of International Folk Art, where they'll learn how milk jugs can become high art. The beauty of northern New Mexico is just as thrilling to children as it is to the Native American tribes who have lived here for centuries, the artists who seek inspiration from the bright

THE  LIST

Albuquerque's Old Town (page 148)

Bandelier National Monument (page 153)

Explora Science Center and Children's Museum (page 148)

Indian Pueblo Cultural Center (page 148)

New Mexico Museum of Natural History and Science (page 149)

The Plaza in Santa Fe (page 155)

The Rio Grande (page 158)

Sandia Peak and Tramway (page 149)

Santa Fe Children's Museum (page 154)

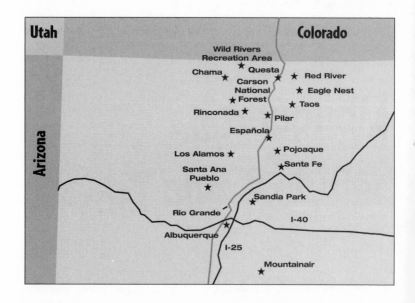

blue skies, and city-weary parents looking for fresh air on the high mesas and pinion-pine mountains.

Albuquerque is the traditional jumping-off point for family travelers, who drive in on Interstate 40 or fly in to the city's airport. But don't make the mistake of stopping only to fill up the gas tank: this city has some of the best museums in the Southwest, including the New Mexico Museum of National History and Science, where your children can walk through a volcano that even has streams of fake lava flowing under their feet. At the nearby Albuquerque Aquarium, kids can snack on fish sticks while they watch sharks devour a similar dinner

> At 7,000 feet above sea level, **Santa Fe** is the highest U.S. capital.

in the 285,000-gallon saltwater tank. At the Indian Pueblo Cultural Center, you can learn how to throw an arrow, grind corn using a mano and metate, and chow down on sugar-drizzled Indian fry bread.

Head north up Interstate 25, but pull off at the Tramway Drive exit to take an 18-minute trip on the Sandia Peak Aerial Tramway. Kids are amazed by the 2.7-mile ride up the side of a mountain on the world's longest single-span tramway. Once on top, they can't wait to roam the well-marked trails. Take a break at the restaurant that's also on top of the mountain, where on a clear day you can almost see into Colorado.

Santa Fe is the state capital and the

destination of most tourists exploring the region. Its cosmopolitan art-gallery scene and upscale inns and bed-and-breakfasts may not seem family-friendly, but with some searching you can find places that are all too willing to cater to kids. The Santa Fe Children's Museum makes for a gem of an afternoon—children can don elaborate animal masks and play Who's King of the Jungle? At the Cowgirl Hall of Fame, you can eat some of the best enchiladas in town while the kids ride stick ponies in the Kiddie Koral play area.

Taos is the place for active-family vacations, from skiing the slopes of Angel Fire and Taos Ski Valley (see page 157) to horseback riding and mountain biking in the Kit Carson National Forest. Children can pitch stones into the Rio Grande or tour an Indian pueblo that is more than 1,000 years old. And older children should see one of the area's museums showcasing Native American art collections, such as the

Millicent Rogers—but don't push it on 3- and 4-year olds (when we told our 4-year-old we were going to look at pottery, his reply was, "Mommy, I don't want to look at potties").

Northern New Mexico is a year-round vacation spot. Winter brings ski weather and summer brings pleasant mountain climes that cool the body and soothe the spirit. Fall is perhaps the best time to visit, because the aspens and cotton-woods turn the mountains gold and the Albuquerque Balloon Fiesta turns the skies into a multicolored mosaic of balloons. Whenever you come, be sure to pack lots of sunscreen and lip balm; humidity levels here are much lower than in the rest of the nation. Also, make sure you always carry water with you to avoid dehydration.

This region—where you feel the huge expanse of time and open space like few other places on earth—has it all: arts, food, and natural beauty that appeals to travelers of all ages.

Albuquerque

CULTURAL ADVENTURES

Albuquerque Biological Park
★★★/$$
A few blocks from Old Town lies this park that combines the Albuquerque

Aquarium and the Rio Grande Botanic Gardens. You can buy tickets to one or get a pass good for both. The botanic gardens are better for older kids, who can appreciate looking at desert plants and don't mind long walks through the park's various habitats. Young children will have a better time at the aquarium. If you're short on time, simply eat lunch at the aquarium restaurant, making sure you grab a tankside seat to watch the sharks, stingrays, and sea tortoises without paying an admission charge. *Central Ave. SW and New York St., Albuquerque; (505) 764-6200; www.cabq.gov/biopark/zoo*

 **Albuquerque's Old Town ★★★/Free** This neighborhood of sun-dried mud-and-adobe buildings dates back 300 years. Located a few miles west of downtown, this was the downtown in the early-19th century, but was bypassed by the railroad and languished until the 1930s when artists rediscovered its charms. Today it's home to the city's museums and several hotels, shops, and restaurants that cater to tourists. Parking can be a problem, so you should look for a space in a city-operated lot, if possi-ble. *Visitors Information Center: 305 Romero St., Albuquerque, across from the church; (505) 243-3215.*

Explora Science Center and Children's Museum ★★★/$ Recently revamped and expanded, this museum targets the under-7 set with a giant loom, a bubble-blowing area, a puppet theater, and arts-and-crafts projects. *2100 Louisiana Blvd. NE, Albuquerque; (505) 842-1537; www.explora.mus.nm.us*

Indian Pueblo Cultural Center ★★★/$ This pueblo is operated by Santa Fe's 19 tribes, which all fall under the Pueblo designation. Kids can beat a drum, grind corn, eat Indian fry bread, and enjoy watching traditional Native American dances. Unlike at other pueblos, photography of the rituals is actively

TACOS, TORTILLAS, AND TAMALES

WEAN YOUR KIDS off burgers and chicken fingers at least once or twice so they can sample New Mexico's unique cuisine, which blends Hispanic and Native American cultures. While their tender taste buds probably aren't ready for extra spicy chili, they will likely love **sopaipillas**, the light, pillow-shaped pastries that are deep-fried and served with butter and honey.

If one of your crew is feeling adventurous, try a breakfast **chorizo burrito**, a flour tortilla with scrambled eggs, potatoes, cheese, chile, and a spicy pork sausage called chorizo. Most children seem to favor **tortillas and fajitas**, strips of sizzling beef or chicken served encouraged here. Call ahead to find out what activities will be taking place. *Corner of Indian School Rd. and 12th St. NW, Albuquerque; (505) 843-6950;* www.indianpueblo.org

MUST-SEE FamilyFun MUST-SEE **New Mexico Museum of Natural History and Science ★★★/$-$$**
Dinosaur central, this museum has more than its share of triceratops and Tyrannosaurus rex. Preschoolers will love playing in the sandpit, where they can dig up fake dino bones, and older kids will have fun riding the Evalator, a ride that travels between eras instead of floors, to the prehistoric days of the dinosaurs. A DynaTheater and an astronomy center are also part of the museum's lineup. Late weekday afternoons are a good time to visit, after-school field-trippers have gone home. *1801 Mountain Rd. NW, Albuquerque; (505) 841-2800;* www. nmnaturalhistory.org

JUST FOR FUN

Rio Grande Zoological Park ★★★/$
The zoo has a primate island, rain forest, and birds-of-prey aviary, but its most unusual attraction is Lobo Woods, where a rare species of small wolves that are extinct in the wild is bred. *903 10th St. SW, Albuquerque; (505) 764-6200;* www.cabq.gov/bio park/zoo

MUST-SEE FamilyFun MUST-SEE **Sandia Peak and Tramway ★★★/$$**
Sure you could drive up the mountain, but taking this tram is so much more dramatic. You'll be whisked up 2.7 miles in 18 minutes, but be ready for the change in temperature (it's typically 20 to 30 degrees cooler on top) and bring a sweater or jacket. At the summit, kids can sign up to be Junior Rangers at the

with onions and peppers. **Tamales** consist of highly seasoned cornmeal with meat, wrapped and steamed in a corn husk. Don't make the mistake of trying to eat the husk!

Some restaurants may offer Native American fare, including the **Navajo taco**, topped with lettuce, tomatoes, refried beans, guacamole, sour cream, and chile. Indian sweet bread is fried bread served with sugar or honey on top.

Finally, **Frito pie**: considered the official state dish, its simplest version is chili topped with cheese and Fritos corn chips, and this is the way most kids like it. Adults tend to add tomatoes and chopped onions, too.

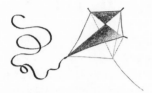

Forestry Service visitors' center and will earn a badge and certificate by completing a questionnaire on the mountain's flora and fauna. There are numerous trails at the top of the mountain, but stay close to young children because some drop-offs are steep. Leave time to enjoy a snack or meal at the **High Finance Restaurant** (reservations required for dinner; *508/243-8742*), also on top, which has a casual atmosphere during the day and a more formal feel at night. In the summer, the tram runs from 9 A.M. to 9 P.M.; hours are shorter in the winter. Lines for the tram ride back down the mountain can get longer toward the end of the day, especially immediately after sunset. *10 Tramway Blvd., Albuquerque; (505) 856-7325;* www.sandiapeak.com

BUNKING DOWN

Cinnamon Morning
★★★/$$-$$$

This small bed-and-breakfast is close to the Rio Grande Nature Center and welcomes families, who typically opt for the inn's guesthouse, complete with two bedrooms and a kitchen. Rooms have VCRs, and guests can check out tapes—including many children's titles—from the main desk. The best part is the menagerie of animals found here—including cats, dogs, chickens, and a peacock. Kids can help gather the morning eggs. *2700 Rio Grande NW, Albuquerque; (800) 214-9481; (505) 345-3541;* www.cinnamonmorning.com

Hyatt Regency Tamaya Resort
★★★★/$$$-$$$$

This resort—located midway between Albuquerque and Santa Fe—is a great base for families exploring both cities. There's a huge spa and yoga center for parents who want some pampering or simply hang out by the huge outdoor pool and watch the kids careen down the water slide. The resort's remote location by the Rio Grande makes for great wildlife viewing. Dining at the resort's Corn Maiden restaurant, you may even see some coyotes. Trail rides and carriage rides are available, or simply hike down to the river and enjoy a picnic under the cottonwood trees. The resort is actually owned by the Santa Ana Pueblo and its activities reflect the connection. At Camp Hyatt, kids can watch Native American dance performances and bake bread in authentic Huruna ovens. *1300 Tuyuna Trail, Santa Ana Pueblo; (800) 633-7313; (505) 867-1234;* www.hyatt.com

Maggie's Raspberry Ranch
★★★/$$

Owner Margaret Lilley says she likes kids so much that she lets them bring their parents to this bed-and-breakfast. Attractions include the Hobbit House, a puppet theater where kids can put on a show; and an assortment of critters, including five turtles, two cats, a goose, two ducks, and a flock of chickens. Visiting this small inn is like going to Grandma's house—if she lived on a farm with a pool by the Rio Grande. *9817 Eldridge Rd. NW, Albuquerque; (800) 897-1523; (505) 897-1523; www.maggiesraspberryranch.com*

GOOD EATS

Garcia's Kitchen ★★★/$$

Kids will love all the oddball collectibles assembled inside this Albuquerque institution. It's a great place for a quick and hearty breakfast. *1113 N. 4th St. NW, Albuquerque; (505) 247-9149.*

High Finance Restaurant
★★★/$$$

This restaurant easily has the best view in town—and of town. Located atop Sandia Peak, it's a relaxing place to wind down after hiking the trails to the top of the mountain. Lunch is a better time for families than dinner, when the menu gets pricier and the atmosphere is more formal. If you have a reservation at the

The Enchanted Circle

Often called one of the most beautiful drives in North America, the Enchanted Circle is an 84-mile loop that takes you down one of the nation's most scenic drives through pinion forests and desolate grasslands. From Taos, the drive is south on U.S. Highway 64 over the scenic **Palo Flechado Pass**, the route used for centuries to get from the plains west over the Cimarron River. Continue west on U.S. 64 to Eagle Nest, a good place to get out and enjoy a view of **Eagle Nest Lake**. From here, go west on Highway 38 and travel through the **Wheeler Peak Wilderness**, a lush valley ringed by mountains.

Take Bobcat Pass to **Red River**, a Wild West town that celebrates its gold-mining past with touristy restaurants and saloons and the occasional staged gunfight. The road follows the Red River through evergreen forests, arriving in **Questa**. Take a side trip on Highway 378 West to see the **Wild Rivers National Recreation site**, stopping at the visitors' center for information on the area's geological history and flora and fauna. Even if you don't have time to hike, enjoy the view from **La Junta Point**.

For a complete guide to the Enchanted Circle, go by the Taos Visitors Center located at Paseo del Pueblo Sur and Paseo del Canyon. (800) 732-8267; (505) 758-3873.

A PRIMER ON PUEBLOS

When the Spanish first explored this region, they found about 100,000 people living in small villages; in an effort to keep things simple, the explorers named them for the Spanish word for village—pueblo. The invading Spanish (and later, American) settlers decimated the Pueblo peoples; today there are only about 40,000 Native Americans living in 19 different pueblos; each has its own government, with its own rules and regulations. In recent years, many of the pueblos have opened casinos along major highways.

If you want to introduce your children to this very different culture, make sure they are respectful of the Pueblo ways:

♦ Interrupting someone or making direct eye contact is considered taboo.

♦ Some pueblos prohibit the taking of photographs; others may charge a fee if you want to take a picture, use your video camera, or sketch a picture. Always ask permission first.

♦ Private homes and kivas (the sites of religious ceremonies) are off-limits to outsiders; be sure your explorations don't lead you or a curious youngster inside an open door.

♦ Don't let the kids climb on any of the buildings; most of them are several hundred years old and can crumble.

♦ If you attend a ceremonial dance, remember it is a religious observance and treat it as such. Don't interrupt the participants with questions; just watch and admire. Also, it isn't necessary to applaud after the dance is over.

♦ If you're going to a pueblo, call ahead to make sure it is open to the public that day (it could be closed for a ceremonial event, such as a funeral).

♦ The best way for children to get a taste of this unique culture is by visiting the **Indian Pueblo Cultural Center**, where they can get a hands-on experience in beating a drum, grinding corn, and watching traditional Native American dances, which are performed most weekends, daily during busy tourism times in the summer and during the **Balloon Fiesta**. *The center is located in Albuquerque at the corner of Indian School Road and 12th Street NW; (505) 843-6950.*

restaurant, the fare to ride the tram is reduced by $5. *(505) 243-9742; www.highfinancerestaurant.com*

Route 66 Diner ★★★/$$
It looks like a gas station on the outside, but inside it's a classic diner that celebrates its location on famous Route 66. The restaurant offers blue-plate specials, like meat loaf and mashed potatoes and ultrathick milk shakes. *1405 Central Ave. NE, Albuquerque; (505) 247-1421; www. 66diner.com*

Santa Fe
CULTURAL ADVENTURES

Bandelier National Monument ★★★★/$$
FamilyFun MUST-SEE MUST-SEE
Fifty miles west of Santa Fe, this National Parks Service site showcases the remains—originally elaborate cliff dwellings—of the ancient Anasazi, ancestors of today's Pueblo Indians. More than 3,000 archaeological treasures, still unearthed (tell the kids to forget the shovels—these findings are left to the pros), consist mainly of caves formed from volcanic rock. Echos of a past culture are felt strongly here. The park has 60 miles of hiking trails, but many are too steep for small children. The park gets oppressively hot (and crowded) in summer and can often be under snow in winter, so try to visit in fall or spring. *From Santa Fe, take U.S. 285 to Pojoaque, then west on Highway 502, and south on Highway 4; (505) 672-3861; www.nps.gov/band*

Bradbury Science Museum ★★★/$-$$
In the 1940s, many of the world's top scientists gathered in this remote region of New Mexico to build the first atomic bomb. This museum explores what is perhaps the most significant development of the 20th century, detailing the effort that went into the project. It's best for older children who can better understand the bomb's historical and moral significance. *From Santa Fe, take U.S. 285; 15 miles to Pojoaque, turn left onto Highway 502 stay left when the road divides and follow to Los Alamos. 15th St. and Central Ave., Los Alamos; (505) 667-4444; www.lanl.gov/worldview/museum/*

Georgia O'Keeffe Museum ★★/Free-$$
Even young children will enjoy the bright, colorful paintings of this favorite American artist who lived and worked in the northern New Mexico town of Abiquiu from 1946 until her death in 1986. O'Keeffe said the New Mexican light inspired

153

her; let her work inspire your children, challenging them to draw their own versions of the region's adobe homes and wildflowers. *217 Johnson St., Santa Fe; (505) 995-0785;* www.okeeffemuseum.org/indexflash.html

Museum of International Folk Art ★★★/$$

If you are going to "do" one artsy museum, make it this one. Housed here is the world's largest collection of folk art and folk toys, from Mexican masks to East Indian dolls. One area of the museum promotes recycling by showing ways trash can be turned into art, providing inspiration for low-cost art projects. There are even oil-barrel drum sets that kids can bang to their hearts' content. Make sure you stop in the gift shop so your youngsters can have a folk-toy souvenir or two to take home and remind them there are alternatives to Nintendo. *706 Camino Lejo, Santa Fe; (505) 476-1200;* www.nmoca.org/mnmfolkart

Santa Fe FamilyFun Children's Museum ★★★★/$-$$

Forget the city's high-end galleries and head to this much more kid-friendly hangout. There's a contraption containing 180,000 metal pins that molds its surface into your child's image, creating a surreal sculpture. Preschoolers won't want to leave the waterworks area,

and the nearby gift shop sells T-shirts if your youngster gets soaking wet. The museum also has an array of animals—from giant cockroaches to snakes and spiders. If those species aren't appealing, there are birds and rabbits outside in the children's garden area. On most weekends, the museum offers arts-and-crafts activities. *1050 Old Pecos Trail, Santa Fe; (505) 989-8359;* www.santafechildrensmuseum.org

JUST FOR FUN

Cumbres and Toltec Scenic Railroad ★★★/$$$-$$$$

Anyone who loves to ride a steam train around mountains will want to board this excursion train, which departs the small town of Chama at 10:30 A.M.; get a seat on the right for the best views. The high altitude here—10,015 feet at the route's highest point of Cumbres Pass—makes it a chilly ride even in the summer, so bring a sweater or jacket. There's an open car in the back, but wear sunglasses or goggles to avoid getting cinders in your eyes. If you're lucky, you may see a deer, mountain lion, bobcat, or brown bear. Lunch options in Osier, the midpoint of the trip, are limited, so you may want to pack a picnic. The train runs from mid-May to mid-October. *Ten miles south of the Colorado/New Mexico line on Hwy. 17; Main St., Chama; (505) 756-2151;* www.cum brestoltec.com

The Plaza in Santa Fe ★★★/Free
FamilyFun MUST-SEE

The plaza, arguably the heart and soul of Santa Fe, can be very difficult to get to given the winding streets, lack of parking, and ever-growing traffic. For older kids, it's worth the trouble to see what was once the center of this region; here you can stroll by the Native American women who sell their silver and turquoise trinkets on beautiful blankets spread on the sidewalk. Unless you get lucky and find parking on a nearby street, plan to walk several blocks—or try to find a parking garage.

Santa Fe Southern Railroad ★★★/$$$$
This is a working railroad, but it offers rides just for fun, too, and is a great half-day adventure for young train buffs.

The Santa Fe Southern Railroad's run goes south to Lamy, where riders get off to enjoy their picnic lunches. During busier times (summer and holiday weekends), a caterer typically meets passengers near the Lamy depot offering Frito pie, a favorite local concoction of chili topped with cheese, tomatoes, onions, and plenty of Fritos corn chips.

On Saturday nights, the railroad runs a barbecue dinner special and around Halloween they add ghost stories. Make sure kids check out the funky *Flintstones-*inspired views en route.

Don't bother paying more for the expensive luxury-car seats; most kids and families prefer the open air and basic benches of the lower-priced car. *Santa Fe Depot, Santa Fe; (505) 989-8600;* www. sfsr.com

AN ERASABLE CLIPBOARD is just right for doodling or playing tic-tac-toe during a long car ride or waiting-room stint. To make one, cover a clipboard with chalkboard Con-Tact paper (sold in most large discount stores) to create a drawing surface your child can chalk up. Use an eraser or damp paper towel to clean your clipboard.

BUNKING DOWN

Santa Fe is famous for its romantic bed-and-breakfast inns and luxury hotels, but many do not welcome younger children. It's best to call ahead and check. Here are three of our favorites:

The Bishop's Lodge
★★★★/$$$-$$$$

This beautiful resort located five miles north of downtown Santa Fe in the juniper-studded Tesuque Valley has been welcoming families with its casual elegance since it opened in 1918. During the high season of summer, there are so many activities going on, it seems impossible to try them all. Children ages 4 to 12 can sign up for the Camp Apaloosa, which includes hiking, swimming, pony rides, and arts and crafts. There's a playground complete with tepee and fishing pond. At night, there's storytelling on the lawn and children's cookouts. Trail rides are a major attraction at the inn and everyone, even if you have never ridden a horse, is encouraged to saddle up. (Parents may appreciate the new spa and wellness center, which offers activities including aerobics.) The property includes a small, exquisite chapel that was once the retreat of Archbishop Lamy, the inspiration for Willa Cather's novel *Death Comes to the Archbishop*. (Bishop Jean-Baptiste Lamy was the first bishop in Santa Fe; the chapel was constructed in 1851.) Even if you can't afford to stay there, stop by for a visit or lunch just to check out the grounds. *Located three and a half miles north of Santa Fe on Bishop's Lodge Road; (505) 983-6377; www.bishopslodge.com*

El Rey Inn ★★★/$$

This is one of the best deals in town, and although the El Rey's location isn't ideal, the funky 1930s-motel ambience and incredible breakfast make up for that inconvenience. Try to reserve a room in the older section of the inn (next to the pool) so you can relax on the patio while the kids frolic in the water. There's also a small playground, the perfect place for youngsters to burn off energy after eating a breakfast of the inn's strawberry or banana tortillas. *1862 Cerrillos*

MAKING FACES

Do an impression of someone whom everyone else in the car knows. It could be a neighbor with an accent or a movie character. The first person to guess correctly gets the next turn at trying an impersonation.

Rd., Santa Fe; (800) 521-1349; (505) 982-1931; www.elreyinnsantafe.com

Fort Marcy Compound
★★★/$$$

This complex of town houses and condominiums is an ideal place for families who want privacy, quiet, and a home away from home. Each unit has two or more separate bedrooms and bathrooms as well as a kitchen/family-room combination. Families love the VCRs and washers and dryers, which are in most rooms. The location is across the street from a park where kids can run around; the inn is also within walking distance of downtown Santa Fe, but families with small children will probably find the five blocks or so too far. A local pizza shop offers fast delivery to any of the apartments, and guests can rent videos at a well-stocked independent rental shop nearby. *320 Artist Rd., Santa Fe; (800) 745-9910; (505) 982-6636.*

GOOD EATS

Cowgirl Hall of Fame ★★★/$$

This restaurant celebrates the cowgirl, but cowboys are welcome too. The kids' menu includes the regional favorite, Frito pie, and buffalo cheeseburgers. New Mexican cuisine is the house specialty, and exotic dishes such as wild-boar burritos are often offered. On Friday and Saturday evenings, there's live

Super Slopes

The high peaks in northern New Mexico provide great skiing from late November to April, depending on the precipitation. In the summer, the ski areas turn to hiking and mountain biking to draw tourists.

The Sandia Peak Ski Area *(505/ 242-9133)* is about an hour's drive north of Albuquerque, or even closer if you take the Sandia Peak Tram to the top of the mountain.

Santa Fe has slopes 30 minutes away from town at the Santa Fe Ski Area on Route 475 *(505/982-4429).*

Taos offers Taos Ski Valley, which has some of the most challenging runs in the West, but also provides easier slopes and family lessons. There's a child-care center and kids' ski camp offered during the season. *Ski Valley Road; (800) 776-1111; (505) 776-2233.*

Angel Fire Resort *(800/633-7463; 505/377-6401)* and **Red River Ski Area** *(505/754-2223)* have less challenging runs and a more laid-back attitude, making them better places for beginning skiers.

music and more of a bar feel. Try to get a table outside on the back patio, where the Kiddie Korral play area is. Call ahead for reservations if possible; this place gets crowded early. *319 S. Guadalupe St., Santa Fe; (505) 982-2565;* www.cowgirl-santafe.com

Hill Diner ★★★/$$

A cozy cabin is the setting for classic diner dishes, from hamburgers to meat loaf. Leave room for the banana cream pie. *1315 Trinity Dr., Los Alamos; (505) 662-9745.*

SOUVENIR HUNTING

Jackaloupe

This famous folk-art emporium has an ice-cream stand, prairie-dog village, and periodic events such as the Mexican Jumping Bean Race. A store carries interesting toys and knick-knacks. *2820 Cerrillos Rd., Santa Fe; (505) 471-8539.*

Santa Fe Farmer's Market

Twice a week, Santa Fe's divergent cultures converge for this event that draws everyone from Hispanic families selling tamales to Polarfleece-clad mountain bikers sipping fresh apple cider. There's a festival atmosphere with strolling musicians, cooking demonstrations, and plenty of tasty samples. This is a great place to pick up breakfast before boarding the nearby Santa Fe train depot. *In the railroad yard off Guadalupe, Santa Fe; (505) 983-4098;* www. farmersmarketsnm.org

Taos

JUST FOR FUN

Kit Carson Park ★★/Free

If the kids need to burn off some energy, take them to this 22-acre park near the center of Taos. Possibly the best treat you can give your youngsters after pueblos and museums is letting them romp. There's a playground, picnic areas, rest rooms, and an outdoor ice rink open in the winter. *209 Paseo del Pueblo Norte, Taos; (505) 758-8234.*

The Rio Grande

FamilyFun ★★★★/Free

This river doesn't look all that impressive, until you remember its water cut most of the Taos Canyon. Older children can ride the river's less advanced white-water sections with local river-rafting companies in Taos (**Los Rios River Runners** operates daily excursions from March through October; *505/770-8854*), while younger ones seem content to cast stones in it for hours. Your best bet for great views of the river is to drive along Highway 68, also known as the Low Road, to Taos from Santa Fe. *To see rafters take on the rocky chute called the Racehorse, pull off Highway 68 between the villages of Pilar and Rinconada.*

Taos Pueblo
★★★/$$

Just north of Taos at the base of a mountain lies this multistoried adobe pueblo that has been in this spot for more than 1,000 years. A trip to this site is better for older children who can understand its history. Make sure they know they are touring someone's home and should be gracious guests. Much of the pueblo is off-limits to visitors, so kids shouldn't just wander inside any open doorways. Other than the structures and the beautiful setting, there's not a lot to see here. If possible, come on a ceremonial dance or feast day. Call for a schedule or look on the Website. Visitors pay a $10 per-person admission and $10 per camera. Photography during dances is prohibited. *Two miles north of Taos on Hwy. 64; (505) 758-1028;* www.taospueblo.com

Taos Youth and Family Center
★★/Free-$

This new facility offers an ice arena, in-line skating, basketball, an arcade, and a snack bar. *407 Paseo del Canon E., Taos; (505) 758-4160.*

Wild Rivers National Recreation Area ★★★/free

This park, about 25 miles north of Taos, is where the Red River and the Rio Grande converge. Stop by the park's visitors' center for hiking-trail maps. Young children won't have the stamina to hike down the gorge to the rivers, but everyone can enjoy the view from La Junta Point. *Hwy. 378; (505) 770-1600.*

Hot-Air Hoopla

This annual 10-day event held in **Albuquerque** during the beginning of October draws hot-air-balloon enthusiasts from around the world for a two-week extravaganza that can be viewed from almost any place in town. The area's unique wind patterns blow balloons to the north in the morning, then back south in the afternoon. The highlight is the mass ascension at dawn, when thousands of balloons go up in an hour, filling the skies with color and patterns in all shapes and sizes. There are also evening Balloon Glows, when the balloons hover above the ground like giant fireflies. The events are held at **Balloon Fiesta Park** off Interstate 25 (Tramway exit). Dress warmly, but in layers. The desert is cold at dawn, but gets short-sleeve comfortable by noon. *(505) 821-1000;* www.balloonfiesta.com

Bunking Down

Casa Benavides ★★★/$$-$$$

Guest rooms here are spread out among several buildings about a block from the Taos plaza. All rooms have VCRs, and kids can choose tapes from the inn's library of Disney classics and other children's favorites. In the afternoon, kids (and their parents) are treated to brownies or other delicious desserts. The inn is not far from a park with a large playground. *137 Kit Carson Rd., Taos; (505) 758-8891; www.taos-casabenavides.com*

Good Eats

Doc Martin's Restaurant ★★★/$$$

Located inside the Taos Inn—the former home of one of the town's prominent physicians—this is the only place we've heard of where you can eat in what was once a birthing room. Don't let that thought dissuade you from trying what is arguably the best restaurant in town. Dinners may be a bit formal for families, so opt for a breakfast trip here instead and chow down on piñon-nut waffles. Kids love the blueberry pancakes and stuffed sopaipillas. *Inside the Taos Inn, 125 Paseo del Pueblo Norte, Taos; (505) 758-2233.*

Dragonfly Café ★★★/$$

This relaxed restaurant has an open

kitchen so kids can watch the bakers making cakes and pies (sorry, you can't lick the bowls). Eat in or get your order to go for a picnic across the street at Kit Carson State Park. These are the best pies and cookies in town. *402 Paseo del Pueblo Norte, Taos; (505) 737-5859.*

The Lodge at Red River ★★★/$$$

A great stop on any Enchanted Circle road trip (see "A Day in Taos" on page 161), this popular restaurant is big on comfort food, so kids can dig into mashed potatoes and fried chicken. *400 E. Main St., Red River, Taos; (800) 915-6343; (505) 754-6280; www.redrivernm.com/lodgeatrr/*

Pizza Emergency ★★/$

This restaurant, with a name you won't forget, serves up great deep-dish pizza, baked pasta, and meatball sandwiches. *316 Paseo del Pueblo Sur, Taos; (505) 751-0911.*

Souvenir Hunting

Taos Drums

You can't miss this store—just look for the tepees as you enter Taos. Inside, kids can watch artisans craft the tom-tom–like drums from logs. The store drums up business with weekly workshops and demonstrations. *Hwys. 68 and 270, Taos; (800) 424-DRUM; (505) 758-3796.*

A Day in Taos

TAOS IS A SMALLER, more intimate town than Santa Fe and well worth visiting, if only for a day.

From Santa Fe there are two ways to get to Taos—the Low Road, a 90-minute trip through Española, then a two- or sometimes three-lane blacktop alongside the Rio Grande; or the High Road, a three-hour trip (if you don't stop) through the Sangre de Cristo Mountains.

Families with young children prone to car sickness and "are we there yet" whining should opt for the Low Road (Highway 68), but be warned that it also has plenty of twists and turns, so keep the Dramamine handy. Take a break in **Española**, a busy town full of fast-food restaurants and gas stations, and make sure you pull off at one of the roadside viewing areas by the Rio Grande. Be ready for your first view of the Taos Valley—it's an awesome sight.

If you are traveling to Taos on a Saturday or Sunday, skip breakfast in Santa Fe, drive 25 miles north to **Rancho de Chimayo** *(505/351-4444)*, and enjoy its bountiful brunch. Be sure to stop by **Santuario de Chimayo**, a small church known for its healing powers. The small towns of Cordova, Truchas, and Ojo Sarco have a quiet, dusty feel and are home to artists' workshops and lovely churches. Drive through the **Carson National Forest**; then stop at **Fort Burgwin**, where U.S. soldiers were stationed after the Taos revolt in 1847. Continue through Talpa to **Ranchos de Taos**, home of the most photographed and painted church in the West, San Francisco de Asis Mission. It's been a famous subject of Georgia O'Keeffe, Ansel Adams, and many other artists; it's also a major photo op.

Once in Taos, check out its plaza, located just west of the main road through town, Paseo del Pueblo. There are several gift shops where you can pick up souvenirs. For lunch selections, see Good Eats on page 160.

Your older kids (best for the over-8 crew) can get an up-close look at the world-famous **Taos Pueblo** (see page 159). Be sure to stop at one of the gravel pull-off areas to let them throw rocks into the **Rio Grande**, a trip highlight for preschoolers.

Carlsbad Caverns is *the* southern New Mexico don't-miss.

Roswell, Ruidoso, and Southern New Mexico

MOST FAMILIES come to southern New Mexico for one reason: a pilgrimage to Carlsbad Caverns. After that—believing they have seen all there is to see in this vast expanse of desert and remote mountain ranges—they leave. What a pity! For while the cave's massive stalagmites and stalactites are amazing, and the dawn and twilight bat flights should not be missed, neither should other treasures—such as the small town of Ruidoso, where Billy the Kid once hid from lawmen in a flour barrel and where Smokey Bear, a singed cub rescued from a nearby forest fire, went on to become a national icon.

Some of the other natural attractions—albeit less spectacular but just as enjoyable as Carlsbad Caverns—include the Gila Cliff

THE **FamilyFun** LIST

MUST-SEE · MUST-SEE

Carlsbad Caverns (page 169)

Ghost Towns (page 165)

Gila Cliff Dwellings (page 166)

International UFO Museum (page 166)

National Solar Observatory (page 167)

Spencer Center for the Performing Arts (page 168)

White Sands National Monument (page 173)

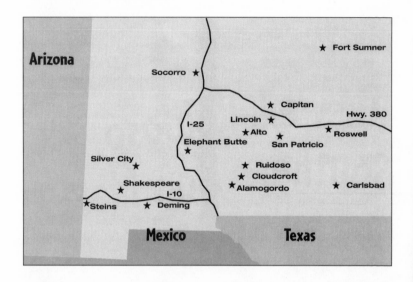

Dwellings, ancient structures built by the prehistoric Mogollon people around 1280 but abandoned a few decades later, and White Sands Monument, with its huge dunes of almost pure white gypsum, stunning by day or on a starry, moonlit night. For a lasting memory, take a picture of your children walking on the strange landscape that looks like a field of clouds.

The open stretch of desert gives southern New Mexico an eerie, almost alien, quality; this perhaps explains the area's fascination with UFOs. In 1947, locals claimed to have witnessed a flying saucer crashing—marking the rise of what would become known as the "Roswell Incident." The "incident" is celebrated at the International UFO Museum, where you and your kids can see the shattered remains of what some say is the famous flying saucer and make up your own minds. Further, you can learn about scientists' attempts to listen to extraterrestrial conversations at the National Science Foundation's Very Large Array, a field of huge satellites that make up the most powerful listening device on earth. And finally, your kids can take a pretend trip to Mars at the International Space Museum and Hall of Fame in Alamogordo, or a parent-approved look directly at the sun at the National Solar Observatory.

The flavor of the Wild West is still very much alive in places like Silver City, with its Victorian architecture and saloons. But while Silver City survived, many of the area's other boomtowns didn't make it. You can tour well-preserved private ghost towns such as Shakespeare, deserted since the 1930s after the nearby silver mine played out (for ghost town etiquette, see "Ghost Towns" on page 261). Travel on the Billy the Kid Scenic Byway in Lincoln County and stop in Lincoln, a city little changed since the famous outlaw walked its streets (for more information, see "Catching Up with Billy the Kid" on page 170).

The region's remoteness makes this a quiet, relaxing place for a family vacation. Even in the high-summer season, it is relatively easy to find a place to stay, and restaurants rarely have long waits. But the remoteness also requires extra preparation: parents of small children should bring extra diapers and a change of clothing with them in case no stores are nearby. If you have older children, make sure they have snacks and toys or games to occupy them during long stretches on lonely highways. Dehydration can set in after a day playing and running in the hot desert sun, so be sure to bring plenty of water and

other liquids. And given the region's bright, sunlit days—up to 350 sunny days a year in spots—make sure everyone (Mom and Dad, too) wears plenty of sunscreen.

CULTURAL ADVENTURES

Ghost Towns
FamilyFun ★★★/Free

Southern New Mexico has several well-preserved ghost towns—a legacy of the boom-and-bust economies of the region's 19th-century mining days. The town of Shakespeare is privately owned, but well preserved, so your kids can get a good idea of what life was like in the Old West. Call ahead to arrange a tour *(505/542-9034)*; if you're in luck, you'll be visiting at one of the occasional times when historical reenactments are performed. (These are performed in April, June, August, and October on the fourth weekend.) There's a small admission to the town ($3 at press time), and tours are generally offered only on the second weekend of the month. *Shakespeare is reached off Interstate 10, exit 22, a half mile south of Lordsburg.*

A few miles west of Shakespeare on Interstate 10, exit 3 (about three miles west of the Arizona-New Mexico line), you can look over from the highway to the ghost town of Steins.

The town has 15 buildings, including the remnants of a hotel, saloons, and stone homes. You can take it in through the car window, stroll around on your own, or arrange for a guided tour. *(505) 542-9791.*

Gila Cliff Dwellings
FamilyFun ★★★★/$

MUST-SEE
MUST-SEE
How often do your kids get to visit 700-year-old homes built on the side of a cliff? They will here as they enter and explore the remains of the Mogollon people, who created these cliff homes between 1280 and the early 1300s. Youngsters love to wander in and out of the small dwellings, but caution them to be careful of any scorpions or snakes that may be hidden inside. Also, be sure they wear sturdy shoes; the one-mile-loop trail through the dwellings is steep in places. Call ahead to find out the schedule of the guided tour of the monument. **NOTE:** It's best to plan ahead on this one—the trip from Silver City can take two hours (heading north) on the very winding New Mexico State Highway 15; *(505) 536-9461;* www.nps.gov/gicl

> **Smokey Bear** received so much mail that on April 29, 1964, he was given his own zip code.

Hubbard Museum of the American West ★★/Free-$$
Your kids can mount a model horse and sit in the saddle or opt for the rocking horse at this museum, which shows how folks got around in the horse-and-buggy days. The striking sculpture of galloping horses outside provides a great photo opportunity. *841 Hwy. 70 West, one mile west of Ruidoso; (505) 378-4142.*

International Space Museum and Hall of Fame
★★★/$

This museum in Alamogordo showcases displays of satellites, astronauts' capsules, and rocket engines. There's a Mars Room, where kids can pretend they're exploring our neighboring planet, and the Clyde Tombaugh Space Theater next door has a planetarium and IMAX theater. *Scenic Drive at Indian Wells Road, Alamogordo; (877) 333-6589;* www.spacefame.org

International UFO
FamilyFun Museum ★★★/Free

MUST-SEE
MUST-SEE
The area around Roswell claims more UFO sightings than anywhere else in the country. In 1947, a Lincoln County rancher said he stumbled onto the remains of a flying saucer that had crashed to earth. Other people in the area said they had spotted unusual flying objects in the sky, but the government downplayed the incident, giving rise to various conspiracy theories. The sightings, which became known as the "Roswell Incident," gave birth to the area's burgeoning UFO industry. This free

museum draws 200,000 visitors a year; there are plans to add more exhibit and parking space. The museum holds an annual children's writing contest for kids creative enough to imagine their own otherworldly encounters. This attraction may not be appropriate for impressionable youngsters, but older (or fearless) ones will be intrigued. *114 N. Main St., Roswell; (800) 822-3545; (505) 625-9495; www.iufomrc.com*

National Radio Astronomy Observatory's Very Large Array (VLA) ★★/Free

If you and your kids (more than likely the older ones) still get a chill watching a space shuttle liftoff, it may be worth a trip down U.S. 60 through the San Agustin Plains to see this otherworldly site where huge satellite dishes search for sounds from the stars. The 27 dishes work together to serve as the world's most powerful and sensitive radio telescope; they're also used to detect regions of space too remote to be viewed by optical telescopes. Some signals monitored here are believed to have come from an estimated six trillion miles away and to have originated out of the Big Bang. There's a small visitors' center where you can view displays that detail the operations. If you're lucky, you may be able to see one of the dishes being moved along railroad tracks for repositioning. *Take U.S. 60, 54 miles west from Socorro; (505) 835-7000.*

National Solar Observatory ★★/Free

This observatory provides a safe way for kids to look directly at the sun. Located 18 miles south of Cloudcroft, it's one of the world's largest solar observatories. There's a visitors' center where your children will enjoy hands-on exhibits explaining the sun's importance to life on earth. Most tours are self-guided, but guided tours are offered Saturdays at 2 P.M. from May to October. The observatory is located in a very remote area, and getting here requires navigating the very winding Highway 6563. *From Cloudcroft, take Highway 130 two miles, turn right onto Highway 6563, and go 16 miles until it ends at the observatory; (505) 434-7000; www. sunspot.noao.edu*

Smokey Bear Historical State Park ★★★/$

In 1950, a fire burned 26 square miles of nearby forests, and firefighters found a small black bear cub clinging to a tree. They named the cub Smokey—and he grew up to become a symbol for forest

FamilyFun GAME

Pretzel Twist

Give your kids a bag of traditional pretzels and challenge them to bite out every letter of the alphabet.

fire prevention. This park celebrates Smokey's life and the importance of fire prevention with interactive computer games and displays that teach kids how to put out campfires and how to make sure they (and their parents) don't start forest fires.

The park details Smokey's life and his death from old age in 1976. (Subsequent generations of Smokeys now carry on the family fire-fighting tradition.) To avoid disappointment, be sure your younger kids know that Smokey himself will not be here. Also be advised that Smokey's grave is located along a scenic hiking trail behind the visitors' center. To get the bear facts before your trip, check out the interactive Website at www.emnrd. state.nm.us/forestry/smokey.htm *The park is located in Capitan on U.S. 380; (505) 354-2748; www. smokeybearpark.com*

 **Spencer Center for the Performing Arts**
★★★★/Free–$$$$

Nestled in a valley outside Alto and north of Ruidoso, this 514-seat, state-of-the-art performance hall brings in some of the nation's top orchestras, ballet troupes, and theatrical productions. Recently, the center has welcomed everything from the Broadway musical *Jekyll and Hyde* to *Cinderella on Ice*, which required transforming the floor into an ice rink. The center also occasionally hosts wonderful children's theater productions such as *The Three Little Pigs* and *The Jungle Book*. Tours are given on Tuesdays and Thursdays at 10 A.M. and 2 P.M. For information on what's doing during your vacation, check the schedule on the Internet at www.spencertheater. com *Located off Highway 48 in Alto; (888) 818-7872.*

FamilyFun READER'S TIP

Road Scholars

As we were planning our family vacation to Steamboat Springs, Colorado, last summer, my husband and I realized that our boys, Nicholas, 7, and Jason 12, weren't as excited about the trip as we were. So my husband devised a fun pre-vacation research project. Each of the boys received questions appropriate for their age two weeks before our trip. They were allowed to choose as many questions to work on as they wished (What's the tallest mountain in Colorado? What states will we cross to get from Wisconsin to Colorado? What kind of animals live in Colorado and not Wisconsin?), and for each question answered, they received $4 of vacation money.

Diane Rush, Thiensville, Wisconsin

JUST FOR FUN

Carlsbad Caverns
FamilyFun ★★★★/$

Formed more than 250 million years ago by water and acids seeping through prehistoric limestone, Carlsbad Caverns includes at least 30 miles of passages. Inside the Big Room, a chamber in the caverns, there's a restaurant, rest rooms, and a gift shop; it's so large that 14 football fields 25 stories high could fit inside it! From May through October, Carlsbad is home to hundreds of thousands of Mexican free-tailed bats, which use the cave as a breeding den. At dawn, the bats swarm into the cave, and at sunset, they stream out of the main entrance; it's a sight that few children—or grown-ups—will forget. During bat season—Memorial Day weekend through late October—park rangers lead a Bat Flight Program, also called the Bat Chat, which details the creatures' habits and migrations. There are a variety of guided and self-guided tours of the caverns offered year round. Kids ages 4 to 13 may enjoy the Junior Ranger Program, which offers a booklet of activities and a certificate upon completion of all activities.

Remember to bring a sweater or jacket when visiting the cave. Even though the temperatures are hot above ground, they stay a cool 56 degrees below. Families with small

In and Around Lincoln and Ruidoso

9 A.M. Grab breakfast and a picnic lunch in **Ruidoso**, then take Highway 48 north to Alto. Pull over at **Alto Lake**, visible from the highway, and drive around the lake. Take a brief hike on the trails by the river. Get back in the car and continue heading north.

11:30 A.M. Stop at the **Spencer Center for the Performing Arts** (see page 168); it makes a dramatic modern-architecture statement in a picturesque valley. Try to catch a matinee if possible.

Noon Enjoy a picnic lunch in Capitan and visit the **Smokey Bear Historical State Park** (see page 167).

2 P.M. Head east to Lincoln on Highway 380 and visit the **Lincoln State Monument** and explore the area's complex history—including the legend of Billy the Kid—at the **Lincoln County Historical Center**.

4 P.M. Take Highway 380 west, then turn left on Highway 214 to **San Patricio**, returning to Ruidoso.

CATCHING UP WITH BILLY THE KID

New Mexico was the stomping ground for many of the Wild West's most colorful figures, but none captured as much attention as William Bonney, better known as Billy the Kid. Born in a New York City tenement in 1859, he moved to Coffeyville, Kansas, with his parents, then later came to Silver City after his father's death. His life of crime began in the 1878 Lincoln County War when he took on a group of hired guns who had killed his mentor, rancher John Tunstall. Legend has it that Bonney shot 21 men before his 21st birthday and frequently hid out from his former-friend-turned-sheriff Pat Garrett.

Although you probably don't want your children to think of Billy the Kid as a role model, it's hard to escape the outlaw's presence in an area that celebrates his name with such "honors" as the Billy the Kid Highway and the Billy the Kid Casino. Challenge your children to look objectively at his short, violent life (with the emphasis on *short*), and draw their own conclusions about a life of crime.

Here are some places to explore Billy the Kid's haunts, including his final resting place at Old Fort Sumner:

The Billy the Kid Museum ★/$
This little museum has a small Billy the Kid exhibit and lots of Indian artifacts and items from the late-19th and early-20th centuries. *1601 E. Sumner Ave., Fort Sumner; (505) 355-2380.*

Casa de Patron ★★/$$
In Billy the Kid's day, this was home to Juan Patron, who served as Speaker of the House in the New Mexico legislature. Patron let Bonney stay here because the custom of the day was to welcome weary travelers—even if they were outlaws. It's now a bed-and-breakfast (for more information, see page 174). *Lincoln; (800) 524-5202; (505) 653-4676; www.casapatron.com*

Lincoln ★★★/Free
Located about 25 miles northeast of Ruidoso, this town revels in its past; much of the downtown is pro-

tected as a national historic monument and is little changed from when Billy the Kid embarked on his life of crime here in the bloody 1878 battle.

Old Fort Sumner Museum
★★/$

There's an emphasis on Billy the Kid at this historical museum, located near the area where he had his final showdown with Garrett. Behind the museum is the graveyard that is Bonney's final resting place. Since vandals have twice stolen his headstone and tried to ransom it, his grave is now in an iron cage. *Billy the Kid Road.*

Ruidoso ★★★/Free

Billy the Kid once escaped detection by hiding in a flour barrel after a shoot-out at nearby Blazer's Mill. Today the main street retains a bit of its Wild West past, but now offers gourmet restaurants and coffee bars. *Ruidoso Chamber of Commerce; (800) 253-2255; (505) 257-7395.*

Silver City
★★★/Free

Billy the Kid lived here with his stepfather and mother. His home was downtown, in the Antrim cabin. The city's jail has the dubious honor of being the first jail he broke out of, at the age of 15. *Silver City Chamber of Commerce; (505) 538-3785.*

children should use the elevator rather than make the steep climb down into the cave on foot. *Located 28 miles southwest of Carlsbad on U.S. 62/180; (505) 785-2232; www. nps.gov/cave*

Elephant Butte State Park
★★★/$

This state park near the town of Truth or Consequences is a popular family getaway. At the visitors' center, kids can check out fossils found in the area, including a Tyrannosaurus rex jawbone. The park has nature trails, a playground, and miles of sand beaches and protected swimming areas. You can also rent a boat at one of the marinas and explore the islands in the lake. And if you want to linger longer, campsites are available. *Five miles east of Truth or Consequences off I-25. Elephant Butte; (505) 744-5421; www.nm parks.com*

Fiesta Drive-In
★★/$

This is one of the few drive-in theaters left in America, and it's a great opportunity for you and your family to drive back in time (don't tell the kids about how you "made out" in the backseat). Cost is $8 a carload or $4 per person early shows, and $4 a carload or $2 per person late shows. Call ahead to check times and features. *401 W. Fiesta Rd., Carlsbad; (505) 885-4126; www.fies tadrivein.com*

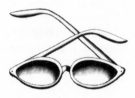

Living Desert State Park
★★★/$

This park and zoo showcases the habitats of the Chihuahuan Desert, with more than 40 native animal species including endangered Mexican wolves, bison, mule deer, antelope, and elk. There's also a walk-through aviary with eagles, owls, and songbirds. Kids can visit the greenhouses for an up-close, but not too close, look at hundreds of cacti. Hit the easy 1.3-mile, self-guided trail if you're up for a 90-minute hike through the desert and a juniper forest, or just enjoy the visitors' center's displays on the area's natural history and ecology. *Hwy. 285, Carlsbad; (505) 887-5516; www.livingdesert.org*

Rockhound State Park ★★/$

"Don't touch" and "put that back" aren't phrases you need to know at this park, tucked in the Little Florida Mountains near Deming. Your kids are not only allowed, they're actually encouraged, to haul as much as 15 pounds of rocks and minerals out of the park. If your rock hounds are lucky, they can find jasper, agate,

quartz, crystals, opals, onyx, or black perlite, but they'll probably be fine with a few of the colorful, plentiful—and hard to identify—red and brown ones. This place gets incredibly hot during the summer, so come early in the day or at a cooler time of year. *The park is located 11 miles southeast of Deming. The park can be reached from Columbus Road (Hwy. 11) or Frontage Road (Hwy. 418); call for directions; (505) 546-6182; www.swlink.net/~southwest/nmex/rock/rock_hound.html*

Sitting Bull Falls ★★★/$

It's a long drive through desolate country, but the reward is a dip in the three natural swimming pools under this 130-foot waterfall. Kids can play in these pools, which have water depths of three to six feet. Adventurous families may want to tackle the half-mile hike to the top of the falls. In addition to the hiking trails, there are picnic tables and rest rooms. *From Carlsbad, take Route 285 about 12 miles north, then take Route 137 southwest for 25 miles and look for the sign signaling the turnoff for the falls (a right turn onto County Road 409). Drive eight miles down a paved road to get to the falls. The first parking lot is for the trailhead, the second lot is for the falls; (505) 885-4181.*

Ski Apache ★★★/$$-$$$$

Skiing is available in the higher elevations of south central New

Mexico generally from late November through much of April. One of the largest resorts is the eponymous Ski Apache—operated by the Native American tribe—located 16 miles northwest of Ruidoso. The area offers a special Kiddie Koral program for those ages 4 to 6, which includes skiing lessons, lunch, a nap, and snow play. Older children can take lessons too. *Located 18 miles northwest of Ruidoso on Hwy. 532; (505) 336-4356;* www.skiapache.com

 **White Sands National Monument ★★★★/$**

Think *Lawrence of Arabia* and you will get an idea of the size and scope of the wavelike white gypsum dunes found in this national park. Stop at the visitors' center, where park rangers present kid-friendly lectures on things like the reptiles who live here and the formation of the dunes (created by water-and-wind erosion of the surrounding mountains). Kids can sign up to be Junior Dunes Rangers; there are three age-specific programs. In each, youngsters fill out activity guides that use games to teach them about the plants and animals in the park and the importance of conservation. Pick up one of the books as you enter the visitors' center. If your kids fill it out during the trip and turn it in on the way out of the park they'll get a patch and a certificate.

An eight-mile drive takes you deeper into the dunes landscape. There's also a boardwalk, which takes you even closer to the sands, and a one-mile Big Dune Trail. The landscape of the white sands and the blue sky can make it appear like you are walking in the clouds. Call ahead if you want information on special tours and workshops, such as the Moonlight Bicycle Tour and summer campfire programs. The shifting sands here—and the often high winds—means you should wear sunglasses or goggles to protect your eyes. *The visitors' center is located on U.S. 70/82, 15 miles south of Alamogordo; (505) 679-2599; (505) 479-6124;* www.nps.gov/whsa

SOME OF THE SMALLER ANIMALS at White Sands National Monument have evolved to match the bleached color of their surroundings. Keep a lookout for the Apache pocket mouse, the Cowles Prairie Lizard, and the Bleached Earless Lizard. Their white coloring helps to camouflage the creatures from predators.

BUNKING DOWN

Bear Mountain Lodge
★★★/$-$$

Set on 160 acres three miles outside Silver City, this 15-room bed-and-breakfast has an on-staff naturalist who can lead your family on hikes or nature walks. Fishing, bicycling, and horseback-riding tours can also be arranged. This place is pretty basic—the attraction is its location and proximity to such parks as Gila National Forest and Rockhound State Park. *2251 Cottage San Rd., Silver City; (505) 538-2538; www.bearmountainlodge.com*

Casa de Patron
★★/$$-$$$

This adobe inn was once home to Juan Patron, a storekeeper and state legislator who hosted Billy the Kid, who spent many nights here. Families should try to book the Casita de Paz, a small adobe cabin with two bedrooms, a full bath, and a sitting area. *Hwy. 380, Lincoln; (800) 524-5202; (505) 653-4676; www.casapatron.com*

Idol Hour Lodge
★★/$$

For a quiet stay under the pines, check out these 12, two-bedroom cabins with kitchens and decks next to the bubbling Rio Ruidoso in downtown Ruidoso. The lodge offers horseshoe pits, a new playground area for kids, and a community campfire. *112 Lower Terrace, Ruidoso; (800) 831-1186; (505) 257-2711; www.idlehourlodge.com*

Lodge at Cloudcroft
★★★/$$$

This three-story lodge has been in operation since the turn of the century. It has a romantic, historic—but a family friendly—atmosphere, and it even claims to have a friendly ghost named Rebecca wandering its halls. From the inn's five-story copper tower, guests can look out over miles of Alpine scenery to the White Sands Monument some 40 miles away—and even beyond that on clear days. *1 Corona Pl., Cloudcroft; (800) 395-6343; (505) 682-2566; www.thelodgeresort.com*

GOOD EATS

Flying J Ranch ★★★/$$$

For a true Old West experience, come to this ranch near Ruidoso, which offers a barbecue dinner served "chuck-wagon style." After chowing down on barbecued beef or chicken, beans, applesauce, and a spice-cookie dessert, join cowboy performers in a family-oriented western show featuring classics like "Home on the Range." Open nightly, Memorial Day through Labor Day, except Sundays. Call ahead to make reservations. *Rte. 48, Ruidoso; (505) 336-4330; www.flyingjranch.com*

Lincoln County Grill ★★/$$

This sandwich-and-burger joint has great desserts, including the Avalanche, a sundae sculpted to resemble a mountain catastrophe with spiraling nuts and swirls of chocolate. *2717 Sudderth Dr., Ruidoso; (505) 257-7669; www.ruidoso.net/grill*

Rebecca's ★★★/$$$

Named after the famous ghost of the Lodge at Cloudcroft (the restaurant's home), this upscale dining room serves gourmet meals in a casual atmosphere. A kids' menu offers pasta, a hamburger with fries, fried shrimp, and other selections. Families are better off at breakfast or lunch than dinner, when the restaurant has a more romantic feel. *1 Corona Pl., Cloudcroft; (800) 395-6343; (505) 682-3131.*

SOUVENIR HUNTING

Bear in the Woods

If you're looking for handmade souvenirs, this shop in Cloudcroft sells all types of homemade dolls. *Rte. 82, Cloudcroft; (505) 682-2094.*

Lincoln County Heritage Trust

The museum shop here sells Western-themed books, including an extensive collection on Billy the Kid, plus comic books, posters, and postcards. *Downtown Lincoln; (505) 653-4025.*

Moore's Trading Post

Want a pound of rattlesnakes? You can buy them here. But if you won't let your kids take home any new pets, let them at least see them at this store that carries a little bit of everything. *215 Rte. 82 East, Alamogordo; (505) 437-7116.*

Who Lives There?

Travel exposes your family to new places and different styles of living. As you pass a lime-green house with a yard full of plastic pink flamingos and a working waterwheel, it's hard not to wonder what type of family lives there. Why not run with that? Suggest that your kids speculate on who lives inside the houses you pass and what they might be doing at that moment. Perhaps the people in the green house invented mint chocolate-chip ice cream. Perhaps they have seven children and three pets— a Lhasa apso, an iguana, and a Persian cat wearing a pink leather collar. If it's dinnertime, perhaps they're gathered around the kitchen table enjoying tuna casserole topped with potato chips that will be followed by a dessert of cherries flambé. They'll be playing a game of Pictionary after dinner and, well, you get the idea.

Arizona

WITH ITS red-rock deserts and deep blue skies, Arizona's incredible natural beauty draws millions of tourists each year. From the restful waters of Lake Havasu to the desolate desert vistas of Monument Valley, your family will find some of the most gorgeous natural landscapes on earth. Its treasures include the Grand Canyon, which alone draws more than five million visitors a year, and Saguaro National Park, where the state's famous cacti reach for the sky.

Southern Arizona is home to the state's two largest cities

Phoenix and Tucson—and offers the best of both worlds—natural beauty and man-made fun. Your family can find mountain hikes only a few miles from city streets.

If you feel like splurging. you'll find some of the nation's most luxurious resorts, which have incredible pools and kid-friendly programs, as well as dude ranches where you can saddle up and enjoy a scenic desert trail ride. Your young shoppers will be glad to see lots of shops with Western duds, Native American jewelry, and even a cactus or two.

And although many of the resorts, ranches, and shops are pricey, you get to keep memories of a great vacation for free.

ATTRACTIONS

$	under $5
$$	$5 - $10
$$$	$10 - $20
$$$$	$20 +

HOTELS/MOTELS/CAMPGROUNDS

$	under $100
$$	$100 - $150
$$$	$150 - $200
$$$$	$200 +

RESTAURANTS

$	under $5
$$	$5 - $10
$$$	$10 - $20
$$$$	$20 +

FAMILYFUN RATED

★	Fine
★★	Good
★★★	Very Good
★★★★	*FamilyFun* Recommended

Take a trip down memory lane by cruising Route 66, America's first paved cross-country highway.

HISTORIC

U.S. 66

ROUTE

Northern Arizona

F EW PLACES ON EARTH offer the incredible natural beauty of northern Arizona— from the Grand Canyon to Sedona's Oak Creek—so it's no surprise that this region is one of America's favorite tourist destinations. Each year, five million people make the pilgrimage to the Grand Canyon and gape at its vast open spaces and burnt red-and-brown cliffs. Some make the mistake of looking around for a few minutes and then turning the car around to head right back home. We hope that you will have time to explore the area longer. You could easily spend a week, if not two or three, discovering the region's treasures. Flagstaff, a surprisingly quaint university town, makes a good base for families exploring the Grand Canyon and the nearby San Francisco Peaks, Sunset Crater, and

THE FamilyFun LIST

MUST-SEE MUST-SEE

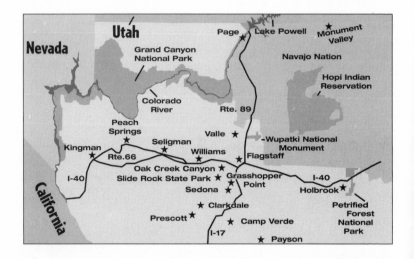

Wupatki National Monument. At the monument your kids will be wowed by the natural blowhole that sucks air in or out, depending on the atmospheric pressure. Native Americans explain the phenomenon as the earth taking a breath.

Some believe Sedona is the vortex of several powerful energy forces. That's up for debate, but there's no arguing that this area, where the Colorado plateau drops off into the southern deserts, is a place of incredible natural beauty. Spend at least a day driving through Oak Creek Canyon. Pull over for a picnic and take a short hike down one of the easy trails, then head back to town or cool off by shooting down a 30-foot

If you're traveling in northern Arizona during December, you can board the Grand Canyon Railroad's version of **the Polar Express**. The train ride offers cookies, cocoa, Christmas carols, and a reading of the Chris Van Allsburg classic on the way to see Santa and his reindeer.

natural water slide at Slide Rock State Park. Train lovers should schedule a ride on the Verde River Canyon Railroad or the Grand Canyon Railroad, which allows you to take in the scenery without worrying about keeping your eyes on the road.

There's a downside to all this heavenly splendor: despite the region's wide-open spaces, you may at times feel crowded by all the tourist buses that travel the same roads you're traveling. This is particularly true at the South Rim of the Grand Canyon in summer, when most families plan their visits. In fact, both the traffic and the fights for the limited number of parking spaces have gotten so bad that the National

Park Service no longer allows individual cars into the Grand Canyon's South Rim; to view the canyon vistas if you're traveling by car, you will have to take a bus to the new Canyon View Information Center. Only families who have reservations at a park property or campground will be allowed to make the drive inside the park. If at all possible, come another time of year. Fall and spring are much slower, and reservations at the fabulous El Tovar Hotel (see page 193) and at other lodgings inside the Grand Canyon can be had with just a few weeks' notice. If you do come in the summer, be prepared to make reservations months, if not a year, in advance—and pack some patience along with your shorts and hiking boots.

One way to get away from the crowds is to take the slow road— and in northern Arizona, this means getting off Interstate 40 and hopping on Route 66, once the central road from the Midwest to the West Coast. Today it is only a few remnants of blacktop lined with old filling stations and hotels. The longest uninterrupted stretch of Route 66 runs from Seligman to Kingman and makes for a fun afternoon detour back in time (see "Get Some Kicks on Route 66" on page 189).

Families enjoy waterskiing, boating, and swimming in Lake Powell, where 2,000 miles of shoreline meld into red-rock formations. And on the Navajo Nation Indian Reservation, you'll take in some of the most magnificent sculptures of the West at Monument Valley Navajo Tribal Park. Near Holbrook, you can see fossilized trees at the Petrified Forest, and at Meteor Crater, a short hop off Interstate 40 between Flagstaff and Winslow, you'll get a physics lesson as you view the 570-foot-deep dent left by a 300,000-ton meteor that hit the earth some 30,000 years ago. Roughly 85 percent of Arizona's 118,000 square miles is national parks, forests, recreation areas, wildlife preserves, and Native American lands. Don't try to see everything all in one vacation, unless you have a month or more. Instead, tackle these natural attractions a few at a time, and savor each one at least a day.

As with any trip to a dry climate, be sure to pack plenty of moisturizer and lip balm. If you hike, carry water to avoid dehydration and wear sunscreen and sunglasses. Temperatures here vary widely. At the

Grand Canyon, the temperature at the base can be 20 to 30 degrees warmer than on the rim. Also, during the day, the temperature may start out at or below freezing but quickly warm up to 70 degrees or more. So it's smart for everyone to dress in layers. Properly armed, get ready to explore one of the great wonderlands of the world.

CULTURAL ADVENTURES

Flagstaff ★★★/Free Local lore has it that this town was first settled in 1876 by Thomas Forsyth McMillan, who built a cabin and on the Fourth of July celebrated the nation's centennial by stripping a pine tree of its branches and from it hanging the American flag—thus giving the town its name. Flagstaff grew in importance in 1882 when the railroad came to town, and trains remain an important part of life here today. Train horns are a frequent sound in the historic downtown; you'll probably hear and see the freight trains hauling automobiles and other consumer goods imported from the Far East to the West, and wheat and other agricultural products from the Farm Belt to the West Coast.

Home of the University of Northern Arizona, this history-rich town has a progressive feel: it's not hard to find a vegetarian restaurant or an acupuncturist. Given the plethora of hotels and good restaurants, it makes sense to make this city a home base for exploring the region. *Tourist office: 323 W. Aspen Ave., Flagstaff; (800) 217-2367; (928) 779-7611;* www.flagstaffarizona.org

Fort Verde Historical State Park ★★/$
Four of this fort's original 18 buildings (the fort was built in 1871–73) remain and have been restored; it's a perfect setting for giving kids an idea of what life was like in these parts a century ago. Volunteers in period costumes occasionally give talks about frontier life, on weekends from spring through fall. On Fort Verde Day, the second Saturday in October, there is a reenactment of an 1882 battle between the U.S. military and Native Americans, and other events. *Hollamon St., 3 miles east of I-17 in Camp Verde; (928) 567-3275;* www.pr.state.az.us

Glen Canyon Dam ★★★/Free-$
This dam provides enough electricity to power a city of 1.5 million; it also aids flood control and irrigation and creates gorgeous Lake Powell. At the Carl Hayden Visitors Center, you can see films on the recreation area, the construction of the dam, and the dam today and how it functions. Pick up brochures

on the surrounding Glen Canyon Recreation Area. The one-hour guided tours take you inside the dam, but may bore kids under 6. *On U.S. 89 at the Colorado River; (928) 608-6404;* www.nps.gov/glea/

⭐ The Grand Canyon
FamilyFun ★★★★/$-$$$$
Probably the biggest thrill of a vacation is this colossal hole in the ground. For more information see "The Grand Canyon" on page 197.

Hopi Reservation ★★/Free-$
The Hopi have received less attention from outsiders than other tribes of the Southwest, due partly to their remote location and partly to their own design. In 1592, Spanish missionaries tried to convert the Hopi to Christianity, but the tribe resisted, preferring their centuries-old religion centered on elaborate dances in a ceremonial kiva. The tribe threw out the priests in 1680 during what's called the Pueblo Revolt. Through the years, the Hopi had to deal with frequent Navajo raids and with smallpox brought by European settlers, which wiped out 70 percent of the tribe in the 1800s. The Hopi are associated with their belief in kachinas, spirits who inhabit the sacred peaks of the San Francisco Mountains, north of Flagstaff. There are more than 500 different kachinas that appear in Hopi ceremonies. According to legend, the kachinas used to live among the Hopi and taught them important ceremonial dances that have a variety of purposes—from bringing rain to the corn crop to assuring peace and happiness. Kachina dances and ceremonies are held from the winter solstice until just after the summer solstice.

The Hopi have now closed almost all of their ceremonial dances to the public because crowds of tourists were turning the dances into spectacles rather than religious observances. If you want a taste of the Hopi culture, it's best to visit the Museum of Northern Arizona in Flagstaff (below)—it's a good choice

---

FamilyFun READER'S TIP

Tic-Tac-Tine

While my sister Barb and I and our seven kids were waiting for dinner at a restaurant, my nephew Josh surprised me with a game he invented using dinner utensils and sugar packets. He set up forks, spoons, and knives in the traditional tic-tac-toe grid and gave me the choice of being the X's (regular sugar packets) or O's (artificial sweetener packets).

Theresa Jung, Cincinnati, Ohio

if you're short on time or have young children. If you want a more in-depth experience, the tribe operates the Hopi Cultural Center; it's located on the tribe's Second Mesa—there are three—near where State Highways 264 and 87 join; *(928) 734-2401.* **NOTE:** For etiquette tips when visiting a pueblo and viewing ceremonial dances, see "A Primer on Pueblos" on page 152; www.psu.com/hopi

Lowell Observatory
★★/$

Photos shot at Lowell, one of the nation's oldest observatories, were the first to capture the planet Pluto. Kids can attend lectures on stargazing and get a firsthand glimpse of the galaxy through a 24-inch telescope. The night programs start every night (except Sunday) at 8 P.M. *1400 W. Mars Hill Rd., Flagstaff; (928) 774-2096;* www.lowell.edu

Meteor Crater
★★/$$

It looks like a big hole in the ground, but it's worth seeing to show kids the power of moving objects. About 50,000 years ago, a meteor between 80 and 200 feet in diameter and weighing some 300,000 pounds crashed to the earth here, leaving a 570-foot-deep hole that is almost a mile across. *From Flagstaff, take Interstate 40 East to exit 233 and drive five miles to the crater; (928) 289-2362;* www.meteorcrater.com

 **Museum of Northern Arizona**
★★★★/$

If you want to give your kids a quick overview of local history, Native American culture, geology, and wildlife, make sure you visit this museum, located three miles north of Flagstaff on U.S. 180. This will probably be your only chance to see what the inside of a Hopi kiva (ceremonial room) looks like, since most are off-limits to the public. The new Hopi Kiva gallery offers hands-on experience that kids will enjoy. The museum also offers specialized educational docent tours and workshops; call ahead to see what is going on during your stay. Walking the short nature trail through the pine grove is an easy way for kids to stretch their legs. The museum also offers a Discovery Program with artistic activities for kids. *Three miles north of downtown Flagstaff on Hwy. 180, 3101 N. Fort Valley Rd.; (928) 774-5213;* www.musnav.org

Sunset Crater Volcanic National Monument ★★★/$

This volcano erupted around 1064 A.D., not that long ago in geological terms, leaving a volcanic cone of red, yellow, green, and black ash. The visitors' center is a hotbed of volcanic information that should help fuel your kids' interest in this topic. *Off 89A, Flagstaff; (928) 556-7134.*

★MUST-SEE★ FamilyFun ★MUST-SEE★ Wupatki National Monument ★★★/$

If you want to give your children an interesting history lesson, head for this monument where they can see the remains of a ball court used a thousand years ago by a group of people called the Sinagua (Spanish for "without water"); you'll also find the remains of a stone amphitheater. Older kids will enjoy the unique learning experience, and younger ones will get a kick out of the natural blowhole on the monument grounds. Air from underground tunnels occasionally blasts up to the surface when the underground air pressure is greater than the pressure above ground. On hot days, cool air blows out of the hole. The visitors' center details what life was like for the ancient Anasazi and Sinagua tribes. *Located 55 miles north of Flagstaff off U.S. 89; (928) 679-2365; www.nps.gov/wupa*

JUST FOR FUN

Bedrock City ★/$-$$

We've given this place only one star, and with good reason: unless your kids are die-hard *Flintstones* fans (or you're simply desperate for a rest room break en route to the Grand Canyon), you should bypass this small, dusty theme park. If you pay the $5 admission fee, you can wander around the Stone Age–inspired cartoon set, which features a post

Holy Crater!

Daniel Barringer, a mining engineer, was the first person to theorize that the giant hole in the Arizona desert (now known as Meteor Crater) was created by a meteor impact. In the early 1900s, he spent thousands of dollars searching for the meteor, but found nothing. Most scientists currently agree that the meteor vaporized upon impact.

office, a beauty salon, and a jail. There's also a small train and a fake volcano. At the Bedrock Theater, grainy, out-of-focus *Flintstones* cartoons are shown on a continuous loop. *Junction 180 and U.S. 64, Valle; look for the giant Fred Flintstone; (928) 635-2600.*

Grand Canyon Caverns ★★/$$

This tourist attraction is classic kid-friendly kitsch—the giant dinosaur in front is a big tip-off. Kids love it and it's a great way to cool off if you're visiting during the hot summer months: the underground caverns have a constant temperature of 60 degrees (temperatures above ground can top 100). This is one of the world's rare dry caves, and its low humidity has preserved everything from a mummified bob-

185

cat to a 1970s-era bridal veil left from a wedding held here. There are even leftover K rations from the 1950s when the cave was a designated bomb shelter. Your kids can see all this, plus a reproduction of a giant prehistoric sloth named Gertie, on the guided tour through the cave that explains the history and formation of the caverns. Be ready when the guides briefly turn out the lights and put you in pitch dark for several seconds.

Unless you drive down Route 66, this spot is a bit off the beaten path, but it's well worth the trip for its wacky appeal. The caverns often get crowded in the summer, but at other times of the year you could easily have them to yourself. There's also an on-site gift shop and restaurant. *Located just outside Peach Springs on Rte. 66; Peach Springs; (928) 422-3223; www.gccaverns.com*

Monument Valley is also the site of two famous buttes, **the Mittens**. The formations strongly resemble their namesake, so see if your children can spot them.

Grand Canyon Deer Farm ★★/$$
Yes it's touristy, but kids don't seem to mind. They just like feeding and petting the residents, which include pygmy and Nigerian goats, antelope, potbellied pigs, and peacocks. *Twenty-five miles west of Flagstaff at Interstate 40, exit 171. 6752 E. Deer Farm Rd., Williams; (800) 926-DEER; (928) 635-4073; www.deerfarm.com*

Grand Canyon Railroad
★★★/$$$$
Rather than fight traffic down the two-lane highway and drive from the interstate to the Grand Canyon, why not sit back and ride this train, which departs daily at 10 A.M. from the Williams Depot. Get there early so your kids can enjoy the staged shoot-'em-up before departure. During the two-hour-plus ride, you will pass through high-desert plains and pine forests before pulling up to the Grand Canyon Depot. You'll have a couple of hours to take in the South Rim before the train begins its return trip. **NOTE:** Be advised that the only view of the Grand Canyon from the train lasts about 20 seconds; for an additional charge, you can take a tram to tour the rim. The train lets you out at a tram stop near El Tovar Lodge. Be careful of the (make-believe) "masked bandits" on the return trip. *1201 W. Rte. 66, Williams; (800) THE-TRAIN; (928) 773-1976; www.thetrain.com*

Lake Powell
MUST-SEE FamilyFun ★★★★/Free
MUST-SEE Houseboating is a huge draw here (see page 289 for more information). Most boat owners require a two-day-minimum rental. If that doesn't fit into your schedule,

DOUBLE-CHECK YOUR WATCH if you travel to the Navajo nation. Arizona does not participate in daylight saving time, but the Navajo nation does, so the clocks in areas like Kayenta, Tuba City, and Chinle may be different, depending on when you visit.

enjoy an hour-long ride aboard the *Canyon King*, a 95-foot paddle wheeler operated by Lake Powell Resorts and Marinas. *Take U.S. Highway 89 two miles north of Page to Carl Hayden Visitor Center to get information on tours; (800) 528-6154*; www.lakepowell.com

Monument Valley ★★★★/Free

The magnificent mesas and buttes here make for the most memorable vistas you or your children will ever see (better still, tell them to be on the lookout for Road Runner and Wile E. Coyote). If this place looks familiar, it's probably because you have seen it in such Hollywood films as *Stagecoach* and *Thelma and Louise* and in numerous television car commercials. Take U.S. 163 north toward the Utah state line. There is a small visitors' center near the state line at Monument Valley Navajo Tribal Park down a four-mile side road; from there, a 17-mile unpaved loop road offers more stunning views of the valley. *You can also opt for one of the organized tours offered at the visitors' center*; www.powellguide.com/lakepowell/monumentvalley.html

Navajo Nation Reservation ★★/Free-$

This is the largest Native American reservation in the United States, occupying parts of Arizona, New Mexico, and Utah. The reservation includes Monument Valley, but don't get so caught up in the scenery that you forget to keep your eyes on the road—and watch out for flocks of sheep or wayward farm animals. (The reservation isn't fenced and animals have the right of way.) Several tours are offered or you can drive around on your own. The main tourist spots are in Window Rock, where there is a tribal museum and a small zoo and botanical park. The week of Labor Day features the Annual Navajo Nation Fair, with its intertribal powwow, rodeo, and song-and-dance demonstrations. *Located in the northeast corner of Arizona, northeast of Flagstaff and Holbrook; (928) 871-6436.*

ᴹᵁˢᵀ⁻ˢᵉᵉ Oak Creek Canyon
FamilyFun ★★★★/Free-$$$

ᴹᵁˢᵀ⁻ˢᵉᵉ A hallmark of scenic Sedona, this canyon is a must-see even if you are just passing through.

187

The creek actually lies on a fault line—one side of the canyon is moving one way while the other side moves another way. The section of Oak Creek that gets the most attention is northwest of Sedona at Highway 89A, where the canyon reaches its narrowest point and the red, orange, and white cliffs are the most dramatic. Pine and juniper forests and colorful red rocks make it a gorgeous hiking, picnicking, and camping spot: the United States Forestry Service maintains six campgrounds in the canyon, picnic spots are plentiful, and hiking is a popular pastime here.

Families with older children can tackle the rigorous six-mile round-trip hike up the West Fork of Oak Creek; those with younger kids can simply enjoy hiking the first mile of the trail as it travels along the creek bed. **NOTE:** If you do hike, make sure you and your kids stay on the trail because poison oak runs rampant. The best view of the canyon is from the Oak Creek Scenic Viewpoint, 16 miles north of Sedona off Arizona Highway 89A. The Canyon is also home to the popular Slide Rock State Park (see page 192); *(928) 282-4119.*

Petrified Forest National Park and the Painted Desert
★★★/Free-$

About 150 million years ago, this area was flooded, creating a great basin of water that left behind iron, copper, and manganese, which give the landscape its brilliant-colored appear-

ance. The waters also washed away trees that were subsequently buried in mud and volcanic ash and which later fossilized. Over the years, erosion and geological uplifts exposed the tree trunks. To avoid any disappointment, however, make sure your children don't get here expecting to see huge, stonelike trees; the forest is really a bunch of horizontal logs.

Before the area was designated a national park, thousands of scavengers made off with pieces of petrified wood. Today, taking the wood fossils out of the park is punishable by fines, and even jail. The visitors' center by Interstate 40 and the larger museum in the park both display letters and notes that modern-day petrified-wood thieves wrote after making off with a stone or two; apparently the guilt got to them and they mailed back the loot. It's a good morality lesson for kids. Samples of petrified wood are readily available for little cost at the gift shop in the visitors' center and at many local shops. Never fear: these are from samples gathered outside the park. *The south entrance of the park is 20 miles east of Holbrook on U.S. 180. The north entrance is 25 miles east of Holbrook on I-40; (928) 524-6228; www.nps.gov/pefo*

Pink Jeep Tours
★★★/$$-$$$$

For a trip off the beaten path—way off—hop in a Pink Jeep and hit the desert back roads. Drivers will take

GET SOME KICKS ON ROUTE 66

ONCE THE MAIN ROUTE from Chicago to Los Angeles, this road was the first cross-country highway to be completely paved (in 1938). Route 66 has nearly faded into oblivion now as travelers opt for Interstate 40 instead. But while much of the road is gone, grown over with weeds in some places, Northern Arizona is home to the longest stretch of the remaining Mother Road, as it was called in John Steinbeck's classic novel *The Grapes of Wrath*, which chronicled the migration of Oklahomans to California on the highway. Today the road welcomes hip Harley-Davidson aficionados, Europeans curious about American culture, and families looking for a road trip down memory lane.

The best stretch of Route 66 to tackle is the link between Kingman and Seligman. To get in the mood for your trip, turn your radio dial to KZKE 103.9 on the FM dial, which plays oldies from the '50s and '60s, the glory days of Route 66. Take the trip at your own pace, but try to stop at the following attractions to make the most of this truly American icon:

Dr. Zs ★★/$$
This old gas station now houses a classic diner that serves up root-beer floats and Corvette burgers. 105 Andy Devine Ave., Kingman; (928) 718-0066.

Grand Canyon Caverns ★★/$$
Kids love the wacky appeal of this cave and will surely remember the mummified bobcat and giant sloth they see inside. For more information, see page 185.

Snow Cap Drive-In ★★★/$$
This place is hard to miss with its giant signs and pink jalopy outside. Pull over for a burger, soda, ice cream—and the monkeyshines of Juan Delgadillo. If your kids ask for straws, he hands them straw, as in hay. No McDonald's could ever have this much personality. Sit on the outdoor patio and enjoy the chili burgers and snow cones. 301 E. Chino St., Seligman; (928) 422-3291.

your family on guided tours by red-rock canyons, Native American cliff dwellings, and scenic overlooks. Families looking for a quick, but memorable, getaway can take the 90-minute Red Rock Range Sunset Tour ($35). Most kids get a kick out of hopping over the red-rock roads (it's way cooler than riding in the family minivan), but some pre-schoolers may get scared, so use your discretion.

Be sure to wear comfortable shoes because some tours involve short hikes to see unique sights such as petroglyphs (Native American drawings etched into stone). **NOTE:** Tours are not recommended for pregnant moms or anyone with back or neck injuries or other serious medical conditions. **ANOTHER NOTE:** The dust kicked up on the tours can wreak havoc with contact lenses, so wear glasses instead. Sunglasses and sunscreen are generally a good idea given the area's intense sun. *The tours leave from 204 N. Highway 89A, north of Sedona.* Advance reservations are recommended; *(800) 873-3662; (928) 282-5000;* www.pinkjeep.com

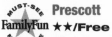

Prescott
★★/Free

The territorial capital of the state from 1864 to 1867, this city retains a large collection of Victorian architecture and a frontier feel year-round, but that especially comes alive in late June during the annual Frontier Days celebration. The town is home to several great museums including the **Sharlot Hall Museum**, which features four gardens and nine restored frontier buildings including Fort Misery, once the home and store of an 1860s-era trader, and a replica of the first public school house in Arizona. *415 W. Gurley St.; (928) 445-3122;* www.sharlot.org Prescott's **Smoki Museum** showcases Native American artists and has a large collection of prehistoric and contemporary pottery, jewelry, baskets, and kachinas. *147 N. Arizona St.; (928); 445-1230;*

I'm So Hungry, I Could Eat an Alphabet

Let your half-starved brood describe how hungry they are in this game, best played about half an hour before you make a pit stop for food. This version of the I'm Packing for a Picnic game begins when you announce, "I'm so hungry, I could eat an aviator" ("alligator," or "apple"). The next player adds on with a *B* word. She might say, "I'm so hungry, I could eat an aviator and a bunny rabbit" ("belly button," or "bologna slice").

See if you can keep it up until your family is eating zoos, zippers, zeppelins, zebras, or zigzags.

www.smokimuseum.org *Prescott is
located 60 miles southwest of Sedona
on Arizona Hwy. 89; (800) 266-7534;
(928) 445-2000;* www.prescott.org

Rainbow Trout Farm ★★/$

If your kids are ready to catch trout,
head to this spot *three and a half
miles north of Sedona on Arizona
Highway 89A*, where they are guaranteed success. *(928) 282-5799.*

Red Rock State Park
★★/Free

If you're up for a hike and picnic
lunch, head to this state park east of
Sedona. There are six hiking trails
ranging in length from less than half
a mile to 1.9 miles. You can fish in
Oak Creek, but swimming is not
allowed here. Park rangers lead
nature walks, bird walks, and moonlit bicycle tours during the busy
summer months. Your older kids
will love it! *Lower Red Rock Loop
Rd., Sedona;* www.pr.state.az.us/
parkhtml/redrock.htm

MUST-SEE Route 66 ★★★★/$$
FamilyFun Lots of fun awaits along
this, the first paved cross-
country highway in the U.S. For
more information, see "Get Some
Kicks on Route 66" on page 189.

MUST-SEE Sedona ★★★/Free
FamilyFun One of the few towns in
the state named after
a woman (early settler Sedona
Schnebly), this town was a popular

location for Hollywood westerns in
the 1940s and 1950s. At the same
time, a growing number of artists,
including surrealist painter Max
Ernst, were drawn by the area's natural beauty and eventually formed
an artists' colony that has made the
city a regional art mecca, today
boasting more than 40 galleries. The
city has grown rapidly in recent years
and is trying to do a better job blend-
ing in with its unique surroundings.
Even the McDonald's sign here has
pastel green arches painted over a
pink background. Sedona has also
become a center of New Age culture because its location is said to be
at the vortex of several powerful
energy flows. **NOTE:** The town is
decidedly upscale, and many families vacation at one of the plush
resorts. There are a few low-cost
options among the older motels
around Oak Creek, but budget
accommodations and reasonably
priced meals can be hard to come by
here. Cheaper digs can be had in
nearby Camp Verde, but they also fill
up fast in the summer. *Sedona is on*

Arizona Highway 179. There is a tourist office at the corner of Highway 89A and Forest Road. Contact the Sedona-Oak Creek Chamber of Commerce at (800) 288-7336 or (928) 282-7722; www.sedona.net

⭐ Slide Rock State Park
FamilyFun ★★★★/$$
The best swimming holes in the area are found here—and on hot summer days so are the crowds. The highlight is a 30-foot natural water slide that sweeps swimmers down the creek bed, hence the park's name. *From Sedona, take Highway 89A for seven miles to the park. Grasshopper Point is another popular swimming spot two miles north of Sedona on the right side of Highway 89A; (928) 282-3034; www.pr.state.az.us*

Don't look down if you're not fond of heights! **The Tonto Natural Bridge** hangs 183 feet over the ground below.

Sunrise Ski Park
★★★/$$$-$$$$
In the winter, this part of the state attracts skiers, including many families who drive up from Phoenix. One of the largest resorts is Sunrise Ski Park (operated by the White Mountain Apache Indian Tribe and located on Arizona Highway 273), which offers children's lessons and child care. (In the summer, the resort features mountain biking and equestrian trails.) *(800) 554-6835; (928) 735-7600.*

Tonto Natural Bridge State Park
★★★/$$
Located 12 miles north of Payson on Arizona Highway 87, this natural bridge formation spans a 150-foot-wide canyon and is more than 400 feet wide itself. Small children will need help navigating the steep stairs to the lookout deck, where you can take a break by a cool, natural pool. There is a short but somewhat steep trail to the bottom of the cavern, *(928) 476-4202; www.pr.state.az.us*

Verde River Canyon Railroad
★★★/$$$$
Restored diesel locomotives take you on a four-hour, round-trip ride into the Verde River Canyon and Sycamore Canyon Wilderness Area. Choose an open-air observation car or closed cabin—either one offers great views—and be on the lookout for bald eagles (the prime viewing season is November to March), blue herons, and deer. Live music and narration that details the area's history helps keep kids entertained during the long ride, but you may want to bring games, books, and other diversions along, too. *300 N. Broadway, Clarkdale; (800) 293-7245; (928) 639-0010; www.verde canyonrr.com*

Bunking Down

in Flagstaff

The Inn at 410 ★★★★/$$$

If you're looking for an intimate (9-room) bed-and-breakfast that doesn't mind kids, this is one of the finest in the state. The 1907-era home has a great front porch made for rocking. The breakfasts are incredible: concoctions feature the inn's trademark oat pancakes and "honey of a fruit cup," but the innkeepers keep boxes of Cheerios on hand if that's what your kids crave. Youngsters can play board games and munch on the inn's popular sugar and oatmeal-raisin cookies, served each afternoon. Best bets for families are the two large suites: Suite Nature and the Dakota Suite, each with a cowboy theme. *410 N. Leroux St., Flagstaff; (800) 774-2008; (928) 774-0088; www.inn410.com*

Radisson Woodlands
★★★/$$-$$$

Comfortable modern rooms with lots of space, plus Nintendo games for young guests (for a small fee), are the draw here. Parents appreciate the hotel's self-service laundry facilities. There is also a pool, an exercise room, and a Japanese steak house where kids enjoy watching chefs chop up meat and vegetables and cook dinner right on the table. *1175 W. Rte. 66, Flagstaff; (928) 773-8888; www.radisson.com/*

in Grand Canyon

Bright Angel Lodge and Cabins
★★★/$-$$

This rustic lodge offers incredible convenience (roll out of bed and see the Grand Canyon) and a low price. Don't expect great decor (maybe someday they'll pull out that shag carpeting)—but you'll be looking at the view, so who cares? A few of the cabins have fireplaces. **NOTE:** Book early, because this place fills up fast; reservations are accepted as far as two years minus two days in advance. *On the South Rim of Grand Canyon; (928) 638-2631; (888) 297-2757.*

El Tovar Hotel
★★★★/$$-$$$$

Who says you have to rough it at the Grand Canyon? If you'd like to take in this grand wonder in grand style, book a room at this posh hotel. It has an old-fashioned ski resort feel, complete with a wood-burning fireplace crackling in the lobby and great restaurants where you will want to eat every meal. Best of all, its proximity to the canyon and the awesome views will appeal to everyone in the family, and you won't hear "when will we get there?"—you are there. **NOTE:** Reserve months (even a year) in advance if coming in the summer; weeks ahead will suffice in slower times of the year. *On the South Rim of Grand Canyon;*

(928) 638-2631; (888) 297-2757;
www.grandcanyonlodges.com

in Page/Lake Powell

Lake Powell Days Inn and Suites ★★★/$-$$

Forget the image you have of this budget chain; this hotel near Page and Lake Mead offers great views of red-rock buttes and canyons and is close to Glen Canyon Dam and Rainbow Ridge National Monument. Suites are available, and guests get a complimentary continental breakfast. *961 Hwy. 89, Page; (928) 645-2800;* www.daysinn.net

in Sedona

Don Hoel's Cabins ★★/$$$

If you want a rustic retreat, this recently renovated place still has plenty of knotty-pine walls (some units have gas-log fireplaces and some have kitchens). There's a playground for kids, and fishing, too (it's catch-and-release only). Ask for a cabin away from the road because truck noise can

---

FamilyFun GAME

Word Stretch

Give your child a word challenge by asking her to make as many words as she can from the letters in a phrase such as, "Are we there yet?" or "When will we be at the zoo?"

---

get loud as the rigs head up and down this steep section of Arizona 89A. *9440 N. Hwy. 89A; (800) 292-4635; (928) 282-3560;* www.hoels.com

Enchantment Resort ★★★★/$$$$

Nestled in a canyon northwest of Sedona, this resort has a great location—especially for hikers. The casitas are large, and two-bedroom units have a kitchenette, kiva fireplace, and deck with built-in barbecue. If you want to hike, a trailhead by the grounds leads to the ruins of an Indian canyon dwelling. Deer are commonly seen munching on the golf course grass in the evenings. Parents in search of pampering can enjoy the resort's famous spa, Mii Amo. *525 Boynton Canyon Rd., Sedona; (928) 282-2900;* www. enchantmentresort.com

Garland's Oak Creek Lodge ★★★★/$$$

People come here year after year for the restful atmosphere and gourmet cuisine made from produce grown in the lodge's organic garden, greenhouse, and orchard. The only problem is getting a reservation in one of the 16 cabins, which are typically booked a year in advance by the same families who return every year. There's a waiting list in case anyone cancels. *8067 N. Hwy. 89A, Sedona; (928) 282-3343;* www.garlandslodge.com

Junipine Resort
★★★/$$$-$$$$
Make this your home away from
home: each one- and two-bedroom
"creek house" has a kitchen, liv-
ing/dining room, fireplace, and deck.
It's a great place for family reunions.
You can have volleyball games on the
grass court, and hiking, swimming,
and fishing are close by; there's also
a restaurant. *8351 N. Hwy. 89A,
Sedona; (800) 742-7463; (928) 282-
3375; www.junipine.com*

GOOD EATS

in Flagstaff

Beaver Street Brewery
★★★/$$
Great wood-fired-oven pizzas for
the whole family and fresh microbrews that Mom and Dad will want
to sample are the main attractions
here. The children's menu includes
Soup of the Moment and Dish of
Dirt (ice cream topped with Oreo
crumbs and gummy worms). *11 S.
Beaver St., Flagstaff; (928) 779-0079.*

Downtown Diner ★★★/$
The place to go for hearty breakfasts before hitting the trail. There
aren't any special kids' meals, but
there are yummy pancakes and hash
browns for breakfast and burgers
and sandwiches for lunch. *Across
from Heratidge Square on E. Aspen
Ave., Flagstaff; (928) 774-3492.*

Galaxy Diner ★★/$-$$
Parked on Route 66, this diner has
a fun feel and serves up great burgers and breakfasts. *931 W. Rte. 66,
Flagstaff; (928) 774-2466.*

Kathy's Café ★★/$-$$
This downtown restaurant has some
of the best desserts in town, including delicious chocolate, strawberry,
and carrot cakes and made-to-order
milk shakes. *7 N. San Francisco St.,
Flagstaff; (928) 774-1951.*

in Grand Canyon

El Tovar Dining Room & Arizona Room
★★★★/$$-$$$$
If you can't stay at the Lodge, at least
eat here: these are among the few
restaurants where the food actually
equals the view. The kids' menu
includes the usual suspects: chicken
fingers, burgers, and sandwiches. It's
open for breakfast, lunch, and din-
ner, though families will feel more
comfortable during the more casu-
al breakfast and lunch times. The
sunrise breakfasts are deservedly leg-
endary. Reservations are advised in
summer. *South Rim of Grand
Canyon; (928) 638-2631.*

in Sedona

Blazing M Ranch Chuckwagon Suppers ★★★/$$$
The folks here make dinner an event
with singing cowboys, pony rides,

and target shooting. There are also shops and a gallery for browsing. As for eats, the fare is your choice of barbecue beef or chicken (vegetarians can opt for the Bordenburger). Your kids will love the homemade spice cake with whipped cream—ours did. Open Wednesdays through Saturdays; closed August and January. Call ahead for reservations. *1875 Mabery Ranch Rd., Sedona; (800) WEST-643; (928) 634-0334; www. blazinm.com*

The Coffee Pot
★★★/$

The casual hangout named after a nearby rock formation is famous for offering 101 types of omelettes. If your kids still can't find a combination they like, opt for the Belgian waffles. *2050 W. Highway 89A, Sedona; (928) 282-6626.*

Cowboy Club and Silver Saddle
★★★/$$-$$$

This place offers upscale regional fare such as Rattlesnake Bites—yes, it really is rattlesnake; try it to see if it's true that it tastes like chicken. Other specialties of the house are buffalo tenderloin and sweet-potato fries. Less adventurous families can opt for traditional burgers and sandwiches. *241 N. U.S. 89A, Sedona; (928) 282-4200.*

Red Planet Diner ★★/$-$$

Offering a cut above standard diner fare, this place makes great burgers

and milk shakes that are out of this world. *1655 W. U.S. 89A, Sedona; (928) 282-6070;* www.redplanet diner.com

SOUVENIR HUNTING

Mother Nature's Trading Company

This store sells nature- and science-oriented toys, games, and puzzles, as well as microscope kits. *336 Hwy. 179, Sedona; (928) 282-5932.*

Sedona Fudge Factory

Rocky road and mocha almond are a couple of the varieties of chocolate concoctions sold here. Buy plenty before hitting the road. Two locations: *257 N. Hwy. 89A; (928) 282-1044 or 162 Coffee Pot Dr. B1, Sedona; (928) 282-7747.*

Sedona Kid Company

The local source for board games, handmade puzzles, Legos, dolls, stuffed animals, and so forth. *333 N. Hwy. 89A in the Madahorn Plaza, Sedona; (928) 282-3571.*

THE GRAND CANYON

IT'S HARD TO DESCRIBE the feeling you get when first glimpsing the Grand Canyon. Its immensity can overwhelm you, then, magically, begin to calm your soul. Kids either love it, offering up the high praise of "Cool," or take a look for a few seconds and then start playing with rocks. Relax and enjoy either reaction. Try to stay in the park at least two days, time enough for the canyon to work its spell on you and the kids. **NOTE:** To make the most of your trip, check out the park's on-line trip planner at www.thecanyon.com/nps, which has details of upcoming activities and camping and lodging amenities as well as general tips, such as bring an extra set of car keys—it's a long wait for the nearest locksmith.

To avoid a daily commute to the park (two hours from Flagstaff and an hour from Williams) and to beat the crowds, make a reservation at one of the campgrounds or accommodations located inside the park that are managed by **Amfac Parks and Resorts** (303/297-2757). The El Tovar is the nicest option, and prices are reasonable given the location and amenities; Bright Angel Lodge and Cabins is a more rustic, less expensive alternative (see page 193 for both). The other properties—including the Kachina and Thunderbird Lodge, Moqui Lodge, and Maswik Lodge—have a utilitarian, almost college dorm-like feel. Phantom Ranch is located at the floor of the canyon and is only accessible by mule, foot, or river raft, methods of transportation not advisable for families traveling with young children. The Grand Canyon Lodge is the only option offered at the canyon's more secluded North Rim.

Each year, five million people visit the Grand Canyon, 90 percent choosing the more easily accessible South Rim. In past years, visiting the South Rim of the Grand Canyon during the busy summer season meant fighting mobs of other tourists for a coveted parking space. To improve the connection with nature and eliminate some of the pollution that was affecting the fragile environment, the National Park Service has instituted a new transportation system that prohibits most cars from entering the park. Now visitors are guided to parking areas away from the South Rim where they board a bus to the Canyon View Information Center at Mather Point. There you can get information about the park's activities, trails, and other programs—even sign your kids up for the Junior Rangers program, where they can earn a badge by correctly answering questions about the

(continued on page 198)

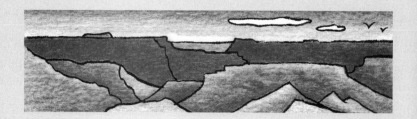

canyon's geology and animal and plant life. From the center, you can walk to the overlook at Mather Point, then board a bus (they run every 15 minutes or so) to see the West Rim. The good news is that the new system eases traffic nightmares and exhaust fumes. The bad news is that many kids will get cranky at the prospect of having to ride two buses. Plan a few diversions—such as a game of "How many (fill in the blank) would it take to fill up the Grand Canyon?"

Before you enter the park to experience the real thing, it's worth stopping at the IMAX theater outside the gate to see the short film on the canyon's history and to take a simulated ride down the Colorado River. Young children ages 3 to 5 may get bored in spots or be scared by a few violent scenes, such as when an early Native American tribe is attacked. If you think that's an issue, one parent can stay outside with the toddler and grab an ice-cream cone here instead. Shows run hourly at half past the hour *(928/638-2468)*. You can save time by buying your car pass into the park from a vending machine outside the IMAX theater lobby.

Once inside the park, pull over at Mather Point, the first overlook, and enjoy the view. Then proceed to the visitors' center, where you can get schedules of special lectures, hikes, and other events. Kids can sign up to be Junior Rangers, earning a patch and certificate when they complete a questionnaire. Shuttle buses leave from here to the West Rim Drive every 15 minutes March through November, when the drive is closed to vehicular traffic.

There are several ways to experience the Grand Canyon. If you are traveling with young children (under 10), you should stick to the safest ways—hiking the rim trail and enjoying the view from a car or tram. **NOTE:** Be sure your youngsters stay on the trail and away from the canyon rim; each year, people fall to their deaths because they get too close to the edge. **ANOTHER NOTE:** If you do decide to hike the Bright Angel Trail, be sure to watch out for mule manure!

Mules are the best option if you want to get to the canyon floor, but riders must be at least 4 feet 7 inches tall, weigh less than 200 pounds, and not be pregnant. Because of these requirements, and the fact that a single trip means spending seven hours on a mule, you might want to think twice before you sign up. Reservations are a necessity during the summer, but walk-ups can often be accommodated in the spring and fall; sign the waiting list at Bright Angel Lodge and hope for the best *(303/297-2757)*.

For a bird's-eye view, take an airplane tour of the canyon. Planes depart from the Grand Canyon Airport, but be aware that this sight-seeing option can be expensive. The benefit is that you get to see remote parts of the canyon not viewable from the rim. Helicopter tours are also available, but they have been a source of controversy among naturalists, who say their loud noise disrupts the tranquillity of the area. You can call **Air Star Air Tours** at *(928) 638-2622*, **Papillian Helicopters** at *(928) 638-2419,* or **Kanai Helicopters** at *(928) 638-2764*.

Rafting the Colorado River is a popular way to experience the base of the canyon and stay cool when summer temperatures here soar to over 100 degrees. A number of companies offer Grand Canyon rafting trips on the mighty Colorado River, but children must be over age 12 to go on the longer, more demanding six-day trips (some companies offer shorter tours for kids ages 9 and older). **Western River Adventures** offers three- and four-day trips that leave out of Las Vegas. For more information, call *(800) 453-7450* or check out www.westernriver.com

A more tranquil water/canyon experience can be had by renting a houseboat on Lake Powell.

But no matter how you do it, do it. The sight, the sensation, the awe will linger long after you've put the last photo in your album.

Take advantage of the famous Phoenix weather—the town boasts more than 300 days of sunshine a year.

Phoenix

P HOENIX IS a modern-day boomtown that has fast become a favorite place for family vacations. Its diverse attractions include Major League Baseball spring training, Wild West theme parks and dude ranches, the Heard Museum, where your children will learn about Native American history and culture, and the Arizona Science Center, where your kids find out, among other things, what it's like to be inside a video game.

Many families make pilgrimages to the Valley of the Sun each spring, arguably the best time to visit, when the desert is in bloom and temperatures climb into the balmy 80s. Most fall and winter days are sunny, with temperatures in the 60s and 70s, but the weather varies, and some days the thermometer hovers

THE FamilyFun LIST

MUST-SEE
MUST-SEE

Arizona Science Center
(page 204)

Bank One Ballpark (BOB)
(page 207)

The Heard Museum (page 204)

Lake Havasu (page 208)

Phoenix Zoo (page 209)

Pioneer Arizona Living History Museum (page 205)

Rawhide Western Town and Steakhouse (page 210)

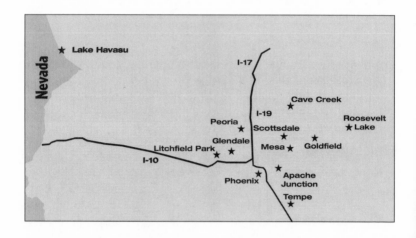

in the 50s, a disappointment if you wanted to hang out by the pool all day. Summer, when temperatures routinely top 100 degrees, is considered the off-season, and many locals leave town for the cooler climes of the mountains two hours to the north. This means that the region's luxury resorts slash their rates to half what they would be during the busier winter and spring seasons, so your family can enjoy incredible pools and lots of pampering at bargain prices.

The **hottest temperature** ever recorded in Arizona was 128 degrees. Lake Havasu City sweltered through that scorcher on June 29, 1994.

Phoenix's weather (more than 300 days of sunshine a year) has drawn legions of transplants, and the region is now home to 2.8 million people, making it the sixth-largest metropolitan area in the country. While the city is generally easy to navigate by car,

it is spread out and you may want to plan your vacation so that you are staying near the attractions you want to enjoy. The sprawling metro area includes tourist-friendly Scottsdale, home to many of the region's luxury resorts, and Tempe, home of Arizona State University and the annual Fiesta Bowl. The Arizona Museum for Youth in Mesa offers child-friendly art exhibits, where works hang at a kid's-eye level, and hands-on art workshops. In Phoenix, you will want to hit the Arizona Science Center and the Phoenix Zoo, which has native desert animals and a simulated rain forest exhibit with gorillas. Youngsters giggle when a goat chews their shoelaces at the petting zoo here, and if they still have any energy after a day of sight-seeing, there's a well-equipped playground.

Your family may also want to get out of town and explore the surrounding mountains, lakes, and historic monuments. For a fun day trip, take a drive on the Apache Trail, originally a path used by Apache Indians to cut through the Superstition Mountains to Roosevelt Lake and the town of Globe. You'll pass sparkling lakes, saguaro cacti, and fields of wildflowers. Or give the kids a history lesson by visiting Montezuma's Castle, a 12th-century Aztec-designed cliff dwelling once home to Pueblo Indians.

If you and your children are sports fans, Phoenix is home to teams from almost every professional sport imaginable. Late winter brings spring training and Major League Baseball's Cactus League. But baseball doesn't end on opening day now that the Diamondbacks are in town. Try to come during a Diamondbacks home stand and check out the amazing Bank One Ballpark, known locally as the BOB. See its retractable roof, which allows the field's natural grass to grow by letting the sunshine in at least every 12 days. There's pro football, too, with the Arizona Cardinals; NHL hockey with the Phoenix Coyotes; and NBA basketball with the Phoenix Suns. Phoenix International Raceway hosts Indy Car and NASCAR events, and the Parada de Sol Rodeo is held every January.

If you're looking for a Wild West adventure, mosey on over to Scottsdale's Rawhide, an 1880s Western town with staged shootouts, pony rides, and a renovated carousel. At the Pioneer Arizona Living History Museum, about 20 miles north of Phoenix, your kids can chat with a female settler churning butter or a blacksmith hammering a horseshoe to find out what living in the Old West was really like. If you want an even more hands-on experience, stay at one of the area's dude ranches. Merv Griffin's Wickenburg Inn welcomes families, even those with little cowpokes under age 6, who want to rope cattle, trail ride, or simply relax by the pool. To learn more about the Native American history of the region, head to the Heard Museum in Phoenix, where your youngsters can wander through a Navajo hogan and see the inside of a Hopi corn-grinding room.

GUESSMASTER

Name a guessmaster—the person who poses a guessing challenge. He or she could ask passengers to guess the color of the next passing car, or how long before you get to the next town. Or, with three clues, what it is that someone else sees.

This area is called the Valley of the Sun for good reason, so come prepared with sunscreen and shades. As with other areas of the arid Southwest, make sure you have bottled water around at all times to avoid dehydration. Then get ready to make the most of all that sunshine.

CULTURAL ADVENTURES

 **Arizona Science** FamilyFun **Center ★★★★/$$**
Plan to spend a day or at least an afternoon at this $47 million museum; it's one of the best children's science centers in the nation and features more than 350 hands-on exhibits. Young children love All About You, which includes the giant sneezing nose and a groovy reflection wall. The second floor showcases a huge ant farm. There's also a virtual-reality game here, which puts your kids inside a video game and a flight simulator. The Fab Lab, on level three, lets kids perform experiments, draw, and play with gears and blocks. On the museum's outdoor terrace, kids can easily spend the better part of an hour in the bubble play area. The center also boasts a state-of-the-art planetarium and a theater with a five-story screen that shows a wide range of films about science from biodiversity to oceanography.

The planetarium offers special shows for children ages 3 to 7, too— these include sing-along songs about the sun and planets. And the location across from Bank One Ballpark makes it a great pregame outing. *600 E. Washington St., Phoenix; (602) 716-2000; www. azscience.org*

Hall of Flame Firefighting Museum ★★/$-$$
Families with firefighting connections or little ones who dream of growing up to be firefighters will enjoy this small museum across from the Phoenix Zoo. It claims to have the largest collection of firefighting apparatus, equipment, and memorabilia in the world. *6101 Van Buren St., Phoenix; (602) 275-3473; www.hallofflame.org*

The Heard Museum
FamilyFun **★★★★/$-$$**
Arizona artifacts and Native American history are the focus of this museum, which looks at the region's indigenous cultures. The exhibits explain the history and social ways of the state's major tribes—Hopi, Zuni, Apache, and Navajo. Kids get to see how members of the tribes actually lived by walking through the Navajo hogan and the Apache wickiup (a hut used by nomadic tribes) displays. There's also a Hopi corn-grinding display and a large exhibit on kachina dolls. But it's not just all look and no

touch. There's an interactive area where kids can pound a drum as they watch a ceremony on a video, learn how to weave, and find out how hard it is to set up a tepee. A 400-seat auditorium hosts music and dance performances most Saturdays. Call ahead for program times and special events. *2301 N. Central Ave., Phoenix; (602) 252-8840; www.heard.org (A smaller satellite site of the Heard Museum is located in Scottsdale and has rotating exhibits and displays. It's located in El Pedregal Festival Marketplace, 34505 N. Scottsdale Rd., Scottsdale; 480/488-9817.)*

Phoenix Art Museum
★★★/$-$$

Older children with an appreciation for fine art will like this museum, which boasts a wide variety of artwork spanning six centuries, including works by Georgia O'Keeffe and Pablo Picasso. Be sure to check out the Thorne Miniature Gallery for an Alice-in-Wonderland experience. (The exhibit features tiny rooms with scaled-down furniture built so that one inch equals one foot.) *1625 N. Central Ave., the northeast corner of Central Ave. and McDowell Rd., Phoenix; (602) 257-1222; www. phxart.org*

Pioneer Arizona Living History Museum
★★★/$-$$

Kids can experience life as it was in pioneer days at this museum, which includes 28 original and reconstructed buildings, among them a carpentry shop, a blacksmith shop, a miner's cabin, a one-room schoolhouse, a church, and a stagecoach station. History comes alive as costumed interpreters go about their everyday activities, explaining what life was like in the pioneer West. Melodramas and occasional gunfights are also staged. The museum's hours vary seasonally: Wednesday through Sunday 9 A.M. through 5 P.M., October through May; Wednesday through Sunday 9 A.M. to 3 P.M., June through September. Be sure to wear comfortable shoes because there's a good bit of walking here. Who said pioneer life was

What If?

Take turns answering these hypothetical questions and then invent some of your own:

♦ If you were king or queen of a country, how would you use your power?
♦ If you could be the best on your block at something, what would it be?
♦ If you could live any place in the world, where would you live and why?
♦ If you were stranded on a desert island and could eat only one kind of food for the rest of your life, what would it be?

easy? *3901 W. Pioneer Rd., exit 225 off I-17, Phoenix; (623) 465-1052; www.pioneer-arizona.com*

Pueblo Grande Museum and Cultural Park ★★★/$

If you want a glimpse into the lives of ancient Native American tribes of this region, this museum—located near downtown Phoenix—is very worthwhile. Your family can walk through the ruins of an ancient Hohokum village that was located along the Salt River between A.D. 300 and 1400. Around 1450, the village and others like it nearby were abandoned, perhaps because of a drought. A small building houses artifacts excavated from the site, but most of the museum is outside, so wear sunscreen and dress appropriately. *4619 E. Washington St., Phoenix; (877) 706-4408 or (602) 495-5645; www.pueblogrand.com*

JUST FOR FUN

America West Arena ★★★/$$$-$$$$

Home to the Phoenix Suns and the Coyotes (the National Hockey League team), this downtown arena is a hot spot in this sports-crazed town. Most of the seats for Suns games are sold out before the season starts, but you might be able to score a few tickets by checking with the box office *(602/379-7800)* either the day before or the day of the game to see if any have been returned.

You can also contact one of the city's ticket agencies, but be prepared to pay a premium. Coyotes tickets can be easier to come by, depending on how their season is going. *Call (888) 255-PUCK or (480) 563-PUCK. 201 E. Jefferson St., Phoenix;* www.american westarena.com

The Apache Trail ★★★/Free

For a fun day trip out of town (best for kids 7 and older), consider driving the Apache Trail, Highway 88, which climbs into the Superstition Mountains. The road begins in downtown Mesa, travels about 20 miles to Apache Junction, then heads northeast to Tortilla Flat into the Tonto National Forest and up to Roosevelt Lake. The road—built in 1904 as an access to the site of the Roosevelt Dam—was named the Apache Trail by the Southern Pacific Railroad to appeal to tourists (although local lore has it that the route was used by the Apaches to travel through the mountains). The trip typically takes two hours each way and includes some hairpin curves, so you may want to give your car-sickness-prone kids some Dramamine before setting out. As the road continues around the Roosevelt Lake, some stretches are unpaved and, while typically passable by car, may be best left to off-road enthusiasts who know their way around. *For more details on enjoying the trail, see "The Apache Trail" day trip on page 210.*

FamilyFun SNACK

Gobbledygook

4 cups oat or crispy rice cereal, 1 cup chopped peanuts, 1 cup raisins or chopped, dried prunes or apricots, 1 cup sunflower seeds,1 cup chopped pretzels, 3 tablespoons butter, melted (optional).

Place all ingredients in a 2-quart plastic bag, seal, and shake to mix.

Bank One Ballpark
FamilyFun ★★★★/$-$$$

MUST-SEE
MUST-SEE

This ballpark is the only Major League stadium we know of that sports a retractable roof and a swimming pool in the outfield. The roof allows fans to enjoy games in cool, air-conditioned temperatures during the heat of summer and then have a few open-air games as the weather moderates. If the roof is open, few seats are better than the ones in the MasterCard Pool Pavilion, located just beyond the right centerfield wall. Groups can reserve the 385-square-foot pool and adjacent spa for $5,250 per game, which includes 25 tickets, 5 parking passes, plus a towel and pair of sandals for each guest. Tickets to games range from $75 for lower level clubhouse seats down to a mere $1 for outfield sections 300 and 332 (on the day of the game only). Families can bring in snacks and water or juice bottles as long as they are in clear bags (such as resealable bags). No coolers, backpacks, or thermoses. If your child needs help seeing the game, guest services can give you a booster seat. You can also watch a game inside the Fridays Front Row Grill, or visit the baseball-themed restaurant on nongame days and simply enjoy the view. There are also concessions throughout the ballpark selling McDonald's, Blimpie, and Little Caesar's Pizza. Tours of the park are offered throughout the year. Tour schedules change based on team playing times and the season, so call ahead. For tickets to a game, call the Arizona Diamondbacks at *(602) 514-8400*; for ballpark tours, call *(602) 462-6799*. *BOB is located at Jefferson and Fifth Sts., Phoenix;* www.bankoneballpark.com

Cerreta Candy Company
★★★/Free

Take this free tour around production time at 10 A.M. or 1 P.M. to see how candy is made and get a free sample. Call ahead and see if your children can get their hands dirty creating a chocolate pizza. *5345 W. Glendale Ave., Glendale; (623) 930-1000;* www.cerreta.com

CrackerJax Family Fun and Sports Park ★★/$-$$

Our pick for the best miniature-golf links in town is this Scottsdale spot. The course has lots of cool colors and can be handled by any would-be duffer ages 3 and up. Other attractions include a huge arcade, go-carts, bumper boats, and batting cages. *16001 N. Scottsdale Rd., Scottsdale; (480) 998-2800;* www.crackerjax.com

Desert Botanical Garden
★★/$-$$

Younger ones may find this boring, but it is a beautiful spot for a picnic and a great place to view desert plants in a natural setting. The Plants and Peoples of the Sonoran Desert Trail exhibit explains how people have used the region's plants to survive and what new plant species they have introduced here. Kids can grind corn and pound mesquite beans to see if they could survive desert living without a McDonald's. There's also a model home that showcases energy- and water-conservation techniques. On spring and fall weekends, the garden hosts musical concerts and lectures. Stay after sunset and you'll see desert flowers that bloom at night. *1201 N. Galvin Pkwy., Phoenix; (480) 941-1225;* www.dbg.org

Dolly Steamboat ★★★/$-$$

Older children will get history and nature lessons while on this boat that tours Canyon Lake. The 90-minute cruise on the reproduction paddle wheeler costs $15 for adults and $8.50 for kids ages 6 to 12. Lunch and dinner cruises are also available (at a higher cost). *Apache Junction at Canyon Lake; (480) 827-9144;* www.dollysteamboat.com

Gameworks
★★/$$-$$$

A video game player's heaven, this complex at Arizona Mills has games for kids of all ages, including a few aimed at 3- to 5-year-olds, but it mainly targets the preteen set with state-of-the-art games. *5000 S. Arizona Mills Pkwy., Tempe; (480) 839-GAME.*

Goldfield Ghost Town and Mine Tours ★★/$

In 1892 gold was discovered here and 4,000 people moved to town. But like so many towns in the West, the mine played out—and by 1925, the town did, too. Your family can pan for gold, tour the old mine, take a ride on a miniature train, and stroll Main Street, keeping a lookout for any gunfights that happen to occur. *4650 N. Mammoth Mine Rd., Goldfield; (480) 983-0333;* www.goldfieldghosttown.com

MUST-SEE FamilyFun Lake Havasu
★★★★/Free-$$$

A great place for strolling, sailing, sleeping—or just crossing London Bridge, this is a must. For more information, see "Lake Havasu" on next page.

Ollie the Trolley ★★/$

If you are staying at a Scottsdale resort, then hop aboard this open-air reproduction trolley, which makes stops at the major shopping and cultural attractions, including

Old Town, Main Street, and Scottsdale Mall. **NOTE:** The trolley runs from November through May and routes are subject to change. Check with your hotel for additional information.

Out of Africa ★★★/$$-$$$

The desert Southwest is just the place you would expect to see a tiger show, right? This wildlife park features tigers, cougars, and other exotic animals and offers feedings and performances throughout the day. The big cats' keepers walk into cages without using whips for protection. There's also a swimming pool where the cats do their laps. *About two miles north of Shea Blvd. off Beeline Hwy. (SR87); 9736 N. Ft. McDowell Rd., Scottsdale; (480) 837-7779.*

Papago Park ★★★/Free

A refuge of red rock and buttes that has a network of trails and picnic areas throughout, this is the place to go to escape the city without really leaving it. *On Gavin Parkway where the cities of Phoenix, Tempe, and Scottsdale merge; (602) 256-3449.*

Phoenix Zoo
FamilyFun ★★★★/$-$$

Home to more than 1,300 animals organized in five different themed areas—among them rainforest and native-desert habitats—the zoo is also home to a baboon colony and some giant Galápagos tortoises. Be sure to get to the large

Lake Havasu

A popular place for Phoenicians to chill out, this lake is one of the busiest recreational areas in the state. The lake itself is beautiful enough, but there's the added fun of seeing London Bridge. Just how did it land in this desert Southwest setting? Chain-saw manufacturer Robert McCullough heard Johnny Carson mention that the famous bridge was for sale, so he bought it—for about $2.4 million—and set it up here. The investment appears to have paid off, as it now ranks as one of the state's most popular tourist attractions, behind the Grand Canyon, and has inspired various mock-Tudor shopping centers and motels.

Spring-break revelers flood the lake in March, but the summer months of June, July, and August are the busiest times for family vacationers. Many families rent houseboats that sleep as many as eight and are available by the half-week or full-week. **Lake Havasu State Park** offers camping facilities and boat launches (*928/855-7851*). Accommodations range from budget motels to moderate upscale resorts such as the **London Bridge Resort** (*1477 Queen's Bay Rd.; 800/624-7939*), where rates range depending on your view of the lake's famous English transplant.

Harmony Farm petting zoo area and the walk-in aviary. You can ride the safari shuttle for a relaxing way to see the animals or get some exercise pedaling around on four-wheel, two-person Deuce Coupe bicycles. *455 N. Galvin Pkwy., Phoenix; (602) 273-1341; www.phoenixzoo.org*

Rawhide Western Town and Steakhouse
★★★★/$$$

Yes, it's a bit corny, but children love visiting this fake Western village that offers stagecoach rides and staged shoot-outs. Take a picture of the kids on the 1880s-era carousel or aboard the steam train. There's also a petting zoo and a town magician. If you don't get your belly full of Old West lore before dinner, head to the Steakhouse Saloon, which must be pretty good—it serves up more than 200,000 pounds of steak each year! More adventurous types can order buffalo and elk burgers. *23023 N. Scottsdale Rd., Scottsdale; (480) 502-1880; www.rawhide.com*

Tempe Town Lake and Rio Salado Park
★★★/Free

This lake is a great place to rent a boat, take an organized sunset cruise, or just look at the water from the shore. Free outdoor concerts are frequently held at Town Lake Beach. Cruises are offered by Rio Lago Cruises (480/517-4050). *The park's offices are at 620 N. Mill Ave. in Tempe; (480) 350-8625;* www.tempe. gov/rio

---

DAY TRIP
The Apache Trail

9 A.M. Start your day with a hearty breakfast—we suggest a dozen doughnuts from **The Iowa Café** (see page 214) in Mesa—then return to downtown Mesa where Main Street becomes the Apache Trail, otherwise known as State Highway 88 as it heads east out of town.

10 A.M. As you approach Apache Junction, look for signs for the **Goldfield Ghost Town** (see page 208). Stop here for a couple of hours and experience the re-created past of an 1890s-era boomtown. Pan for gold, tour the mine, and stroll down Main Street. Be ready for a staged gunfight to erupt at any time.

1 P.M. Head northeast on the Apache Trail to **Tortilla Flat** (see page 214). Stop here to pick up lunch, with a scoop of prickly pear ice cream for dessert, and a few souvenirs. Head southwest back down Highway 88 to Canyon Lake. Hop aboard the **Dolly Steamboat** (see page 208) for a relaxing 90-minute cruise, or head back into Phoenix if you or your kids are ready for an afternoon nap.

BUNKING DOWN

Arizona Biltmore Hotel
★★★★/$$$–$$$$

This lavish, 652-room Art Deco resort was built under the inspiration of Frank Lloyd Wright, who lived in the area in the '30s and '40s. The grounds include gorgeous lawns sprinkled with Adirondack chairs for relaxing. Kids will delight in the fact that the hotel has eight pools and a popular water slide. Families can play with the life-size lawn chess set or enjoy a sedate game of croquet. *2400 E. Missouri Ave., Phoenix; (800) 950-0086; (602) 955-6600; www.arizonabiltmore.com*

Holiday Inn SunSpree Resort
★★/$$–$$$

Though not as plush as some other resorts in town, this middle-of-the-road hotel offers comfort at affordable prices. Some rooms boast mountain views; if you like to spend a lot of time in the pool, ask for a room with a poolside patio. The facilities also offer a volleyball court, croquet, and horseshoes. *7601 E. Indian Bend Rd., Scottsdale; (800) 852-5205; (480) 991-2400; www.holiday-inn.com*

Hyatt Regency Scottsdale
★★★★/$$$$

Families love this resort's fountains (dozens of them), waterfall pools, water slide, and artificial beach. Amenities also include activities at the adjacent Gainey Ranch and the Native American Learning Center. Camp Hyatt Kachina is available for ages 3 to 12. *7500 E. Doubletree Ranch Rd., Scottsdale; (800) 55-HYATT; (480) 991-3388; www.hyatt.com*

Marriott's Camelback Inn
★★★/$$$–$$$$

The 447 rooms at the posh resort all have private patios or balconies and Native American–inspired decor. That said, you probably won't spend too much time inside because the resort offers everything from horseback rides to desert Jeep tours to keep your family busy. There's a full children's program during busy family travel times, including most holidays. Called Hopalong College, the program for kids ages 5 to 12 includes arts and crafts, nature walks, tennis clinics, ice-cream socials, and computer classes. *5402 E. Lincoln Dr., Scottsdale; (800) 24-CAMEL; (480) 948-1700; www.marriott.com*

Mesa/Apache Junction KOA ★★/$

This campground has great views of the Superstition Mountains and offers amenities, including a heated pool and hot tub. It makes a good base for exploring the region and seeing spring training. The camp offers one-room Kamping Kabins that sleep up to six, but remember to bring bedding. *1540 S. Tomahawk Rd., Apache Junction; (480) 982-4015; www.koakampgrounds.com*

Phoenician Resort
★★★★/$$$-$$$$

Amazingly gorgeous, this luxury resort is a real splurge in the winter, but becomes a bargain in the summer when rates are cut in half. Kids can sign up for the Funicians Kids Club, where they have the run of a whimsical clubhouse with computers, a hamster habitat, an arts-and-crafts studio, and a library of books and videos. Children also love the hotel's 165-foot water slide, game arcade, and water-volleyball court. For dining, get spiffed up for a meal at the Windows on the Green, or go casual at the hotel's ice cream parlor that also serves up lunch and breakfast. Rooms and private casitas are ultraluxurious, and tired parents will enjoy being pampered at the Centre for Well-Being Spa. *6000 E. Camelback Rd., Scottsdale; (800) 888-8234; (480) 941-8200;* www.the phoenician.com

Pointe Hilton Resorts
★★★★/$$$-$$$$

Hilton operates two area resorts in Squaw Peak and Tapatio Cliffs. The Tapatio Cliffs resort includes an incredible pool and waterfall, plus a 130-foot water slide. Meanwhile, over at Squaw Peak, you'll find seven pools and a lazy river. While both hotels offer first-rate amenities, plenty of pampering, and large two-room suites, Squaw Peak also has a Coyote Camp for kids ages 4 to 12 with plenty of Southwest–themed activities, which include creating sand art and making bolo ties. Special family packages are offered. *Tapatio Cliffs: 1111 North 7th St., Phoenix; (602) 866-7500; (800) 684-4261. Squaw Peaks: 7677 N. 16th St., Phoenix; (602) 997-2626;* www.hilton.com

The Wigwam ★★★★/$$-$$$$

Built by Goodyear in 1918, this resort is now owned by Starwood Hotels.

Counting the Miles

Last summer, we set out on our first big road trip. To get us through the first long day of driving (500 miles), I strung a long string with a marble-size bead for every 25 miles we would travel. Every fourth bead was a white bead. As we completed each 25 miles, the children moved a bead to the other end of the string. Our children could visualize how far we had to go by how many beads were left. After 100 miles, the white bead was moved, signaling a treat from Mom's bag. Every day, our kids stayed occupied counting the beads, comparing how far we had come to how far we had to go. Our first grader added the 25's and informed us often of our progress.

Jane Rice, Maple Grove, Minnesota

A favorite with active families, the resort offers a dizzying array of activities that change seasonally. The 331-room lodge also offers more than a few ways to burn off energy. There are three 18-hole golf courses, nine tennis courts, two pools, stables, a volleyball court, shuffleboard, Ping-Pong, and croquet. Kids ages 5 to 12 can enroll in Camp Pow Wow, where they can hear Indian stories or take nature hikes. *300 Wigwam Blvd., Litchfield Park; (800) 327-0396; www.wigwamresort.com*

GOOD EATS

Don & Charlie's American Rib and Chop House
★★/$$$-$$$$

This restaurant is famous for its barbecue ribs and baseball memorabilia. If you or your kids are big baseball fans, you could spend an hour just looking at all the autographs and souvenirs on the walls. The children's menu includes a miniature version of the famous ribs, plus cheeseburgers, grilled cheese sandwiches, and pasta. *7501 E. Camelback Rd., Scottsdale; (480) 990-0900;*

Ed Debevic's Short Orders Deluxe ★★★★/$$

Youngsters will love this fifties flashback complete with Elvis jukebox. The owners keep a supply of Hula Hoops by the cash register for active diners. Best of all, your little ones can sing and dance without getting scolded (by the management, that is). The burgers and milk shakes are the best in town—and kids shouldn't have trouble saving room for the World's Smallest Sundae. *2102 E. Highland Ave., Phoenix; (602) 956-2760; www.eddebevics.com*

El Bravo
★★★★/$$-$$$

For a taste of local cuisine, head to this Arizona-Mex restaurant that offers machaca burros, green-corn tamales, and Navajo popovers. Young diners can look forward to a chocolate chimi, the Arizona-Mex version of a s'more. *8338 N. Seventh St., Phoenix; (602) 943-9753.*

Greasewood Flat
★★★/$-$$

This ultracasual stop is an interesting mix of hamburger joint, farm, and dance hall. Kids love the farm animals out back, and parents will appreciate the live music offered most evenings. Your family will also enjoy the restaurant's hearty, but basic, fare such as cheeseburgers, hot dogs, and chicken sandwiches. *27500 N. Alma School Pkwy., Scottsdale; (480) 585-7277.*

Harold's Cave Creek Corral
★★★/$$

This burgers-and-ribs joint also offers live music and a dance floor that's been known to tempt kids away from the video games. *6895 E.*

Cave Creek Rd., Cave Creek; (480) 488-1906; www.haroldscorral.com

The Iowa Café
★★/$

The place for homemade doughnuts. They only offer two kinds—plain and jelly-filled—so kids won't fight over who has more sprinkles. Get here early, before they run out. *5606 E. McKellips Rd., Mesa; (480) 985-2022.*

Rainforest Café
★★★/$$-$$$

Amidst all the waterfalls, trumpeting elephants, and chattering cheetahs, your children can choose from a variety of kids' meals, from chicken fingers to pizza to Gorilla Grilled Cheese. The selection of smoothies is pretty good, too. *Located inside Arizona Mills. 5000 S. Arizona Mills Circle, Tempe; (480) 752-9100;* www.rainforest cafe.com

Rock Springs Café
★★★★/$

About 30 miles north of Phoenix lies this famous café renowned throughout the state for its pies made by local chef extraordinaire Penny Cooley. Her bakery churns out all different types all day long, so you should have a pretty good selection. Eat your slices here or order a pie to go. *Take exit 242 off I-17 and look for the full parking lot; (623) 374-5794.*

Sno-to-Go ★★/$

What better way to cool off from 100-degree summer temperatures than a frosty treat from this roadside stand. Open May through October. *2757 W. Windrose Rd., Phoenix; (602) 375-0403.*

Tortilla Flat ★★★/$$

This former stagecoach stop on the Apache Trail managed to survive and thrive in the era of automobiles by offering hungry tourists plenty of good grub and lots of conversation pieces. Consisting of a restaurant, saloon, and general store, it's definitely an all-purpose stop. *Located on Arizona Hwy. 88, about 20 miles east of Apache Junction; (480) 984-1776.*

Souvenir Hunting

Awesome Atom's

Located in the Arizona Science Center, this store has kid favorites such as ant farms, fake snakes, rocket sets, and wrist walkie-talkies, too. *600 E. Washington St., Phoenix; (602) 716-2000.*

Lisa Frank Clubhouse

Little girls will love this shop, which draws them in with bright pink-and-purple ponies, unicorns, and kittens. *770 W. Bell, Glendale; (623) 773-3490.*

PLAYING AROUND

ONE OF THE BEST WAYS for kids to rub elbows with their ball-playing idols is by taking a trip to one of Arizona's many spring-training facilities. Without the pressure of the regular season, players are more relaxed and have more time to chat and sign autographs. And tickets are cheap, generally a few bucks. Arizona is the spring-training home of ten professional clubs, known together as the Cactus League. (Florida teams are called the Grapefruit League.) With the exception of the Los Angeles Dodgers, all the West Coast clubs train here. Both Chicago teams and the Milwaukee Brewers and Colorado Rockies come, too.

Of the spring-training ballparks, Tempe Diablo Stadium, home of the 2002 World Champion Anaheim Angels, offers the best view, combining red-rock boulders with green outfield grass. For an old-fashioned feel, go to Hi Corbett Field in Tucson's Randolph Park, home of the Colorado Rockies. The Diamondbacks and the White Sox share the new Tucson Electric Park. The Chicago Cubs have the largest spring-training park, Hohokam Park, which holds 12,500.

Some clubs start selling their exhibition-game tickets months in advance, while others don't open the box office until a few days before the players report to training. Call ahead to get ticket information and schedules. For more information, contact the Cactus League Baseball Association, *(800) 283-6372*, or the individual clubs:

Anaheim Angels, Diablo Stadium *(2200 W. Alameda Dr., Tempe; 480/350-5205)*

Chicago Cubs, Hohokam Park Stadium *(1235 N. Center St., Mesa; 480/644-4451)*

Milwaukee Brewers, Maryvale Baseball Park *(3600 N. 51st Ave., Phoenix; 623/245-5500)*

Oakland A's, Phoenix Municipal Stadium *(5999 E. Van Buren St., Phoenix; 602/495-7239)*

San Diego Padres and Seattle Mariners both play at the Peoria Sports Complex *(16101 N. 83rd Ave., Peoria; 623/878-4337)*

San Francisco Giants, Scottsdale Stadium *(7408 E. Osborn Rd., Scottsdale; 480/312-2580; www.ci.scottsdale.us/stadium)*

The following teams play in nearby Tucson:

Chicago White Sox and Arizona Diamondbacks both play at Tucson Electric Park *(2500 E. Ajo Way, Tucson; 520/434-1000)*

Colorado Rockies, Hi Corbett Field *(3400 E. Camino Campestre, Tucson; 520/327-9467)*

Stay at the Lazy K Bar Ranch and take a once-in-a-lifetime ride among the giant saguaro cactii.

Tucson

I F YOUR FAMILY IS looking for a change of scenery, then a trip to Tucson can put you into a new world. The area's trademark saguaro cacti aren't found anywhere else on earth. The mountain ranges that ring the town are a gorgeous backdrop for hikes or for just sitting and viewing the pink-and-purple desert sunsets. It seems almost impossible to get too depressed in a place that claims to be the sunniest city in America, with more than 350 days without rain each year. The warm climate draws many retirees (you may be coming here to visit golfing grandparents) and northerners looking for a respite from snowy winters. Many families come here during their spring break in March to catch preseason action of the Colorado Rockies, the Chicago White Sox, and the Arizona Diamondbacks. (For

THE FamilyFun LIST

MUST-SEE ★ MUST-SEE

Arizona-Sonora Desert Museum (page 219)

Biosphere2 (page 220)

Flandrau Science Center and Planetarium (page 221)

Kartchner Caverns State Park (page 223)

Kitt Peak National Observatory (page 221)

Sabino Canyon (see page 225)

Saguaro National Park (page 226)

Tombstone (page 226)

Tucson Children's Museum (page 222)

217

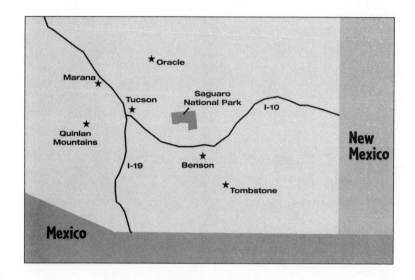

more information on Cactus League Spring Training, see "Playing Around" on page 215.) If you do come during Tucson's high season of October through April, be prepared to pay a bit more for a hotel room and find longer waits at restaurants. If you come during the off-season, generally May through September, call ahead to attractions and restaurants because many close their doors early or don't open them at all during the heat of summer.

Tucson's population of 750,000 makes it the state's second-largest city behind Phoenix, but Tucson seems to have just as many restaurants and resorts as its sprawling neighbor to the north. Your family can find all types of places to stay and eat—from upscale, spalike retreats to guest ranches with trail rides and square dancing. City officials boast that Tucson has more Mexican restaurants per capita than any other American city, not surprising given its proximity to the border. Even if your kids aren't big burrito fans, it's worth trying one of the city's more famous Mexican eateries, such as El Charro (see page 230).

The area's unique desert vistas and sunny climes make it a prime spot for outdoor pursuits, so bring your hiking boots. You can hike trails in the Saguaro National Park, then reward your kids with a dip in the cool swimming holes of Sabino Canyon. There are also plenty of reasons to go underground. Kids will be fascinated by the Biosphere2 project, where a group of scientists attempted to live partially underground, and they'll have fun exploring the giant terrarium. Kartchner Caverns, south of Benson, remained a secret for years but opened to the public in 1999, allowing visitors to see one of the world's rare dry caves.

Tucson is also a mecca for stargazers. At night, the desolate desert and its lack of light pollution make the area a perfect place to gaze into the heavens. Several observatories are located here; one of the most kid-friendly is the Kitt Peak National Observatory, where your family can check out the world's largest solar telescope. If your kids want a basic primer on the planets, consider the Flandrau Science Center and Planetarium, where they'll learn the constellations in the Night Sky Room and see how exploding asteroids create space debris (it will put your kids' messy rooms in perspective).

NOTE: No matter what time of year you travel here, be sure to tote a water bottle. You should always have at least one gallon per person, per day to rehydrate your family. Sunscreen and sunglasses are also must-haves. As you map out your Tucson itinerary, be ready with back-up plans. Despite the very sunny climate, rains pop up suddenly, so it's good to have a nice indoor option ready just in case. In all, a visit to this unique valley is a trip you'll never forget.

Kartchner Caverns State Park is the home of the longest **soda straw stalactite** in the world. The formation is 21.16 feet long and only about as wide as a drop of water!

CULTURAL ADVENTURES

Arizona-Sonora Desert Museum ★★★★/$-$$

To call this a museum is to use the term loosely. It's actually a combination zoo, botanical garden, and educational exhibit that celebrates the plant and animal life of the region's Sonoran desert. Your kids will learn that deserts are far from deserted as they see all the varieties of plants, insects, fish, reptiles, and mammals that make their home here. Coyotes, black bears, mountain lions, beavers, otters, prairie dogs, and javelinas (wild boars) live here, too. Bug-crazy youngsters will want to get up-close looks at scorpions and tarantulas (don't worry; they're behind protective barriers). Docents bring some of the animals out of their cages, so your children may be able to pet a gopher snake or similar creature. And one of the highlights has to be the Hummingbird Aviary, where the tiny birds flutter by, buzzing your face and hands. Two restaurants are above average and either makes for a nice resting spot during your busy day. Ironwood Terraces serves up cafeteria-style fare while Ocatillo Café offers sit-down

219

service. The museum is open daily from 8:30 A.M. to 5 P.M. from October through February and daily from 7:30 A.M. to 5 P.M. from March through September. *2021 N. Kinney Rd., Tucson; (520) 883-2702; (520) 883-1380;* www.desertmuseum.org

Arizona State Museum
★★/Free
This museum is home to some of the area's best Native American artifacts and is a good place for older kids to learn more about the prehistoric and contemporary Native American cultures of the Southwest. The exhibits include a Paleo-Indian spear point that is more than 12,000 years old. The lifestyles and cultural traditions of modern-day Native Americans are explored in the North Building, located across the street. Because the exhibits are mostly behind glass, it's better to bypass this museum if you are traveling with kids under age 7.

But older kids will get a more detailed look at desert cultures than they ever will from their history textbooks. *On the University of Arizona campus, at University Blvd. and Park Ave., Tucson; (520) 621-6302;* www.state museum.arizona.edu

Biosphere2
FamilyFun ★★★★/$$$
In 1991, four men and four women entered this three-acre, airtight greenhouse as part of a grand $150 million experiment to create a separate earth on earth. Life under glass wasn't all it was cracked up to be, and the experiment ended two years later when the air became too low in oxygen and too high in nitrous oxide (laughing gas). The Biospherians emerged with tales of food hoarding and mind games (consider it a precursor to the popular *Survivor* television show). In 1996, Columbia University took over

---

FamilyFun **READER'S TIP** -

Window Box Organizer

In the past on family road trips, I've found that keeping books and games organized and within reach (instead of under the seats) was a challenge for my boys, Joshua, 6, and Brooks, 4. I finally figured out the perfect solution: I purchased a plastic window planter and cut two parallel slits through the bottom of one end. I threaded the middle seat belt through the slits, so the box stays safely attached to the backseat. I even attached battery-operated lights (the kind you clip to books) on both sides of the box so the boys each have a lamp for reading. Best of all, the box keeps them on their own sides of the car, reducing the fight factor tremendously.

Angela Ruder, San Antonio, Texas

the facility, shifting its focus to research and education and opening the doors to curious tourists.

A trip here begins with a short video explaining the original project; after that, there's a guided tour through the massive steel-and-glass structure, including stops in the apartments that once housed its famous residents and walks through the small forests, fields, and algae-laden ponds. Biosphere2 is best for kids ages 9 and over who can appreciate the science and ecology involved in the experiment, but even preschoolers will enjoy walking through the giant terrarium. Three gift shops sell everything from T-shirts to Biosphere shot glasses. Our pick was the snow globe. *32540 South Biosphere Rd., Oracle; (520) 896-6200;* www.bio2.columbia.edu

 **Flandrau Science Center and Planetarium**
★★★/$-$$

Located on the campus of the University of Arizona, the Flandrau Planetarium offers stargazers of all ages a chance to learn more about the universe. The Arizona Night Sky program is open to everyone and focuses on what's going on in the Arizona sky. There are also morning programs for kids. The exhibit halls contain a mineral museum (the largest in the state) and hands-on science exhibits for people of all ages. On clear nights (Wednesdays through Saturdays), you can gaze through the planetarium's 16-inch telescope. (Closed Mondays.) *On the University of Arizona campus, at 1601 E. University Blvd., Tucson; (520) 621-STAR;* www.flandrau.org

Fort Lowell Park ★★/Free

Your kids get to see what Old West life was like at this park, which was once home to the area's cavalry outpost, Fort Lowell. A museum highlights the history of the fort and details the lives of the soldiers stationed here. Youngsters will enjoy seeing some of the ruins of the original fort. The site was also once home to a Hohokam village, and your family can see artifacts uncovered from archaeological digs. *2900 N. Craycroft Rd., Tucson; (520) 885-3832.*

International Wildlife Museum ★★/$$

While the Arizona-Sonora Desert Museum focuses on local animal life, this nearby museum is a grab bag of exhibits that includes an extensive collection of stuffed animals. Kids get a realistic look at now-extinct species such as the Irish elk and the woolly mammoth. *4800 W. Gates Pass Rd., Tucson; (520) 617-1439.*

 **Kitt Peak National Observatory**
★★★★/Free-$

This is arguably the most famous observatory in the region, and it's easily the most family-friendly—but still best for kids 7 and over. Located about 56 miles southwest of Tucson in the Quinlan Mountains, the observatory sits on a 6,882-foot peak. There are 24 major telescopes here, including the McMath Telescope, the largest solar telescope in the world. Three are open to the public, including the McMath. This telescope uses a system of mirrors that reflect the sun's image, reducing it to a 30-inch-diameter figure. The observatory also boasts a 158-inch Mayall telescope, which can peek into the far regions of the universe. There are tours offered of the telescopes and of the adjacent museum, which explains the telescopes and how they are used. There's also a gift shop and bookstore. Plan a nighttime visit during a stargazing program. *56 miles southwest of Tucson, or about 90 minutes. Take Hwy. 86, 44 miles to the Quinlan Mountains; (520) 318-8200; www. noao.edu*

Old Tucson Studios' **Reno Locomotive** was used in the Will Smith summer flick *Wild Wild West*.

Pima Air and Space Museum ★★/$$

This museum claims to have one of the largest collections of historic aircraft in the world. Your kids can get a good idea of the history of American aviation by walking through the more than 250 aircraft displayed here, including replicas of the Wright brothers' 1903 Wright Flyer and the X-15, the world's fastest aircraft. Guided tours are available. If you have aviation buffs in your family (this place will be of interest to kids ages 7 and older who love airplanes), consider the museum's guided tour of Davis Monthan's AMARC (Arizona Maintenance and Regeneration Center) facility, which also goes by the nickname The Boneyard. You can see thousands of planes neatly stored in rows. Tours last just under an hour and cost $6 for adults, and $3 for children 12 and under. Be sure to make tour reservations in advance. *6000 E. Valencia Rd., Tucson; (520) 574-0462; www.pimaair.org*

★MUST-SEE★ Tucson FamilyFun Children's Museum ★MUST-SEE★ ★★★★/$-$$

If you need a fun indoor activity for your kids, consider this hands-on museum where kids can do everything from broadcasting the news to managing a pretend grocery store. In fall 2000, the museum unveiled a robotic dinosaur exhibit and recently opened the Sonoran Sea Aquarium, which is a replica of the oceanic habitats found in the Sea of Cortez. Kids can experience life in a pseudo-submarine, hear whale songs, and see everyday products made with things from the sea.

There is a special area for kids ages 4 and under that has a tree house; there's also a puppet theater where shows are staged daily. In the "bubbles" area children can stand inside a bubble and watch it grow bigger around them. There are plenty of playacting opportunities, too, with a kid-size television studio where they can forecast the weather or deliver the news or a sportscast. Another section offers a place for kids to play firefighter. The museum is closed on Mondays. *200 S. 6th Ave., Tucson; (520) 792-9985;* www. tucsonchildrensmuseum.org

JUST FOR FUN

Breakers Water Park ★★/$$
If you need a break from all that culture, this 20-acre water park features five giant water slides, Splash Canyon, a wave pool, a restaurant, and a snack bar. *8555 W. Tangerine Rd., Marana; (520) 682-2530.*

Funtasticks Family Fun Park ★★/$$
True to its name, this place is home to two miniature-golf courses, go-carts, bumper boats, batting cages, a kiddie theme park, and the city's largest arcade. *221 E. Wetmore Rd., Tucson; (520) 888-5739.*

Golf N' Stuff Family Fun Center ★★/$$
This park has two miniature-golf courses, go-carts, bumper boats, batting cages, laser tag, and The Rock, a rock-climbing area. There's also an arcade and snack bar. *6503 E.*

Tanque Verde Rd., Tucson; (520) 296-2366; www.golfnstuff.com/

 Kartchner Caverns State Park ★★★★/$$

Arizona's latest geological gem opened to the public in 1999 and has quickly become a major tourist attraction. The cave is considered a "living cave," which means it is still growing new formations. It was discovered in 1974, but its existence was kept quiet so it would not be overrun with tourists who could ruin its delicate ecosystems. **NOTE:** Even though it has opened to the public as a state park, access is tightly controlled. Visiting the cave requires making reservations months in advance for a spot on one of the three tours offered each hour or waiting in line at 6 A.M. for the small number of same-day tickets, which go on sale at 8 A.M. Be ready for the misting system that kicks in as you enter the tour (the man-made misting system is used at the entrance to keep the moisture in the cave at a constant

FamilyFun GAME

Crazy Menu
On a paper restaurant menu, take turns crossing out key words. Then have your kids read aloud the new and often grotesque combinations they've created. Anyone for Pepperoni Cake with Strawberry Lettuce?

level despite the many people going in and out), and warn kids not to touch the fragile formations. Thankfully, there is a fake stalagmite they can grab in lieu of the real thing at the adjacent Discovery Center, which also houses the 80,000-year-old bones of a giant ground sloth and exhibits on cave formation. Inside the cave, you'll see red, gray, and brown stalactites and stalagmites, which may remind your family of everything from popcorn to soda straws. **ANOTHER NOTE:** The tour guides focus on geological facts, and preschoolers may be bored by this dry approach—or they may be scared by the strange surroundings. Consider forgoing the 70-minute tour if you have children ages 5 or under. Older kids love the tour's climax—a music-and-light show that starts with the sound of a drop of water (the powerful force that formed the caverns) and ends with an orchestral explosion. *Located 10 miles south of Benson*

The Saguaro
SENTINEL OF THE SONORAN DESERT

The saguaro cactus is a study in survival. In a lifetime that can reach 175 to 200 years, each saguaro produces some 40 million seeds, but only one will likely survive to full maturity. Seeds and young saguaros with the best odds of making it are cared for by "nurse trees," species such as paloverde or mesquite that shelter the young cacti from the intense desert heat, harsh winter cold, and rats, birds, and other desert animals that eat them.

Saguaros are very slow growers. By its first birthday, a young saguaro will have reached only a quarter of an inch in height. A 10-year-old cactus may only be 6 inches tall. At 30 years, a saguaro is old enough to produce fruit and flowers. At 50 years, it can get as tall as 7 feet. And at about 75 years, it begins to grow arms. Saguaros that live the longest—150 years and up—can attain heights of 50 feet or more, and weigh more than 8 tons. But even at these massive sizes, they are vulnerable, often victims of lightning strikes, high winds, and severe droughts. Saguaros rely on a highly efficient root system that can reach 100 feet in diameter. The roots suck up water after a rain, storing enough to survive two years with no additional water. Each spring, waxy white flowers bloom on a saguaro's arms, drawing white doves and bats, which help pollinate the plant and continue its tenuous reproduction cycle.

Biologists believe that harsh freezes are the main reason for saguaro deaths in **Saguaro National Park** (see page 226), which lies at the northernmost extreme of their range. But humans can also be culprits in their demise. Today the park must battle cactus rustlers—vandals who come in and try to remove cacti from the park, to resell to landscapers.

on Hwy. 90. Reservations: (520) 586-2283; other information: (520) 586-4100; www.pr.state/az.us/parkhtml/kartchner.html

Old Tucson Studios
★★/$$–$$$

Once a Wild West movie set originally built for the 1940 film *Arizona*, these studios are now the home to staged shoot-outs, barroom brawls—and amusement rides. The studios are sometimes used as movie sets today, and, if there is something going on, your family can watch the productions. The admission price is good for all games, rides, and entertainment. The studios host a lot of special events such as Halloween Horror shows in October and the Christmas-themed Winter West Fest in December. *201 S. Kinney Rd., Tucson; (520) 883-0100;* www.oldtucson.com

Reid Park Zoo ★★★/$

Smaller than the neighboring Arizona-Sonora Desert Museum, this zoo is an important breeding center for several endangered species, including giant anteaters, white rhinoceroses, tigers, ruffed lemurs, and zebras. Kids either love or hate the exhibit of the South American capybara, whose claim to fame is being the largest rodent in the world. Come early in the day to avoid crowds and afternoon heat. There's a nice playground in the adjacent park, where your young-

sters can work off any leftover energy. *Lake Shore Lane and 22nd St., Tucson; (520) 791-4022.*

Sabino Canyon
MUST-SEE FamilyFun ★★★★/Free–$
MUST-SEE This desert oasis remains a magnet for the thousands of visitors who hike its trails and hang out in the waters and waterfalls of Sabino Creek, especially when spring showers fill its natural swimming pools. The Bear Canyon tram is used by hikers heading from the parking lot to the 2.6-mile trail that leads to picturesque Seven Falls. If you don't feel like hitting the trail, stay on the tram and enjoy the narrated tour and gorgeous scenery of cacti-studded mountain ridges while the driver does all the work. The park occasionally offers moonlight tram rides, a special treat given the desert's beauty under a full moon. The rides are a cool way to let kids stay up past their bedtimes. *5900 N. Sabino Canyon Rd., Tucson; (520) 749-2861; moonlight-tour reservations: (520) 749-2327;* www.sabinocanyon.com

It's a Draw

The **Bird Cage Theater** in the city of Tombstone claims to be the location of the longest poker game in Western history.

The game ran continuously for eight years, five months, and three days; players could opt out of the game whenever they wanted and were immediately replaced by another player who had paid the $1,000 entry fee.

Saguaro National Park
FamilyFun ★★★★/Free-$

This park is divided into two sections—east and west—that serve as bookends to Tucson. The west section is the more popular, both because of its proximity to the Arizona-Sonora Desert Museum and for its dense saguaro forests along the scenic Bajada Loop Drive. Several short, but informative, trails off the drive are easy enough for families traveling with preschoolers—our favorites are the Desert Discovery Trail, located one mile north of the Red Hills visitors' center, and the Signal Hill Petroglyphs Trail, which zigzags up a small hill for a quarter mile to a view of ancient Indian artworks.

To reach the west section of the park, take Speedway Boulevard west from downtown Tucson (it becomes Gates Pass Boulevard). If nothing else, check out the cactus garden behind the visitors' center, which gives you a primer on the desert's major plants.

The east section of the park contains an older area of forest at the foot of the Rincon Mountains. This section is popular with hikers and bikers who tackle the Cactus Forest Loop Drive. Your family can enjoy several trails located along the drive including the quarter-mile Desert Ecology Trail, which has signposts along it explaining the role of water in the desert (this trail is also accessible to people with disabilities). The Freeman Homestead Nature Trail is a one-mile loop located by the Javelina Picnic Area that features informative signs detailing the history of Tucson. For a detailed map of trails, stop at the visitors' center. There is a $6 entry fee per car ($3 per hiker or bicyclist) charged at the east entrance. *To reach the east section, take Speedway Boulevard east, then head south on Freeman Road to Old Spanish Trail. The east district visitors' center is located at 3693 S. Old Spanish Trail; (520) 733-5153. The west district visitors' center is at 2700 N. Kinney Rd.; (520) 733-5158;* www.nps.gov/sagu

Tombstone
FamilyFun ★★★/Free-$$$

Billed as The Town Too Tough To Die, it's now a celebration of the Wild West (both real and imagined). Some families bypass the corny staged gunfights and barroom brawls found here; others love it. But if your "pardners" enjoy Westerns and the Old West, then you'll probably spend the better part of a day exploring this historic town turned Western theme park. The town is a combination of restored buildings and attractions—each one has a separate admission charge, so bring plenty of cash.

The **Historama**, located at Allen and 3rd Streets, is a good starting point for your tour; a 30-minute multimedia presentation highlights the town's colorful history. Next door is the famous **OK Corral** where the shoot-out between Wyatt Earp and Ike Clanton occurred in 1881. There's a staged reenactment every day at 2 P.M. **NOTE:** Tickets cost $4.50 and should be purchased early in the day because they sell out during popular tourist times. Other shoot-outs are staged here as well, and you may find several vying for your attention (and cash).

The **Pioneer Home Museum**, located at Fremont Street (Highway 80) shows what life was like for the typical family 100 years ago. After seeing the town, head over to

Boothill Graveyard, just north of the city limits on Highway 80 where your family can look over some 300 gravestones with some of the most colorful epitaphs you'll ever see. One of the most famous: "Here Lies Lester Moore, 4 slugs from a 44, No Les, no more." *From Benson, take Arizona Highway 80 twenty-one miles southwest to Tombstone; (520) 457-3829;* www.tombstoneweb.com

BUNKING DOWN

Lazy K Bar Ranch
★★★/$$$$

This comfortable, all-inclusive dude ranch is located adjacent to the Saguaro National Park and offers trail rides into the saguaro forests. Rooms are basic, but roomy and comfortable—a definite plus for families. Kids ages 6 and up can join in on the trail rides, and riding lessons are available if you or your little wranglers need some horse sense. Activities include twice-weekly hayrides, square dances, and cookouts by the ranch's incredible 10-foot waterfall and pond. There's also

PERSONAL ADVENTURES

Take turns sharing the memorable events of your lives. What was the scariest thing that ever happened to you? The funniest? The best? The worst? The most embarrassing? What have you done that you are most proud of?

Homemade Energy Bars

These granola bars are chock-full of goodies and will sustain all ages of travelers. Wrap them individually and make extras for tucking into backpacks.

INGREDIENTS

♦ 1 egg
♦ $1/2$ cup brown sugar
♦ 1 teaspoon vanilla extract
♦ 1 cup granola
♦ $1/2$ cup raisins (or any chopped dried fruit)
♦ $1/2$ cup chopped hazelnuts (or your favorite nut)
♦ 1 1.69-ounce package M&M's chocolate candies

Preheat the oven to 350°.

Generously butter or oil an 8- by 8-inch square pan (preferably non-stick). Crack the egg into a medium-size bowl. Add the brown sugar and vanilla extract and mix thoroughly. Stir in the granola, raisins, hazelnuts, and M&M's and mix until combined.

Transfer to the prepared pan and distribute evenly over the bottom, pressing firmly with your hands. Bake for 25 minutes. Cool and cut into bars or squares. Serves 8 to 12.

a library of books and board games you can check out. Telephones and televisions aren't in the rooms, but you can watch a communal set and make calls in the main lodge. Guided nature hikes are also offered. All meals are enjoyed in the main dining hall. This is a relatively small ranch, with only 23 rooms, and it makes for a great family reunion spot. During peak tourist times, the ranch requires a three-night minimum stay. *8401 N. Scenic Dr., Tucson; (520) 744-3050;* www.lazykbar.com

Skywatcher's Inn
★★★★/$-$$

If your kids are avid astronomers, check out this unique inn situated on the grounds of the privately owned Vega-Bray Observatory. The inn provides a bed for the night—they're pretty basic; don't expect room service—and the opportunity to check out the stars through the observatory's telescopes. You can pay a little extra and get some professional guidance from one of the observatory's staff members, or you can do the stargazing on your own. The grounds also include a small science museum, a mile-and-a-half-long nature trail, and a small pond for boating and fishing. Guests can have access to a small kitchen. *The inn is located four miles outside Benson on I-10. For reservations and directions, call (520) 586-7906;* www.communiverse. com/skywatcher

Tanque Verde Ranch
★★★★/$$$$

Spread out over 640 acres in the Rincon Mountains' desert foothills, this ranch offers comfortable casitas complete with fireplaces. This isn't exactly roughing it. There's a giant communal hot tub that's the perfect place for post-trail-ride rejuvenation. In-room massages are also an option. Riding is the big attraction here, and each day brings a variety of options—from breakfast rides to the Old Homestead, to picnic rides in Cottonwood Grove. A ranch program for children is offered including arts and crafts, games and activities, and of course, riding lessons on gentle horses. Kids ages 7 to 11 can enter the Wrangler program, where they go on trail rides (parents are welcome, but don't have to ride along). If horses aren't your thing, there are five tennis courts, a nature center, indoor and outdoor pools, mountain biking, and daily hikes led by a naturalist who discusses the ecosystems of the cacti-and-sagebrush-covered hills. Evening activities include country western dances, and all meals are provided in the main dining room. *14301 E. Speedway Blvd., Tucson; (800) 234-DUDE; (520) 296-6275;* www.tanqueranch.com

Westin La Paloma
★★★★/$$$-$$$$

Located north of Tucson in the Santa Catalina Mountains, this is the kind of place where every family member can kick back and relax. The resort has tennis and volleyball courts, but what your kids will really remember is the huge pool and water slide, which management claims to be the longest in the state. The hotel offers a comprehensive Kids Club, with complementary kid-friendly gifts and amenities. Parents can also request Safety Kits, which include bandages, electrical-outlet covers, and identification bracelets. The kids program costs extra but includes arts and crafts, games, and nature hikes under the supervision of attentive staff members. *3800 E. Sunrise Dr., Tucson; (800) WESTIN-1; (520) 742-6000;* www.westinlapalomaresort.com

Windmill Inn at
St. Phillips Plaza ★★★/$$

This moderately priced hotel has a great location and rooms big enough so your family won't feel squeezed. All the rooms are suites with two televisions, a mini kitchen with refrigerator and microwave, and three telephones (in case you have a family conference call). Other family-friendly amenities include a nice pool, a small library with books and board games you can borrow, and complimentary use of bikes you can use to hit the Rillito River Bike Trail, which starts right behind the hotel. *4250 N. Campbell Ave., Tucson; (800) 547-4747; (520) 577-0007;* www.windmillinns.com/

GOOD EATS

El Charro Café—
★★/$$$$

Located in an old stone building in Tucson's El Presidio Historic District, this restaurant claims to be the city's oldest family-operated Mexican restaurant. Look at the roof of El Charro as you approach, and you might see a large metal cage containing beef drying in the sun. This is the main ingredient in *carne seca*, El Charro's well-known specialty reminiscent of beef jerky. Since *carne seca* is a special Tucson thing, your kids should try it even if they think it will taste like shoe leather. (Who knows? They might like it and

DAY TRIP
Going Underground

I
T'S EASY to make a day trip to Kartchner Caverns and Tombstone if you're staying in Tucson. If possible, make reservations for an early-morning tour of the caverns at least a month or two before your trip here. If you don't have reservations, set your alarm clock extra early and try to get to the park by about 6:30 A.M. to line up for the tickets available for that day. The ticket office opens at 8 A.M. and tickets are generally gone by 8:15.

9 A.M. Tour Kartchner Caverns State Park (see page 223). Be sure to wear something warm because the cave is cool and moist (believe it or not, your clothes will be wet when you leave). Wear comfortable walking shoes for the tour and your stroll through the adjacent Discovery Center (see page 223). Plan to spend at least three hours at the park.

Noon Head over to Tombstone (see page 226). If your kids are up for it, try to get tickets for the 2 P.M. gunfight show at the OK Corral. Grab lunch at the OK Cafe and see if you or your kids are game for the restaurant's exotic burgers (opposite page).

1 P.M. Visit the Historama (see page 227), located at Allen and 3rd Streets, for a quick take on this Wild West town. Then mosey on over to the OK Corral (see page 227) for the big showdown at 2 P.M. If you want to skip the show, go on to the Boothill Graveyard (see page 227) just north of town and check out some of the most interesting epitaphs West of the Mississippi.

3 P.M. Head back to Tucson after enjoying your in-depth (sorry, we couldn't resist) exploration of southern Arizona.

want to lug a bunch home in their suitcase!) Be aware that this place is extremely popular, so make a reservation a day in advance. *311 N. Court Ave., Tucson; (520) 622-1922. (You can also try one of the other locations, including a site at 6310 E. Broadway, Tucson; 520/745-1922.)*

Hidden Valley Inn
★★★★/$$-$$$

Near Sabino Canyon, this restaurant is a great place to rest up after enjoying the canyon's trails. Kids like the colorful cowboy-motif interior, which includes glass cases displaying miniature Western scenes carved from wood. *4825 N. Sabino Canyon Rd., Tucson; (520) 299-4941.*

Horseshoe Café ★★/$$

This restaurant sports an old-time western motif and is a nice respite after your tour of Kartchner Caverns. Save room for the homemade apple pie for dessert. *154 E. 4th St., Benson; (520) 586-3303.*

OK Café
★★/$-$$

If you're looking for a nice place to take a break in Tombstone, head to this casual joint on the main drag. See if your kids are adventurous enough to try a buffalo, ostrich, or emu burger (our 3-year-old "taster" *loves* the emu). Pint-size PETA members can opt for the veggie burgers. *220 E. Allen St., Tombstone; (520) 457-3980.*

SOUVENIR HUNTING

B&B Cactus Farm

Even if you don't buy anything, this store is a showcase for the different varieties of cacti. If you do want to do some shopping, the store will pack your purchase for traveling or ship it so you won't have to cram it in a trunk or an overhead bin. *11550 E. Speedway Blvd., Tucson; (520) 721-4687.*

Picante

Preteens who want to jazz up their rooms with a few "Day of the Dead" skeletons will enjoy stopping at this shop that specializes in Hispanic folk art and accessories. *2932 E. Broadway, Tucson; (520) 320-5699.*

Western Warehouse

If you need to get duded up for the dude ranch, hit this store, which stocks jeans, hats, and boots for big and little cowpokes. *3030 E. Speedway Blvd., Tucson; (520) 327-8005.*

Yikes!

The name of this toy store should be a tip-off that it's not for the faint of heart. Inside are a plethora of rubber spiders, lizards, snakes, and frogs. Kids can also find yo-yos, marbles, and other more traditional toys. *2930 E. Broadway, Tucson; (520) 320-5669.*

Nevada

THE Silver State is a place of extremes—the beautiful natural landscape of Lake Tahoe and the high Sierras and the extravagant creation that is Las Vegas. They couldn't be more popular or more different. What they have in common are great possibilities for a family vacation.

Lake Tahoe (some of which is in California) is a top destination for outdoor enthusiasts. The lake mirrors the gorgeous Sierra Peaks that ring its shores. Your family can ski all morning, picnic on the lake, and catch a boat ride in the afternoon.

The state's mining history

and railroad heritage linger in Virginia City, where a writer named Mark Twain chronicled the hard lives of tough pioneers.

Las Vegas has billed itself as a family-friendly destination, but many parents may disagree. In general, the casinos remain more interested in providing adult fun and games than children's diversions. The trick is looking past the casinos. The famous Strip is a visual treat, but get out of town and enjoy the natural beauty of Lake Mead and Red Rocks State Canyon. If you can't leave Las Vegas, opt for child-friendly attractions like the Lied Discovery Children's Museum.

Whether your family is coming to experience the wonders of nature or human construction, you can bet Nevada has it all.

ATTRACTIONS

$	under $5
$$	$5 - $10
$$$	$10 - $20
$$$$	$20 +

HOTELS/MOTELS/CAMPGROUNDS

$	under $75
$$	$75 - $100
$$$	$100 - $150
$$$$	$150 +

RESTAURANTS

$	under $5
$$	$5 - $10
$$$	$10 - $20
$$$$	$20 +

FAMILYFUN RATED

★	Fine
★★	Good
★★★	Very Good
★★★★	*FamilyFun* Recommended

Combine the natural wonders of the desert with the man-made wonders of the Strip and the Fremont Street Experience *(shown here)* for a grand Vegas vacation.

Las Vegas

L AS VEGAS is proof that excess knows no bounds. Once a dusty, desert train-and-truck-stop and railroad town, it grew into the nation's premier tourist destination as casino operators vied to create the biggest, busiest, and most outlandish resort along an unlikely stretch of desert-cum-concrete now known as the Strip. Where else can you see a volcano erupt—on schedule—watch pirates do battle, tour the Eiffel Tower, and take a gondola ride on Venetian canals—all on the same city block? Your kids will be wide-eyed taking it all in: the seemingly endless dancing lights and color-that-hurts-your-eyes flashing neon, where even the McDonald's sign glitters. In fact, once youngsters experience this city's sensory overload, the "swinging" neighborhood pizza parlor and

THE FamilyFun LIST

MUST-SEE
MUST-SEE

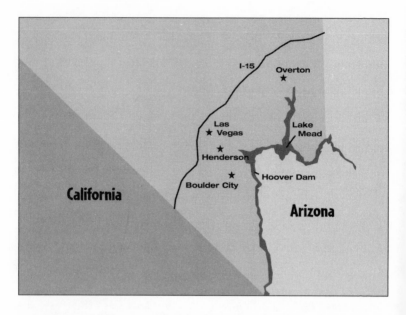

"glitzy" arcade back home will never seem the same.

About three million children accompany their parents to Vegas each year, but be aware that the idea that this place is a family vacation mecca may be a desert mirage. While some resorts tout their children's activities and offer amenities such as circus clowns and roller coasters, the bottom line here is luring Mom and Dad into the casino—where kids aren't allowed to linger. So before you pack your bags, think about why you really want to go. Is it the excitement of the craps tables? The thrill of hitting 21 or catching a lounge act? If so, make the trip without your kids. Too many parents say they are going to Vegas for a family trip, but end up parking their kids in child

care or arcades for hours on end. And though many casinos offer these arcades, specifically aimed at youngsters, they also stress that these facilities should not be considered free baby-sitting. If you want a break to try your luck or indulge in a romantic dinner (and there's certainly nothing wrong with that—even on a family vacation), then check out the licensed child-care centers offered at the MGM Grand, Sunset Station, and Orleans resorts.

That said, Las Vegas can work as a family destination, if you truly decide to experience it as a family—which means spending time together touring the city's nongaming attractions such as the Lied Discovery Children's Museum, taking in one of the handful of family-friendly shows such as Tournament of Kings at Excalibur, or, even better, getting out of town altogether for a swim in Lake Mead, a tour of the Hoover Dam, or a drive through Red Rock Canyon. (To help you beat the crowds, we've focused on some of the less promoted sites that are popular with families who actually live in the city.)

As for your choice of accommodations, remember that your kids will naturally be curious about the pinging slot machines and roars from around the roulette tables, but they are, by law, forbidden from playing, watching, or even being near any casino games. If you have to walk through a casino to get to your room or other attractions—a common problem—make sure you keep moving. Better still, when choosing a place to stay, consider a noncasino hotel or find one that has a direct path from the parking lot to the room elevators so you won't have to walk the kids through casinos that stretch the length of several football fields. You may want to stay in nearby Boulder City, the only town in Nevada that outlaws gaming, which boasts a charming downtown and views of Lake Mead.

Some things are unavoidable, however—Las Vegas isn't dubbed Sin City for nothing. Be ready for a brush with the city's seamier side. It could be as mild as a performance of the Fountains of Bellagio, featuring the provocative tune, "Hey,

Big Spender," or as direct as finding one of the thousands of flyers promoting escort services and topless bars, which are handed out, then cast aside, on the Strip each night. Your 7-year-old daughter may ask you, "What's a table dance?" Bringing your kids to Vegas can mean having that birds-and-bees talk a lot earlier than you had planned. NOTE: Be warned that, as with any large, crowded area, pickpockets can be a problem here.

Forewarned and forearmed, you can have an (almost) all-for-the-family Las Vegas vacation. Whether you want to explore the natural wonders of the desert or take in the man-made wonders of the Strip, the best of Vegas can be enjoyed—with some planning and, of course, a bit of good luck.

CULTURAL ADVENTURES

MUST-SEE Hoover Dam
FamilyFun ★★★★/Free-$$$$
MUST-SEE Want to see what really powers Vegas? Head about 30 miles southeast of town to this marvel of 20th-century engineering. Construction began in 1931, and it took more than 5,000 laborers working 24 hours a day to complete it in 1936. Visit in the early morning (the visitors' center opens at 9 A.M.) to avoid the crowds and

summer heat. If you are on a tight schedule or are traveling with an impatient preschooler, just take a quick look and a few photos (that's the free part) and head to one of the snack and gift shops. The Arizona side of the dam is generally less crowded and may be a better bet if you have young kids in tow. If you want a more in-depth look at the marvel, take the guided, 30-minute Discovery Tour, which leave from the visitors' center lobby every 15 minutes ($10). The tours are not recommended for claustrophobics because you take an elevator down 561 feet and walk through a tunnel to get to the dam's base and mon-

FamilyFun TIP

The Earache Solution

You can often lessen ear discomfort on airplanes by nursing infants, giving tots bottles or pacifiers, and letting older kids chew gum (buy it on your way to the airport because many terminals do not sell chewing gum—workers are tired of cleaning it off floors and chairs). But if your child experiences real ear pain, you can try this funny-looking but often effective trick. Ask the attendant for two plastic cups. Fold a napkin into the bottom of each cup and pour in just enough hot water to moisten the napkins. Then, place the cups over your child's ears, making sure you hold them tightly against his head.

strous turbines. The guides explain how the dam was built—at a cost of $165 million and 96 workers' lives—and the tour is best for kids ages 8 and up. *Hoover Dam is located on U.S. 93 at the Nevada/Arizona state line; (702) 293-8321;* www.hooverdam.com

Las Vegas Natural History Museum ★★★/$-$$

This cultural destination has some good hands-on exhibits—for example, kids can dig for dinosaur fossils and shake a tube of sand to hear what a rattlesnake sounds like. The Wild Nevada Room is a tribute to regional wildlife—from bighorn sheep to the desert tortoise. There's also a new Out of Africa exhibit. The main attraction for your youngsters will be the animatronic dinosaurs that roar as you walk by. *900 Las Vegas Blvd. N., Las Vegas; (702) 384-3466;* www.lvnhm.org

Lied Discovery Children's Museum ★★★★/$-$$

High-tech and hands-on, this museum complex is within walking distance of downtown Las Vegas. There's a musical keyboard mounted on the floor where kids can "hop" or "play" their way through "Twinkle, Twinkle, Little Star." At the Discovery Grocery Store, youngsters get to play postman, sorting mail by zip code, or dress up like a firefighter, which includes donning some very heavy fire-fighting gear. One permanent exhibit even teaches what it's like to play basketball when confined to a wheelchair. At KKID radio studios, kids can do karaoke, while parents sing backup. *833 Las Vegas Blvd. N., Las Vegas; (702) 382-3445;* www.1dcm.org

JUST FOR FUN

Circus Circus Grand Slam Canyon Adventuredome
★★★/Free-$$$

This five-acre theme park has a flume ride, roller coaster, bumper cars, kiddie rides, the Rim Runner boat ride, the new Frog Hopper (which offers the thrill of hopping up and down from a height of 18½ feet; kids must be 36 inches or taller) and laser-tag games. It's behind the hotel, so from Industrial Road to avoid Strip traffic jams. *2880 Las Vegas Blvd. S., Las Vegas; (702) 734-0410;* www.adventuredome.com

Ethel M Chocolate Factory
★★/Free

Got chocoholics? The free, self-guided manufacturing-plant tour and museum here show kids how chocolate candy gets made—and even offers free samples, a clever bid to make you want more from the gift shop. There's an adjacent two-and-a-half-acre cactus garden next door. *2 Cactus Garden Dr., Henderson; (702) 458-8864.*

Fountains of Bellagio
FamilyFun **★★★★/Free**

One of the best shows in Vegas is this $35-million water spectacle that plays—or should we say sprays—in front of the opulent Bellagio resort. The musical accompaniment runs the gamut—from Sinatra to Pavarotti—but the spraying jets of water, all backlit by bright white lights, are guaranteed to enchant folks of all ages. Shows are every 30 minutes from 3 P.M. to 8 P.M., more frequently after 8 P.M. *3600 Las Vegas Blvd. S., Las Vegas; (888) 744-7687.*

Gameworks
★★★/Free-$$$

This is video-game heaven, featuring the latest creations and even "old classics"—like Pac-Man. Instead of pumping quarters into the machines, buy a $10-or-more credit card; it automatically deducts the proper amount until you reach your limit. *3785 Las Vegas Blvd. S., Las Vegas; (702) 432-4263;* www. gameworks.com

★ᵁˢᵀ⁻ˢᴱᴱ Lake Mead
FamilyFun ★★★/**Free**

ᴹᵁˢᵀ⁻ˢᴱᴱ   This surreal, man-made lake looks even bluer against the backdrop of red desert; and the fact that you can swim and boat in the middle of the desert makes this a fun—and unique—place to spend a day or afternoon. The Alan Bible visitors' center, about four miles northeast of Boulder City on U.S. 93, is a good starting point. Inside you can get information about trails, activities, scenic drives, and local wildlife. Several operators rent canoes, fishing boats, or patia boats, and a few offer lake cruises. Boulder Bay, about a mile beyond the visitors' center, is the closest swimming area. In the summer, the water is bath-water warm; in the winter, unless you're a polar bear, it's too chilly for swimming; *(702) 293-8906;* www. nps.gov/lame

Sweet Fortune

It may not be scientifically proven, but the tastiest method of fortune-telling we know involves a big bowl of M&M's.

Grab a small handful and interpret them according to the list below. The more of each color, the greater that particular influence in your life. If you don't like your fortune, eat up and try again!

R E D Self-confidence

O R A N G E Love

Y E L L O W Geekiness (can be canceled out if you also have red and blue)

G R E E N Wishes. For each one you get, you can make a wish that will come true.

B L U E Wealth

B R O W N Health

M&M World ★★★/$

Kids who love this chocolate candy will probably want to see this museum/huge advertisement. A seven-minute film tells the tale of how Red the M&M found his M. Riveting stuff for 4- and 5-year-olds. *In the Showcase Mall, 3785 Las Vegas Blvd. S., Las Vegas; (800) 651-2437; (702) 736-7611;* www.m-ms.com

MGM's Grand Lion Habitat
★★★/**Free-$$$**

The MGM hotel features a Lion Habitat which gives families an up-close encounter with the king of the jungle. You can actually walk inside a see-through tunnel where you are surrounded by the habitat's five lions. Admission to the habitat is free. *Located inside the MGM Grand at 3799 Las Vegas Blvd. S., Las Vegas; (800) 929-1111;* www.mgm grand.com

NEVADA'S NAME was adopted when Congress established the territory in 1861. The state name means "snowcapped" in Spanish.

Race for Atlantis ★★/$$

This 3-D thrill ride simulates a race to the center of Atlantis. Each rider gets a headset and goggles before embarking on a wild ride that thrills some, sickens others. Not for kids under age 10 or anyone subject to motion sickness. If you're up for it, it's one of the best thrill rides in town. *Inside the Forum Shops at Caesars Palace, 3500 Las Vegas Blvd. S., Las Vegas; (702) 893-4800; www.imax.com/raceforatlantis*

Rebel Adventure Hummer Tours ★★★/$$$$

If you don't have a car to tool around in during your Las Vegas stay but want to get out of town, then hop in a Hummer and head for the desert. Rebel Adventure Tours offers air-conditioned Hummer Adventure Tours, which run five hours and include lunch and drinks. The price is a whopping $169 per person, but considering the price tag of a Hummer, it's not a bad deal (you may be able to secure a 10 percent discount for kids, so be sure to ask). The guided tours take you on a unique trek by (and sometimes up) canyon walls. The company also offers Jet Ski tours of Lake Mead and one-day rafting adventures on the Colorado River. Both are best for older kids who can stomach high adventure (meaning they won't get carsick) and parents looking for a cure for the "been there, done that" blues. *713 E. Ogden St., Las Vegas; (800) 817-6789; (702) 380-6969; www.rebeladventuretours.com*

MUST-SEE Red Rock Canyon
FamilyFun ★★★/$$

MUST-SEE Worlds away from the glare and blare of Vegas, but only 20 minutes by car, lies this almost-200,000-acre preserved desert vista of statuesque red-rock formations. Stop at the visitors' center, where kids can sign up to be Junior Rangers (they have to complete a booklet answering questions on local wildlife, to earn their badge and certificate). The park maintains 24 miles of trails, but the best one for kids is the 0.7-mile Children's Discovery Trail, located seven miles past the visitors' center at the turnoff for Willow Springs/Lost Creek. The trail starts in a low-lying valley and climbs up to a stand of trees with benches by a small creek. It's very easy to get lost here, so be sure everyone stays on the trail—and bring plenty of water. *Located 15 miles west of Las Vegas via Charleston Blvd. on State Rd. 159; (702) 363-1921; www.redrockcanyon.org*

Ron Lee's World of Clowns
★★★/Free

Anyone crazy for clowns will love this place, which produces clown figurines and other fanciful creations. Kids can watch as artists mold and paint figures. *330 Carousel Pkwy., Henderson; (800) 829-3928; (702) 434-1700; www. ronlee.com*

Scandia Family Fun Center
★★/$$-$$$

If you're longing to get some outdoor exercise, try this place a few blocks from the Strip that has three miniature-golf courses, miniature-car racing, batting cages, arcade games, and bumper boats. *2900 Sirius Ave., Las Vegas; (702) 364-0070.*

Star Trek: The Experience
★★★/$$$

Trekkies converge on this $70-million attraction that is part museum, part movie, and part ride. You enter through a futuristic version of a casino to begin the wait in line. (Be aware that the wait can stretch two hours or more during peak times.) During your wait, you are entertained by televisions running clips from the famous show and by assorted memorabilia. As you approach the ride, costumed characters advise that you've crossed over into the 24th century. You then begin an out-of-this-world "experience" that combines live theater, a motion-simulation ride, and dazzling special effects. One of the coolest parts is getting "beamed" aboard the *Starship Enterprise.* You also get involved in a wild, and sometimes nausea-inducing, chase through space, but you can skip this part of the ride by simply walking through the spaceship doors instead of taking a seat. **NOTE:** Given the vivid presentation and some of the characters portrayed by the live actors (including evil Klingons), the ride is not suitable for preschoolers and may bore those who never "got" the appeal of Captain Kirk and his crew. It's best left to kids over age 7 and their Spock-loving parents. *Located inside the Las Vegas Hilton, 3000 Paradise Rd., Las Vegas; (702) 732-5111; www.startrekexp.com*

Stratosphere Tower
MUST-SEE FamilyFun MUST-SEE ★★★★/$$

The best overview of town can be had from this vantage point, some 1,150 feet above the Strip. And if the view isn't thrilling enough, there are several roller coasters at the top that will probably frighten all but the most fearless coaster connoisseurs. Don't bother taking preschoolers or kids who are afraid of heights—they'll probably be too scared to look anyway. There's a small charge. Rides cost extra and there are combination tickets offered. *2000 Las Vegas Blvd. S., Las Vegas; (702) 380-7777; www.stratospheretower.com*

MUST-SEE **Treasure Island Pirate**
FamilyFun **Battle** ★★★★/Free
MUST-SEE A pyrotechnic blowout between pirates and sailors, this is one of the best free shows in money-hungry Vegas, which means it is also always very crowded. Shows are performed every 90 minutes (weather permitting) beginning at 5:30 P.M. Stay a bit after the show to watch the captain come back up with his ship—a full three minutes after it sinks. Earlier shows are typically less crowded, but shows after dusk offer a better view of the cannon blasts. For a more private viewing spot, head inside to the Buccaneer Bay Club, an inexpensive restaurant where the waitstaff will hold your order until after the show if you request it. *3300 S. Las Vegas Blvd. S., Las Vegas; (702) 894-7111; (800) 944-7444.*

DAY TRIP

Leaving Las Vegas

A LL THAT NEON can become grating after a while. Here's a great one-day alternative.

9 A.M. Head for **Hoover Dam** (see page 237), arriving well before the heat and crowds take over. Take the 30-minute tour and wander around the huge complex. For grins, head over to the Arizona side to check out another time zone (in winter) and for views from the top of the dam.

Noon Drive back toward **Boulder City.** From Highway 93, turn left at Business 93 (alias Nevada Highway) and wind around the mountainous blacktop until you reach this charming city of bungalows that was built for the workers who constructed the dam.

1 P.M. Head back over to **Lake Mead** (see page 240), checking in at the Alan Bible Visitors Center at U.S. 93 and State Highway 166. Kids can sit in on nature programs, and you can check out opportunities for exploring the lake. One of the best is a lake cruise on the paddle wheeler *Desert Princess*, where you'll also get a narrated tour. The boat departs from the **Lake Mead Lodge** *(322 Lakeshore Dr.; 702/293-6180 for reservations).* Or simply head down to the beach a mile down from the center and take a swim. If it's summer, water temperatures are typically a bath-water warm 80 degrees or higher.

3 P.M. If you still have any energy left on your drive back to Vegas, exit in Henderson for the **Ethel M Chocolate Factory** tour (see page 239)—and some free samples. Nearby is **Ron Lee's World of Clowns** (see page 242), which makes clown figurines and has a working carousel. Pick one or choose to do them both, depending on your stamina.

Your Shows of Shows

Going to Las Vegas without seeing a show would be like taking a trip to Paris and not stopping at the Louvre. Entertainment is considered high art on the Strip and in the surrounding environs, and you will be bombarded with scores of options from the second you get to the airport or tune to a local television station. Some shows are obviously not suitable for children (the word "topless" is a good clue), but many times it is difficult to tell. A magic show may seem like a perfect family outing, until you get inside only to hear profanity and see scantily clad assistants. We have tried to recommend a few shows that are acceptable for families (see "Kid-Friendly Shows" on page 251), but because performers change and shows evolve, you should make sure by asking others who have made recent visits, or question a concierge to get the latest reviews.

If possible, make reservations ahead of time. Be sure to tell the reservations agent that you have children and how old they are; many shows offer discounts for kids. The agent may tell you that your children are too young, some shows ban those under age 6—a good sign you shouldn't be there, anyway. Also ask if there is a certain minimum charge for drinks, another big warning sign. If your child is sensitive to smoke, make sure the theater is smoke-free and request seats as far as possible from any onstage "explosions."

 **Valley of Fire State Park**
★★★★/$

This park gets its name from the unusual coloration of its rocky scenery, which can change from purple to orange to lavender, depending on the vista. Kids will enjoy looking at the rock formations and trying to spot the shapes of birds, snakes, or whatever else they can imagine. Don't miss the petroglyphs, etchings carved into the rocks by ancient Native American tribes. Try to time your visit at sunrise or sunset when the heat is lower and the park's colors are most vibrant. *Valley Fire Rd. (169), Overton; (702) 397-2088;* www.state.nv.us/stateparks

Wet 'n' Wild
★★★/$$$-$$$$

If your hotel pool hasn't saturated your family's desire for aquatic adventures, head to this 26-acre water park on the Strip. The rides include a simulated white-water-rafting adventure and a lazy river. Older kids like the thrill rides such as Der Stuka, billed as the world's largest and highest water chute, and Banzai Baizai, a water roller coaster where you hop on a plastic slide and careen down a 45-degree, 150-foot chute to skip across a 120-foot pool. Younger kids can hang out at the children's water playground, with its gentle waterfalls and water spouts. Discount coupons for admission abound, but call ahead for hours of operation, which vary depending on the time of year. *2601 Las Vegas Blvd. S., Las Vegas; (702) 871-7811; www.wetnwildlv.com*

BUNKING DOWN

Best Western Lighthouse Inn and Resort Boulder City ★★/$

If you're looking for a plain but functional room with breathtaking views of Lake Mead and only 23 miles from the Strip, Boulder City is the place. It's quiet, even relaxing, and close to all the activities in and around Lake Mead and Hoover Dam. Because this is the one town in Nevada that prohibits casinos, Boulder City—and, in particular, this motel—has a more family-friendly feel than anything you can find in Sin City. *110 Ville Dr., Boulder City; (800) 934-8282; (702) 293-6444;* www.bestwestern.com

The number of segments on a **rattle-snake's rattle** shows how many times the creature has shed its skin.

Excalibur
★★★/$$$

This hotel/casino's architecture was inspired by castles in England, Scotland, and Germany. It's full of family-friendly attractions such as the Fantasy Faire, a dark but very large video arcade, and the Court Jester's Stage, where magicians and puppeteers entertain small audiences. Kids love to climb the dragons outside the Sherwood Forest Café, and the Tournament of Kings is one of the few family-oriented entertainment extravaganzas in town. Avoid taking a room in Tower 2 if you want to sleep before 11 P.M.; screams from the nearby New York, New York roller coaster may keep you up. *3850 Las Vegas Blvd. S., Las Vegas; (800) 937-7777; (702) 597-7777;* www.excalibur-casino.com

Four Seasons
★★★★/$$$$

If money is no object, then this is a wonderful place to stay. Don't look for a big Four Seasons sign on the Strip; the hotel is actually tucked inside four floors of the Mandalay Bay Hotel. Given its exterior anonymity, it's one Vegas hotel that actually manages to be quiet and somewhat calming (and there's a separate entrance that does not go through the Mandalay's casino). Four Seasons guests are welcome to use Mandalay Bay's incredible pool and lazy river (there's a separate entrance and lobby) or the Four Seasons' private pool. The concierge desk can provide board games, videos, and video games upon request, and the resort is the only one we know of in town that offers childproofed rooms upon request. *3960 Las Vegas Blvd. S., Las Vegas; (877) 632-5000; (702) 632-5000;* www.fourseasons.com

A TRIP DOWN THE STRIP

THE STRIP, otherwise known as Las Vegas Boulevard, is the spine of Las Vegas and one of the most cruised streets in the world. It's so busy that on many weekend nights traffic doesn't move during rush hour—that's midnight to 2 A.M. in Vegas. If you want to take this very Vegas trek with your children, we suggest going early, around sunset, when all the neon really starts rising and the crowds are still in the casinos. Here's our guide to a quick trip on the Strip.

Enter the Strip from the south at Russell Road (exit 36 off Interstate 15) and look for the famous "Welcome to Las Vegas" sign. It's been a famous landmark and perfect photo op since the 1950s. **NOTE:** The sign is in an island in the middle of the street, so venture out of the car *verrry* carefully—maybe when there's a lull in traffic (ha!).

Head north past Mandalay Bay and the pyramid-shaped Luxor; the Excalibur; New York, New York; and the MGM Grand. Keep going, passing Bellagio; the Aladdin; and Paris, Las Vegas. Pull into the Mirage, find parking, then check out the erupting volcano (which spews every 15 minutes). Head to the **Secret Garden of Siegfried and Roy**, where you can view the duo's famous white tigers. A 15-minute tour takes you through an aquarium of bottle-nosed dolphins and concludes with a film of a dolphin birth. If you exit the Mirage at the south end, you can pick up the Caesars people mover to get to the **Forum Shops**. You could spend hours at this upscale mall; the huge FAO Schwarz could take a day by itself. Mythology comes alive at the Festival Fountain, where the Roman god and goddess statues "put on a show" every hour on the hour with lasers and music. The similar Atlantis show, at the east wing of the mall, tells the tale of a king who must decide whether his son or daughter should get his throne.

Inside Caesars, view a 3-D film at the Omnimax theater.

You will have to quickly move through Caesars' casino and wander by the valet parking lane to get to the small sidewalk back to the Strip (casinos let you get in, but not out, easily). Once you reach the Strip, head toward Bellagio. The upscale hotel and adjacent shops are not child-friendly, and they've actually posted a sign that prohibits anyone under age 18 who is not a hotel guest. But the free Fountains of Bellagio show, which runs every 15 minutes after 7 P.M. on weeknights in the lagoon area in front of the hotel, shows what Old Faithful would be

like if it had spotlights and Sinatra accompaniment.

From Bellagio, cross the pedestrian bridge over Las Vegas Boulevard to get to Paris, Las Vegas. Take an elevator up to the observation deck at the top of the faux Eiffel Tower for a great view of the city; inside the hotel, you'll see a recreation of a bustling Paris neighborhood—only this one has slot machines and blackjack. *Sacré bleu!*

Return to the Strip, walking down to the new Aladdin and the Venetian. Inside the Venetian, head toward the **Venetian Shops,** where you can take a stroll through a simulated Venice and even go on a gondola ride through the fake canals. The lighting on the sky-painted ceiling makes it feel like it is perpetually 4 P.M. Enjoy the ambience, then amble back to the Strip and either head back to your car at the Mirage or take a cab, exhausted and/or energized by your stroll down excess lane.

Hyatt Regency Las Vegas Resort
★★★★/$$$-$$$$

This new resort is located about 20 minutes from the Strip on 25 acres designed to evoke a lush, Mediterranean oasis. Built to cater to conventioneers and golfers, the resort is also family-friendly, with such amenities as a 320-acre lake that includes a swimming lagoon (open March through October). Your family can rent fishing poles and tackle, kayaks, and paddleboats, too. Nature lovers can order free bird-watching backpacks and amateur astronomers can get stargazing guides. The resort also offers Camp Hyatt, a day (and sometimes evening) camp for kids ages 3 to 12. Another plus: families can get a second room for half price, based on availability. *101 MonteLago Blvd., Henderson; (702) 567-1234;* www. hyatt.com

MGM Grand
★★★/$$$-$$$$

This huge hotel has the feel of an international airport as guests wander through its giant casino and adjacent restaurant row, theme park, and shopping mall. If you want to enjoy a few hours without the kids along, you can drop them off to be entertained at the 3,000-square-foot MGM Youth Center; it's the only licensed child-care facility on the Strip and accommodates children ages 3 to 12 for up to five hours. Activities include sports, arts, and video games. Hourly fees vary. *3799 Las Vegas Blvd. S., Las Vegas; (800) 929-1111; (702) 891-7777;* www. mgmgrand.com

Orleans
★★★/$$-$$$
Located a mile west of the Strip, this resort/casino has a family-oriented feel to it, despite its Bourbon Street theme. It's also one of the best bargains in town. Family entertainment includes a 12-screen movie theater and a concert hall called the Branson Theater, which hosts classic rock-and-roll and country acts. Guest rooms are spacious, and all have a small seating area of two chairs and a sofa. There's a view of the Strip from the small shower window in east-facing rooms. Parents appreciate the low rates and easy access from the west parking lot directly to the room elevators. Also available here is the Kids Tyme child-care center for kids 2½ up through 12-year-olds, if you want to leave the kids and enjoy a show or a romantic dinner. The center has a large play structure,

FamilyFun SNACK

Cranberry-nut Snack Mix
Measure 2 cups raw sunflower seeds; 1 cup pine nuts; 1 cup raw pumpkin seeds; 1 cup sweetened, dried cranberries; and 1 cup raisins into a mixing bowl and stir with a wooden spoon. Makes 6 cups.

which costs $5.40 an hour per child, with a maximum stay of three hours. *4500 W. Tropicana Ave., Las Vegas; (800) 675-3267; (702) 365-7111;* www.orleanscasino

Sunset Station
★★★/$$-$$$
This hotel/casino, and its relative, Boulder Station, merit mentioning because Kids Quest, a drop-in day-care facility, has gotten raves from kids who love its huge climbing walls, giant video screens, and three-story Barbie House. Babies (over 6 weeks) are kept in a separate quiet room, while older kids are free to run and jump in the main arena. There is at least one counselor for every eight children; more counselors for younger ones. We've even known some parents who bring their kids here and don't even leave—they just watch the kids have fun. Parents pay from $5.50 to $6.75 an hour and don't have to be guests of the hotel, but they do have to stay on the premises. *1301 W. Sunset Rd., Henderson; (702) 547-7773;* www.sunsetsta tion.com

Treasure Island ★★★/$$$
If your kids like Disney's Pirates of the Caribbean ride, they will love this resort based on the tales of Robert Louis Stevenson. There's a pirate-ship battle staged on Buccaneer Bay, a lagoon facing the Strip, and inside there are plenty of talking skeletons and treasure chests.

The resort also boasts a large pool and game arcade and is home to *Mystère*, the Cirque du Soleil production many consider the best show in town. *3300 Las Vegas Blvd. S., Las Vegas; (800) 288-7206; (702) 894-7111;* www.treasureisland.com

GOOD EATS

Buccaneer Bay Restaurant
★★★/$$
This restaurant inside The Treasure Island Hotel serves up standard kids' fare. It also offers a great view (above the crowds) of the Treasure Island Pirate Battle. Time your visit to the battle so that you can enjoy a feast for the eyes, too. *3300 Las Vegas Blvd. S., Las Vegas; (702) 894-7111.*

Krispy Kreme Doughnuts
★★★/$
Children and parents love these airy, Southern-fried confections; parents have even been known to maneuver across several lanes of traffic when the HOT DOUGHNUTS NOW sign signals a fresh batch. Kids love watching the doughnuts move down the conveyer belt, and hit the gooey wall-of-glaze finish line. *7015 Spring Mountain Rd., Las Vegas; (702) 222-2320;* www.krispykreme.com

McDonald's ★/$
Want to see the Golden Arches all decked out in neon and flashing lights? Check out this glitzy

High-Flying Games

Games that use a pen or pencil are perfect to play on airplanes, since you can lean on the tray top. The following ideas are especially enjoyed by players who are sitting in a row. Unlike backseat games, which can get fairly boisterous, these airplane pastimes are a bit quieter, so you won't make enemies of your fellow fliers.

CRAZY CREATURES
Create strange-looking people, beasts, or any combination of both by folding a piece of paper into three equal sections. One person draws the face in the top section, then folds down the paper so the next person can't see it. That person then draws the midsection of the body, folds down the paper, and passes it to the third person, who sketches the legs in the bottom section. Finally, unfold the paper and name your creature.

TOUCHY TELEPHONE
This is a good game for people sitting in a row. Player 1, on one end, thinks of a word. Player 2, next to 1, closes his or her eyes and holds out an arm. Using a finger, Player 1 "writes" the word on Player 2's arm. The word gets passed down the row—and maybe across the aisle—until it reaches the last person in your party. That person says the word he thinks was written on his arm out loud, and Player 1 says the original word. Let Player 2 start the next round, and so on.

location. *2880 Las Vegas Blvd. S., Las Vegas; (702) 731-1575; www. mcdonalds.com*

Rainforest Café
★★★/$$$

This jungle-theme restaurant has animatronic beasts that take turns sounding the calls of the wild. If this isn't noisy enough (it is!), the decibels rise dramatically when a simulated thunderstorm strikes (about once every hour). The food is so-so—during our visit, our orders of Tuscan chicken and Mogambo shrimp were average at best—but portions are large and you might consider splitting an entrée. Kids' meals include mini hot dogs and Castaway Pizza (plain cheese or pepperoni) and each comes with a souvenir cup. If you want to avoid the large lunch and dinner crowds, consider coming for breakfast, served from 8 to 11 A.M. *Inside the MGM Grand at 3799 Las Vegas Blvd. S., Las Vegas; (702) 891-8580; www.rainforestcafe.com*

Sherwood Forest Café
★★/$$-$$$

This coffeehouse with a kids' menu inside Excalibur is open 24 hours a day and serves breakfast all day long. It's close to the kid-friendly attractions of the hotel, including the lavender dragons that preschoolers love to climb and the Court Jester's Stage, where performers do juggling and clown routines. You can skip

dessert here and head instead to the hotel's food court, which includes a Krispy Kreme outlet and the Cold Stone Ice Cream shop. *3850 Las Vegas Blvd. S., Las Vegas; (702) 597-7777.*

SOUVENIR HUNTING

Dragon's Lair
Inside Excalibur's Realm shops, this store has knightly specials, including a full set of armor. *3850 Las Vegas Blvd. S., Las Vegas; (702) 597-7777.*

FAO Schwarz
Look for the five-story-high Trojan horse to spot the entrance to this toy and game wonderland inside the Forum Shops at Caesars. *3500 Las Vegas Blvd. S., Las Vegas; (702) 796-6500; www.fao.com*

Houdini's Magic Shop
Located inside New York, New York, this magic shop typically has performers who are all too eager to show little ones tricks and even reveal the secrets to performing them. (For a modest fee of $15 or so, your whole family can head into a small room where one of the magicians shows you how his or her tricks are done.) Of course, the kids will want to stock up on magic gear sold at the shop, so be ready to watch your cash disappear. *3790 Las Vegas Blvd. S., Las Vegas; (800) 693-6763; www.houdini.com*

KID-FRIENDLY SHOWS

Cirque du Soleil's *Mystère* and *O*

These two New Age circus shows are among the hottest tickets in town. Most audience members rave about everything from the acrobatic ballet moves to the haunting classical music on mesmerizing sets, but others complain it's just overpriced eye candy. *Mystère* is less expensive and more accessible to children than *O*, which uses a unique stage/pool that has rising and falling water levels. *O* also features a few menacing, ghostlike characters that may frighten young children. But more than likely, the relaxing, repetitive music will actually put them to sleep—a waste considering the high cost of tickets ($100+ for *O*; $80 for *Mystère*). Tickets to both shows are available to guests of Mirage resorts until 28 days before the show dates, when they are released to the general public. Go ahead and order tickets before you get there. Mirage is now offering tickets to *O*, *Mystère*, Danny Gans, EFX, and Siegfried and Roy—use Ticketmaster's Website at www.ticketmaster.com *Mystère*: *Treasure Island Hotel and Casino,* *3300 Las Vegas Blvd. S., Las Vegas;* *(702) 894-7722. O: Bellagio, 3650* *Las Vegas Blvd. S., Las Vegas; (702)* *894-7722;* www.cirquedusoleil.com

Lance Burton: Master Magician

Year after year, this show draws rave reviews from parents and kids alike. While the performance is about as clean-cut as Vegas acts get, Burton did mention, in a recent show, that he and his staff liked to "get drunk." Don't sit in the balcony unless you want to see some of his magic secrets revealed. Kids will like close-up seats with the best views of his stunts (and the possibility of being pulled onstage)— they include pulling a gaggle of geese out of thin air. Tickets (at press time) run $54 to $59 per person; no shows on Sunday or Monday. *Monte Carlo Hotel and Casino, 3770 Las Vegas Blvd. S., Las Vegas; (702) 730-7777.*

Tournament of Kings

This musical version of the legend of King Arthur is not Camelot, but kids like the rowdy antics that include a jousting show. They can yell and scream and even eat with their fingers (no utensils allowed). The food—Cornish hen, potatoes, and tarts (no kids' options)—is average given the $40-plus price per person, for everyone over 4. *Excalibur Hotel and Casino, 3850 Las Vegas Blvd. S., Las Vegas; (702) 597-7600.*

The waters of Lake Tahoe are so clear that kids can see plants and creatures 75 feet below the surface.

Reno and Lake Tahoe

I<small>T'S SMALLER</small>, friendlier, and more scenic than Las Vegas, but the Reno and Lake Tahoe area of Nevada has remained a regional tourist destination, drawing visitors primarily from northern California, Oregon, and Washington State. The area has a bit of a split personality, attracting both gamblers and outdoor enthusiasts in equal numbers. But for families looking for nature next door to plenty of city fun, this alpine wonderland is tough to beat.

Unless you're driving in from the California side, Reno is your likely starting point. Called the Biggest Little City in America, it has many of the same casino names found in Las Vegas but is smaller, friendlier, and less overwhelming than the Strip. Families can comfortably take advantage of the restaurant and entertainment offerings at the

THE **FamilyFun** LIST

Boomtown Family Fun Center
(page 257)

Cave Rock (page 257)

Children's Museum of Northern Nevada (page 255)

Lake Tahoe (page 258)

National Automobile Museum
(page 255)

Virginia and Truckee Railroad
(page 260)

Virginia City (page 260)

Wilbur May Great Basin Adventure Park
(page 261)

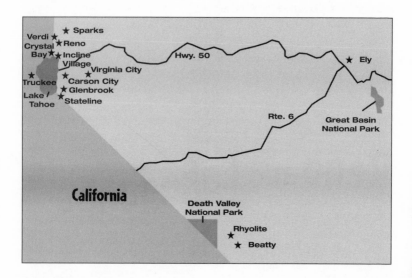

casino resorts while avoiding the gaming areas, where anyone under 21 is prohibited from lingering. Be sure to visit the Wilbur May Center in Reno's Ranch San Rafael Park, where kids can ride ponies and mine for gold in the small theme park or relax in the tranquil indoor arboretum by waterfalls and koi and goldfish ponds.

Before the casinos cashed in, this was mining country. For a historical perspective on the area's past, head to

FamilyFun GAME

Car Scavenger Hunt

Hand your kids a pack of index cards and ask them to write or draw pictures of 50 things they might see on a trip. Keep the cards for scavenger hunts in which players vie to match what they see with the cards.

Virginia City, where you can tour an old mine and ride a steam train on the Virginia and Truckee Railroad. Carson City, the state capital, offers the area's best museums—including the Children's Museum of Northern Nevada and the Nevada State Museum, where you can wander through a full-size replica of a ghost town and an underground mine.

The real jewel of the region is Lake Tahoe and the surrounding mountain peaks, filled with trails for skiers in the winter and for hikers, bikers, and horseback riders in the summer. With its almost perfect climate of warm, dry summers, mild springs and falls, snowy winters, and 300 days of sunshine a year, Tahoe is always an ideal destination. The lake is so clear that underwater life can be seen down to 75 feet. (The lake used to be even clearer and cleaner, but development and the resulting algae growth have muddied the waters a bit.) On busy summer days, when almost 100,000 cars clog the roads around the lake, families can find a respite from the crowds by renting a boat or heading upstream to fish in one of the 63 streams that flow into the lake from the surrounding mountains.

While this guide focuses on the Nevada side of Lake Tahoe, *Family-Fun Vacation Guide: California and Hawaii* looks at the California side of the lake, home to many family-friendly ski resorts, parks, and other attractions. For our part, here are the best, most fun, and most kid-appealing pleasures to be found in and around Nevada's high Sierras.

CULTURAL ADVENTURES

 **Children's Museum of Northern Nevada ★★★/$**

This interactive children's museum, aimed at youngsters ages 2 and up, lets kids do everything from ring up sales in a pretend store to explore the power of wind. There's a stage with dress-up costumes, a pretend emergency room, and collections of Barbie and Ken dolls and antique rocking horses. There's also a huge piano keyboard like the one featured in the film *Big*, and a wall of fun-house

mirrors. *813 N. Carson St., Carson City; (775) 884-2226;* www.cmnn.org

Fleischmann Planetarium ★★/$

Kids can learn more about the stars at shows at this planetarium on the University of Nevada-Reno campus. There's also a small space museum, a public telescope viewing on Friday nights, and the Skydome, a large-format theater. *N. Virginia St., Reno; (775) 784-4811;* http://planetarium.unr.nevada.edu

National Automobile Museum ★★★/$$

The extensive car collection of gambling magnate William Harrah evolved into this museum with 220 classic cars. Many are displayed in period vignettes, making this a nice history lesson on automotive changes through the 20th century. The collection also includes a 1960 Beatnik Bandit, which sports an acrylic bubble top, and a Cadillac once owned by Elvis Presley. A short film tracks America's love affair with cars and how they reflect our dreams. *10 Lake St., South Reno; (775) 333-9300;* www.automuseum.org

Nevada State Museum ★★★/$

Formerly a U.S. Mint, this museum makes for a nice primer on Nevada's history, from how it was formed geologically some 1,750 million years ago to how those rocks panned out later in the state's silver boom and bust. Kids love seeing the Imperial

Lake Tahoe

ALTHOUGH many families love to take to the ski slopes that rim Lake Tahoe, summer is the most popular vacation time here. Here's an itinerary for a summer day at the lake:

8 A.M. Start the morning with a breakfast hayride at the **Ponderosa Ranch** (see page 258) outside Incline Village, then continue driving south on State Highway 28 to U.S. 50 to reach **Stateline**.

Noon Buy provisions for a picnic at **Austin's General Store** (see page 264), then take the Heavenly tram up the mountain and enjoy hiking one or more of the trails there. The Lake Tahoe trail system can be accessed from the Stagecoach parking lot.

3 P.M. Spend the afternoon at **Zephyr Cove Resort** (see page 262), or take a cruise on the *Dixie II* stern-wheeler or the Woodwind glass-bottom boat.

Mammoth, which was found in Nevada's Black Rock Desert. There are replicas of a ghost town and mine and a re-creation of a Great Basin Native American camp. Children can also see some of the state's wildlife (stuffed) including a coyote, mountain lion, badger, and black bear. Check out Under One Sky, too, an exhibit that tells the history of Native Americans in Nevada. *600 N. Carson St., Carson City; (775) 687-4810;* www.nevadaculture.org

Nevada State Railroad Museum ★★/$

This is a great stop for train buffs, but others will be bored. The museum includes antique rolling stock from the Virginia and Truckee Railroad. During the summer, a steam train occasionally makes a loop around the museum, but a motorized car is on hand at other times to offer a short ride. *2180 S. Carson St., Carson City; (775) 687-4180;* www.nsrm-friends.org

Sierra Nevada Children's Museum ★★★/$

This museum just over the California line makes a great morning or afternoon outing. Its interactive exhibits include a pretend grocery store, an art center, and computer corner. The museum is open Wednesday through Saturday and often offers special workshops and events. *11400 Donner Pass Rd., Truckee, California; (530) 587-KIDS.*

JUST FOR FUN

★ Boomtown Family Fun
FamilyFun Center ★★★/$-$$

The place to go for miniature golf, an arcade, and a handful of rides, including an antique carousel, an Old West-style Ferris wheel, and a bucking bronco ride. *I-80 at Boomtown (exit 4) in Verdi; (775) 345-8668.*

★ Cave Rock ★★★/Free
FamilyFun This huge cliff at the south end of Lake Tahoe is sacred to the Washoe Indians, who use it as a burial site. Rock climbers view it as a shrine; in fact, its popularity with climbers forced wildlife management officials to prohibit rock climbing here. The rock is actually the mouth of an ancient volcano and is reputed to be the home of Tahoe Tessie, a distant cousin of the Loch Ness monster. *Cave Rock is located at U.S. 50, three miles south of Glenbrook.*

Circus Circus Hotel and Casino ★★/Free
Jugglers, trapeze artists, and high-wire daredevils are part of the scenery at this huge casino/resort. There's no charge to wander through, but try to stay out of the casino area, where children are not allowed to stop. The family appeal here is mostly on the mezzanine level, where parents and kids can try their hand at carnival games. *500 N. Sierra St.,* Reno; (800) 648-5010; (775) 329-0711; www.circuscircusreno.com

Heavenly Ski Resort ★★★★/$$$$
Located on the California/Nevada border near Stateline, this is the only Tahoe-area resort that offers a licensed child-care center accepting infants as young as 6 weeks. Parents can enroll 3- to 5-year-olds in a special program called Snow Play where they will get comfortable with the idea of skiing while enjoying the snow. If you want to ski and learn along with the kids, opt for the special Tag-a-Long lessons, which include tips on how to get a small child out of a lift—and how to recognize fatigue. The resort's five-minute tram ride up the mountain offers such great views that it's worth a trip even if you don't ski. *From Carson City, take U.S. Highway 50 to the State Line of California. Drive one mile, turn left on Ski Run Blvd. Stateline, Nevada; (800) 243-2836; www.skiheavenly.com*

Idlewild Park ★★★/Free
A shady spot with plenty of picnic tables, this is a great outdoor destination. There's a large children's playground and an outdoor swimming pool, all along the Truckee River. The highlight for younger children is Playland, an amusement park aimed at kids ages 2 to 7 with a merry-go-round, train ride, and small roller coaster. *West of downtown Reno, off California Ave; (775) 334-2270.*

257

⭐ Lake Tahoe
FamilyFun ★★★★/$-$$$
⭐ The lake itself is the thing—be it winter or summer (See "Lake Tahoe" page 256 and Tahoe Rim Trail page 260.)

Magic Carpet Golf ★★/$$
You'll find three themed courses, video games, and rides here. *6925 S. Virginia St., Reno; (775) 853-8837.*

Ponderosa Ranch
★★★/$$-$$$
Maybe your kids aren't old enough to remember even the reruns of *Bonanza*, but they can still have fun at this popular tourist spot that replicates the Cartwright family ranch. Mom and Dad will recognize wax figures of Pa, Adam, Hoss, and Little Joe. Get here early to enjoy the breakfast hayride, which offers bacon and pancakes—and a view of Lake Tahoe. Breakfast is served from 8 to 9:30 A.M. daily from Memorial Day through Labor Day. *100 Ponderosa Rd., Incline Village; (775) 831-0691;* www.ponderosa ranch.com

Pyramid Lake ★★★/$
A nice day trip out of Reno is a jaunt to this lake, a remnant of a sea that once covered 8,000 square miles but which now is only 30 miles long. Take State Highway 445 north from Reno and follow the 37 miles of shoreline on the western side of the lake, on the nationally designated scenic byway. The lake is home to the Paiute tribe, who believe the lake was created by Stone Mother. According to the legend, two sons fought so much that their father decided to separate them, putting one to the north of the valley and one to the south. When their mother learned her sons had been cast away, she started crying and her tears filled the valley, creating the lake. **NOTE:** The tribe still controls the lake, and you must acquire a permit from the tribe before fishing, boating, or camping in the area. For information, call the **Pyramid Lake Marina** *(775/476-1156).* Your kids may enjoy seeing the lake's endangered fish species, the cui-ui sucker, at the **Marble Bluff Fish Facilities** *(775/574-0187),* about one mile north of Nixon on State Highway 447. Be sure to take

IN THE 1860S, Carson City was one of the stops for the Pony Express. The mail service ran from Missouri to California and delivered letters and packages far more quickly than shipboard mail did. The Pony Express ceased service after just a year and a half when telegraph service became available nationwide.

a photo of the 400-foot-high pyramid rock formation that rises from the middle of the lake. *State Hwy. 445, northeast from Sparks.*

Rink on the River ★★★/$

This seasonal ice skating rink operated by the Reno Parks and Recreation Department on the banks of the Truckee River recently moved to a larger location offering an 85-foot by 200-foot skating surface. Skate rentals and arcade games are available. *First and Virginia Sts., Reno; (775) 334-2262;* www.cityofreno.com

Riverwalk ★★/Free

Reno's Riverwalk offers a lovely two-block stroll in the heart of the city. It's also home to many of the city's festivals and arts events, including Artown, a summer arts festival held from July 1 to July 31. After dark the city's homeless tend to converge here. *River Avenue, from Virginia to Arlington Sts., Reno.*

Sand Harbor Beach ★★★★/$-$$

Located in the Lake Tahoe Nevada State Park, this popular sunning spot is typically packed by noon on summer weekends. In late July/early August, it's home to the state's Shakespeare Festival, where performances are housed in a unique amphitheater that offers the audience a gorgeous lake-and-mountain view as a backdrop. The park is also a good picnicking spot, with plenty of shaded

One Minute of Words

Everybody gets a pencil and paper. Someone has to be the timekeeper (a good job for a grown-up). The timekeeper picks a letter, tells it to everyone else, and shouts, "Go!" Players write as many words as possible that start with that letter. When a minute is up, the timekeeper says, "Stop!" and all the players put down their pencils. Whoever has the most legitimate words wins. Decide in advance whether you can finish writing a word you've already started when the game ends. Now, give yourself one more minute to write a sentence with as many of the words as you can.

tables. Swimming and boating are other attractions, and there is a boat launch. Rest room facilities are available. *Located south of Incline Village on Hwy. 28, Lake Tahoe; (775) 831-0494.*

Sierra Safari Zoo ★★/$$

Just north of Reno, this small zoo is home to more than 200 animals, including lemurs, a rare Siberian tiger, a bison, a camel, and a hyena. Kids can also pet and feed the deer. Open April through October. Mondays are free. *10200 N. Virginia St., Reno (exit 78 off U.S. 395 North); (775) 677-1101;* www.sierrasafarizoo.com

Tahoe Rim Trail ★★★/Free

This 150-mile system of hiking and horse trails—with mountain biking allowed in designated stretches—provides hiking families with a great trail that overlooks scenic Lake Tahoe. While the trail is popular during the summer months, don't expect to find fast-food restaurants and flushable toilets along the trail. Pack plenty of water and bring your own toilet paper. Most of the trails are moderate in difficulty with a ten-percent average grade. One of the more family-friendly stretches can be accessed at Heavenly Ski's Stagecoach parking lot. Trail maps are available at Chamber of Commerce sites around the lake. Camping is permitted in the Lake Tahoe Nevada State Park in designated areas. *948 Incline Way, Incline Village; (775) 298-0912;* www.tahoerimtrail.com

Victorian Square Fountain ★★★/Free

Here's an ideal place to cool your heels—literally. The ornate fountain shoots streams of water 30 feet in the air. Everyone's encouraged to frolic through the spray. *Victorian Avenue, Sparks.*

Virginia and Truckee Railroad ★★★/$$$

The 1916 Baldwin steam locomotive runs nine times a day every day from the end of May to the end of September, and on weekends in October and November, weather permitting. The 40-minute, six-mile round-trip ride to the Gold Hill depot travels through the Comstock Mining Area. You aren't able to change cars once you are on board, so you may want to play it safe and opt for the partially covered cars instead of the open-air ones, unless you love wind and are wearing lots of sunscreen. *The depot is located at Washington and F Sts., Virginia City; (775) 847-0380;* www.steamtrain.org

Virginia City ★★★★/Free

This city was booming back in the 1860s after miners discovered the rich silver and gold deposits of the Comstock Lode. The boom lasted about 20 years, but residents held on during the lean times—keeping the city from becoming one of Nevada's 600 or so ghost towns. Though only about 1,000 people live here today, it is one of the best-preserved frontier towns in the country. The Ponderosa Saloon on C Street offers a guided tour that includes a foray into a restored portion of an old mine and a railroad tour (for more information, call *775/847-0380*). **NOTE:** If you go, wear a jacket; the temperature in the underground tunnel and the mine is about 52 degrees. The **Mark Twain Museum** (*775/847-0525*) is a must for Tom Sawyer and Huck Finn fans. The museum details the time Twain spent here as a newspaper reporter, which he wrote about in the book *Roughing It.* Avoid the Red Light Museum unless you want the kids to learn about life in a boomtown brothel and see antique sexual aids. *For more information,*

stop at the Virginia City Chamber of Commerce at Avenue C across from the post office, or call (775) 847-0311.

 **Wilbur May Great Basin Adventure Park**
★★★★/$

This park caters to the 2- to 12-year-old set with a log flume, petting zoo, and pony rides all in one spot and surrounded by Rancho San Rafael Park. There's also a replica of a mine, complete with shafts and a gold-

Ghost Towns

The boom and bust times of the 19th-century mining craze drew people from around the world, but when the economy faltered and/or the mineral deposits ran out, most people moved on, leaving more than 600 ghost towns in the state of Nevada. Most of the towns are little more than dust today—thanks to Mother Nature and scavengers who carted away bricks and other artifacts. But a few remain, offering an eerie view of what happens to places that people and time leave behind.

A few guidelines about visiting ghost towns: the first rule of etiquette is to not take anything. Be aware that not all ghost towns are totally abandoned, so be careful about approaching an occupied home. Because of their desolate locations, it's best to make sure you have plenty of gas for your automobile and water for yourselves before heading out on a ghost-town trip. Finally, be careful

to watch for spiders, snakes, and other creatures that have taken up residence.

One of the best-preserved ghost towns is **Rhyolite**, located about two hours northwest of Las Vegas off State Highway 374, west of Beatty, at the edge of Death Valley National Park. Gold was discovered nearby in 1904, and by 1907 the desert town had more than 6,000 people. Now it is totally abandoned. Kids will marvel at the world-famous bottle house—a miner/saloon owner built it out of 20,000 whiskey bottles for lack of any other building material. The large stone ruins here make for great photographs, particularly at sunset. Rhyolite artifacts are on display at the **Beatty Museum** *(Death Valley Hwy. 374; 775/553-2303).*

For a listing and map of the state's ghost towns, contact the **Nevada Commission on Tourism** *(800/945-3281; www.travelnevada.com).*

panning activity area; guided tours are offered, but you can tour on your own if you prefer. In the nature-walk area, kids can climb on

What Makes Sunsets Red?

It's a lovely phenomenon that replays day after day. When the sun rises in the morning, it's a brilliant orange-red; as it climbs into the sky, it seems to gradually lose its color, fading to white; come afternoon, it warms to a fiery red again as it sinks in the west. Seen from space, the sun is a rather ordinary yellow-white star, but viewed through the gassy veil of our atmosphere, its color changes. As white sunlight (which actually consists of a rainbow of colors) passes from outer space into air, it encounters gas molecules that scatter blue light out of the beam. This makes the sky look blue and the sunlight appear more yellow. When the sun is low in the sky, we view it through the thickest bottom layers of our atmosphere. Here, the light encounters extra gas molecules, dust, and pollutants, scattering even more blue light and leaving mostly orange and red light in the beam.

dinosaurs that are about one third the size of what they were when they actually roamed the earth. For quiet times, check out the indoor arboretum and Honey's Garden, with rock gardens, gazebos, waterfalls, and goldfish ponds. Don't forget your camera. Open Tuesday through Sunday, Memorial Day through Labor Day. *1502 Washington St., Reno; (775) 785-4319*; www.may center.com

Wild Island
★★★/$$$
The family amusement complex has a water park called Wild Waters, with a wave pool, lazy river, and children's play area. There's also Adventure Golf, a 36-hole miniature-golf course with elaborate decorations, including a 41-foot castle, and a raceway that offers electric mini cars for younger children and adult-size Indy cars for older drivers. *250 Wild Island Ct., Sparks; (775) 359-2927*; www.wildisland.com

Zephyr Cove Resort
★★★/$-$$$$
One of the best beaches on the lake, Zephyr Cove offers jet-ski and boat rentals through companies such as **Action Watersports** (*775/831-4386*). Your family can also take a relaxing cruise aboard the *Dixie II*, a sternwheeler that operates out of Zephyr Cove Marina (*775/588-3508*). The boat tour gives you a gorgeous view of the lake and includes narration

Foil Boredom

This one is so simple you won't believe it. Just buy a roll of aluminum foil (make sure to remove the saw on the box), and toss it into the backseat. Although foil is hardly a traditional sculpture material, it works. In the hands of your kids, aluminum foil can be turned into snakes, crowns, masks, and more. (You might need to switch activities when it turns into a bat and balls.)

Angela de la Rocha, Sterling, Virginia

explaining its ecosystem. There's also a glass-bottom-boat tour available aboard the *Woodwind* (*775/588-3000*) if you would like the view down under the water. For another water's-eye view, your family can see the lake on a relaxing two-hour tour via a 55-foot catamaran called the *Sierra Cloud* (*775/832-1234*). Horseback riding is here, too, at the **Zephyr Cove Stables** (*775/588-5664*). *On Hwy. 50, just north of Stateline.*

BUNKING DOWN

All the larger resorts on the Nevada side of the state line also house casinos, so keep to the California side if you want to stay in a larger property and avoid the gaming scene. Another option is to rent one of the area's many vacation homes, cabins, or condominiums through a local real-estate agency. *For information about local rental agencies, call the Incline Village and Crystal Bay Visitors Bureau at (800) 468-2463;* www.gotahoe.com

Cal-Neva Resort
★★★/$$$-$$$$

Once owned by Frank Sinatra, this was a playground for the Brat Pack and other Hollywood stars, including Marilyn Monroe. The lodge actually straddles the state line, so your kids can swim from California to Nevada in the pool that overlooks Lake Tahoe. Although the resort attracts mostly couples seeking romance (and time at the craps table), kids are welcomed, too; they can have a "gaming" experience at the hotel's video arcade. Families can opt for one of the 12 cabins with living room and bedroom, or select from one of the 7 two-bedroom chalets. *2 Stateline Rd., Crystal Bay, Nevada; (800) 225-6382; (775) 832-4000;* www.calnevaresort.com

Hyatt Regency Lake Tahoe
★★★★/$$$-$$$$

A $60-million refurbishing is still underway at this lakeside casino resort that's tucked away in the pine trees. Families can still enjoy the two-bedroom suites near the hotel's private beach. As of the fall of 2003, a new and fun-filled Camp Hyatt (for kids ages 3 to 12) will return with plenty of activities. The updated amenities will include a three-tiered heated pool, a newly finished tennis court, and a video-game arcade. *111 Country Club Dr., Incline Village; (800) 233-1234; (775) 832-1234; www.hyatt.com*

GOOD EATS

Austin's Restaurant and General Store and Pie Shoppe ★★★/$$

This restaurant offers hearty home-cooked favorites, plus such kid-friendly "feasts" as chicken strips and grilled cheese sandwiches with fruit on the side. Next door, the general store is picnic-shopping central. Stop here for munchies, quiches, and the trademark homemade pies. *120 Country Club Dr., Lake Tahoe; (775) 832-PIES.*

Johnny Rockets ★★★/$$

You won't have to sing for your supper; the waiters and waitresses here will do it for you. That's part of the fun at this retro '50s diner that serves up burgers and milk shakes inside the Reno Hilton. *2500 E. Second St., Reno; (775) 333-5200; www.johnnyrockets.com/*

Planet Hollywood ★★/$$$

There are two members of this chain in the Northern Nevada galaxy: one at Harrah's Reno *(775/323-7837)* and one at Caesars Tahoe *(775/588-7828)*. Both have zebra-striped tablecloths and plenty of movie props, photos, and TV screens covering the walls. Reno's location features the dress Barbara Stanwyck wore in *The Big Valley* and Vanna White's letter S from *Wheel of Fortune.* At Lake Tahoe, you can check out the phone booth used in *Bill and Ted's Excellent Adventure* and an animatronic penguin from *Batman Returns.* The menu changes, but rest assured—cheeseburgers will always be there. www.planethollywood.com

Sierra Bagel Factory ★★★/$-$$

This is the place to load up on carbs, including fresh bagels, deli sandwiches, wraps, and omelettes. Kids can even get bagels topped with peanut butter and jelly. *Raleys Center, 930 Tahoe Blvd., Incline Village; (775) 832-2245.*

SOUVENIR HUNTING

Mark Twain Books

This bookstore specializing in Western literature is located inside the Mark Twain Museum in Virginia City. *111 South C St., on the corner of C and Taylor Sts., Virginia City; (775) 847-0454.*

GREAT BASIN NATIONAL PARK

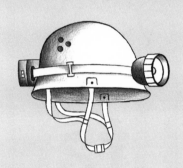

THIS NATIONAL PARK is one of the system's youngest, created in 1986, and most desolate. Its out-of-the-way location on the Nevada-Utah border makes it a great destination for families who want to escape crowds and enjoy the amazing beauty of the Great Basin, so named because most of the area's streams and rivers find no outlet to the sea so water collects in desert salt lakes and marshes until it evaporates in the desert air.

The park's highlights are the **Lehman Caves**, open year-round, and the **Wheeler Peak Scenic Drive**, open seasonally from late spring through early fall. During the summer, the park offers guided bristlecone hikes, campfire programs, and the Junior Rangers program, which allows kids to earn a badge for answering age-appropriate questions on local plant and animal life.

The Lehman Caves are filled with a fantastic collection of stalagmites and stalactites, columns, drapers (cave formations that look like drapes), and rare shield formations.

Three different cave walks are offered: 30-minute, 60-minute, and 90-minute. Children 7 and under should take the short, 30-minute tour. The hour-and-a-half-long tour should only be taken by older children with a very active interest in spelunking (exploring caves). The caves are a constant 50 degrees, so wear a sweater or jacket. All tours include a brief period when the guide turns off the lights to demonstrate darkness. If you think this will be too scary for your child, either opt out of the tour or advise the guide before you leave. You can purchase advance tickets by calling *(775) 234-7331, ext. 242.* All tickets must be paid for at the time of purchase and advance sales are final. www.nps.gov/grba

Reservations may be made as early as 30 days before the tour.

There are a small number of motels available in Baker, Nevada, and campsites inside the park. Because gas and grocery options are limited in Baker, you should gas up and load up your car when you pass through Ely, about 70 miles west of Baker. www.nps.gov/grba

Utah

FROM its snowcapped peaks to its desolate desert canyons, Utah is a place of amazing natural beauty, and its history is as colorful and diverse as its natural landscape. From settlement by the ancient Anasazi to its designation by the Mormons as their final stop, your family can trace the history through museums, cultural centers, and archaeological sites.

The family-oriented national parks, such as Bryce Canyon, are great for showing kids the workings of erosion up close: in the Capitol Reef National Park, your children can learn the quirks of geology as they explore

Salt Lake City

Southern Utah:
Desert Wonderland

lush orchards that grow in a fold of the earth's crust; and at Zion National Park, you can hike past hanging gardens, places where pockets of water nurture life in the desert.

Salt Lake City, the state's capital, has plenty of cultural offerings, including a great zoo and children's museum.

Skiing brings many families to the state's mountain towns, such as Park City and Deer Valley. Only an hour from Salt Lake City's airport, these resorts are a great getaway if you want to hit the slopes in style.

And, although the 2002 Olympics are over, Utah still scores a 10. In fact, there are wonders here you and your family will treasure for a lifetime.

ATTRACTIONS

$	under $5
$$	$5 - $10
$$$	$10 - $20
$$$$	$20 +

HOTELS/MOTELS/CAMPGROUNDS

$	under $50
$$	$50 - $100
$$$	$100 - $200
$$$$	$200 +

RESTAURANTS

$	under $10
$$	$10 - $20
$$$	$20 - $30
$$$$	$30 +

FAMILYFUN RATED

★	Fine
★★	Good
★★★	Very Good
★★★★	_FamilyFun_ Recommended

Kids are always impressed when tour guides drop three straight pins to demonstrate the incredible acoustics of the famous Tabernacle.

Salt Lake City

S ALT LAKE CITY is locked in between the high peaks of the Rocky Mountains to the east and the Great Salt Lake Desert to the west. Now a major airline hub, it lies at the crossroads of Interstate 15 and Interstate 80, earning it the nickname Crossroads of the West. More and more families are discovering the city's cultural attractions, and its proximity to high peaks and ponderosa forests make this a vacation spot that combines arts with altitude.

Once you arrive, you may notice the large number of kids and families here. Utah has one of the highest fertility rates in the country and is statistically the youngest state in the Union. For your family, this means it's easy to find child-friendly hotels and restaurants.

The state's history, culture, and

THE FamilyFun LIST

Children's Museum of Utah
(page 271)

Dinosaur National Monument
(page 271)

The Great Salt Lake and Antelope Island (page 273)

Hogle Zoo (page 274)

Lagoon Amusement Park
(page 276)

Park City (page 277)

Park City Mountain Resort
(page 282)

Wheeler Farm (page 279)

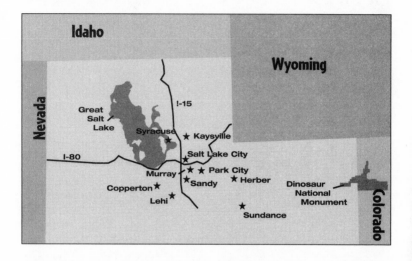

society are dominated by the Church of Jesus Christ of Latter-day Saints, or Mormons, who make up three fourths of the state's population and about half the population of Salt Lake City. Because many Mormons observe Monday as a time for doing things together as a family, many attractions offer special discounts on Monday evenings; your family can also take advantage of these deals—regardless of your religious affiliation. Mormons also believe in the redemption of those already dead, a tenet that has made the church's Family History Library one of the best genealogical resources in the country. If your kids are interested in tracing the family tree, a trip to this center can help uncover a few branches (for

Utah's name comes from the language of the Ute tribe. It means "people of the mountains."

more information, see "Family History Library" on page 278).

Mormon settlers came here in 1847 under the leadership of Brigham Young to escape persecution they faced in New York and Illinois. Today, the Salt Lake Valley is home to more than one million people, including many recent transplants from California and other Western states; most are drawn by the area's vibrant economy and recreational opportunities—child-friendly hiking trails, scenic picnic spots, and gorgeous pine-covered canyons abound.

For the 2002 Olympics, the city was spruced up, widening freeways, building a light-rail system, and adding hotel rooms. If you are driving, you may notice the city's wide streets, a legacy of Brigham Young who decreed they should be 132 feet wide, or wide enough for a covered wagon led by four oxen to pass. Young laid out the streets in a grid pattern, centered on Temple Square, the world headquarters of the Mormon Church. Street addresses can be confusing, but should become clearer if you remember they basically describe how far each site is from Temple Square. For example, the Children's Museum of Utah is located at 840 North 300 West, or about nine blocks north of Temple Square and three blocks west. Don't worry if you don't quite get the system—most locals are willing to help you get to your destination by offering directions.

CULTURAL ADVENTURES

 **Children's Museum of Utah** ★★★★/**$**
This museum was created especially for kids ages 2 to 12 and delights them with hands-on exhibits such as the archaeological dig, where they can actually dig up dinosaur bones (a great prelude to Dinosaur National Monument). There's also a switchboard where they can play operator, a jet they can pilot and land (well, pretend to anyway), and a make-believe area with face paint and other makeup that will keep kids entertained for an

hour or more. *840 North 300 West, Salt Lake City; (801) 328-3383;* www. childmuseum.org

Dinosaur National Monument ★★★★/**$$$**
This park offers two things: gorgeous red-rock canyons and dinosaur bones. To get to the scenery and some easy kid-friendly hikes, enter from the Colorado side of the park. To see the bones, come in from the Utah side on Highway 149 from Jensen. Just so you know, the roads do not meet. From the Colorado side, your family can stop at Monument Headquarters and pick up directions for the self-guided drive and a map of hiking trails. An easy hike for kids is a walk along the half-mile Plug Hat Trail, located by the Plug Hat picnic area on the Harpers Corner Scenic Drive. Exhibits along this easy, level trail describe local history and geology. The Utah side of the park has the Dinosaur Quarry Visitor Center, a working lab where kids can watch scientists at work at the quarry wall. During the summer, rangers give talks about the quarry and the excavation process.

In general, the park is better suited to children ages 7 and older. Younger kids only want to know "Where are the dinosaurs?" Luckily, they aren't far away. The **Utah Field House of Natural History and Dinosaur Garden** in Vernal *(235 E.*

GOLD RUSH

The United States won more medals at the 2002 Salt Lake City Olympic Games than in any previous Winter Olympics. With 34 total medals, the U.S. athletes shattered their previous record of 13 medals, won at the 1998 games in Nagano, Japan.

Main St., Vernal; 435/789-3799) has 18 life-size prehistoric reptiles certain to amaze kids—and their Moms and Dads. If you come here in the summer, and most families do, plan to buy a combination sunscreen/bug repellant; the summer sun and the mosquitoes can be oppressive. *4545 U.S. Hwy. 40, Dinosaur, Colorado; (970) 374-3000;* www.nps.gov/dino

Temple Square
★★/Free
The headquarters of the Church of Jesus Christ of Latter-day Saints, or Mormons, this four-block area is enclosed by 15-foot walls with a gate in the center of each. There are visitors' centers on the north and south sides of the square. **NOTE:** The Temple is closed to non-Mormons, but the Tabernacle is open to the public and is home to the Mormon

Tabernacle Choir. Your family can learn more about the Mormon religion (and get a taste of the church's famous missionary zeal) by taking a free 45-minute tour—best enjoyed by youngsters 7 and older—that leaves from the front of the Tabernacle every 10 to 15 minutes. Kids are impressed when tour guides demonstrate the Tabernacle's incredible acoustics by dropping three pins that sound as clear as a bell even if you stand at the back of the seats. *Bounded by North Temple St., West Temple St., South Temple St., and Main St.; (801) 240-2534.*

Thanksgiving Point Institute
★★★★/$$
Families can spend a day (or two or three) checking out this attraction located midway between Salt Lake City and Provo, which includes botanical gardens, a farm and animal park, and a huge dinosaur museum. The 55-acre botanical gardens include the world's largest man-made waterfall and the Noah's Ark-water park, plus replicas of artist Monet's famous garden and one inspired by the classic children's novel *The Secret Garden*. At the Fox Family Farm, kids can learn where milk comes from, how chicks hatch, and even help slop the pigs. Pony and wagon rides are also part of the experience. If you need an indoor activity, then head for the North American Museum of Ancient Life, which calls itself the world's largest

dinosaur museum. There are plenty of hands-on activities such as fossil-rubbing and building dams and canyons at the Erosion Table. The Village at Thanksgiving Point has shops that showcase Utah arts and crafts and restaurants such as Chubby's Soda Fountain and Huckleberry's Family Restaurant. Thanksgiving Point Institute is open seasonally from April through October and is closed on Sunday. *3003 North Thanksgiving Way (take exit 287 off Interstate 15), Lehi; (888) 672-6040; (801) 768-4971; www. thanksgivingpoint.com*

Just for Fun

Gallivan Center ★★★/Free

A major gathering spot in downtown Salt Lake City, this complex includes a skating rink and amphitheater and frequently hosts arts festivals and free concerts. In winter, it's a great place for a family skate and in summer it's a welcome place to hang out and people-watch. *239 S. Main St., Salt Lake City; (801) 535-6110; www.galli vanevents.com*

 **The Great Salt Lake and Antelope Island**
★★★★/Free-$$

A trip to this lake, one of the most unusual natural landmarks in North America, will be something your children won't soon forget. The lake

has no outlet, so everything that flows into it—more than two million tons of minerals—pretty much stays there. As water evaporates from the lake, the mineral concentration gets higher, making it at least six times saltier than the ocean. (You may see front-loaders scooping up salt at the big Morton Company plant on Interstate 80.) All that salt also means your youngsters will be able to float without floats, a unique thrill; regardless, be careful about non-swimmers going out too deep (please see Note, below). If your kids want to get into the lake, head to the designated beach at Bridger Bay on Antelope Island, where you'll find picnic tables and, most important, public showers where you can wash off the salt after splashing around. **NOTE:** Don't say we didn't warn you—swimming here *is* an unforgettable experience. BUT because of the high saline levels, you need to be extra careful about closing your eyes and mouth when swimming. Also, be prepared for the stench of rotting algae that can waft over the lake. If you're lucky, you'll be upwind of the worst of the odor, or the lake levels will be high enough and it

WATER LEVELS IN THE GREAT SALT LAKE

are inconsistent. In 1963, the water levels were so low that eight of the lake's islands were landlocked. However, twenty years later, the overflowing lake forced Utah to construct pumps to move the excess water to the desert region.

won't be a big problem. You'll probably also notice the brine flies. They shouldn't be too much of a bother since they don't bite, but their presence can be annoying. Interestingly, the "sand" here is made from the crushed bodies of brine shrimp that inhabit the lake.

It's worth a trip to Antelope Island, the largest island in the lake, for its hiking and biking trails (you have to bring your own bikes because there is no rental agency). You can also drive by the island's buffalo corrals and get a photo of your kids with the buffalo in the background. The visitors' center highlights the lake's wildlife, including its importance to migratory birds. *Antelope State Park, 4528 West 1700 South, Syracuse. Take Interstate 15 to exit 335 and go six and a half miles west to the causeway; (801) 773-2941; www.saltlake.org*

Heber Valley Historic Railroad
★★★/$$-$$$
Affectionately dubbed the Heber Creeper, the train trip leaves Salt Lake City on a scenic excursion trip, and takes you through a lush valley, past a large lake, and through a deep

canyon before reaching Vivian Park in Heber City, where your kids can frolic during the half-hour stop before heading back to Salt Lake City. If you're traveling with young children, consider buying one-way tickets and having one parent meet the family at the park instead of taking the 90-minute ride back; spending close to four hours on a train may be too much for a preschooler (and some older children, too).

The train is usually pulled by a vintage steam engine, but occasionally it is replaced by a diesel engine, so you may want to call ahead if you want to hear that whistle blowing (a thrill for little train lovers). The railroad often offers seasonal theme rides, including summer barbecue trains and a special Santa train in December. *450 South 600 West, Salt Lake City; (801) 581-9980; (435) 654-5601; www.hebervalleyrr.org*

 **Hogle Zoo**
FamilyFun ★★★★/$-$$
This zoo is a bit smaller than those in other major cities, but its size makes it easy to navigate. There's a miniature-train ride that

makes a loop past some of the zoo's residents. The unique giraffe house has a balcony so kids can see eye to eye with the tall creatures. Daily programs here include Meet-A-Keeper, where your young explorers can ask zookeepers what it's like to feed tigers and bears. Try to get here early (the zoo opens at 9 A.M.) if you visit in the summer because the animals are not as active during the heat of the afternoon. The zoo has several concession stands for snacks, plus a gift shop. *2600 E. Sunnyside Ave., Salt Lake City; (801) 582-1631;* www.hoglezoo.org

Jordan Commons Super Screen ★★/$-$$

If your kids love movies, a trip to this 70-mm-format center with a screen that measures 60 feet high by 80 feet wide is sure to impress. Part of a 17-screen multiplex, the theater runs popular IMAX films on animals and natural phenomena; showing during a recent visit were *Whales, Wildfires, and Michael Jordan. 9400 S. State St., Sandy; (801) 304-4636;* www.jordancommons.com

Kennecott's Bingham Canyon Mine ★★★/$

Seeing the world's largest open-pit copper mine may amaze your kids or depress them (given the wreckage to the environment). There aren't any guided tours, but the observation area does offer an unforgettable view. If you're lucky, your family may get to see an explosion as workers blast away the rock to get to the copper ore. The visitors' center offers a film that explains the mine's geology and the history of the mine and its operations. There's also a gift shop for copper souvenirs. Closed November through March. *Outside Copperton on Hwy. 48.*

Colors and Numbers

COLOR SAFARI

This all-ages game is easily adaptable to your kids' attention spans. All you do is agree on a basic color—such as red or blue—challenge your kids to find 100 items that are this color. Younger kids can play a shortened version—counting items to 25; older kids will be challenged if you set a time limit and make them race against one another. You can also give each player a different color to search for.

BUZZ

This is a team effort to try to reach 100 without making a mistake. Take turns counting, beginning with one. Every time you get to a number that's divisible by seven (7, 14, 21, . . .) or has a seven in it (17), say "Buzz" instead of the number. If one person forgets to say "Buzz," everyone has to start over. If this is too hard, say "Buzz" for every number divisible by 5.

Lagoon
FamilyFun ★★★/$$-$$$$

This amusement park offers three attractions in one: a traditional theme park with thrill rides and kiddie favorites; a water park with chutes and slides; and a re-creation of a pioneer village. The theme park's history dates back a hundred years, when families came here to swim and ride some newfangled contraption called a roller coaster. The attraction has since grown to include 125 rides, games, restaurants, and shows and can take the better part of a weekend to fully enjoy. It remains a roller-coaster lover's heaven, with every type from the old-fashioned wooden classic to Colossus the Fire Dragon, a steel coaster that reaches speeds of 55 miles per hour as it

FamilyFun TIP

Boning Up

If you go to the **Dinosaur Quarry** visitors' center, you'll be able to see one entire wall filled with more than 1,500 fossils. You and your kids might be wondering why there are so many bones in one area, so we'll tell you.

Long ago, the quarry was part of a river channel and when the river overflowed, it picked up the bodies of deceased dinosaurs. As the waters disappeared, hundreds of dinosaur bones came to rest in the bottom of the riverbed.

hurls you through loops 65 feet in diameter. A ride called the Samurai looks like a giant propeller that spins riders around as their feet dangle. Younger kids will enjoy the kiddie-ride area, which includes a small dragon-themed roller coaster, bumper cars, and a Bulgy the Whale ride.

The Lagoon-A-Beach water park includes waterfalls, bubbling fountains, and a lazy river ride. Thrill seekers can run the Rapids, riding down a 65-foot tube to plummet 70 feet into a wave pool.

Pioneer Village is a re-creation of a Utah town from the 1880s and includes a one-room schoolhouse, log cabin, cobbler shop, music house, and town hall. Be forewarned that gunslingers are common in these parts, so watch for mock shoot-outs.

One admission ticket covers all of Lagoon's many attractions; it is all but impossible, however, to do everything in one day. We suggest hitting the theme park early on the first day, then heading to a show or two in the afternoon before ending the day with a carriage ride through the pioneer village. Come back the second day (if you expect to spend two days here, you can get two-day tickets at a discount rate), again early, and enjoy the water park at a relaxed pace. The park is open weekends only during May and September and daily June through August. *375 N. Lagoon Dr, just off I-*

15, Salt Lake City; (800) 748-5246; www.lagoonpark.com **NOTE:** If your kids scream that they don't want to leave, consider camping at the **Lagoon RV Park and Campground**, adjacent to the park. Amenities include laundry machines, rest rooms and showers, and sandwich and ice-cream shops. *375 Lagoon Dr., Salt Lake City; (800) 748-5246, ext. 3100; (801) 451-8100; www.lagoonpark.com*

Nascart ★★/$

Race each other at this indoor speedway with computerized timing and scoring. Choose between an oval track and a road course. *600 South 4650 West, Salt Lake City; (801) 973-4735; www.nascart.net*

Park City
MUST-SEE FamilyFun ★★★★/Free
MUST-SEE A former silver town, Park City now mines its excellent ski slopes for economic riches, so be prepared to pay resort prices both here and at neighboring Deer Valley, Utah's answer to Aspen. If you're looking to trim costs, consider staying in Salt Lake City and driving here for the day. Despite its name, parking in Park City is a major hassle. Unless you luck into one of the few spots downtown, plan on heading for a satellite lot and getting around via the extensive bus system. The area's ski season generally runs from mid-November to mid-April. All of the three major

Seeing Salt Lake
From the Bottom to the Top

8 A.M. Grab breakfast at **Dee's Family Restaurant** (*143 W. North Temple; 801/359-4414*). This Salt Lake diner serves up great pancakes and omelettes, but you can also order your kids a bowl of cereal.

10 A.M. Hit the **Hogle Zoo** (see page 274). At 11 A.M. your kids can catch the Meet-a-Keeper program offered on weekdays and learn what it's like to feed lions, tigers, and bears.

2 P.M. If the kids (and you) still have energy to burn, check out **This is the Place State Park**, which gets its name from what Brigham Young said when he first saw the Great Salt Lake Valley and led Mormon settlers here. The park is located at *2601 Sunnyside Avenue* and has an admission charge of $1.50 for adults and $1 for children 6 to 12. Head to **Old Deseret**, a pioneer village with authentic cabins from the 19th century. In summer, the park comes to life with costumed workers in period clothes; they'll show kids how many more chores they would have had to do if they had lived back then. After visiting the village, drive around and see if you or your crew can spot a mule deer or hawk.

ski resorts—Deer Valley, The Canyons, and Park City Mountain Resort—offer first-rate ski schools for children ages 3 and up. Deer Valley offers a posh, pampering ski experience. Wolf Mountain has some of the area's steepest runs and may be best left to experts. Park City Mountain Resort is the largest resort and was a training ground for the U.S. Olympic team. For more information on our picks for the area's best ski resorts, see "Snow Business— *FamilyFun*'s Picks" on page 282. *Take I-80 east about 20 miles to the Park City exit; (800) 453-1360*; http://216.122.157.25

Utah Fun Dome ★★★/$

Located in Murray, about 20 miles south of Salt Lake City, there are indoor rides, bowling, and a huge laser tag arena. There's also a year-round fun house and bungee jumping. A kiddie ride area is perfect for the preschool set. Tickets that allow unlimited rides range from $10 for children to $20 for adults. *4998 South 360 West, Murray; 801-265-FUNN (3866);* www.fundome.com

Utah Olympic Park
★★★/$-$$

This facility was home to the bobsled, luge, cross-country skiing, and ski-

Family History Library

With more than two billion names culled from a variety of records, this is arguably the largest genealogical research center in the world. Most of the records date from about 1550 to 1910 and were gleaned from government records, church rolls, and individuals. There is a substantial amount of information on families in the United States and Great Britain, and the center is constantly adding data from other countries around the world. The library grew from the Mormon belief that families are united forever when one of them is baptized in the church. This means baptism applies not just to modern-day believers but to their deceased ancestors as well—which makes it important to know exactly who those forebears were.

To make the most of your visit, come with whatever information you have on your family's history, names, birth dates, and places of residence. Call the library before your trip to receive its visitors' kit. And, when you arrive, you can watch the 15-minute film that explains how to use the center's computers and microfilm, or ask one of the staff members to assist you.

Obviously leafing through thick books and doing computer searches isn't very entertaining to a preschooler, but mature elementary school students and middle school students can make history come alive. Knowing an ancestor fought in the Civil War or came to America through Ellis Island can pique their interest in these and many other historical events. *35 N. West Temple, Salt Lake City; (801) 240-2331.*

jumping events in the 2002 Winter Olympics. Your family can take a tour of the park, its lodge, and its educational displays. You may even catch occasional ski-jump shows featuring quadruple twisting back somersaults—flipping 60 feet in the air before landing in the 750,000-gallon training pool! *3000 Bear Hollow Dr., Park City; (435) 658-4200;* www.utah olympicpark.org

Wheeler Farm
FamilyFun ★★★/$

Your family can enjoy a hayride in the summer or a tractor-pulled wagon ride year-round. If your kids have never milked a cow they can have their chance at 5 P.M. any afternoon. And if you happen to show up in December you can sit down to a hearty breakfast with Santa. *In Cottonwood Regional Park, 6351 South 900 East, Salt Lake City; (801) 264-2241;* www.wheeler farm.com

BUNKING DOWN

Cherry Hill Family Campground & Resort ★★★/$
Stay here and your kids will think you've checked into a theme park. They can splash around at the water park (complete with fountains and a giant pirate ship), hit the miniature-golf links, or learn the finer points of aeroball, a new version of basketball. Whoever said camping

was roughing it obviously didn't stay at this campground. *1325 S. Main St., Kaysville; (801) 451-5379;* www. cherry-hill.com

Salt Lake Hilton
★★★/$$-$$$

The rooms here are spacious, but your kids will be more interested in the hotel's indoor pool. This is also one of the few hotels that welcomes pets (under 25 pounds), in case your child has to bring along a gerbil or poodle. *255 S.W. Temple, Salt Lake City; (800) HILTONS; (801) 328-2000;* www.hilton.com

GOOD EATS

Hard Rock Café
★★★/$$

Located in the city's Trolley Square historic district, this outpost of the popular rock-and-roll chain features memorabilia from Utah's most famous rockers—the Osmond family. It also serves classic cheeseburgers and chicken fingers that are sure to please. *505 South 600 East, Salt Lake City; (801) 532-7625;* www. hardrockcafe.com

Mayan
★★★★/$$

Talk about diving into dinner: at this Acapulco-themed restaurant, Mexican cliff divers entertain while you and your family scarf down tacos and enchiladas. You enter through a stone labyrinth intended to simulate the feel of entering an ancient Mayan temple; your assigned table may be on any of four levels surrounding a huge atrium that affords everyone a view of the cliffs and waterfall, which is center stage for the diving show. Before and after the show, animatronic toucans and iguanas sing, talk, and ask you how you like your burrito (and yes, they expect an answer). For youngsters who get bored with all this excitement, there's an amphitheater with a 36-inch television screen and a computer-game arcade on the third floor. The menu is pretty standard Mexican fare, and the kids' Little Mayan Meals, for ages 9 and under, includes the choice of beef taco, chicken fingers, cheese enchilada, bean burrito, or the Poco PB&J. Kids' meals come with a beverage and dessert for $4.99. The menu has a note that says, "Any person over the age of 4 must purchase a meal." Be forewarned that the restaurant has a large gift shop, selling its trademarked characters, that can be a real kid magnet. Mayan has been a smash since it opened in the spring of 2000, and the wait for a table can be long; try to get here for lunch when it opens (at 11 A.M.) to beat the crowds. *9400 S. State St., Sandy; (801) 304-4600;* www.jordan commons.com

Squatters Salt Lake Brewing Co.
★★★/$$

Despite Utahans' reputation as teetotalers, the city has its share of good brewpubs, including this one with two locations. The kids' menu

---

FamilyFun READER'S TIP

Taste Testers

While traveling cross-country on vacation a few years ago, my husband and I grew tired of our children's requests to visit the same old fast-food places for the latest kids'-meal prize.

So we instituted the no-fast-food rule: when our family hits the road on vacation, we only stop at restaurants we can't visit back home. The idea is to convince the kids to try new things and to find some regional flavor. The rule has an added benefit of taking us off the beaten path a bit. As it gets closer to meal time, we look for one-of-a-kind diners, rib joints, custard shops, and the like.

Thanks to this new rule of ours, we have eaten Indian fry bread in the Badlands, great sloppy ribs in Tennessee, sensational seafood in South Carolina, and more.

Lisa Tepp, Milwaukee, Wisconsin

includes the standard burgers and hot dogs, and families can chill in the outdoor beer garden in the summer or warm by the inside fireplace in the winter. *There is a location inside the airport's Concourse C, and the main site is at 147 West 300 South, Salt Lake City; (801) 363-2739.*

Souvenir Hunting

Chocolate Covered Wagon
Kids can watch an old-style machine pull saltwater taffy, then try it themselves (by hand) at this candy shop in Trolley Square. *335 Trolley Sq., Salt Lake City; (801) 364-3394;* www.trolleytraffic.com

Park City Factory Stores
This discount center includes Carter's Childrenswear and Osh-Kosh B'Gosh outlets. *It's located along I-80 at 6699 N. Landmark Dr., Park City; (435) 645-7078;* www. shopparkcity.com/

United States Olympic Committee Spirit Store
Get your Winter Olympic gear—including sweatshirts, coffee mugs, and key rings—at this nonprofit retail store whose sole purpose is to raise funds for the Olympic movement. *Located in Park City at the base of Main Street beside the Town Lift. 751 Main St., #5, Park City; (435) 655-7597;* www.usolympic team.com

Your Own Olympic Adventure

Give your family a taste of Olympic training at **Gold Medal Adventure day camps**, offered from 10 A.M. to 3 P.M., Tuesday through Friday, from mid-June to mid-September. Sign up for one, two, three, or four days and master new skills such as push-starting a wheeled bobsled, maneuvering a kayak or canoe, even freestyle skiing on a trampoline.

Depending on which day you choose, your coaches could be figure skaters, Nordic ski jumpers, or members of the national luge team. You'll also get to meet world-class athletes and tour the Olympic venues where they train.

Gold Medal Adventure camps are open to children 7 and older. The cost of $55 per person per day (discounts are available for multidays) includes coaching, all equipment, lunch, tours, transportation between venues, and a souvenir. You need reservations for June and September programs, and they are recommended for July and August sessions. For more information or to make reservations, *call (518) 523-1655, ext. 250.*

SNOW BUSINESS—*FAMILYFUN'S* PICKS

I N CASE you haven't noticed, Utah's license plates have a not-so-subtle message: "Ski Utah! The Greatest Snow on Earth." For families, Utah's resorts offer extensive kids' programs, plenty of après-ski activities, and sometimes, lower-priced lift tickets than you'd find next door in Colorado. Here are three resorts that go out of their way to entertain, enlighten, and educate kids on and off the slopes.

Brian Head Resort ★★★/$$$

This out-of-the-way resort in southern Utah between Las Vegas and Salt Lake City (see map page 286) has a laid-back feel and carefully planned kids program at attractive prices. Lift tickets are $40 for adults during peak holiday periods and $38 much of the rest of the year. Kids age 5 and under ski free. The kids' camp is designed for kids under age 12, including a Tiny Tracks program for ages 3 to 5 and a snowboard Mountain Explorers program for ages 6 to 12. Day care is offered for kids who don't want to hit the slopes. Snow Tube Park lets you burn rubber at one of the state's best tubing hills. In spring and summer the focus is on hiking and biking. *329 South Highway 143, Brian Head; (435) 677-2035; www. brianhead.com.* Lodging is available in area condos ranging from $85 to $500 and up per night. A family favorite is the Cedar Breaks Lodge, which offers one-, two-, and three-bedroom suites with kitchens. Fuel up at the Columbine Café breakfast with buttermilk pancakes or *huevos rancheros. 223 Hunter Ridge Rd., Brian Head; (888) 282-3327; www.cedar breakslodge.com*

Park City Mountain Resort ★★★/$$$$

The largest of the major Park City ski resorts, it offers a learn-to-ski or snowboard program designed specifically for youngsters ages 7 to 12. The resort's Legacy Lodge offers one-stop shopping, dining, and ski services—including equipment rental and lift tickets. In the summer, kids can rocket the bobsled run—which has a 550-foot vertical drop—or putter around the 18-hole miniature-golf course. Preschoolers will love Little Miner's Park and its kiddie rides, while pre-teens can take the ski lift up the mountain and hike or bike down. There's also a giant trampoline where your young acrobats can jump, flip, twist, and spin through the air while safely snapped in a harness. **NOTE:** Rather than getting nickel-and-dimed to death paying for each ride individually, consider buying a $25 wristband that gives each person unlimited access to all the rides, except horseback riding. The catch is you have to come Monday through Thursday from 3 to 6 P.M. *(800) 222-7275;* www.park citymountain.com

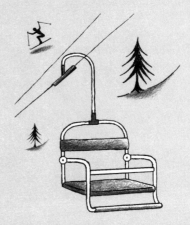

The Sundance Institute
★★★★/$$-$$$$
Actor Robert Redford fell so deeply in love with this land in the shadow of 12,000-foot Mount Timpanogos that he bought it in 1969 and turned it into this resort, which reflects his love and appreciation of the outdoors and the arts. Your family can ski all day and take in a play or concert at night. The Institute also promotes environmental awareness— you'll even find your bathroom stocked with ecosensitive soaps.

Sundance Kids Ski School offers many different programs, including group lessons for children ages 6 and older. The resort is also famous for its Nordic Center, and kids under age 12 can cross-country ski for free. There are also some great hiking trails, including a wonderful hour to hour-and-a-half hike on the Sundance Nature Trail, which winds through forests and alpine meadows before reaching a waterfall.

But Sundance really excels in its plethora of arts activities for youngsters of all interests and abilities. In summer, the resort offers Sundance's Art Shack, where kids ages 8 and older can craft a vase on a potter's wheel and learn the finer points of papermaking, printmaking, pho-

tography, and woodcutting. The resort also offers animation workshops for children ages 5 and up.

Both the Sundance Kids' Camp and Junior Camp offer hands-on art projects, science study, environmental activities, theater games, cooking classes, and daily mountain recreation. Kids' Camp (for ages 6 to 12) runs Monday through Saturday from 9:30 A.M. to 4 P.M. Prices are $50 for the first day and $32 for each additional day. For younger campers, the Junior Camps (for ages 4 to 6) run every day from 9:30 A.M. to 1 P.M. Prices are $35 for one day and $30 for each additional day; *(801) 223-4140.*

Sundance offers one-, two-, and three-bedroom suites that range from $235 to almost $450 a night, depending on the time of your visit (summers and Christmas holidays are the priciest). Cottages nestled in the mountains are also available; *(800) 892-1600; (801) 225-4107;* www.sundanceresort.com

Desert tortoises may live more than 100 years in the wild. They are rarely seen by visitors, but you may get lucky enough to spy one, especially if you're visiting in the spring.

Southern Utah: Desert Wonderland

SOUTHERN UTAH offers some of the most gorgeous landscapes on earth: desolate canyons, ponderosa-covered peaks, and stunning rock formations sculpted over the ages. Zion National Park, Bryce Canyon, Lake Powell, Glen Canyon—the amazing beauty of these spots and others has made southern Utah a huge tourist destination in recent years, drawing more than three million people annually. Families come to the region for its unique scenery and unlimited opportunities for hiking, biking, horseback riding, and rafting. This isn't the typical theme-park, chain-hotel, and fast-food family vacation experience, however: it's a drive through remote areas to enjoy desert vistas. And if you come in summer, you can expect to enjoy those vistas with hundreds of others. But don't

THE **FamilyFun** LIST

MUST-SEE
MUST-SEE

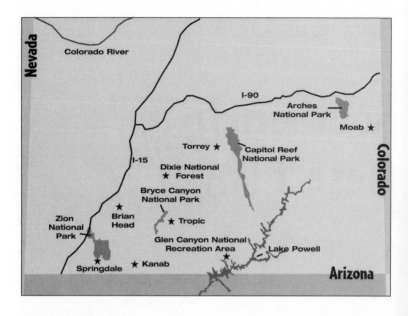

worry, we'll help you get off the beaten trail and find some places where your family can get in touch with nature and each other.

With so many national parks and monuments in the area, some families make the mistake of trying to cram them all in during a week-long driving vacation that combines Bryce Canyon, Zion National Park, Monument Valley, and Arizona's Grand Canyon. Better not to take the hurry-up-and-enjoy-the-view-so-we-can-make-the-next-stop approach; instead, choose two or three of the parks and leave plenty of time for hikes, horseback rides, or a rafting trip. The slower pace will let your family appreciate

Zion is an ancient Hebrew word that means sanctuary or refuge.

the awesome red-rock deserts, not at 75 miles per hour, but at a relaxing crawl; the sites have been here for eons—why rush through them?

Bryce Canyon National Park and Zion National Park are the biggest attractions here, and have the largest crowds in the hot summer months. At Bryce Canyon, erosion has shaped stones into thousands of spires, fins, pinnacles, and mazes, all collectively called hoodoos. Zion is home to massive sandstone monoliths such as the Great White Throne, a 2,000-foot-tall sandstone sculpture shaped like a king's throne. If these sights don't excite your kids, give them time: before long, they'll be scampering up and down the sandstone and playing hide-and-seek in the rock crevices.

Southern Utah isn't all rocks and desert brush, however. In Capitol Reef National Park, a bulge in the earth's crust helps retain water and creates the lush landscape of Fruita, a small town with apple, cherry, peach, and pear orchards where your family can literally pick their favorite snacks. Glen Canyon and Lake Powell are also popular vacation spots, particularly for families who enjoy houseboat vacations (for more on renting a houseboat, see "Float Your Houseboat on Lake Powell" on page 289).

Finally, when you are in southern Utah, take time to look up at the sky at night. The lack of major cities and their resultant pollution makes stars appear brighter here. You may want to pack an astronomy book to help you point out constellations.

As in any arid, remote area, be sure to always have bottled water at hand (figure on a gallon of water per person per day if you are camping or hiking in the backcountry). We also suggest that you always carry basic supplies like drinks, diapers, and snacks with you; grocery stores can be few and far between. And tell your children not to approach wildlife here. Unfortunately, the bacteria that causes bubonic plague has been found here in fleas on the prairie dogs in the area, so avoid getting too close to them. These precautions will help your family make the most of a visit to this strange, magnificent desert wonderland.

JUST FOR FUN

Arches National Park
FamilyFun ★★★★/$$

MUST-SEE If the only arches your kids recognize are golden and hold the promise of a Happy Meal, then a trip here will broaden that definition. This park is full of naturally formed rock arches—at least 1,700 of them, with more being discovered

Coyote Run Camp

Sure you can pack up your minivan, give the kids Game Boys, and point out scenic canyons and mesas as you speed to the next chain hotel, but we've got a better idea. Why not hit the Colorado River in a canoe, learn to make a birdhouse out of a gourd, and sleep in a tepee at Coyote Run Camp on the Colorado River? Operated by veteran outfitter Sheri Griffith, the camp offers several multiday outdoor adventures from family rafting expeditions to sea kayaking tours. Trips may include horseback riding, mountain biking, hiking, or even scenic airplane flights. *For the latest tour information, call (800) 332-2439; (435) 259-8229, or visit* www.griffithexp.com

IN ORDER TO BE CATALOGUED as an arch in Arches National Park, the formation must have at least a three-foot opening. Landscape Arch is the largest arch in the park, measuring 306 feet from base to base.

all the time. Children of almost any age are fascinated that the arch formations were caused by water, that the eroding effect of water freezing and ice thawing eats away at the stone, eventually dissolving it to form these creations. Pick up a map at the visitors' center and let your youngsters discover stone sculptures such as the Penguins, Tower of Babel, and Eye of the Whale. Then see if they can come up with better names for them. The park's famous Delicate Arch has also been named Old Maid's Bloomers and Cowboy Chaps. During the summer, park rangers lead nature talks and conduct a three-hour guided hike along the Fiery Furnace trail twice a day. Evening campfire programs are also held, focusing on topics such as geology and wildlife (For a full schedule, check at the visitors' center when you arrive or go to the park's Website at www.nps.gov/arches). The park is fairly easy to see in a day. Be ready to deal with temperatures near 100 in the summer; fall and spring are better times to visit—the heat abates and hiking is pleasant. *The park is located outside Moab on U.S. 191; (435) 259-8161; www.nps.gov/arch/index.htm*

Bryce Canyon National Park ★★★★/$$$$

MUST-SEE FamilyFun MUST-SEE

Land of the hoodoos, Bryce Canyon is one of the most magical, inspiring places in the Southwest. The intricately sculpted figures are like silent sentinels who hover in congregations in stone-cliff cathedrals decorated with windows and arches. Mormon pioneer Ebenezer Bryce, who tried raising cattle in this area that now bears his name, had another take on the canyon, calling it "a helluva place to lose a cow." Bryce is like a concentrated Grand Canyon and, as is true of its larger neighbor, is a fabulous spot for sunrise and sunset viewing. The visitors' center has exhibits on the geology of the area and hosts ranger programs on plants and animals of the park, among other subjects. Rangers also lead hikes, including a special midnight hike three times a month (reservations are required), and there is a wheelchair-accessible rim walk.

The park offers a Junior Rangers program that rewards kids who complete a questionnaire on the park's plant and animal life. If you are looking for a picnic spot, try Rainbow Point, the highest (and often coolest) point in the park, which has plenty of tables and rest rooms. If you're in good shape and your children are old enough to stay away from the rim, consider the three-hour hike down to the canyon along the Navajo Loop. Whatever you do, get to Inspiration Point to see the Silent City, which looks like a city of people who were cast in stone. The image may bring to mind the Biblical tale of Lot and the cities of Sodom and Gomorrah. To see the canyons as the pioneers (and outlaws who used it as a hideout) did, take the two-hour horseback trail ride to the canyon floor and back offered by **Canyon Lake Rides** (*435/679-8665*). Rides are offered April through October, and riders

must be over 6 years old and weigh less than 220 pounds. If possible, try to stay in the park, either at one of the two campgrounds or at the Bryce Canyon Lodge (see Bunking Down). The campgrounds are filled on a first-come, first-served basis and are often full by 1 P.M. in the summer. To make the most of your trip, call the park before your visit to get a schedule of events, or access

Float Your Houseboat on Lake Powell

The best way to see Lake Powell is from the water, and many families rent houseboats to explore all the canyons on their own. Generally, anyone who can drive a car should be able to take the helm of a houseboat; no lessons or license are required. Still, you should spend some time practicing turning and stopping before heading too far from the marina. Also, be sure to get tips from your rental agency on navigating the lake's currents, and make sure you have a map before heading out. Summer is the high season and rentals are booked months, even years, in advance. Prices are higher then, too. A 44-foot boat can run $1,500 for three days in May through September, versus $1,000 the rest of the year. Unless you really love the water (and each other), we recommend a three- or five-day vacation; experienced houseboaters can opt for longer excursions. Also, be sure everyone on board knows how to swim. We don't recommend houseboat trips for families who have preschoolers that are apt to wake up and wander at night. Lake Powell is very popular with jet ski enthusiasts, so don't be surprised if the loud watercrafts wake you up in the mornings. *For more information, call Lake Powell Vacations, 800 Elm St., Page, Arizona; (800) 530-3406.*

its Website www.nps.gov/brca *The park is located in the Dixie National Forest off Hwy. 63; (435) 834-5322.*

Butch Cassidy's King World Waterpark ★★/$$

Named after the famous outlaw who holed up in the area after robbing banks (the pond here is supposedly where Cassidy watered the horses and cattle he rustled), this park offers three large slides, two kiddie slides, three pools, including an activity pool and sand volleyball. There is a small snack bar and picnic tables. It's open from mid-May through mid-September. *1500 N. U.S. 191, Moab; (435) 259-2837;* www.moab utah.com/waterpark

⟨MUST-SEE⟩ Canyonlands National FamilyFun Park ★★★/$$

⟨MUST-SEE⟩ Utah's largest national park is also the most difficult to see. Its vast backcountry is accessible primarily on hiking trails or (arguably the best way to see it) aboard a raft or canoe on the Green River or Colorado River. If you are traveling by car, you will probably enter the park on Highway 313 and view the intricate Maze District from the Grand View Point at Island in the Sky. If you enter from the east, you'll get the best view of the park at Confluence Overlook. Canyonlands is home to rock arches and sculptured spires, grassy meadows where the two rivers meet, and wildlife including deer, bobcats, beavers, and coyotes.

This is remote country, so be aware that there are no stores or restaurants in the park. Occasionally, rangers do give nature programs at the park's two campgrounds during the summer and a short morning program may be offered at the Island of the Sky visitors' center.

Frontier Movie Town

Where is the best place to see the Old West as you best picture it? On a movie set, of course. The town of **Kanab** is called **Utah's Little Hollywood** because so many Western films and television shows have been filmed here—among them, *Gunsmoke, The Lone Ranger*, and *The Outlaw Josie Wales*. Some of those sets—including a livery stable and saloon—have been assembled at this attraction, where your family can don Wild West costumes and get an old-fashioned-looking photograph as a souvenir. During the summer, mock gunfights and cowboy-style buffet dinners served on tin plates, with lemonade served in tin cups, add to the kitsch appeal. The gift shop sells Native American trinkets, including silver jewelry and kachina dolls. *297 West Center, Kanab; (800) 551-1714;* www.onlinepages.net/frontier_ movie_town/

This is also a mecca for four-wheel-drive fans, and the White Rim Road, also used by mountain bikers, is a favorite trail. For a more intimate view of this mammoth park, consider contacting an outfitter (see "Coyote Run Camp" on page 287). *For more information, stop by the Moab Information Center on Main St. and Center St., Moab; (435) 259-7164;* www.nps.gov/cany

Capitol Reef National Park ★★★★/$

While Zion and Bryce canyons have gotten all the attention (and tourists), this gem of a park has been relatively undiscovered. That's changing, but it still has fewer visitors than its famous neighbors—and is just as gorgeous. The colors of the rocks change here with the sun's light and the composition of the rocky canyon walls. The Navajos called this place Land of the Sleeping Rainbow and settlers compared it to a coral reef, hence the park's name. The area's unique geology comes from the earth's surface, which is folded here in a thick, uneven crust. The large fold runs about 100 miles and is called the Waterpocket Fold because it holds rain in small pockets that encourage wildlife and plants to flourish.

The pioneer village of Fruita, inside the park beside its visitors' center, is well worth a visit. Morman settlers found the area's soil to be perfect for growing fruit, and there are still orchards covering the area; during harvesting season, your family can pick their own snacks of apples, cherries, and pears. Echoes of the lives of those early settlers can be found in the historic Gifford House and Barn and at the Fruita Schoolhouse. Fully restored, it gives youngsters a sense of what life was like 100 years ago and how their school days are the same, but different—there are still chalkboards and desks, but the pioneers had to make do without computers.

For a relatively easy hike, go on the two-mile Capitol Gorge Trail, which is mostly level and takes you by rock walls where pioneers and prospectors carved their names. Or consider taking a horseback ride on the park trails. Crazy C. Coyote Trailrides offers anything from one- and two-hour rides to half- and full-day trips. *Capitol Reef National Park is located 11 miles east of Torrey on Hwy. 24; (800) 425-3791;* www.nps.gov/care

Glen Canyon National Recreational Area ★★★★/Free

The sight of deep blue water surrounded by desert is surreal yet beautiful and remains a testimony to the power of nature and the determination of mankind. This huge water park is built around man-made Lake Powell (named for Major John Wesley Powell, who led an expedition down the Colorado River in 1869).

The lake is 186 miles long and has more than 1,960 miles of shoreline—more than the West Coast of the continental United States. One of the best ways to enjoy the scenic canyons that surround the lake is via houseboat (see "Float Your Houseboat on Lake Powell" on page 289). The famous Rainbow Bridge, a natural stone bridge that is sacred to the Navajo tribe, is accessible only by boat or a very strenuous hiking trail. The area also holds ancient Anasazi ruins, the 1870s stone fort at Lees Ferry, and Glen Canyon dam, which provides electrical power for a good portion of the West. For a fun, quick trip over the lake, follow Highway 276 to Bullfrog Crossing Marina and take the 20-minute ferry ride across the lake to Halls Crossing. *For one of several guided boat tours, call the Lake Powell Marina at (800) 528-6154; www.lakepowell.com*

Hole 'n the Rock ★★/$

If people who live in glass houses shouldn't throw stones, does that mean that people in stone houses shouldn't throw glass? It's something to ponder as you tour this 5,000-square-foot cave home of solid stone built by Albert and Gladys Christensen. Even some of the furniture is all rock, a real selling point to families with active youngsters. Tours of the 14-room home are offered every 10 minutes. *La Sal Route, 15 miles south of Moab on U.S. 191; (435) 686-2250.*

★ Lake Powell
FamilyFun ★★★★/$$$$
This is one fantastic body of water. Grab a houseboat and see what we mean. For more information, see "Float Your Houseboat on Lake Powell" on page 289.

★ Moab ★★★★/Free
FamilyFun Founded by Mormon missionaries, Moab—once a sleepy desert town—is now a mountain biker's mecca. But be forewarned that the world-famous Moab Slickrock bicycle trail, a very challenging 9.6-mile trail over Navajo sandstone, is not recommended for children—or anyone without extensive experience. Opt for the Gemini Bridges Trail, a 13.5-mile, one-way trip that is mostly downhill. For information on bike rental and shuttle services, call **Coyote Shuttle** *(435/259-8656).*

Moab is a small town by most standards, with about 4,000 year-round residents, but that's enough to make it the biggest city in southwest Utah. Moab is still home to some hippie, outdoorsy types, but they are increasingly being elbowed out by upscale yuppies who demand state-of-the-art hiking and biking equipment and gourmet fare. (Believe it or not, gas stations here can fill you up with leaded or unleaded espresso!) Moab is a good base of operations for touring Arches and Canyonlands national parks and offers a couple of places to cool off—including the city's public pool *(181 W. 400 North St.)*, which is open year-round; *(435) 259-8226;* www.moab.net

Zion Canyon Giant Screen Theatre ★★★/$-$$

If the idea of seeing Zion National Park in air-conditioned comfort appeals to your family, consider visiting this theater and seeing the film—appropriately shown on a towering six-story, 80-foot-high screen. Offering an overview of the area's history and wildlife, it's actually a great introduction to the park. You'll get a unique hawk's-eye view and learn about the history of the ancient Anasazi. The complex includes a gift shop, art gallery, film processing, ATMs, and picnic tables. *145 Zion Park Blvd.; (435) 772-2400;* www.zioncanyontheatre.com

Zion National Park
FamilyFun ★★★★/$$$$

Mormon pioneers named this area after the Biblical Promised Land. Today the park welcomes more than 2.6 million visitors a year, drawn by its vast canyons, stone cliffs, cascading waterfalls, and deep, green pools. Protected within Zion's 229 square miles is Kolob Arch, the world's largest arch, with a span measuring 310 feet. Wildlife, such as mules, deer, golden eagles, and mountain lions, also inhabits the park.

Summer is by far the busiest, and hottest, time of year—temperatures hover at 95 to 100 degrees during the day; evenings cool down to a comfortable 65 to 70. Afternoon thunderstorms are common from mid-July through mid-September, so do your hiking in the morning if possible. Storms may produce waterfalls as well as flash floods.

While exploring the park, look for "spring lines," or hanging gar-

FamilyFun TIP

Pass It On

If you're planning on visiting multiple national parks on your vacation, you might consider purchasing a National Parks Pass. For a fee of $50, the pass will admit either you and the other passengers in your vehicle or you, your spouse, parents, and children to any of the national parks for a full year (it depends whether the park admits visitors on a "per vehicle" or "per person" basis). For more information, call 1-888-GO-PARKS or go to the National Park Service's Website at www.nps.gov

dens that cling to the cliffs where water percolating through the sandstone is stopped by harder rocks.

The park recently opened a new visitors' center and, in an ecologically friendly move, closed the six-mile-long Zion Scenic Canyon Drive to automobiles from March through October, making it accessible only by a park shuttle bus, by foot, and by bicycle. It is recommended that you park in Springdale, where you can pick up the shuttle buses.

Each shuttle bus leaves the visitors' center at the park's south end and travels northward through the canyon, making eight stops along the way. The bus is free, and visitors can board and reboard at any point. You can drive your car to the visitors' center or take another shuttle, also free, from the town of Springdale, just outside the park boundaries.

NOTE: The new system has made it more difficult for families who want to get away from the crowds and discover the park on their own, but it is still possible. Get off the bus at the Temple of Sinawava and take the easy two-mile hike on Riverside Walk, which follows the Virgin River through a narrow canyon. The hike takes between two and four hours round-trip. Another trail leaves Zion Lodge and leads to the park's famous Emerald Pools; the walk takes about an hour round-trip. The nod to the park's fragile environment extends to the pools—swimming and wading are not permitted here. Kids also

love the Weeping Rock trail, which takes them to a rock that oozes water.

The Pa'rus Trail offers a paved, car-free alternative for bicyclists, pedestrians, and people with strollers or wheelchairs who want to visit lower Zion Canyon and access the Scenic Drive.

During the summer, children can join a park ranger to learn more about the park's geology, plants, animals, human history, and other features. Programs also include guided walks, short talks at the visitors' center, and evening programs at the campground amphitheater, which often include musical performances. Check the weekly schedules, posted at the visitors' center and on bulletin boards throughout the park, for times, places, and subjects. *You can access park information on the Internet at* www.zioncanyon.com *or by calling (435) 772-3256.*

BUNKING DOWN

Best Western Ruby's Inn
★★★/$-$$$

This huge motel offers one-stop living. You can spend the night, get a haircut in the beauty salon, eat at the restaurant, do your laundry, fill up at one of the gas stations (there are two), develop your film, grab some souvenirs at the general store, and check the concierge's desk to arrange a horseback-riding or four-wheel drive excursion. Oh, yeah, it's right next to Bryce Canyon, too. *Located on Utah 63, one mile north of Bryce Canyon National Park entrance; (800) 528-1234; (435) 834-5341; www.rubysinn.com/*

Bryce Canyon Lodge
★★★★/$$-$$$

If you travel with kids, you know that location can make all the difference. And if your kids get tired and cranky, you're better off staying at the hotel. Well, if that hotel is actually inside the park (as this one is), you can have it all. Try to get one of the spacious lodge suites, which have separate sitting rooms, or opt for one of the cabins, which have two bedrooms with queen-size beds. The regular hotel rooms aren't bad, just a bit plain given the spectacular setting. Staying here gives your family easy access to the horseback trail ride and hiking trails, so you can beat the crowds that throng the park by midmorning on most summer days. The lodge is closed mid-November through April. Reserve six months before your stay. If you can't get in, keep checking—there may be some cancellations. *Bryce Canyon National Park. (435) 834-5361; www.bryce canyonlodge.com*

Canyon Livery Bed-and-Breakfast ★★★/$$

Just outside Bryce Canyon, this simple bed-and-breakfast offers proximity plus an authentic Western feel

Zion in a Day

I F YOU ARE on a tight schedule, here's how we recommend seeing this massive park in a limited amount of time:

9 A.M. Catch the big-screen film at **Zion Canyon Theater** (see page 293); pick up film and postcards (plus sunscreen and bottled water) at the souvenir shop.

10 A.M. Head into **Zion National Park** (see page 293). Stop at the visitors' center for a schedule of events and trail maps, then catch the shuttle bus. Get off at the Temple of Sinawava and, if you're up for it, hike a portion of the two-mile trail along the Riverside Walk.

11:30-Noon Take the bus to **Zion Lodge** (see page 296) for lunch.

1 P.M. Walk to the **Emerald Pools**; the trailhead is next to the lodge. This trail takes you through a forest of cottonwood trees, oaks, maples, and firs to a waterfall, hanging garden, and green pool. Listen for the frogs, but don't jump in yourself—swimming (even dipping in a big toe) is not permitted.

2:30 P.M. Return to the lodge and check out the gift shop. Board the tram and head back to the visitors' center.

with delicious breakfasts of peach or elderberry pancakes and "skillet potatoes." *50 S. 660 West, Tropic; (888) 889-8910; (435) 679 8780; www.canyonlivery.com*

Zion Lodge ★★★/$$-$$$

Location is everything here, too, putting you inside magnificent Zion National Park so you avoid some of the "when will we get there" whines. Built in 1925 by the Union Pacific Railroad, the lodge offers charming cabins, each with two double beds, and porches for relaxing and viewing the park's red cliffs. Rooms in the motel are basic, but clean and comfortable. Some suites offer sitting rooms and refrigerators. Ranger programs are offered in the lobby and a gift shop sells postcards, T-shirts, and Native American jewelry. Book early, because this place fills up fast. *(435) 772-3213;* www.amfac.com *or* www.nps.gov/zion

FamilyFun TIP

Weather Watch

Bryce Canyon only receives an average of ten inches of rainfall in the valley each year. Most of the rainfall comes from summer monsoons, in which one to two inches of rain can fall in under an hour. Hail frequently accompanies heavy storms, so keep your eyes on the sky if you're hiking in the canyon.

GOOD EATS

Bit & Spur Restaurant and Saloon ★★★/$$

This saloon has a family feel, with an outdoor patio where even boisterous kids don't seem to bother anyone. The menu is standard Mexican fare, with burritos, enchiladas, quesadillas, and the like; there are smaller versions of the regular adult fare for youngsters. Save room for the desserts, which include brownies, peach cobbler, and crème brûlée. *1212 Zion Park Blvd., Springdale; (435) 772-3498.*

Bryce Canyon Lodge ★★★/$$

Even if you don't stay here, it's worth coming for a meal or two. The lodge is casual at breakfast and lunch, but goes a bit more upscale at dinner, when cheese tortellini and roast beef au jus may be on the menu. The fresh mountain trout is outstanding. There's a kids' menu with all of the usual suspects; they'll especially love the ice cream flavors such as wild berry crunch. *Located inside the park, near the Rim Trail; (435) 834-5361;* www.brycecanyonlodge.com

Foster's Family Steak House ★★★/$-$$

A popular locals' hangout, Foster's serves up great steaks and steamed Utah trout. The kids' menu offers grilled cheese sandwiches, corn dogs, chicken fingers, and a shrimp plate. *Located about 1.5 miles west of Bryce Canyon National Park's main entrance on Hwy. 12; (435) 834-5227.*

Jailhouse Café ★★★/$

Who says prison food isn't good? Housed in the old courthouse (the kitchen actually used to be jail cells), this spot serves breakfast all day. Kids ages 8 and under can choose from eggs, pancakes, or French toast, served with bacon, sausage, and potatoes, for $3.75. Older kids and their parents can get the delicious Southwestern eggs Benedict, with a spicy hollandaise sauce. *101 N. Main St., Moab; (435) 259-3900;* www.moabutah.com/jailhouse

Zion Pizza and Noodle ★★★/$$

Housed in a former Mormon church, this pizza joint serves up chewy pies in offbeat flavors like Southwest Burrito. Never fear, you can get basic cheese and/or pepperoni, too. Takeout and delivery are available. *868 Zion Park Blvd., Springdale; (435) 772-3815.*

Souvenir Hunting

Moab Rock Shop

You can't take them out of the national parks, but you can buy rocks, minerals, geodes, gems, dinosaur bones, and fossils here. *600 N. Main St., Moab; (435) 259-7312.*

Our Favorite Boredom Busters

Vacation downtime—the "I'm bored" variety—can be easily filled with these fun and challenging pastimes, good for kids of all ages.

♦ Make a paper-bag puppet

♦ Paint a face on a rock

♦ Construct a cootie catcher

♦ Design a paper airplane

♦ Juggle sock balls

♦ Build a couch-cushion fort

♦ Blow bubbles

♦ Play slapjack

♦ Fly a kite

♦ Sing along with your favorite tunes

♦ Read a story together

♦ Start a collection (rocks, buttons, bottle caps – whatever's easy to find around the house or the yard)

♦ Make a paper-clip chain

♦ Draw your favorite person (or place, cartoon character, sport, etc.)

♦ Bowl with a tennis ball and a few empty plastic soda bottles

♦ Cut up a catalog and make a collage

♦ Do a jigsaw puzzle

♦ Make a greeting card for your best friend

Colorado

EVERYONE from John Muir to John Denver has documented Colorado's natural beauty, and families who travel here today will find the Rocky Mountains just as awesome a sight. It's truly an outdoor lovers' paradise, where summer brings hiking and white-water rafting, and winter transforms the landscape into a paradise for cold-weather sports. The spring heralds gorgeous wildflowers, and the fall offers the golden colors of aspens quaking in the wind. It's no surprise that this state is one of the most popular family vacation choices in the country.

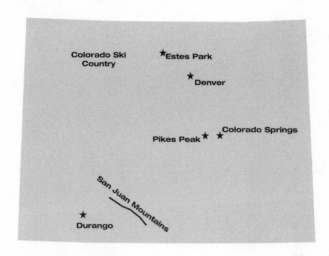

Many families start a Colorado trek in Denver, which has hands-on museums and theme parks that will please your kids.

Colorado boasts some of the best skiing in the world, and the fun continues after the snow melts; most ski resorts shift gears from skiing to hiking, horseback riding, and fishing.

The state's pioneer past comes alive in places like Durango; Mesa Verde and the nearby Anasazi Cultural Center teach the ways of ancient Native American civilizations; in South Park City, your family can wander through the remains of a ghost town.

From its Eastern plains to the Rocky Mountains, Colorado is a great family vacation.

ATTRACTIONS
$	under $5
$$	$5 - $10
$$$	$10 - $20
$$$$	$20 +

HOTELS/MOTELS/CAMPGROUNDS
$	under $100
$$	$100 - $150
$$$	$150 - $200
$$$$	$200 +

RESTAURANTS
$	under $5
$$	$5 - $10
$$$	$10 - $20
$$$$	$20 +

FAMILYFUN RATED
★	Fine
★★	Good
★★★	Very Good
★★★★	_FamilyFun_ Recommended

The big Colorado ski resorts offer family programs on and off the slopes, winter and summer.

Colorado Ski Country

THE HIGH PEAKS of the Rockies were of little interest to families 100 years ago. They were largely the domain of miners and a few hearty ranchers and railroad workers. Now the region and its numerous ski resorts—including Vail, Aspen, and Steamboat Springs—draw millions of vacationers each winter and an increasing number of summer visitors as well, lured by mountain biking, white-water rafting, and arts festivals.

Downhill skiing is the big attraction here, although cross-country skiing and snowboarding are gaining in popularity. When making travel plans, ask about each resort's kids' program, the number of instructors per student in the children's ski school, and what other nonski children's activities there are. We are only listing resorts that are exceptionally child-friendly, and our picks range from modest to pricey. We looked for value because wonderful

THE **FamilyFun** LIST

MUST-SEE · MUST-SEE

Aspen/Snowmass (page 316)

Beaver Creek (page 316)

Breckenridge (page 316)

Copper Mountain Resort (page 317)

Country Boy Mine (page 308)

Dillon Reservoir Recreation Center (page 309)

Steamboat Springs (page 317)

Winter Park (page 318)

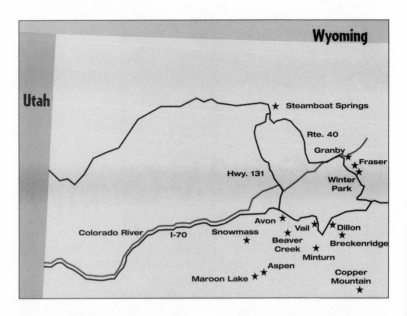

amenities can often justify a high price. Resorts have come a long way in improving their kids' programs over the last decade, particularly for preschoolers where instructors now build in some playtime. Improvements to kids' ski equipment have helped too, enabling skiers as young as 3 or 4 to glide down a bunny hill. If your child doesn't want to ski, explore other activities such as snowmobile tours, sleigh rides, ice-skating, snow tubing (sliding downhill on an inner tube), or snow-biking (riding a bike fastened to skis). Or opt to relax, reading *The Snowy Day* by the fireplace.

The ski season runs from December through March, but resorts may start operations as early as October and stop in May or June, depending on the weather and the snowfall. Be prepared to pay high prices if you come between Christmas and New Year's, during the Martin Luther King, Jr., holiday weekend, or in March, when resorts charge their highest prices. If you can manage to make the trip in February or April during the week, you can get a much better deal. It may also be worth checking travel Internet sites for last-minute bargain ski packages. **NOTE:** Be warned that many ski resorts and the area restaurants and hotels virtually shut down between the end of the ski season and mid-June, and then between Labor Day and the start of the new season. If you are traveling during these times, call ahead to your destination so you won't get there only to find a "CLOSED" sign.

Summer used to be the off-season, but increasingly it is a prime travel time as resorts add special programs, festivals, and events. Many resorts use their ski lifts to transport hikers and mountain bikers. We realize that mountain biking in the Rockies is not exactly a family-friendly activity; our suggestion is to take the lift up, enjoy the view and a picnic on top, and then head down again.

Your family may want to pick one resort and spend the entire trip there, enjoying the amenities without worrying about driving. But if you do have a car and some time, it's worth exploring some of the out-of-the-way gems this region offers. For example, the railroad junction of Minturn has several great restaurants with prices half what you would pay in the neighboring resorts of Vail and Beaver Creek.

Because of the high altitudes here and the reflective power of snow, it's imperative that you don sunscreen every morning. Also, be sure to pack sunglasses and a hat (this goes for the summer, too). Know the symptoms of high altitude sickness (see page 305), and bring pain medication to deal with possible headaches. This is one of the few negative aspects of traveling to Colorado's ski meccas. But armed with our tips, planning your vacation will be a downhill ride.

NOTE: For your convenience, we've highlighted attractions within each area and then listed accommodations and eating places together.

Aspen

The fact that Aspen is a skier's paradise (see "Super Ski Spots" on page 316) is obvious. What follows are all the other things to do in this year-round town.

CULTURAL ADVENTURES

Wheeler Opera House
★★/$-$$$$
Built in 1889, this 500-seat theater hosts the area's top music events, the most popular being the annual summer extravaganza, the Aspen Music Festival, which typically stages productions geared to children, such as storytelling sessions and children's concerts. The theater is also open for daily tours from 9 A.M. to 5 P.M. *320 E. Hyman Ave., Aspen; (970) 920-5770; www.wheeleroperahouse.com*

Wheeler/Stallard Museum
★★★/$
For a great history lesson, take the kids to this house built in 1888 by a

303

man named Wheeler whose wife refused to ever move here. It was bought by a family named Stallard, who lived here for 40 years, and today your kids can get a look at what their own lives might have been like 100 years ago by walking through the children's room and seeing the period toys and pictures of kids playing back in 1900. This museum goes out of its way to cater to youngsters, offering special children's tours. Call ahead to check schedules. **NOTE:** Though the museum does welcome children, you should probably not bring smaller ones—ages 6 and under—who might be tempted to touch or play with the artifacts. *620 W. Bleeker St., Aspen; (970) 925-3721;* www.ahistory@ros.net

JUST FOR FUN

Ashcroft Ghost Town
★★★/$
Kids can walk around this collection of log cabins that was a thriving silver-mining town a hundred years ago. In its heyday, back in the 1880s, the town had 2,500 residents and 20 saloons. Guided tours of the abandoned buildings are offered at 11 A.M. and 1 P.M. Thursdays through Saturdays in June, July, and August. Ashcroft is located 10 miles south of Aspen. *To get there, take Highway 82 to Castle Rock Road and look for the parking area on the left; (970) 925-3721.*

Aspen Center for Environmental Studies ★★★/$
This research center and wildlife refuge is also a sanctuary from tourist crowds. In winter, you and your youngsters can learn to snowshoe, or take a guided hike with one of the naturalists on staff. In the summer, there are also guided hikes, plus workshops that help your children learn how to create a wildlife habitat in their own backyard. Summer also brings the Special Little Naturalist programs for kids ages 4 to 7, which include nature hikes and arts and crafts. *100 Puppy Smith, Aspen; (970) 925-5756;* www.aspen nature.org

Aspen Ice Garden ★★/$
Kids can take to the ice almost year-round at this indoor rink operated by the city of Aspen's recreation department. Hours vary seasonally, and the rink is closed from mid-April to early June. *233 W. Hyman Ave., Aspen; (970) 920-5141.*

Hyman Avenue Mall Fountain ★★/Free
This water fountain in the middle of Aspen's outdoor mall is a great place to let your kids do what they want to do when they see water: get soaking wet. The fountain shoots jets of water in a random pattern, and kids love the challenge of getting through without any water touching them. The admission charge—nothing— is a great wallet break in pricey

Aspen. *At Mill and Hyman Sts. in the Hyman Avenue Mall, Aspen.*

Maroon Lake
★★★/$

One of the most photographed scenes in the state is the view overlooking Maroon Lake toward two 14,000-foot-plus mountains called the Maroon Bells. The best (and often only) way to get here is on a shuttle bus (cars are prohibited most of the time due to the area's fragile ecosystem). Buses run every 20 minutes from the Aspen Highlands and Ruby Park Transit Center, located at Durant Avenue and Mill Street in Aspen (*970/925-8484*). The cost is $5 for adults, $3 for kids ages 6 to 16 and seniors ages 65 and up; children ages 5 and under ride free.

The narration during the bus tour explains some of the geology and nature of the area; if this piques your kids' interest, you can learn even more by going on one of the free guided tours offered to summer visitors at the end of the bus ride (tours are every hour on the hour between 10 A.M. and 2 P.M.). Guided tours around the lake take about 45 minutes; on the tour, you'll learn about wildflowers and the active beaver dam. If you don't want the guided tour, don't worry: trails are well marked. There are picnic tables and rest rooms but no food is available, so pack a picnic in town before heading here. *Call the Forrest Service at (970) 925-3445.*

Dealing with High Altitudes

The high Rocky Mountains are gorgeous, but a tour of the towering peaks is not always without side effects. High altitude sickness can strike children and adults alike. Pregnant women, or anyone with a heart condition or other severe medical condition, should consult a doctor before traveling 7,000 feet or more above sea level. At these altitudes, the amount of oxygen in the air begins to decrease and your body has to work harder for you to breathe. You slowly adjust to the change but can become ill in the meantime. Symptoms to watch out for are headaches, weakness, light-headedness, nausea, difficulty sleeping, shortness of breath, and confusion. The best way to prevent altitude sickness is by giving your body time to adjust to the changes. For example, try to spend a night in Denver (elevation: 5,300 feet) to acclimate your body. Take it easy on your first day instead of heading right to the hiking trail or horseback riding. Encourage your kids to take naps and drink lots of water, and set an example by doing the same yourself. Finally, don't ignore symptoms in hopes they will go away; in some cases, altitude sickness can be fatal. Don't be afraid to go to the hospital or contact a doctor, who can offer prescription medicine to alleviate the symptoms.

Silver Queen Gondola
★★★/$$$–$$$$

This gondola ride to the top of Snowmass's Ajax Mountain is operated in the summer. Your family can ride up, have lunch at the Sundeck Restaurant, and take a guided nature tour sponsored by the Aspen Center for Environmental Nature Studies. Adventurous (or kamikaze-style) travelers can take a mountain bike up and grip the breaks all the way down. In the winter, two-hour snowshoe tours led by a naturalist are offered. Mom and Dad: the mountaintop also provides a stunning setting for free classical music concerts offered most Saturdays around 1 P.M. during the Aspen Music Festival held in summer. *On Durant Ave., near corner of Galena St., Aspen; (970) 925-1220;* www.aspen.com

Wagner Park Playground
★★/Free

If you or your kids aren't into the Aspen shopping scene, opt for this playground with swings, slides, and monkey bars. *It's conveniently located just off the west end of Hyman Avenue Mall, Aspen.*

Snow Mountain Ranch
YMCA OF THE ROCKIES

Operated by the YMCA, this ranch/resort offers a camplike experience, including campfires around a gaslit fire ring. Like its counterpart, the YMCA of the Rockies in Estes Park, Snow Mountain Ranch in Winter Park is a great place for family reunions; you can find accommodations—including five-bedroom cabins—to suit groups of 15 or more people. In the summer, campsites are available and activities include hiking and hayrides. In winter, the focus is on Nordic activities such as snowshoeing and cross-country skiing. For more information, see page 318. *Take I-40 to Highway 40, continue past Fraser, take a left on County Road 53; (970) 887-2152, or call the ranch's Denver line at (303) 443-4743, ext. 4110 for reservations.*

BUNKING DOWN

Limelite Lodge ★★/$$–$$$

One of the less expensive options in Aspen, this family-operated lodge offers two key features for families: a laundry, and Nintendo in the rooms. The inn also has two heated pools and several whirlpools. Après ski, families can gather by the huge fireplace for complimentary hot cider, hot chocolate, and tea and coffee. Each room has a refrigerator for storing snacks. *228 E. Cooper St., Aspen; (800) 433-0832; (970) 925-3025;* www.limelitelodge.com

Wildwood Lodge
★★★/$$–$$$$

This upscale condominium complex offers two- and three-bedroom units suited for families who like to spread out. There are in-room Nintendo units, but a more old-fashioned option is to check out the board games available in the lobby. *40 Elbert Lane, Snowmass; (800) 837-4255; (970) 923-3550; www.wildwood-lodge.com*

GOOD EATS

Boogies Diner ★★/$$$

Aspen is known more for its haute cuisine than kid-friendly diners, but this boutique with an upstairs restaurant is an exception. Boogies welcomes kids by providing crayons, and it's always willing to split the very large portions if you ask. But kids can also choose from among their own personal faves, such as macaroni and cheese, hot dogs, and spaghetti. Parents are welcomed with entrée prices below $10, a rarity in pricey Aspen. The chefs take a healthy approach to cooking, using canola oil and low-fat mayonnaise. *534 E. Cooper Ave., Aspen; (970) 925-6610.*

Paradise Bakery ★★/$-$$

The place where Aspen congregates each morning for caffe latte and huge, gooey cinnamon buns and muffins. *320 S. Galena Ave., Aspen; (970) 925-7585; www.paradisebak ery.com*

SOUVENIR HUNTING

Geraniums 'n Sunshine

An eclectic collection of clothes (mostly for girls), accessories, jewelry, ceramics, furniture, gifts, toys, and games. *208 E. Main St., Aspen; (800) 925-1648; (970) 925-6641; www.gnsaspen.com*

Short Sport

You'll find a complete selection of kids' skiwear and toys from all over the world here, as well as stroller and infant-backpack rentals. *Two locations: one in Aspen in the Aspen Square Building (970/920-3195) and another in Snowmass at the Snowmass Village Mall (970/923-5010).*

Breckenridge

If you think skiing in Aspen is awesome, better check Breckenridge (see "Super Ski Spots" on page 316). And there's lots more—from ice-skating rinks and play-in fountains to ghost towns and wildlife sanctuaries—read on.

JUST FOR FUN

Breckenridge Recreation Center ★★★/$-$$

Youngsters will burn off some energy at this huge complex that includes tennis courts, swimming pools, and basketball courts. There also are two indoor rock-climbing walls—but you have to take a brief, $19 class before you can use them—and a pool where kids can frolic on the water slide or play on the rope swing that drops them into the water. Admission prices here are a modest $5 to $10, making the place a bargain cure for cranky kids. *880 Airport Rd., Breckenridge; (970) 453-1734.*

Breckenridge Super Slide
★★★/Free-$$

Visitors during the summer (late May to September) will enjoy the ride down this concrete chute—it's short, but the memories will last a lifetime. Board the chairlift to the top of Peak 8, then get in a sled and head downhill. You can (somewhat) control the speed of the sled with a center lever. Sleds are big enough for a parent and a child to ride together in, and kids ages 2 to 6 must ride with an adult. Discounts are offered if you want to ride more than once. *At the Breckenridge Ski Resort, 535 S. Park Ave.; (970) 453-5000.*

Country Boy Mine
MUST-SEE FamilyFun ★★★★/$$-$$$

Kids can get a handle on the area's mining past (and present) at this working gold mine two miles from Breckenridge. During the 45-minute guided tour, you can watch miners run the drills, get a history lesson on Rocky Mountain mining, and walk in the mineshaft, where

The Perfect Summer Day in Beaver Creek

9 A.M. Pick up breakfast (sticky buns or muffins) at the **Columbine Bakery** (see page 320).

10 A.M. To Beaver Creek; get your parking pass and a map. Head to the **Beaver Creek Children's Museum** (see page 311; Wednesday through Sunday only) and watch for actors from the **Beaver Creek Children's Theater** (see page 312); see their show in the plaza.

12:15 P.M. Buy lift tickets and ride the **Centennial Express Lift** (see page 314) to the top of the mountain. Enjoy lunch at the **Spruce Saddle Lodge**, followed by high-altitude playtime.

2 P.M. Walk the mile-long **Spruce Saddle Loop** trail, then bike or hike down the mountain. Play **miniature golf** next to the lift at the base.

5 P.M. Have dinner at the **Blue Moose** pizza parlor (see page 320), then finish the day with ice-skating at **Black Family Ice Rink** (see page 313), which opens at 6 P.M.

workers are still clearing out rubble from a 1990 rockslide. After the tour, your kids can pan for gold in a creek; even if they don't find any big nuggets, the mine does yield tiny gold specks, and you can buy small vials of water (which magnifies the specks) to help you see them better. In the summer, the mine offers evening hayrides with marshmallow roasting and hot chocolate, but reservations are required. *0542 French Gulch Rd., Breckenridge; (970) 453-4405;* www.countryboymine.com

Dillon Reservoir Recreation Center
★★★/Free-$$$$

This 3,300-acre lake surrounded by mountains is a gorgeous place for a boat ride. Rent a pontoon boat, fishing boat, sailboat, or kayak at the Dillon Marina. The pontoons are the most popular family option because they offer a smooth ride and can seat eight or nine people and still have wiggle room. A two-hour rental goes for about $80. On the shore, near the marina, are picnic grounds, a playground, a concession stand (open in the summer), and rest rooms. Swimming, waterskiing, and jet skiing are not allowed in the lake. *Interstate 7, exit 205, Dillon; (970) 468-5100;* www.dillon marina.com

Maggie Pond ★★/$

Great place to paddleboat during the warmer months. *535 S. Park Ave., Breckenridge; (970) 453-2000.*

BUNKING DOWN

Village at Breckenridge
★★★/$$-$$$$

The term "village" here means a huge complex of rooms, restaurants, and shops. Accommodations range from lodge-style single rooms to huge three-bedroom condominiums. Kids will enjoy the indoor/outdoor pool. *535 S. Park Ave., Breckenridge; (800) 800-7829; (970) 453-2000.*

Steamboat Springs

Steamboat Springs has some of the most kid-friendly slopes in the U.S. For further information, see "Super Ski Spots" on page 316. Other great adventures in town include natural springs hot tubs, giant mazes, and fabulous hiking.

JUST FOR FUN

Amaze 'N Steamboat ★★/$-$$

If your kids know the old rat-in-a-maze experiment, they'll understand the premise of this people-size maze and will want to see whether they, like the rats, can get through faster the second time around. The wooden maze is open daily from Labor Day through Memorial Day. There's also a miniature-golf course, and you can get a package deal that includes both the maze and the mini golf. *1255 Lincoln St., Steamboat Springs; (970) 870-8682.*

Fish Creek Falls ★★★/Free-$

Fishing used to be the main reason folks gathered here, but now families make the short, 200-yard hike from the parking lot to see the glorious 283-foot waterfall. At the base of the falls, there's a wooden footbridge that makes a great viewing spot. Picnic facilities are available, too. Depending on where you park, there may be a small fee. *To get to the falls, go north on 3rd Street from Lincoln Avenue and look for signs.*

Steamboat Springs Health and Recreation Association ★★★/$-$$

The official-sounding name of this attraction doesn't indicate what it really is: a collection of giant hot tubs all powered by Mother Nature (water temperatures range from 98 to 102 degrees year-round). Kids love scooting down the enclosed slide, and if they get tired of swimming, there's an adjacent playground, but you'll need to sign your child up for child care for them to use it. You can rent swimsuits and towels and pick up snacks at the small concession stand. The association's central location, right in the middle of downtown, is convenient for families staying in town. In the winter, few things delight kids more than swimming next to snow. *136 Lincoln Ave., Steamboat Springs; (970) 879-1828*; www.steamboat springs.com

BUNKING DOWN

Sheraton Steamboat Resort ★★★/$$$-$$$$

This huge hotel complex recently underwent a $20 million renovation, which spruced up its decor and added new restaurants and a larger fitness center. The resort is just steps away from the Silver Bullet Gondola, making it extremely convenient for

---

FamilyFun GAME

To the Letter

The next time your family hits the road, invite everyone to put their vocabulary skills to the test with this fun word game. Have one person begin by stating a category and a number of letters and then naming an appropriate item. He might pick the category of animals and the number 3, then say "yak." Players take turns coming up with three-letter animals until everyone is stumped. The player who contributed the last word wins the round and starts the next one.

families hitting the slopes. Families will also enjoy the new Morningside Luxury Condominium Tower, which has two-, three-, and four-bedroom units with fireplaces and kitchens. For a less expensive alternative, try the Village Inn Condominiums or the standard hotel rooms, which can accommodate four. The concierge here can help families sign up for activities such as sleigh rides, snowmobile tours, and fishing trips. *2200 Village Inn Ct., Steamboat Springs; (800) 848-8878; (970) 879-2220; www.sheraton.com*

Good Eats

Steamboat Smokehouse ★★★/$$

At this casual barbecue joint, your youngsters can open and munch the peanuts served in baskets—and then toss the shells right on the floor. Kids' meals include the standard peanut-butter-and-jelly and chicken fingers, or they can split a buffalo roast with Mom and Dad. Go before 6 P.M. to avoid lengthy waits during the ski season. *In the Thiesen Mall, 9th St. and Lincoln Ave., Steamboat Springs; (970) 879-5570.*

Winona's ★★★/$

This small café has landed in the pages of *Bon Appétit* for its famous cinnamon buns topped with honey-and-cream-cheese frosting. The breakfast burritos and eggs Benedict aren't bad, either, but your kids (and you) will probably stick with the buns. There's also a kids' menu. *617 Lincoln Ave., Steamboat Springs; (970) 879-2483.*

Souvenir Hunting

Toys & Moore

Stock up on board games here if your kids are bored. *119 9th St., Steamboat Springs; (970) 879-8697.*

Vail/Beaver Creek

Beaver Creek is among the most family-friendly spots in the area. For more information, see "Super Ski Spots" on page 316. From a great museum and children's theater to ice rinks and high-flying gondola rides, Beaver Creek is a family paradise.

Cultural Adventures

Beaver Creek Children's Museum ★★★/Free

A new addition to this already family-friendly mountain, this

A River Runs Through It

It starts in the high peaks of Rocky Mountain National Park, and by the time it flows through central Colorado, it is a powerful river. Some sections of the Colorado River are treacherous and left only to experts to navigate, but there are other sections tame enough to provide a great afternoon float trip for families with kids ages 3 and older. Many outfitters make the journey—we suggest **Lakota River Guides** in Vail *(800/274-0636; 970/476-7238)*.

Outfitters will provide you with life jackets and paddles—even booties for your feet. You'll also get lunch (usually ham and turkey sandwiches) and brownies for dessert when your guides pull over for a break by some old miners' cabins (abandoned by people, but not prairie dogs).

The rapids are mostly Class 2 and 3, just challenging enough to make you feel like you are on a very small roller coaster. Kids love the splash factor with little fear of actually going overboard. Of course there are opportunities for swimming along the way, but be prepared for the shock of jumping into very cold water. The scenery is gorgeous, and if a train goes by on the neighboring tracks, the engineer won't mind blowing the horn—if you wave hard enough.

museum offers everything from computer games to Tinkertoys. There's a huge trunk filled with outfits so that kids can play dress-up and perform shows on the small stage, or they can simply sit down and enjoy a short story from the small library of books. Three computers and a nice library of educational software are available, but your child will have to get one of the docents to load any programs into the computer. In Professor Quackenbush's Workshop, youngsters get to build their own toys out of blocks, Legos, or Tinkertoys. There are also special arts-and-crafts workshops, visits by Smokey Bear, and natural-science talks given by representatives from the Denver Museum of Nature and Science. The museum is open June through September only, Wednesday through Sunday from 10 A.M. to 4 P.M. and is located by the escalators leading to the Centennial Express Lift (see page 314). *Beaver Creek Plaza; (970) 926-5855.*

Beaver Creek Children's Theater ★★★/Free

This theater's small, zany troupe of actors doesn't mind acting really silly if it means getting kids to laugh. In the summer, the actors perform in various places around the resort's central plaza at 11 A.M. Wednesdays through Fridays. Their skits teach lessons on things like the importance of doing homework and overcoming shyness, but they are so funny that your kids won't realize they may be learning some valuable lessons. During July and August, the troupe stages Children's Theater Workshops for kids ages 5 to 12. Young thespians learn to create stories and characters and then actually put on a show. *(970) 926-5855.*

Colorado Ski Museum/ Ski Hall of Fame ★★/Free

Your kids may find it amusing to see the bare-bones equipment people used to use for skiing and the fashions they wore. This small museum in Vail showcases the evolution of skis and the now-antiquated equipment people used with them. There's also a short video on the history of skiing in the area. This attraction is best for kids 8 and older and should probably take less than an hour. *231 S. Frontage Rd., in the Vail Village Transportation Center, Vail; (970) 476-1876;* www. skimuseum.net

JUST FOR FUN

Avon Recreation Center ★★★/$$

After an active day on the mountain, or on a cloudy day when you can't think of anything else to do, your family can unwind in the waters here— a lap pool, diving pool, play pool, and 150-foot water slide with a lazy river and mushroom-shaped slide. There's also a kiddie pool with bubble beds and fountains. *Near Nottingham Park at 325 Benchmark Rd., Avon; (970) 949-9191;* www. avon.org

Beaver Creek Summer Camp ★★★/$$$

This resort offers the top-notch Five Star Camp for youngsters ages 5 to 12, which includes such challenging activities as rock climbing, rafting, fly-fishing, horseback riding, and ceramics. **NOTE:** Camp isn't cheap. At press time, rates were $85 for one day and $280 for five days, but it's worth it given the quality of the instruction and facilities. Our 7-year-old is still talking about going up the indoor rock wall. There is a less intense—but just as fun—Discovery Camp, offered for kids ages 5 to 7, which includes nature hikes, arts and crafts, face painting, and panning for gold. Rates are $65 a day. Rates for Adventure Camp, for children ages 8 to 12—which includes activities such as swimming, in-line skating, and archery—are $75 a day or $335 a week. *The camp is located in Village Hall, across from Beaver Creek Lodge, Beaver Creek; (970) 845-5464.*

Black Family Ice Rink ★★★/$

Even in the summer, this outdoor ice rink continues operation, giving your kids a fun way to cool off. The rink is covered during the heat of the day but opens again in the late afternoon. Skate rentals are available for a few dollars; there is a small admission fee. *In the middle of Beaver Creek's central plaza; (970) 845-5248.*

Black Mountain Ranch
★★★/$$$$

This working cattle ranch opens its gates to city slickers who want to go on an all-day cattle drive through aspen groves and spruce forests. If you don't want to saddle up, your family can sit back by the trout pond and reel in a catch or just enjoy a barbecue dinner. *Located between Vail and Steamboat Springs on Hwy. 131, 21 miles north of I-70; (800) 967-2401; (970) 653-4226;* www.black mtnranch.com

Centennial Express Lift
★★★★/$$$-$$$$

Catch this open-air chairlift in Beaver Creek for a gorgeous ride up to a view of the surrounding mountains. The chairs seat four adults, but you can manage a family of five on board with no problem; caution your kids not to fidget too much. At the top, you can have lunch at the **Spruce Saddle Lodge**, which offers burgers, corn dogs, and chicken fingers for kids and grilled chicken sandwiches, burgers, and salads for adults. Youngsters can amuse themselves with a variety of games at the top, including horseshoes and volleyball. Your family can also go on a nature hike on one of several well-marked trails; pick up a map detailing all the trails when you buy your lift ticket. The lift and the restaurant operate daily in summer and winter, but close in late September until the beginning of the ski season and again from mid-April to mid-June. *The lift is located next to the Hyatt Regency Beaver Creek; (970) 845-9090.*

Time in a Bottle

Our kids (Kiersten, 12, Nicolai, 10, Jarin, 4, and Micah, 1) love to collect rocks, so whenever we go someplace special, we choose one to mark the trip. We write on them—where we went, the date, the initials of those who were there, and other notes, if there is room—and save them in glass jars. We love looking at the rocks and remembering the places we've been and the people who were with us. For instance, one rock says "Horseback Riding, September 27, 1997" and includes the names of family members and the horses we rode (and some we will never try to ride again, like the one that loved to try to buck us off!). Memories of Sunday drives, camping trips, fairs, birthday parties, and family vacations are all recorded and "bottled."

Ron and Marci Clawson, Sandy, Utah

Dobson Ice Arena ★★/$

If the weather gets too nasty, head to this indoor ice rink for a fun way to spin your time. Hockey games and other special events often preempt open skating, so call ahead to check the schedule. *321 E. Lionshead Cir., Vail; (970) 479-2270; (970) 479-2271.*

Eagle Bahn Gondola and Adventure Ridge ★★★/$$$-$$$$

This is a great way to see the gorgeous mountain views of the Vail Valley. Pile your family into one of the gondolas, which hold as many as six, and ride up about a mile to the top of the mountain. Once there, you can check out Adventure Ridge, the site of seasonal activities, restaurants, a small nature center, and an observation deck. In winter, your family can ski, ice-skate, snowmobile, sled, snowboard, or snowshoe—or even hop on an inner tube and slide down the slopes. In summer, there are great nature trails and mountain biking, but be careful: it's very hard to stop once you get going down the mountain. *In the center of Lionshead, Vail; (970) 476-9090.*

Ford Park ★★★/Free

Vail's version of a city park and green space is just as upscale as the resort itself. Set by the Betty Ford Alpine Gardens, the kids' play area features a huge wooden play structure next to a gorgeous man-made waterfall. In the summer, it's the perfect place

C Lazy U Ranch

A dude ranch that mixes the rustic and the upscale, this is one of the best in the business. The wide choice of accommodations includes everything from secluded cabins to suites (all with twin beds for kids), fireplaces, and whirlpool tubs. Every guest, ages 6 and up, is assigned a horse at this 5,000-acre ranch in the Rocky Mountains (younger wranglers enjoy pony rides in the supervised children's program). Families eat breakfast together, and then typically go their separate ways. Among the favorite activities are fishing, paddleboat rides, and hayrides. Nightly entertainment features square dances, cookouts, and campfire sing-alongs. Your weeklong stay culminates with the kids' show-off Showdeo. *3640 Colorado Hwy. 125, Granby; Mailing address: P.O. Box 379, Granby 80446; (970) 887-3344; www.clazyuranch.com*

to watch paragliders drift down the mountain and land—sometimes right next to you. The park is also home to the Gerald R. Ford Amphitheater (the former president and his wife have a home in the area and spend a lot of time here). There's also a great playground on the adjacent Gore Creek school grounds

SUPER SKI SPOTS

Colorado ski resorts are family-friendly, and many offer great kids' programs and activities, but we think the following resorts really go all out to please kids—and their parents.

Aspen/Snowmass
FamilyFun ★★★★/$$$$

Often billed as the most upscale of Colorado's ski resorts, Aspen is also one of the most child-friendly. Buttermilk Mountain has primarily beginner and intermediate runs; it's best for kids and parents still perfecting their technique. The ski program for those ages 3 to 6 offers a separate ski hill and chairlift, and lunch and snacks are provided. Older kids can enroll in full-day lessons, and children 8 to 19 can take the three-day, learn-to-ski package deals that include lift tickets, equipment, and instruction (lunch is included for kids 8 to 12). Be aware that Aspen prohibits snowboarding, a plus in the eyes of families who don't like having to dodge the fast-moving and often out-of-control boarders on the slopes. If you want to snowboard, nearby Snowmass welcomes it.

The resort also has a children's play area called Fort Frog that has a mock jail, saloon, and tepee village. Characters such as Max the Moose and Colonel Frog inhabit the area, and kids can take them on in ski races. If your youngsters can go faster than the moose, they can get a button that says, "I Waxed Max"; if the moose wins, your kids get a button that reads, "I Made Tracks with Max." For older kids, there is a snowboard park and a snowboard half pipe. *(800) 525-6200; (970) 925-1220;* www.aspen snowmass.com

Beaver Creek
FamilyFun ★★★★/$$$$

This resort in Avon is one of the most family-friendly ski areas in the state. It can be expensive, but worth it given the low students-to-instructor ratio at the children's ski school and the resort's compact size, which makes getting around quick and easy. If you don't feel like walking, there are free shuttles available. Ski instruction is available for kids as young as 3 (they must be potty trained). To get and keep younger kids interested, the resort recreates a gold mine, a bear cave, and a tepee village. And each week, there is a big ski competition where everyone gets a ribbon. *(970) 845-9090;* www. beavercreek.com

Breckenridge
FamilyFun ★★★/$$$

This resort is ideal for active families looking for lots to do. In winter, the resort offers a comprehensive ski school for ages 3 and up, and snowboarding classes for ages 7 and up. Off the slopes, sign up for snowmobiling, dog sledding, and horse-drawn sleigh rides. In summer the focus shifts to hiking, biking, horseback riding, fishing, and rafting on the nearby Colorado and Arkansas rivers. The town has a state-of-the-art recreation center with tennis courts, rock-climbing walls, and a pool with a 150-foot water slide. The Breckenridge Ice Rink is open year-round and the town's Backstage Theatre has an active children's program, staging productions such as *A Christmas Carol.* If parents want a night out, the resort's Café Breck offers a three-hour supervised program for kids with food, activities and entertainment. *(970) 453-5000;* www.breckenridge.snow.com

MUST-SEE FamilyFun MUST-SEE Copper Mountain Resort ★★★/$$$

Already a winner with families, this resort recently completed a huge renovation that makes it even better. Head to the Union Creek day lodge, where you can get lift tickets and sign up for ski lessons (eight levels offered) and snowboarding instruction (for ages 12 and up). The Mill Café, located upstairs in the day lodge, has a kid-size buffet, and the kids' ski school has a cafeteria with kid-size tables and chairs and a play area. In addition to hitting the slopes, kids over

age 4 can ice-skate, sled, and build snow sculptures in the children's program. The resort also offers 30 acres of mostly easy terrain that's designated as the Family Ski Area, and is separate from the serious downhill trails on the other side of the mountain; *(866) 656-1539; (970) 968-2882;* www.coppercolorado.com

MUST-SEE FamilyFun MUST-SEE Steamboat Springs ★★★/$$$

Steamboat pioneered the Kids Ski Free concept back in 1982, and the family-friendly resort treats more than 10,000 kids ages 12 and under to skiing, lodging, and rental equipment each year. The Kids Vacation Center has a day-care center and a protected ski area where kids ages 2 to 7 receive an hour of instruction each day. The resort also offers regular lessons for children ages 6 and up and snowboarding for those ages 8 and up—plus special teen classes during the holidays. Kids' Night Out, a special night of supervised fun for kids ages 3 to 12, is held every evening except Sunday and Monday. Families can wander around the scenic downtown, go ice-skating, or hit the soothing warm waters at the Steamboat Springs Health and Recreation Association. *The resort is at 2305 Mt. Werner Circle in Steamboat; (970) 879-6111;* www.steamboat.com

(continued on page 318)

Winter Park
FamilyFun ★★★/$$-$$$

Kids' ski programs here start with 3-year-olds (who must be potty trained) and focus on creating an easygoing first-time experience with lots of fun and games. By ages 5 and 6, youngsters learn how to get on and off the ski lift, and instruction for kids ages 9 to 13 is geared to the proficiency of the child. Beginning skiers get 25 acres of trails called Discovery Park, which is isolated from the trails that have faster-moving, more experienced skiers and where they can practice their ski-lift skills away from the main lifts. The resort (*800/729-5514*) is renowned for its ski program for the physically challenged and uses adaptive equipment that helps those with any of more than 40 types of disabilities. To get here hop aboard the Ski Train (*303/296-4754*), which runs up the mountain from Denver on weekends from December through April; www.ski winterpark.com

Snow Mountain Ranch, operated by the YMCA of the Rockies, offers a family-friendly experience similar to Estes Park's YMCA program (see page 333). The 5,000 acres of meadows, aspen groves, and fir trees make for great cross-country skiing, and you can pull your little one along in a small, enclosed sled called a pulk. *(970) 887-2152.*

with tire swings and slides. *Located about a quarter of a mile east of the main Vail Village (near Gerald R. Ford Amphitheater, 530 S. Frontage Road); (970) 476-0103.*

Four Eagle Ranch
★★★/Free$$$$

If your family gets tired of the upscale scene in Vail and Beaver Creek, head to this down-home ranch for a taste of the Old West. The ranch offers horseback riding year-round, with hot cider served on winter trail rides and lemonade on summer treks. In the winter, sleigh rides are also available. Kids can also visit some of the ranch's other animals, including a buffalo named Reject. Lunch is offered daily, with the menu ranging from grilled chicken sandwiches to buffalo bratwurst—don't worry, it's not from Reject. Complimentary hayrides make a fun postmeal activity. *Hwy. 131, about four miles north of I-70; (970) 926-3372;* www.4eagle ranch.com

Nottingham Park
★★★/Free-$$

Yet another great outdoor attraction in Beaver Creek, this place offers more activities than you can cram into an afternoon. The 48-acre park in Avon, next to Beaver Creek, has everything from canoes to croquet. In the winter, ice-skating is available on the park's lake (from about Christmas through February, depending on weather conditions). In the summer, the lake becomes a place to canoe, kayak, and ride paddleboats. Your family can also rent equipment at the park's headquarters and mountain-bike, in-line skate, or play croquet, Frisbee, football, basketball, or soccer. *From I-70, exit at Avon/Beaver Creek; follow Avon Road to West Beaver Creek Boulevard to the park, 325 Benchmark Rd.; (970) 949-9191.*

Vail Athletic Club
★★★/$$$$

We've listed this facility because its indoor climbing wall is a huge hit with youngsters ages 5 and up. Sign up your kids for a lessons-and-climbing package, which teaches them the basics of rock climbing in a 90-minute class. It's well supervised, so if you like, steal away for a romantic lunch or dinner at one of the nearby restaurants while your kids climb away like little spiders. *352 E. Meadow Dr., Vail; (970) 476-7960;* www.vailmountainlodge-spa.com

Vilar Center ★★/$-$$

This swanky theater hosts the Family Film Series (held last summer on Friday evenings), with showings of family-friendly movies like *Toy Story* and *Matilda.* The theater's other events include theatrical productions geared to kids, such as *The Three Little Pigs* and *The Wizard of Oz. 68 Avondale Lane, Beaver Creek; (888) 920-2787; (970) 845-8497;* www.vilarcenter.org

BUNKING DOWN

The Charter at Beaver Creek
★★★/$$-$$$$

This sprawling, upscale hotel has units that include two bedrooms, a kitchen, washer/dryer, and VCRs. Add a huge fireplace (with wood supplied daily) and balcony and you have a true home-away-from-home experience. Kids love the huge pool and the videotape vending machine, where you put in your money and make your pick from the selection of Disney favorites and teen-oriented titles. *120 Offerson Rd., Beaver Creek; (800) 525-6660; (970) 949-6660;* www.thecharter.com

Hyatt Regency Beaver Creek
★★★★/$$-$$$$

This posh, slope-side hotel offers great convenience by being close to the ski runs and Beaver Creek's wonderful children's programs. The ski school runs in the winter. Camp Hyatt for kids ages 3 to 12 offers activities from 9 A.M. to 10 P.M. year-round. The Hyatt also has one of the area's top spas. **NOTE:** Be careful if you have young children because the rooms have heated towel racks. You may want to unplug your unit. *136 E. Thomas Pl., Beaver Creek; (800) 233-1234; (970) 949-1234;* www.hyatt.com

GOOD EATS

Blue Moose ★★/$

Parked inside the posh Beaver Creek Plaza, this casual pizza parlor is a place your family can unwind, after a busy day on the mountain, with innovative pizzas (they have lasagna pizza and buffalo wing pizza, among others) or calzones. Save room for a dessert of homemade chocolate-chip or oatmeal-Cheerios-raisin cookies. *122 Beaver Creek Pl., Beaver Creek; (970) 845-8666.*

Chili Willy's
★★★/$-$$

Why pay high resort prices when you can drive a few miles to Minturn, a small railroad town between Vail and Beaver Creek, and get great food at bargain prices at places like this Mexican restaurant run by Texas transplants? Kids can get quesadillas or tacos, and parents can unwind with one of the delicious margaritas. *101 W. Main St., Minturn; (970) 827-5887.*

Columbine Bakery
★★★/$-$$

This simple but cozy bakery is a great place to load up on carbs before skiing or hiking. Breakfast (served from 7:30 to 11 A.M.) includes freshly baked Danish, muffins, and croissants. Lunch (served from 11 A.M. to 3 P.M.) features everything from Philly steak sandwiches to peanut-butter-and-jelly. You can also come here to stock your picnic hamper or order a birthday cake. *51 Beaver Creek Pl., Avon; (970) 949-1400;* www.co-biz.com/columbinebakery

Minturn Country Club
★★★/$$

Don't look for the golf course; there isn't one. This down-home steak place does, however, offer top-quality sirloins and filets, and—here's the fun part—you cook 'em yourself. Kids who may never help out at home suddenly get interested in cooking when the tables are turned at a restaurant. Obviously, younger kids shouldn't take on this task, but they can look on from a safe

COLORADO IS NICKNAMED "the Centennial State" because it attained statehood in 1876, 100 years after the United States declared its independence.

distance as Mom and Dad "make dinner." Older children can grill their steak just like they like it, so there's no complaining. *131 Main St., Minturn; (970) 827-4114.*

Splendido
★★★★/$$$$
Yes, it's swanky, but this upscale Beaver Creek restaurant is surprisingly child-friendly. If your kids have a modicum of manners and you want to celebrate with a delicious—albeit pricey—meal, then splurge here. Chef David Walford doesn't mind downsizing the meals on the menu for kids and has even been known to grill a burger or two to please young ones who like the tried and true. Come early, between 6 and 7 P.M., before the place gets really busy, and Walford will even treat your kids to a tour of the kitchen, where they will no doubt be most impressed with the ice-cream machine. *17 Chateau Lane, Beaver Creek; (970) 845-8808.*

Up the Creek
★★★/$$
How many restaurants let your kids frolic in a creek while you wait for your meal? This one—located on Gore Creek next to the Children's Fountain—does, and it's a great lunch or dinner stop. Kids can order hamburgers, grilled cheese sandwiches, or pasta. The mom-and-Dad menu includes salads, pasta, and fresh fish, and all are priced rea-

sonably, particularly given the unique setting. *223 E. Gore Creek Dr., Vail; (970) 476-8141.*

SOUVENIR HUNTING

Treasure Island Toys
This shop has a wide selection of toys, including a great section with educational toys, craft kits, and puzzles—all at what the owners promise are "Denver prices." *In Chapel Square, Avon; (970) 748-1708.*

Verbatim Booksellers
This bookstore has thousands of books for kids—from Harry Potter to Beatrix Potter. *Located across from the Lionshead parking area in Vail; (970) 476-3032.*

Estes Park's camps, cabins, and hotels are reserved months in advance by families who return summer after summer

Estes Park

WHEN SUMMER heats up the American Plains, families start packing for Rocky, the affectionate nickname of Rocky Mountain National Park. Each year, the park draws more than 3.4 million visitors, most during the summer-vacation season. The reasons: incredible mountain vistas, meadows dotted with wildflowers, and the occasional photo opportunity with an elk. The park, formed in 1915 after a decade of lobbying by photographer and naturalist Enos Mills, is about a two-hour drive from Denver. You and your family can either make your own fun, packing a picnic and planning an easy nature hike, or turn to professional outfitters who can take you on a horseback ride or fishing expedition. Either way, your kids are bound to have fun chasing chipmunks and having a summer snowball fight along the stunning Trail Ridge Road.

Estes Park is the logical base of operations for a family stay. The central downtown is three blocks of pizza parlors, gift shops, and

THE **FamilyFun** LIST

MUST-SEE
MUST-SEE

Grand Lake (page 326)

Rocky Mountain National Park (page 326)

Trail Ridge Road (page 329)

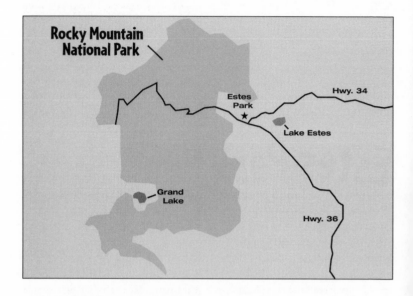

Rocky Mountain National Park

Hwy. 34

Estes Park
★

Lake Estes

Grand Lake

Hwy. 36

sporting-goods vendors clustered along a four-lane main street that gets clogged in the busy summer season with throngs of tourists. But don't despair: you can take the bypass to avoid the jams and spend your time in the family-owned lodges nestled in the pines by the Big Thompson and Fall Rivers. Camping sites are a popular alternative, but a few are located near horse stables; unless you want a natural experience that includes horseflies and the smell of manure, ask before booking. **NOTE:** Because the supply of Estes Park's 6,000 or so hotel rooms and campsites doesn't always meet demand, it is imperative to plan a vacation in the peak summer season at least three or four months in advance. Don't think you can stumble into town and find a

room on a July or August weekend. Staying at the popular YMCA of the Rockies, for instance, involves making a donation and getting on a waiting list.

A vacation in Estes Park will enable your youngsters to appreciate the wonders of nature up close and personal. The National Park Service offers ranger-led programs called Children's Adventures for those ages 6 to 12, which focus on hands-on activities that teach kids

about Rocky's geology and wildlife. In the Skins and Skull program, kids get to touch animal skulls and stuffed animals while learning about moose, elk, bighorn sheep, and bobcats. We'll also spotlight a couple of great hikes inside the park that won't wear you out too much, and suggest a few prime picnic spots. In addition, we'll help you saddle up on a trail ride and show you a fishing hole where a catch is almost guaranteed.

This area isn't the place to come for gourmet meals, but that's fine for most families. Generally, the restaurants cater to kids with the standard pizza, burgers, and corn dogs. Since many accommodations include kitchens, you will likely spend some time at the large Safeway grocery store, just off Highway 34 in the Stanley Village. To save a few dollars, sign up for a Safeway frequent shopper's card. Even if you never use it again, you could rack up significant savings. There's also a handy place to wash clothes called Dad's Laundromat in the same shopping center as the grocery store, making it convenient for one person to shop while the other watches the spin cycle.

Most families come here for a week, or at least five days, which is enough time to drive most of the park's roads, hike several trails, enjoy two or three picnics, have a day of horseback riding or river rafting, and perhaps even take a trip to the other side of the park for

FamilyFun GAME

Race to 20

Two players take turns counting to twenty. On each turn, a player can say one or two numbers. (If the first says "One," the second might say "Two, three.") Try to force your opponent to reach twenty first.

the glorious vistas of Grand Lake. **NOTE:** If you are coming from an area that's near sea level, consider spending at least one night in Denver to get acclimated to the 5,200-foot elevation before coming to the high peaks here, which reach 12,000 feet and higher. Also, as in any high-altitude area, wear lots of sunscreen and take a break when you or another family member becomes too winded. With some advance planning, your trip to Rocky Mountain National Park will become what it is to many others—a family tradition.

JUST FOR FUN

Cascade Creek MiniGolf and Ride-A-Kart ★★/$-$$

If your kids get bored with all the nature and wildlife interaction, head to this commercial attraction where they can spend a couple of hours riding go-carts, playing miniature golf, and riding bumper boats. There also are baseball batting cages, an arcade and family game room, and a miniature-train ride. *Located two miles east of town on Hwy. 34; (970) 586-6495.*

Estes Park Aerial Tramway
★★/Free-$$

If you don't have time to drive Trail Ridge Road to see mountain vistas, a quick trip up in this small gondola car is another option for getting a panoramic view of the area. Be forewarned that lines to board the tram can get long in the late afternoon, so get there early. There are picnic tables and a small snack bar at the top of the mountain. *420 E. Riverside Dr., Estes Park; (970) 586-3675;* www.estes-park.com

Fishing ★★★/Free-$$

The Big Thompson and Fall rivers offer great trout-fishing opportunities. For more information, see "Fishing for Fun" on page 329.

Grand Lake
FamilyFun ★★★/Free

MUST-SEE

MUST-SEE

A haven for boaters and fishermen, this mountain lake is a less crowded alternative as a base camp for exploring Rocky Mountain National Park. According to Ute legend, the fog that shrouds the lake each morning represents that spirits of women and children whose boat capsized as they were fleeing attacking Cheyennes and Arapahoes. You can rent a pontoon boat at one of the marinas; *Trail Ridge Marina*

(970) 627-3586 or *Beacon Marina (970) 627-3671*. Rates range from $50 for two hours to $145 for an all-day rental.

Rocky Mountain National Park
FamilyFun ★★★★/$$

MUST-SEE

MUST-SEE

This jewel of the National Park Service covers 417 square miles of the Rockies, stretching from Estes Park across the Continental Divide to Grand Lake. The first thing families should do here is stop by one of the park's visitors' centers. There are several—the Kawuneeche center on the west side of the park, the Lily Lake, Fall River, and Beaver Meadows centers on the east side, and the Alpine Center on Trail Ridge Road. We suggest entering the park at the Fall River entrance station, which has some interactive play activities—kids can dress up in a park-ranger uniform, pioneer garb, or traditional Native American outfits. At all the visitors' centers, youngsters can sign up for the Junior Rangers program and, after completing a work sheet quizzing them on local flora and fauna, earn a badge. You'll want to pick up a schedule of events and find out about daily ranger-led programs such as Rocky's Engineers, a look at the importance of beavers, and adventure programs, for kids ages 6 to 12, offering hands-on activities that teach about the animals, plants, and rocks in the park. Each center is also a great place to pick up sou-

HORSING AROUND
at Sombrero Stables

I F YOUR KIDS are into horsing around, be sure to book a trail ride during your stay here. The most popular local stable in these parts seems to be **Sombrero**; its owners have been in the business here for more than 50 years and they welcome kids, even preschoolers, who can ride double with a parent. A guided horseback ride takes you to amazing vantage points for awesome views, while skilled wranglers describe points of interest and provide a bit of history and humor along the way—like detailing the silly things previous riders have done. On our one-hour ride out of the main Estes Park stable, the guides pointed to a large tree dubbed the Grandfather Tree and told us to touch it for good luck. Take it from us: the sight of your youngsters on horseback for the first time by themselves touching that big tree and smiling is priceless.

The one-hour ride is long enough for kids under age 8 and city slickers with little riding experience. If your family is up for more trail time, consider the popular two-hour breakfast ride, which leaves at 7 A.M. and includes a breakfast of sausage, pancakes, eggs, and orange juice. There's also a Steak Fry dinner ride where the cowboy chefs cook up steaks, Dutch-oven potatoes, and baked beans on open fires—just like

cowboys would on a real roundup. All meal rides require advance reservations, available by calling *(970) 586-4577*, but it is possible to walk up and saddle up for the one- and two-hour nonfood trail rides. *Sombrero is located at Estes Park on Hwy. 34;* www.sombrero.com

The same owners also operate **Hi-Country Stables**, which offers rides inside Rocky Mountain National Park at the Moraine Stable and Glacier Creek Stable. Rides range in length from two hours—the most popular option—to ten hours, a trek which crosses the Continental Divide and goes down to Grand Lake. Rides in the park tend to book a day or two in advance during the summer, so call ahead—and opt for a morning ride to avoid risking an afternoon thunderstorm. The stables operate from May 20 to September 20. *Moraine Park Stable; (970) 586-3244; Glacier Creek Stable; (970) 586-2327.*

FamilyFun FACT

Male and female bighorn sheep have horns. Unlike animals with antlers, the sheep retain their horns for their entire lives. The size and shape of the horns help to distinguish the age and sex of each sheep. In rams, the horns grow continuously to nearly a full curl. The horns of female sheep grow into a sharp, straight point.

venirs, books on the park's history, and wildlife and trail guides. Your kids can ask the rangers at the information desk if any bears have been sighted recently; there are no grizzlies here, but there are brown bears, and you probably won't want to go into areas where they have been spotted.

If possible, get an early start. The park gets crowded by the afternoon, and it can be difficult finding a parking space at some of the popular stops—such as Sprague Lake—after 10 A.M. A shuttle is offered in the summer from Glacier Basin to popular Bear Lake, but if you get there early enough, you may be able to find parking at the lake. The hikes around Bear Lake and Sprague Lake are easy for kids. For a longer, more strenuous, hike by several waterfalls, take the Fern Lake Trail, located just west of the **Moraine Park Museum.**

The museum is a nice place to stop if you have been driving awhile and want to stretch your legs. It fea-

tures exhibits created by the Denver Museum of Nature and Science. Kids like playing the Animal, Vegetable, or Mineral game, where they get to test their newfound knowledge of the park's ecosystems and natural history. If you need to brush up on your Rocky knowledge, there are also frequent lectures and displays of the park's flora and fauna and its geological history. The museum is open seasonally from May through September. *Take U.S. 36 into the park, and drive two miles on Bear Lake Road; (970) 586-1206.* **NOTE:** There's not much in the way of food or drinks sold inside the park, so you should pick up something in town before heading out. When looking for a picnic spot, be a bit leery of those around the lakes (lots of mosquitoes) or near stables (where flies are a problem). We prefer those near creeks or streams, specifically the group of tables on Bear Lake Road by Mill Creek (if you are coming from the Moraine Park Museum, it's the first picnic turnoff on the left). *The park is about five miles outside Estes Park on U.S. 36 or U.S. 34; (970) 586-1206; (970) 586-1333;* www.nps.gov/romo *or* www.explore-rocky.com

Stanley Park ★★★/Free-$
Families can enjoy the great outdoors here with picnic facilities, a playground with a large climbing structure and three slides, a sand volleyball court, and a skateboard

park. In winter, the park offers public ice skating. *Highway 36 and Community Drive on the south shore of Lake Estes; (about 45 miles southwest of Denver; take I-70W and highway 9S), (970) 586-8191.*

Trail Ridge Road
FamilyFun ★★★★/$$

The highest continuous paved highway in the United States, Trail Ridge Road travels through the heart of Rocky Mountain National Park from Estes Park to Grand Lake, providing access to the delicate beauty of the Alpine Tundra, which comprises a full third of the park's 415 square miles. This route, with 11 miles of pavement above the tree line, climbs from Beaver Meadows Park Headquarters visitors' center (7,840 feet above sea level) to more than 12,000 feet. It is open year-round. The road is one of the most gorgeous drives in North America, right up there with Glacier National Park's famous Going to the Sun Road and the Blue Ridge Parkway. Even in the heat of summer, snow is found at the higher elevations and daytime temperatures can be quite chilly, so plan on wearing sweatshirts or light jackets. It takes about three to four hours to drive from Estes Park to Grand Lake, including stops at several overlooks.

Fishing for Fun

Estes Park is an angler's paradise. That's because the Big Thompson and Fall rivers provide ample opportunities for catching brown, brook, rainbow, and cutthroat trout.

Fishing is permitted in designated areas of **Rocky Mountain National Park**, including **Mills Lake, Sprague Lake,** and **Arrowhead Lake.** To preserve the park's fish population, there are very detailed rules and regulations on the size of fish you are permitted to possess and the types of lures permitted. For example, you are allowed to catch two rainbow and brown trout per day, but they must be 10 inches or longer. Greenback trout must be released if you catch one. All anglers ages 16 and over must have a valid Colorado fishing license, which costs $18.25 for a five-day permit. Fishing regulations are available at the park's information centers. For a detailed guide to fishing these waters, check out the book *Fly Fishing in Rocky Mountain National Park*, by Todd Hosman (Pruett Publishing Co., 1996).

If you'd rather let someone else handle the regulations and other details, **Estes Park Mountain Shop** (*358 E. Elkhorn Ave., Estes Park;* 970/586-6548) offers lessons, guided excursions, and gear rental. Guided fishing trips—including a four-hour, half-day excursion that's ideal for beginners—start at $100 per person (at press time).

329

Trout Haven ★★★/$-$$

This fishing pond almost guarantees a catch—and the people who run the operation provide the fishing poles and worms, too. You only pay if you catch a fish, and they will clean and even smoke your trout. (Their slogan is "You hook 'em, we cook 'em.") For even better odds, call ahead to see when they've recently restocked the pond. The operators don't allow catch-and-release because they say it causes the released fish to succumb to a fungus that kills them. *810 Moraine Ave., Estes Park; (970) 586-5525;* www.trouthaven.com

BUNKING DOWN

Aspen Lodge ★★★/$$$-$$$$

A great place to stage a family reunion, this resort offers numerous packages and has a reunion coordinator available. You can choose between a room in the main lodge or a rustic cabin. During the summer, meals are included in the cost of a room, making this an expensive but convenient option for those who don't want to worry about cooking. There's a comprehensive kids' program with activities geared for both pre-kindergartners and older kids, including a nature hike up to a tepee where there's a cookout and campfire sing-along. The program also offers local field trips to a climbing gym, a rock museum, and a glassblower's studio. *6120 Hwy. 7, Estes Park; (800) 332-6867; (970) 586-8133;* www.aspenlodge.net

Evergreens on Fall River ★★★/$$-$$$

This complex of cabins along the Fall River is less than two miles from the national park's entrance and three miles from Estes Park, but it feels secluded, particularly if you can get one of the cabins on the other side of the river and not one by the road. Most families appreciate the clean, two-bedroom units with decks that overlook the river. Kids love fishing, or just throwing rocks in the river and taking a dip in the outdoor hot tub. *1500 Fish Hatchery Rd., Estes Park; (970) 577-9786;* www.estes.park.com/evergreens/

Grand Lake Lodge ★★★/$$

The best place to stay if you want to be on the west side of the park, this lodge is famous for its huge front porch that overlooks scenic Grand Lake and Shadow Mountain. It offers secluded two-bedroom cabins in the hills and has a playground and a game room to occupy the kids. There's also a pool, a hot tub (handy after hiking or horseback riding), this scenic restaurant that overlooks Grand Lake. Famous for its mesquite-grilled fish and meats, the lodge also offers a kids' menu that includes all the usual suspects. *Off Hwy. 34, north of Grand Lake; (970) 627-3967.*

Mountain Home Café ★★★/$$

This place is a great breakfast spot, famous for its German potato pancakes (served with applesauce and sour cream) and its Arizona hash browns, which come with Monterey jack cheese and salsa. Kids can get the made-from-scratch pancakes shaped like Mickey Mouse. Open 7 A.M. to 9 P.M. *Located in the Stanley Village Shopping Center, just down from the Safeway at 451 E. Wonderview, Estes Park; (970) 586-6624.*

Penelope's World Famous Burgers and Fries ★★★/$-$$

The name tells it all—almost. If your kids don't like hamburgers, the menu offers chicken fingers and "trout nuggets." Also on tap are old-fashioned flavored colas in cherry, lemon, chocolate, vanilla, strawberry, and lime. *229 Elkhorn St., Estes Park; (970) 586-2277.*

Village Pizza
★★/$$

Thick crust or thin—either way, this is one of the best pizza spots in town. There's also a small video arcade to entertain the kids. *543 Big Thompson Ave., Estes Park; (970) 586-6031.*

A Day in "Rocky"

8 A.M. Breakfast at the **Mountain Home Café** (see page 332). Pack a picnic lunch (there is a Kentucky Fried Chicken in the same shopping center), then take U.S. 34 west to the Fall River entrance.

9:30 A.M. Go to the **Fall River** visitors' center (see page 326); check on ranger-led programs held later in the day. Pick up snacks and souvenirs.

10 A.M. Pull over at West Horseshoe Park to see if you can spot any deer or elk. At Deer Ridge Junction, get on U.S. 36, then take a left on Bear Lake Road. Go to the Sprague Lake parking lot and head out on a hike around the lake or go on a two-hour trail ride at the stables there (call ahead for a reservation at **Glacier Creek Stable**; *970/586-3244*).

12:30 P.M. Picnic **by Mill Creek** (look for the pull-off on the right after you pass the Mill Creek Basin Trailhead on Bear Lake Road).

2 P.M. Go to the **Moraine Park Museum** (see page 328) to see exhibits created by the Denver Museum of Nature and Science and play a Rocky version of I Spy (Animal, Vegetable, or Mineral) that tests your kids' knowledge of the area's geology and wildlife.

Grand Lake Lodge Restaurant
★★★/$$

Your family will definitely get the feeling of eating in a grand lodge at this scenic restaurant that overlooks Grand Lake. Famous for its mesquite-grilled fish and meats, the lodge also offers a kids' menu that includes all the usual suspects. *Off Hwy. 34, north of Grand Lake; (970) 627-3967.*

Mountain Home Café ★★★/$$

This place is a great breakfast spot, famous for its German potato pancakes (served with applesauce and sour cream) and its Arizona hash browns, which come with Monterey jack cheese and salsa. Kids can get the made-from-scratch pancakes shaped like Mickey Mouse. Open 7 A.M. to 9 P.M. *Located in the Stanley Village Shopping Center, just down from the Safeway at 451 E. Wonderview, Estes Park; (970) 586-6624.*

In the fall, you may hear the **bull elk bugling**. Males emit this call during mating season in order to intimidate rivals. Bugling sounds like a series of low, resonant sounds that quickly rise to a high-pitched squeal before dropping to grunting sounds.

Penelope's World Famous Burgers and Fries ★★★/$-$$

The name tells it all—almost. If your kids don't like hamburgers, the menu offers chicken fingers and "trout nuggets." Also on tap are old-fashioned flavored colas in cherry, lemon, chocolate, vanilla, strawberry, and lime. *229 Elkhorn St., Estes Park; (970) 586-2277.*

Village Pizza
★★/$$

Thick crust or thin—either way, this is one of the best pizza spots in town. There's also a small video arcade to entertain the kids. *543 Big Thompson Ave., Estes Park; (970) 586-6031.*

SOUVENIR HUNTING

Geppetto's Toy Factory

This old-fashioned toy shop offers lots of games and puzzles, plush animals, educational toys, and a book nook. There's also a supply of travel toys so you can restock your car's toy bin. *160 W. Elkhorn Ave., Estes Park; (970) 586-5709.*

In the Groove

Teens and preteens will think this shop is way cool, with its supply of tie-dyed shirts and other '60s- and '70s-inspired paraphernalia. Just don't tell them you used to wear this stuff. *149 E. Elkhorn Ave., Estes Park; (970) 577-0490.*

Seybold's Gifts

This shop stocks everything from Southwest pottery to Beanie Babies, making it a good bet if you have kids with divergent interests. *135 E. Elkhorn Ave., Estes Park; (970) 586-3495; www.seybolds.com*

YMCA OF THE ROCKIES

THIS 820-ACRE RESORT is one of the best places for family reunions in North America. The reasons: great programs, great facilities, and great prices. The only negative is the challenge of getting in here in the busy summer season. Securing a reservation for one of the 200 cabins in the popular summer months takes some tactical planning. Operated by the YMCA of Denver, the facility takes reservations from its members first (membership is $150 annually). Paying the fee gets you first dibs on the popular cabins, which have kitchen facilities. Members have to apply for the weeks they want; each request is processed according to seniority and when the request was mailed in. After a specific date in late spring, nonmembers can make reservations. If you don't want a cabin, it's much easier to get a standard hotel room.

Sound complicated? Maybe, but many families wouldn't dream of staying anywhere else. The YMCA offers fabulous kids' programs for ages 3 through 17, which include nature hikes, horseback riding, and hayrides. In the winter, youngsters can cross-country ski, snowshoe, or ice-skate. The resort also has three restaurants, a church, a museum, and a library. You might want to warn your kids that there aren't any televisions in the rooms because the Y wants to encourage family interaction. A few TVs are available for rent, but don't expect great reception. Also, accommodations can be a bit cozy, another Y effort to encourage family togetherness. If that's your style, consider one of the cabins with rooms that sleep six to eight in bunk beds.

Large groups and family reunions are welcome—the resort even has reunion coordinators who will help plan activities for your clan. If your family wants a campfire, the staff will get the fire going and supply marshmallows and song sheets. They will also help organize relay games or educational lectures on outdoor survival or Native American history. One of the Y's more popular accommodations is the Pattie Hyde Barclay Reunion Lodge, which has its own hostess on the grounds. The lodge sleeps 72 people and has four extra-long dining tables.

There is also a sister center in Winter Park, outside Denver, called Snow Mountain Ranch, which is typically less busy in the summer but heats up in winter during ski season. For more information on Winter Park, see the Colorado Ski Country chapter, page 318. *The YMCA of the Rockies is located five miles southwest of Estes Park at 2515 Tunnel Rd.; (970) 586-3341.*

The Denver Zoo is home to nearly 4,000 animals, including a black rhino that paints, a pair of brotherly lions, and a polar bear named Cranberry in honor of her Thanksgiving birth.

Denver

DENVER IS CALLED the Mile High City because its elevation is approximately 5,280 feet above sea level, but it isn't the mountainous city some visitors expect. It's actually quite flat; in fact, its other nickname is Queen City of the Plains. The city spreads out like a green blanket of trees and parks with straight streets that are easy for visiting families to navigate. For mountains, look to the west, where the base of the "Front Range" of the Rocky Mountains rises, creating an impressive horizon of snowcapped peaks. As you drive in from the Great Plains, the mountains look at first like clouds, then maybe a mirage. Only when you get almost into the city do the peaks come into focus. For kicks, ask your kids to imagine that they are making the journey in a covered wagon and that to head

THE FamilyFun LIST

MUST-SEE
MUST-SEE

Butterfly Pavilion and Insect Center (page 340)

Children's Museum of Denver (page 338)

Colorado's Ocean Journey (page 340)

Coors Field (page 341)

Denver Museum of Nature and Science (page 339)

Denver Zoo (see page 342)

Six Flags Elitch Gardens Theme Park (page 346)

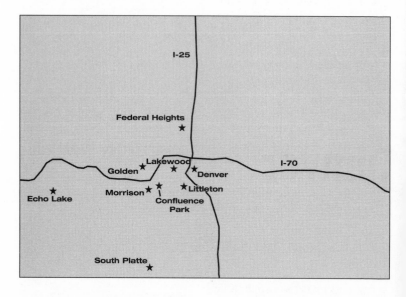

west, they will have to cross over those mountains, some more than 14,000 feet high.

Denver grew into a city in the latter part of the 19th century, when miners and other settlers realized the mountains created a shield that protected the area from severe storms. (The city actually gets more than 300 sunny days a year.) The climate and location made it an ideal trading center, and it weathered booms and busts along with the state's gold and silver mines. A taste of the city's Wild West past is easy to sample in Golden, about 15 miles west of town, home to the Buffalo Bill Museum and the Colorado Railroad Museum.

Denver also has plenty of modern-day attractions for kids, including theme parks like Six Flags Elitch Gardens, nationally recognized

museums such as the Denver Museum of Natural History, and such state-of-the-art sports venues as Coors Field, where kids have their own food stand and playground. You may not expect it, but this inland city is also home to one of the top aquariums in the country, Colorado's Ocean Journeys. There's more than enough to keep you busy for a week, but many families come here for three- or four-day weekends on the way to Colorado's famous ski resorts or Rocky Mountain National Park.

The Rockies are Denver's most popular playground, and the region's 2.5 million residents take to the hills for skiing, mountain biking, hiking, and rafting. (The city's outdoor lifestyle helps make Denver one of America's fittest cities; less than 20 percent of the locals are overweight compared with more than 50 percent of the general American population.) Your family can enjoy this outdoor way of life with a picnic and a hike in one of the parks that ring the city.

Be aware that the high altitude here can cause problems for you and your kids. Some people experience shortness of breath, although you generally have to be above 9,000 feet for this to happen. If you're traveling on to higher elevations and are not used to the altitude, it's a good idea to spend a day in Denver to let your body adjust. Also, be sure to put on sunscreen and wear sunglasses because Denver receives 24 percent more ultraviolet light than cities that are near sea level.

Most families find that a car comes in handy if, but if you want to avoid wheels, pack some comfortable walking shoes, check into a downtown hotel, and hike around the bustling 26 blocks of Lower Downtown (called LoDo)—kids can even rock climb and mountain bike without leaving the air-conditioned confines of the REI outdoor superstore.

CULTURAL ADVENTURES

Black American West Museum and Heritage Center ★★★/$

A third of the working cowboys in the Old West were African Americans, many of them freed slaves who migrated west after the Civil War. Their story isn't often portrayed in larger history museums, which makes a stop at this small center all the more important. Although it may not be interactive enough for younger children, those ages 8 and over can learn from the displays and artifacts housed in the former home of Dr. Justina Ford, Denver's first African American doctor (she delivered more than 7,000 babies). Through photographs, personal artifacts, clothing, and oral histories, the exhibits tell the story of Buffalo Soldiers, African American cowboy pioneers, and business owners who helped settle the west. You can reach the museum from downtown by taking the light-rail east to the last stop. The museum is across the street from the train station. *3091 California St., Denver; (303) 292-2566.* www. coax.net/people/lwf/bawmus.htm

Buffalo Bill's Grave and Museum ★★★/$

Located on top of Lookout Mountain, with spectacular views of both the snowcapped Rocky Mountains and the high plains of Denver, this is the final resting place of the famous frontier scout Buffalo Bill Cody. The museum provides a well-rounded look at his exciting life, from Pony Express rider and buffalo hunter to the world's greatest showman (he often performed before the crowned heads of Europe). There are posters from his shows and mementos from his life—including guns, costumes, and historic photographs. *987½ Lookout Mountain Rd. (exit 256 off I-70), Golden; (303) 526-0747;* www. buffalobill.org

About 15 minutes away, your family can see a buffalo herd maintained by the city of Denver, grazing in a field off Interstate 70 at exit 270.

Children's Museum of Denver ★★★★/$$

Hands-on heaven for kids 2 to 8, this museum lets youngsters shop and ring up sales in a mock supermarket, or make cars or trucks from recycled materials. The Discovery Center has a place to learn about the environment, and the Center For the Young Child offers interactive activities in a pretend village with playhouses. At Alphabet Soup, your preschoolers can play with large colorful letters, shapes, and numbers that can be attached to a 28-foot-long activity wall. Older kids will enjoy the museum's special events like the Saturday Family Theater, which includes sing-alongs and plays such as *The Three Little*

Pigs. I-25 at 23rd Ave. (exit 211), Denver; (303) 433-7444; www.cm denver.org

Colorado History Museum ★★/$

A bit dull for younger kids, but interesting to those 8 and older, this museum—through models, paintings, and photographs—tells the tales of Colorado's Indians, gunfighters, wagon trains, mining operations, railroads, sodbusters, explorers, Spanish conquistadors, gold miners, mountain men, and buffalo hunters. A detailed diorama depicts Denver in 1860, before it was destroyed by fire and flood. *13th St. and Broadway, Denver; (303) 866-3682;* www.colo radohistory.org

Colorado State Capitol ★★/Free

Colorado's State Capitol Building is best known for its brilliant dome, which is decorated with 200 ounces of 24-karat gold leaf. Free tours of the building, erected in 1908, offer a visit to the chambers of the Senate and House of Representatives. And even if the legislature isn't in session, a trip to the capitol building offers free tours all year long. On the Capitol's west staircase, you can stand on the step that is exactly "one mile above sea level." The marker was carved into the steps in 1947, but 20 years later, and proving that grown-ups aren't always right, some students discovered that the measurement was wrong; in 1967, a geodetic-survey marker was placed in the correct spot, three steps above the original marker. Go kids! *200 E. Colfax Ave. (Broadway at Colfax), Denver; (303) 866-2604;* www.state.co.us

 Denver Museum of Nature and Science
★★★★/$-$$

This is the fourth-largest museum of its kind in the nation, with three floors of incredible exhibits about our planet and the creatures that live on it. Egyptian mummies, rare gems and minerals, colorful butterflies, and Native American totem poles are interspersed with 80 world-famous dioramas that depict animals from around the globe in realistic settings. Prehistoric Journey is a $7 million exhibit that transports you back to a time when dinosaurs ruled the planet. Visitors walk through displays dubbed "environamas" that duplicate the sights and sounds of prehistoric earth, complete with fighting dinosaurs. The Hall of Life explores the amazing human body through a series of fun, interactive experiments and exhibits. The museum also has an IMAX theater (separate admission required), which has featured such movies as *Adventures in Wild California* and *Dolphins* on a huge screen (four and a half stories tall); film subjects change—call for schedule. *2001 Colorado Blvd., Denver; (303) 370-6357;* www.dmnh.org

Denver in a Day

IT ISN'T RECOMMENDED, but it is possible to hit a few Denver highlights in a day if you are on a quick trip through town:

9 A.M. Early start at the **Denver Zoo** (see page 342).

11:30 A.M. Lunch at the **Hungry Elephant** restaurant (located by the entrance of the park). You should be able to beat the lunch crowds. It's easy, fast, and reasonably priced, but don't expect gourmet fare.

12:30 P.M. **Denver Museum of Nature and Science** (see this page).

2:30 P.M. Browse the **Cherry Creek shopping district** (exit the museum onto Colorado Boulevard and drive south until you get to 1st Avenue). Afterward, head back to the hotel and rest up for dinner.

4:30 P.M. Dinner at **Casa Bonita** (see page 348)—take Interstate 6 west to Lakewood. **NOTE:** Try to get a table next to the waterfall and pool because most kids love getting splashed by the divers as they hit the water.

JUST FOR FUN

Butterfly Pavilion and Insect Center ★★★/$-$$

Bring your camera into this huge greenhouse filled with thousands of butterflies and lush tropical plants. If you're lucky, you might even get a photo of one of nearly 3,000 butterflies perched on your child's shoulder. The 40,000-square-foot facility is the world's largest pavilion of its kind, featuring more than 50 species of butterflies from nine countries. Also included in the museum space are a research laboratory, greenhouse, outdoor habitat, and cultural center. Your kids, however (and you), will be fascinated by the grace and beauty of the butterflies. They will then want to get a close-up look at the less beautiful black widows, giant cockroaches, centipedes, and giant African millipedes. Signs through-out the insect exhibit detail the lifestyles of the creepy crawly creatures and occasionally museum officials bring some out for your kids to touch. Make sure they then wash up before lunch. *6252 W. 104th Ave., Denver; (303) 469-5441; www.butterflies.org*

Colorado Railroad Museum ★★★/$

Forget those stuffy rail museums that say "hands off our choo-choos"—this one welcomes kids on board several vintage trains, including an old mail car where they can play railroad postmaster. In the museum's basement, youngsters can watch a miniature train chug through a mining town and the mountains—but parents have to cough up 25 cents to get it going. On most summer weekends, the museum offers "steam-ups," where a locomotive is fired up to take your family for a short run around the grounds. Call ahead to check the schedule. There's also a bookstore and gift shop, which includes a large selection of Thomas the Tank Engine paraphernalia. *17155 W. 44th Ave., Golden; (303) 279-4591; www.crrm.org*

Colorado's Ocean Journey ★★★★/$$$

This $93 million, world-class aquarium—which opened in June 1999—showcases more than 15,000 fish, plants, and mammals,

---

FamilyFun TIP

Good Golly, Miss Molly

While in Denver, *Titanic* buffs may wish to visit the former home of Margaret Tobin Brown, better known as "the Unsinkable Molly Brown." Ironically, the rags-to-riches society lady was never called Molly during her lifetime; instead, she was known as Maggie.

---

which live in tanks that together hold more than a million gallons of water. Visitors to the aquarium have two distinct "river journeys" they can follow by walking through the exhibits. Both rivers start at 12,000 feet above sea level and flow to the Pacific Ocean, yet they are on opposite sides of the globe and represent completely different ecosystems. The Colorado River journey follows mountain waterfalls and trout streams down to the arid red-rock canyons of the Southwest, and ultimately to the Sea of Cortez. The Kampar River journey begins in the mountains of Sumatra in a tropical rain forest and flows to a coral reef in Indonesia. Kids especially love seeing Sumatran tigers, sharks, and colorful tropical reef fish. *The aquarium is located in Denver's Platte Valley and is connected to the Children's Museum on the South Platte Trolley line. 700 Water St. (exit 211 off I-25), Denver; (303) 561-4450; www.oceanjourney.com*

Coors Field
FamilyFun ★★★★/$-$$$$
One of the most family-friendly ballparks in Major League baseball, this stadium is worth a trip even if your family members are not baseball fans; there's plenty of stuff to do without even watching a game. If you are going to a game, the cheap bleacher seats in center field ($1 for kids, $4 for adults) are one of baseball's best bargains; there are also special family sections in the ballpark where alcoholic beverages are prohibited. To amuse the rest of the family: kids ages 6 and under will enjoy the small playground located on the concourse in the park's left-field corner, and there's a special kids' concessions stand called Buckaroos next to the playground with smaller portions (and prices) than other stands. Another favorite activity is watching the trains in the yard adjacent to the ballpark, easily viewed from the wall behind Buckaroos. If you want to save money, consider bringing in your own food (no glass or aluminum cans and no coolers or backpacks) and buying souvenirs from street vendors instead of inside the park. *Corner of 20th and Blake Sts., Denver; (800) 388-ROCK; 303-ROCKIES; www.coloradorockies.com*

Denver Botanic Gardens ★★/$
Kids enjoy running around the paths of these lush gardens and playing in the Japanese Garden's teahouse. Regarded as one of the top five botanic gardens in the nation, this facility has more than 15,000 species of plants on 23 acres in its Rock Alpine Garden and Water Gardens. An extensive waterway system meanders through the gardens and has become home to a collection of more than 450 species and varieties of aquatic plants. *909 York St., Denver; (303) 331-4000; www.botanicgardens.org*

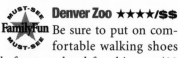

Denver Zoo ★★★/$$

Be sure to put on comfortable walking shoes before you head for this vast (80 acres) zoo. Rather than risk having to carry your kids, you can rent one of the Safari Wagons; these wagons (they look more like mini-jeeps) can accommodate one or two little ones and are perfect for navigating the huge, but well-designed, complex. Once you get a map, let your kids select the animals they most want to see and base your plan of attack on their wishes. If gorillas are their first choice, head to the right to check out the Primate Panorama—you can actually get within a few feet of one of the gorillas (viewing him through a thick pane of glass). Other highlights include elephants, puffins, and polar bears. For a nice break, take the little ones on the miniature-train ride; it's a brief, but restful, trip. Be aware of the various peacocks roaming around the park; young kids love to chase them. A recent addition is an endangered species carousel, where kids can ride on hand-carved pandas, elephants, and tigers. **NOTE:** This is a very popular attraction, so try to get here as soon as the doors open, to avoid the crowds, which get very heavy on most summer weekends. The zoo is open every day of the year, even holidays. *City Park, E. 23rd St. and Steele St., Denver; (303) 376-4800;* www.denverzoo.org

Dinosaur Ridge ★★/Free

An interesting attraction for kids ages 4 and over, this scenic mountain ridge 12 miles west of Denver is where the world's first large dinosaur bones were discovered. The visitors' center has interpretive displays that tell the story of how, in 1877, a schoolteacher named Morrison was poking around

DENVER'S GREEN SPACES

Denver offers plenty of places where families can enjoy the great outdoors. Here are some of our favorites:

Take a stroll through the **South Platte River Greenway**, a 30-mile paved trail by the Platte River that travels through Denver from Chatfield State Park to **Confluence Park**, where the Platte meets Cherry Creek. To get to Confluence Park, take Interstate 25 to the 23rd Avenue exit and drive north to the first parking area on the right. The trail includes some historic markers, and it doesn't leave the city. There's even a kayak course, so your family can watch kayakers paddle the rapids. *(303) 698-4900.*

Located in one of Denver's upscale neighborhoods, **Washington Park** is another popular spot for family outings. The park, located at South Franklin and Downing Streets in Denver, has an extensive trails system, and its open fields are on the ridge when he discovered the fossil of an enormous bone. Within weeks, the area became known as the Morrison Dinosaur Quarry. The world's first stegosaurus was found here, along with the bones of an allosaurus and a brontosaurus, among others. The discovery set off the Great Dinosaur Rush, and dozens of scientists from the east came to Denver in search of additional fossil sites. Today, the area has been designated a National Natural Landmark and preserves over 300 dinosaur footprints. Seventeen interpretive signs along a mile-long path describe and show what dinosaur bones look like to scientists when they are still encased in rock. Guided tours may be scheduled by calling the information center. On your own, the attraction takes about an hour. *16831 W. Alameda Pkwy., Morrison; (303) 697-3466;* www.dinoridge.org

Four Mile Historic Park ★★/$

This former stagecoach stop—constructed from hand-hewn pine logs in 1859—is now operated as a 14-acre farm in southeast Denver. There are self-guided tours of the barns and grounds (guided tours are available on the hour), and on weekends, your family can take a horse-drawn-stagecoach ride around the park. Numerous events are held here throughout the year, including an old-fashioned Fourth of July celebration. *715 S. Forest St., Denver; (303) 399-1859;* www.fourmilepark.org

Heritage Square ★★/Free

A reconstructed Colorado mining town from the 1870s, this square has an old fort, elaborate Victorian buildings and storefronts, shops, restaurants, and a cabaret theater. Amusement-park rides, a water slide, a bungee tower, go-carts,

filled with soccer players and dogs jumping for flying discs. *(303) 698-4962.*

The city also oversees the extensive Mountain Parks system, which covers more than 13,000 acres of green space and mountaintops around the city. Established in 1913, the parks provide excellent opportunities for families to watch birds, hike, picnic, or just hang out. **Genesee Park** is the largest park and is located about 20 miles west of the city off Interstate 70, exit 254. It has picnic areas with fireplaces, and buffalo and elk herds are special attractions.

Echo Lake is another popular park, located about 34 miles west from Denver. Take Interstate 70 west to Highway 103 south. The park offers fishing, hiking, picnic spots, a restaurant, and a gift shop. *For more information on Denver's Mountain Parks, call (303) 697-4545.*

miniature golf, miniature railroad, and an alpine slide are some of the other attractions. The center features more than 35 specialty shops and restaurants. *18301 W. Colfax Ave., Golden. From I-70, take 6th Ave. west to Hwy. 40; turn left and watch for signs; (303) 279-2789.*

Invesco Field at Mile High
★★/$

The new home of the city's beloved Broncos, this facility offers more than 76,000 seats. Moms will appreciate the expanded rest room facilities and the plentiful concession stands. Kids love spotting Bucky Bronco, a steel-and-fiberglass horse modeled on Roy Rogers's Trigger, atop the south scoreboard. The Broncos sculpture of horses roughly one and a half times their natural size at the south entrance makes a great photo opportunity. Tours are offered Tuesday through Saturday from 10 A.M. to 2 P.M. and include stops in the locker room and the stall of team mascot, Thunder. *For reservations, call (720) 258-3888. 1701 Bryant St., Denver; (720) 258-3050;* www.invescofieldat milehigh.com

Lakeside Amusement Park
★★★/$$$

If Six Flags Elitch Gardens (see page 346) is too overwhelming (or expensive) for your taste, then head to this small park west of downtown Denver. With 24 main rides and 15 kiddie rides, the vintage theme park (built in 1908) is probably a better bet anyway for families with kids under age 6. The miniature-train rides aboard engines called Puffing Billy and Whistling Tom are a hit with small kids—and a great way to relax in the heat of the day. A larger train circles the 1.25-mile track, providing nice views of Lake Rhoda. The park also has a vintage carousel and classic Cyclone roller coaster. Refreshment stands are housed in the park's bell tower. *I-70 and Sheridan Blvd., Denver; (303) 477-1621;* www.lake sideamusementpark.com

Littleton Historical Museum
★★/Free

This free museum in southeast metro Denver has two working farms—one from the 1860s, when Littleton was first founded, and one from the turn of the century. You can

A Good Egg

Hard-boiled eggs are a perfect road food if you peel them first, wrap them in plastic, and chill them. Here's a foolproof recipe: place eggs in a nonaluminum saucepan and cover with cold water. Bring to a boil, reduce heat to low, and simmer, uncovered, for 15 minutes (add 2 minutes if eggs are straight from the fridge). Drain eggs and plunge in cold water. Keep in the cooler or eat within two hours.

tour the farmhouses and barns and see cattle, sheep, chickens, ducks, and other farm animals. After the museum, take a walk in the lovely park that surrounds it. *6028 S. Gallup St., Littleton; (303) 795-3950; www.littletongov.org/museum/*

LoDo ★★★/Free

Denver's lower downtown, nick-named LoDo, is home to scores of shops, restaurants, businesses, and homes. Tourists come here to check out the shopping scene, including the huge new REI store (page 349) and the restaurants. Your family can take a horse-drawn-carriage ride in nearby Larimer Square, grab a bite to eat, and browse the shops, then walk over to Coors Field or the new Pepsi Center for a game. *LoDo is a 30-block-square area north of Larimer Square to the South Platte River between 14th and 22nd streets.*

Pepsi Center ★★★/$-$$$$

Home of the Denver Nuggets and the Colorado Avalanche, the $160 million Pepsi Center opened in 1999. The arena sits in between Denver's Lower Downtown (LoDo) and Six Flags Elitch Gardens. If you are planning to catch a game while you are here, make sure you take advantage of the special kids' clubs both teams offer, which include game and food discounts. The Avalanche also offer a special Family Nights package, which includes four tickets, pizza, and a game program for $90. If you just want a tour of the arena, they are offered Monday and Wednesday at 10 A.M., noon, and 2 P.M., and Fridays at 10 A.M. and noon. *1000 Chopper Circle, Denver. Game ticket information: (303) 405-1111; tour ticket information: (303) 405-8556; www.pepsicenter.com*

Platte Valley Trolley ★★★/$

A fun way for families to get around town without wearing out shoe leather, this yellow "Breezer" trolley is operated by the Denver Rail Heritage Society. The trolley (it's actually a bus that looks like a trolley) takes a half-hour tour along the Platte riverfront and then an hour-long-ride to Sheridan Boulevard; pick it up at the Denver Children's Museum, where the station is located. The route will take you by Colorado's Ocean Journey, Six Flags Elitch Gardens, Mile High Stadium, Confluence Park, and downtown Denver. It's a nice way to unwind after a morning at the Children's Museum or Ocean Journey. *To reach the trolley, take Interstate 25 to exit 211 (23rd St.) and turn east on Water Street. Follow the signs to the Children's Museum and look for the station; (303) 458-6255; www.denvertrolley.org*

Red Rocks Amphitheatre ★★★/$-$$$$

One of the most gorgeous places in America to watch a concert, this 9,000-seat, acoustically perfect amphitheater was created in 1936 by carving out seats between two gigantic red-rock boulders. The unique venue has played host to many historic concert performances, from Igor Stravinsky to the Beatles. A special sunrise service is held each Easter Sunday. The park surrounding the theater is open year-round and is free, except when there is a scheduled performance. A well-marked nature trail winds through the rocks; signs explain their geologic history, which dates back 70 million years. There is also a gift shop and snack bar located in the park. *Fifteen miles west of Denver, south of I-70 (exit 256), Morrison; (303) 697-8801;* www.red rocksonline.com

MUST-SEE FamilyFun MUST-SEE Six Flags Elitch Gardens Theme Park
★★★★/$$–$$$$

Six Flags Elitch Gardens is really two parks in one—an amusement park with more than 40 rides, and a water theme park with water rides and pools. The 58-acre amusement park offers a variety of thrill rides, including the new high-speed Flying Coaster. Twister II is one of the nation's top-rated wooden roller coasters. Other theme park attractions include Boomerang and the Tower of Doom, where you are hoisted up a 210-foot steel tower and dropped in a free fall that reaches speeds in excess of 60 miles per hour.

Kids must be 48 inches or taller to ride most thrill rides. Younger kids can head to Looney Tunes Movietown, which has smaller rides geared to little ones ages 6 and under.

The other side of Elitch Gardens is Island Kingdom, a 10-acre water park that resembles a Caribbean island, with water slides, tube rides, and wave pools. Highlights include Commotion Ocean, a 28,000-square-foot wave pool perfect for body surfing or just relaxing, and Hook's Lagoon, a five-story tree house offering lots of wet-and-wild adventures and over 100 water gadgets, several lagoon playgrounds, and a giant barrel overhead that drenches everyone below. **NOTE:** Be advised that you cannot bring food into the park, so you are stuck with the high prices and mediocre fare here. To cut back on expenses, pick up discount coupons, available at area hotels, restaurants, and grocery stores. *2000 Elitch Circle, Denver; (303) 595-4386;* www.sixflags.com/elitchgardens

Tiny Town and Railroad ★★★/$

Nestled in a scenic mountain canyon just 30 minutes west of Denver, Tiny Town is a unique, one-sixth-scale village with its own authentic steam locomotive. Originally opened to the public in 1920, it is the oldest miniature village and railroad in the United States. There are more than

The 20th row of the upper deck at **Coors Field** is painted purple and marks the area of the stadium that is exactly one mile above sea level.

100 handcrafted structures, including the Tiny Town Tribune newspaper building, the Diesel Engine Round House, and a steam-powered locomotive that takes children around the tiny village, making stops along the way. Families can enjoy picnics, snacks, and a gift shop in this quaint mountain town. There's also a large playground. *6249 S. Turkey Creek Rd., Tiny Town; (303) 697-6829;* www.tinytownrailroad.com

Water World ★★★★/$$$-$$$$

One of America's largest family water parks, this place features more than 40 attractions on 64 acres, including two oceanlike wave pools, twisting water slides, and mock white-water raft adventures. Thrill rides include Voyage to the Center of the Earth, a five-minute trek to the prehistoric era; the Screamin' Mimi, a water roller coaster; and Lost River of the Pharoahs, a family raft ride that blends white-water thrills and Egyptian history. Slides, two wave pools, a lazy river ride, a fun house, and Calypso Cove—a place where preschoolers can splash around—are other highlights. *1800 W. 89th Ave., Federal Heights; (303) 427-SURF;* www.waterworldcolorado.com

BUNKING DOWN

Embassy Suites ★★★/$$$

Located within walking distance of Coors Field and the shops and restaurants of the Sixteenth Street Mall and LoDo, this all-suite hotel is perfect for families. Each unit has a separate bedroom, a pull-out sofa, and a wet bar. Kids love the free breakfast bar, which includes doughnuts, waffles, and made-to-order omelettes. *1881 Curtis St., Denver; (303) 297-8888;* www.embassysuites.com

Golden Gate State Park ★★/$

Only 30 miles west of Denver, this park has more than 150 campsites and great hiking trails. For a special adventure, reserve one of the five cabins or two yurts, round tents on wooden frames. The yurts have two bunk beds and a twin bed and can sleep as many as six. Cabins are the same size. Be advised that you have to bring your own bedding and a cooler since there isn't a refrigerator. The yurts and cabins do have lights, propane heaters, showers, and outdoor grills. Cost is $30 per night, plus $5 per person and a $7 nonrefundable reservation fee. *3873 Hwy. 46, Golden; (303) 582-3707; (800) 678-2267; (303) 470-1144;* http://parks.state.co.us/Golden_Gate/index.asp

Westin Hotel Tabor Center ★★★★/$$$-$$$$

Located right in the middle of downtown, this hotel offers large rooms and a swimming pool that affords views of the Rockies. For young guests, the hotel has the Westin Kids Club, which upon check-in gives kids a goody bag filled with a cup (a sipping cup for toddlers or a sport bottle for older kids). *1672 Lawrence St., Denver; (303) 572-9100;* www.westin.com

GOOD EATS

Casa Bonita
★★★★/$$
This huge restaurant spreads out over 52,000 square feet and has seating for 1,100 diners, but youngsters seem to love all the activity, including cliff divers plunging from a spectacular 30-foot waterfall, strolling mariachi bands, puppets, and piñatas. Kids can also explore Black Bart's secret hideout, then watch as the Sheriff and Black Bart engage in a shoot-'em-up Western gunfight. Children love the chips and salsa and the sopaipillas (hot fried dough topped with honey). The wait for a table can be an hour or more on weekends and other holidays, so try to come early for lunch (about 11 A.M.) or in the middle of the afternoon (around 3 P.M.) to beat the crowds. *6715 W. Colfax Ave., Lakewood; (303) 232-5115;* www.casabonitadenver.com

ESPN Zone
★★★/$$
Named for the sports cable channel, this chain celebrates all this sport with interactive games and plenty of big screen playing, what else, ESPN. *Located inside the Tabor Center, 1187 16th St., Denver; (303) 595-3776.*

The Fort ★★★★/$$$
You don't get too many opportunities to chow down in a fort, or at least a replica of one. This restaurant combines history and haute cuisine. Kids love exploring the center courtyard, which has a tepee and a warming bonfire. If that's not enough to keep them busy, they also get to paint with watercolors in special menus while they wait for the meal. Every once in a while, a drumbeat echoes through the place to celebrate someone's birthday or anniversary. The lucky person gets his or her photo taken in a coyote or buffalo hat (much like a coonskin cap). The kids' menu features western cuisine, including buffalo burgers. *19192 Hwy. 8, Morrison; (303) 697-4771;* www.thefort.com

Liks ★★/$
A Denver ice-cream tradition, this parlor offers such flavors as Chocolate Decadence and Cherry Cheesecake. Its central Denver location makes it a good place to take a break if you're hitting the downtown attractions. *2039 E. 13th Ave., Denver; (303) 321-2370.*

White Fence Farm
★★★★/$$-$$$
This restaurant/attraction rivals Casa Bonita for kid appeal. The for-

mer farm features a backyard petting zoo and tree house where your kids can pass the time while you wait for a table. Your family can also ride in a horse-drawn carriage around the grounds, weather permitting. The fare is down-home cookin' with fried chicken, coleslaw, and corn fritters. To avoid long waits, come early—it opens for dinner at 5 P.M. Tuesdays through Saturdays, for lunch at 11:30 A.M. on Sundays. *6232 W. Jewell Ave., Lakewood; (303) 935-5945; www. whitefencefarm.com*

SOUVENIR HUNTING

Caboose Hobbies

Billed as the largest model-railroad store in the world, this is a must-stop for train-crazed kids and their parents—it's a virtual supermarket of toy trains in all sizes with half a dozen working layouts. Plus it also carries books, videos, and railroad memorabilia. *500 S. Broadway, Denver; (303) 777-6766; www.caboosehobbies.com*

REI

Who needs the great outdoors when you have such a great indoors without pesky mosquitoes or snakes? This superstore, the flagship of the outdoor-gear retailer, gives kids an active shopping experience that includes climbing a 45-foot-tall mountainside, testing hiking shoes on a faux trail, and stepping inside a meat-lockerlike room to test down jackets in temperatures as low as minus 30 degrees. If that's not enough, check out the 318-foot-long outdoor mountain bike test track that runs through the store's beautifully landscaped courtyard. This can all be cheap entertainment—unless of course you buy something. *1416 Platte St., Denver; (303) 756-3100.*

The Tattered Cover Bookshop

Denver residents love their bookstores, particularly this one, with two locations—in Cherry Creek and LoDo. Head downstairs for the children's section, where you can read books to your kids while sitting on comfy sofas or chairs. *Locations are at the corner of 1st and Milwaukee (303/322-7727) and the corner of 16th and Wynkoop (303/436-1070); www.tatteredcover.com*

The Wizard's Chest

If your youngsters are Harry Potter fans, they will love a trip inside this castle. (How many times do you get to shop in a castle?) The store stocks magic paraphernalia and wizard regalia. There's typically a magician on duty performing tricks. Kids love the costume section, where they can don robes and wizard hats. There are also several sections of masks and an area devoted to body parts, with spare arms, legs, skulls—you get the idea. *230 Fillmore St., Cherry Creek North, Denver; (303) 321-4304; www.thewizardschest.com*

Ever been sand sledding? Check out America's highest dunes (some are 700 feet tall) at Great Sand Dunes National Monument.

Colorado Springs and Pikes Peak

LOCALS LIKE TO POINT OUT that the words to "America the Beautiful" were penned by Katherine Lee Bates after a visit to Pikes Peak in the summer of 1893. Now, a hundred years later, families still come to the region for the "purple mountain's majesty above the fruited plain." This area has more than its share of natural and human-made wonders, including Royal Gorge, Cave of the Winds, and Garden of the Gods, all places that will impress even the most jaded preteen. Elementary-school-age kids like to watch would-be Olympians train at the U.S. Olympic Center and marvel at the sight of hundreds of Air Force cadets marching to lunch at the U.S. Air Force Academy. The region is also home to hokey tourist attractions like the North Pole, where Santa is in residence 364

THE **FamilyFun** LIST

MUST-SEE
MUST-SEE

Arkansas River (page 354)

Cheyenne Mountain Zoo (page 357)

Garden of the Gods (page 357)

Great Sand Dunes National Monument (page 357)

Pikes Peak (page 358)

Royal Gorge (page 360)

United States Air Force Academy (page 354)

United States Olympic Training Center (page 354)

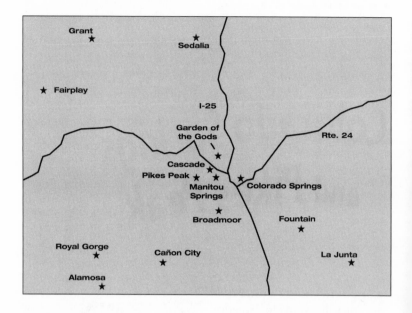

nights a year, a delight for younger children. Whatever your family's interests are, there are enough attractions here to fill a weeklong vacation—or you can just hit a few highlights in a day trip from Denver.

If your troops enjoy outdoor adventures, a trip down the Arkansas River is fun, with just enough white water to add excitement without causing you to go overboard. Be sure to pack some hiking boots too, so you can enjoy the trails in Pike National Forest. A trip here wouldn't be complete without a visit to Royal Gorge Bridge, where you can walk some 1,000 feet above the canyon floor or take an enclosed tram that slides you across the chasm, a better choice for younger kids and anyone with vertigo.

Colorado Springs was founded by General William Palmer (an early president of the Denver and Rio Grande Railroad), who set out to build a utopian village in the late 1870s. It's easy for kids to get a taste of the town's early history at places like Rock Ledge Ranch Historic Site, where they can talk to a pioneer woman as she churns butter or ask a blacksmith if he's hurting the horse when he nails on a horseshoe. To go back further in the area's history, visit the Manitou Cliff Dwellings Museum, where your family can wander inside an Anasazi pueblo. Even if your kids are too young to learn much about this ancient Native American culture, they can have a great time climbing up the ladders and waving from the balconies of the stone homes.

The area enjoys a mild, sunny climate year-round, but be sure to dress in layers if your family heads up the mountain, where temperatures are generally 30 to 40 degrees cooler. Given the high altitudes, it's imperative to slather everyone with sunscreen and smart to pack sunglasses, too. Afternoon thunderstorms are common in the higher elevations during summer, so try to sight-see in the morning. Avoid going outside if you are on a mountain and see dark clouds approaching; lightning can strike before any raindrops hit the ground. Finally, be aware that high-altitude side effects can include tiring easily, headaches, nosebleeds, and nausea. For more information on altitude sickness, see page 305.

CULTURAL ADVENTURES

Children's Museum of Colorado Springs ★★★/$

Located inside a mall, this museum offers plenty of hands-on activities that will get your kids smiling. There's the Creation Station, where they can color, draw, and make collages; the Home Depot House, a half-constructed playhouse where they can don hard hats and stack pretend bricks; and a science lab, where they can create huge bubbles that surround their bodies. In Recollections, kids walk inside a dark room and see their shadows projected on a giant, colorful screen. There is also a music area and a theater, where films and live performances are presented. A special section called Small Wonders, reserved for kids ages 4 and under, has pint-size computers, toys, and hand puppets. *750 Citadel Dr. East (next to JC Penney in Citadel Mall), Colorado Springs; (719) 574-0077; www.iex.net/cm*

Colorado Springs Pioneers Museum ★★/Free

This museum, housed in a restored courthouse, may interest older kids who want to see Native American artifacts and antique toys. The toy collection also includes popular toys from today, making it fun for youngsters to compare their favorite playthings with those of their parents and grandparents. *215 S. Tejon St., Colorado Springs; (719) 385-5990; www.cspm.org*

Pro Rodeo Hall of Fame and American Cowboy Museum ★★★/$$

Even if your kids aren't that familiar with rodeos and cowboy culture, they will have a good time at this well-organized museum. The tour starts with two films, one explaining the history of rodeos and one detailing modern rodeos; together they run about 20 minutes. The displays highlight famous cowboys and the evolution of the cowboy hat, spurs, boots, and saddles. Much of

353

EVERY GRADUATION CEREMONY at the United States Air Force Academy includes a performance by the legendary Thunderbirds, an elite team of Air Force demonstration pilots.

the museum may bore little kids, but they can look forward to seeing a few real animals, including a retired champion bronco and bull. *101 Pro Rodeo Dr., Colorado Springs; (719) 528-4764; www.prorodeo.com*

 **United States Air Force Academy**
★★★/Free

You probably don't get saluted that often, but you will as you pass the guardhouse at this service academy that grooms officers for the United States Air Force. The visitors' center has maps for self-guided tours, displays detailing life at the academy, a snack bar, and rest rooms. If you are traveling during the academic year, you can see the cadets marching in formation to the dining hall at 11:35 each weekday—a sight sure to wow your family. The massive Cadet Chapel is a popular attraction and your family can attend Catholic and Protestant services there at 9 and 11 A.M. Sunday, and Jewish services at 8 P.M. on Fridays. In the summer, the academy offers planetarium shows; call for a schedule. *Take exit 156B off I-25N and follow signs; (719) 333-8723; www.usafa.af.mil Planetarium: (719) 333-2778*

 **United States Olympic Training Center**
★★★★/Free

Athletes train year-round at this 37-acre complex, where they prepare for the next Summer Olympics in 2004. (Winter Olympic hopefuls are trained in another state.) The one-hour walking tour takes you through gyms, weight-lifting rooms, the aquatics center, and the shooting arena. Your kids may see gymnasts going through their floor exercises or swimmers perfecting their strokes in a water treadmill. Be advised that most of what you see at this place is "look, don't touch," which makes it a bit boring for preschoolers. But it can be an inspiring trip for budding elementary-school athletes. *1750 Boulder St., Colorado Springs; (719) 866-4618.*

JUST FOR FUN

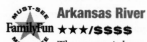 **Arkansas River**
★★★/$$$$

The upper Arkansas River offers experts the challenges of Class V rapids, but the river eventually slows down a bit, offering more moderate Class III rapids, easily navigated by novices. Families can sign up for a full-day or half-day float trip with one of the area's outfitting companies. **Echo Canyon River Expeditions** offers a three-hour rafting trip through Bighorn Canyon, which has rapids with names such as Devil's Hole, Shark's Tooth, and Maytag (it spins you around). The full-day trip includes lunch of sandwiches and watermelon slices. *45000 Hwy. 50, Canon City; (800) 748-2953; (719) 275-3154;* www.raftecho.com

Bear Creek Regional Park and Nature Center ★★/Free-$

If it's a nice day and your kids want to hit the trail, head out to this park, which offers easy hiking trails and interactive wildlife displays. If you want a guided tour that explains the region's plant and animal life, call ahead for a reservation. Even if you go on your own, the staff naturalists are helpful and will point out highlights of each trail. The nature center has a diorama of the area's common animals and a bear cave (don't worry, it's empty) that kids can play in. *254 Bear Creek Rd., Colorado Springs; (719) 520-6387.*

Bent's Old Fort ★★★/$

Get a sense of life in the Old West at this fort on the Arkansas River built in the early 1830s as a rest stop on the Santa Fe Trail. This is actually a replica of the original, but it's an interesting living-history museum with costumed guides who explain what it was like to live in pioneer days. A blacksmith gives demonstrations on fashioning horseshoes. The gift shop sells Old West trinkets such as beads and beaver hats. The fort is open year-round, but try to

Wilderness on Wheels

The idea came from a son who wanted to build a trail that his wheelchair-bound father would enjoy. Years of volunteer labor and generous donations from lumberyards later, the Wilderness on Wheels boardwalk trail became a reality, allowing disabled people access to the joy of outdoor hiking and camping. The trail has numerous pull-off areas with picnic tables, and it takes you past a mountain stream and gradually up a hillside. One part of the trail descends to an outdoor amphitheater where concerts and other events are staged. Wilderness on Wheels is located on U.S. 285, 60 miles southwest of Denver or 3.8 miles west of Grant, Colorado. Reservations are required for entry. There are no fees, but donations are requested to support the nonprofit organization that maintains the trail. Pets are not allowed. Trash must be brought out. The facility is open between mid-April and mid-October. *Contact W.O.W. by telephone at (303) 751-3959 or through the Website* www.wildernesson wheels.org come in late July. This is when it stages the Santa Fe Trail Encampment, which further re-creates the bustling days of the Old West. *Seven miles east of La Junta on Hwy. 194; (719) 383-5010;* www.nps.gov/beol

Buckskin Joe Frontier Town and Railway ★★/$$$

Cowboy kitsch reigns supreme in this fully restored Wild West town that has been featured in such movie Westerns as *True Grit* and *Cat Ballou.* Much of the town is made up of gift shops filled with Western-themed tourist trinkets like fake Indian headdresses or kid-size pistols. Youngsters can watch staged gunfights and hangings, which may fascinate them even if they horrify you. You'll also want to take the pleasant 15-minute train ride to Royal Gorge (page 360). At night, the theme town puts on a chuck-wagon dinner. (For a more authentic, and cheaper, Wild West experience, consider going to South Park City— page 361—outside Fairplay instead.)

Eight miles west of Canon City on Hwy. 50; (719) 275-5149; www.buck skinjoes.com

Cave of the Winds ★★/$$$

This heavily promoted attraction is a bit corny, but kids love crawling up and down the cave's winding paths and think the laser shows and colored lights focused on the crystal formations are way cool. Be ready to deal with crowds and a few come-ons (for instance, a staff member will take your family photo at the beginning of the tour, then try to sell you a copy at the end). There are several tours offered. The Discovery and Lantern Tours are advised with children. There are also laser light shows during the summer months. Tours last around 45 minutes, but that can seem long to a cranky toddler or preschooler. During the tours, at some point, the lights are cut off, an experience that frightens many kids (and adults). *Take I-25 to exit 141; go 6 miles west on Hwy. 24; (719) 685-5444;* www.caveofthewinds.com

Hitting the Trail in Colorado Springs

8 A.M. Breakfast trail ride at **Academy Riding Stables** *(4 El Paso Blvd., near the south entrance to Garden of the Gods; 719/633-5667).* **NOTE:** Riders must be at least 8 years old and weigh less than 220 pounds.

Noon Spend the afternoon at the **Pro Rodeo Hall of Fame and American Cowboy Museum** (see page 353).

6 P.M. Chuck-wagon dinner at the **Flying W Ranch** (see page 362).

Cheyenne Mountain Zoo ★★★★/$$

FamilyFun
MUST-SEE

Visiting this zoo is a real workout. Its 75 acres run straight up the side of a mountain, making pushing a stroller or pulling a wagon a real head (and shoulder) ache. We suggest taking the tram to the top of the mountain, where your kids can visit the petting zoo and ride a carousel for 50 cents, then working your way downhill through the exhibits. The zoo's 500 animals include rare okapi (zebralike animals that actually are giraffe relatives). Kids love feeding the giraffes and checking out the bat colony. A pride of peacocks wanders the grounds, dodging preschoolers who delight in chasing them. Plan on spending at least a couple of hours, and consider packing a picnic to avoid the standard hot dog and hamburger fare offered at the concession stands. **NOTE:** After the zoo, consider driving to the Shrine of the Sun, located just up the mountain. The shrine offers one of the best views in the area and is dedicated to humorist Will Rogers. You can hear a tape of him speaking and see photos from his life, which ended in a 1935 plane crash. *4250 Cheyenne Mountain Zoo Rd., Colorado Springs; (719) 475-9555;* www.cmzoo.org

Garden of the Gods ★★★★/Free

FamilyFun
MUST-SEE

This famous 1,350-acre park is home to majestic red-rock sculptures—including Three Graces, the Siamese Twins, and Kissing Camels—formed more than 300 million years ago. At the visitors' center, your family can watch a 12-minute film that explains how the rock formations evolved; there's a small fee—$1 for kids, $2 for adults. The center also has displays on the area's wildlife, a café, and two gift shops. Be sure to get a map, because some of the formations can be difficult to find. If you are here in the summer, you can take the 30-minute narrated bus tour. To keep your youngsters interested (which can be difficult with even the most rock-obsessed preschooler), challenge them to name the abstract monoliths themselves. Consider combining a trip here with a visit to Rock Ledge Ranch Historic Site (page 359). *1805 N. 30th St., Colorado Springs; (719) 634-6666;* www.gardensofgods.com

Great Sand Dunes National Monument ★★★★/$

FamilyFun
MUST-SEE

Consider this place a humongous sandbox—your kids will, and they'll beg to stop and play awhile. The unique geology of the area has trapped the sand in this valley, where wind constantly moves the shifting dunes. Kids love watching their footprints disappear as the winds continually reshape the landscape. Some of the dunes tower 700 feet high, and we noticed on our trip that a few kids had brought plastic sleds and were using them to dash downhill. If you're lucky, you may be able to spot deer, elk, eagles, and other wildlife. Start your trip at the visitors' center, where you'll find exhibits on the geological and natural history of the dunes and a 15-minute film that explains how and why the dunes were—and continue to be—created. The desert landscape is actually held in place by huge amounts of water beneath the surface. Kids can also sign up for the Junior Ranger program and earn a badge for completing a quiz about the dunes. *35 miles northeast of Alamosa off Colorado Hwy. 150 from the south; Colorado Hwy. 17 from the north; (719) 378-2312;* www.nps.gov/grsa

During the third weekend in August, several hundred people take part in the **Pikes Peak Marathon**, a grueling race from Manitou Springs, up to the summit, and back to town.

Manitou Cliff Dwellings Museum ★★★/$-$$

If you want to give your kids a real hands-on history lesson in a place where they are encouraged to climb up and onto the displays instead of being shooed away, come to this museum that showcases ancient Native American history. The cliff dwellings at this outdoor museum were actually assembled in modern times, but they were modeled after ancient pueblos. The advantage to this is that your children can crawl up the ladders and run inside the dwellings—which is strictly prohibited at most ruins sites. Youngsters will want to play here for the better part of an hour. In the summer, Native American dancers entertain the crowds. The gift shop stocks handmade Native American jewelry, drums, and other items, and they will ship your purchases home if you don't have room in your suitcase. *West of Colorado Springs on Hwy. 24, Manitou Springs; (719) 685-5242;* www.cliffdwellingsmuseum.com

Pikes Peak
FamilyFun ★★★★/$$

The road up Pikes Peak isn't for the faint of heart (or the unsure of steering wheel). Before you head up the 19 miles of twisting curves, be sure everyone has had their dose of Dramamine. The drive, which requires paying a toll, can take less than two hours round-trip, but don't let it; take it slow and enjoy activities at places such as the Crystal

Reservoir visitors' center, which offers boat rides and fishing. You'll also find a picnic area midway up the mountain if you want to pack lunch. Kids can watch the changing landscapes as you climb past the tree line, and they'll appreciate the stunning view from the top, which inspired Katherine Lee Bates to write "America the Beautiful" in 1893. Be sure to pack a sweatshirt or light jacket because mountaintop temperatures can be 30 to 40 degrees lower than those in the valley. If you forget, there's a souvenir stand at the top where you can buy Pikes Peak logo sweatshirts and T-shirts that say, "Real Men Don't Need Guardrails" for $19.95 and up. There's also a small snack bar, but you may want to forgo a huge meal given the fact that you've got to go back down the mountain. **NOTE:** Parents traveling with kids under 5 might want to enjoy the view from the bottom of the mountain. *Ten miles west of Colorado Springs off Hwy. 24;* www.pikespeak.com

Pikes Peak Cog Railway
★★★/$$$$

You have two options for getting to the top of Pikes Peak—the winding highway or this scenic train ride, which leaves from a depot in Manitou Springs. The train ride takes about three and half hours for the round trip, including a stop at the summit. If you think your kids will enjoy a trip this long, taking in some of the state's most gorgeous scenery, then consider taking the train—but be forewarned that there are no rest rooms or snack bars on the train (though there are some at the top of the mountain). It's smart to take a picnic to enjoy while on board and some games or toys for the kids to play with. Also, pack a sweatshirt or jacket because the temperatures at the top of Pikes Peak are 30 to 40 degrees cooler than at its base. *515 Ruxton Ave., Manitou Springs; (719) 685-5401;* www.cogs railway.com

Rock Ledge Ranch Historic Site ★★★/$

An alternative to the touristy Wild West show towns like Buckskin Joe Frontier Town and Railway (page 356), this living-history ranch gives a realistic depiction of life on the range without gunfights and magic shows. In the summer, the ranch comes alive with costumed workers who tell your kids what life was like a hundred years ago as they go about doing such pioneer chores as churning butter. The blacksmith shop is a favorite stop for most youngsters. Skip the tour of the 1907 estate house if you are short on time. The ranch is next to Garden of the Gods (page 357), making it an easy combination trip in an afternoon. *On Gateway Road, just before the entrance to Garden of the Gods; (719) 578-6777;* www.community.colorado springs.com/cs/rockledgeranch

★ Royal Gorge
FamilyFun ★★★/$$$

The 1,053-foot-deep Royal Gorge—often called the Grand Canyon of Colorado—draws 500,000 visitors each year. Carved by the Arkansas River for some three million years, the gorge is spanned by the world's highest suspension bridge. Signs by the bridge note boldly, "Who says you can't improve on nature?" The bridge was originally built in 1929 as a tourist attraction, and today the attraction feels like a theme park, with costumed characters—Little John the bear and Stryker Rick the gold miner among them—strolling about in the summer. You can drive or walk across; some daredevils prefer crossing the bridge on windy days, when it sways. You can also ride the aerial tram for a dramatic glide across the canyon on 2,200 feet of cables. Lines for the tram, which only holds 35 people, can get long, so consider walking over and making the return trip on the tram. There is also an incline railway that takes you down to the base of the canyon, where you can walk by the river.

To avoid crowds at this popular site, consider coming in the fall or spring on a weekday. If you are traveling in summer, get there early, just after the park opens its gates, at 9:30 A.M. To get to the bridge, take Highway 50 West from Canon City. **NOTE:** Take care to avoid the entrance to Buckskin Joe Frontier

FamilyFun TIP

Postcard Journal

Document your travel adventures by bringing along a small photo album that fits 4- by 6-inch pictures. Then, wherever you go, have your child pick out a few postcards of scenic landmarks, quirky roadside attractions, or native wildlife. On the back of each card, she can jot down the date and a brief note describing her impressions of the place or an account of something memorable that happened during your stay there before inserting it into a photo sleeve in the album.

Town and Railway, unless you want to go there. The theme park has a confusing sign that says ROYAL GORGE COUNTRY, which fools some drivers. *You should continue driving all the way up the hill to get to Royal Gorge Bridge; (719) 275-7507;* www.royalgorgebridge.com

Santa's Workshop/North Pole
★★★/$$$

Do your little ones still believe in Santa Claus? They can meet the Jolly Old Elf himself at this outdoor amusement park. It's hokey, but little kids think the candy-cane slide is cool. Santa (who has a real beard) holds court each day and eagerly listens to your child's Christmas desires, even though the holiday may be months away. The rides include a carousel and Ferris wheel, and you can ride them as often as you like, so take your time. The park is at a high elevation and can get chilly even in the summer, so pack a light jacket. If you're traveling here in summer, come early (the park opens at 9:30 A.M.) because the area frequently gets afternoon thunderstorms. *Ten miles west of Colorado Springs on Hwy. 24; (719) 684-9432;* www.santas-colo.com

Seven Falls ★★★/$$
Adults tend to be more impressed than kids with this attraction, which features seven separate waterfalls that drop 250 feet into a canyon. You can walk up 224 steep steps to the top (kids seem to have the energy, but you may not) or take the elevator to the observation deck. The falls are gorgeous, but younger kids are more interested in the fish in the canyon's pond and may get bored quickly. *2850 S. Cheyenne Blvd., Colorado Springs; (719) 632-0765;* www.sevenfalls.com

South Park City ★★★★/$-$$
If you want to experience a Wild West town without all the fake gunfights and overpriced gift shops, try this collection of buildings, all salvaged from ghost towns in the area. The 30 or so structures include a bank, jail, blacksmith shop, and livery stable, all furnished as they would have been in a thriving 19th-century mining town. Show your kids the

scary implements in the dentist's office and they won't forget to brush their teeth for a while. The experience is great for kids 7 and older, but will probably bore preschoolers. *100 4th St., Fairplay; (719) 836-2387;* www.southparkcity.org

World Figure Skating Museum and Hall of Fame ★★/$
This museum celebrates the world of figure skating and includes photos, costumes, and even medals of famous skaters. There's a tribute to local hero Scott Hamilton, whose gold medal is showcased behind glass. Kids can also watch a movie on the life of Sonja Henie and see costumes worn by Peggy Fleming and Debi Thomas. Needless to say, this is boring stuff for preschoolers or folks who aren't big figure-skating fans, but anyone with an interest in the sport will enjoy a spin around. *20 1st St., Colorado Springs; (719) 635-5200;* www.worldskatingmuseum.org

BUNKING DOWN

The Broadmoor ★★★★/$$$$
If your family is looking for a place where they'll be pampered, this resort is well worth the price. Frequently named one of the top hotels in the country, the Broadmoor can be a self-contained luxury vacation all by itself. The resort covers 3,500 acres, which include a private lake, tennis courts,

an arcade, two outdoor pools, one indoor pool, and an on-site movie theater that only shows movies rated G, PG, or PG-13. Kids ages 3 to 12 can join the Bee Bunch, which offers daytime and evening activities such as nature hikes, swimming, and field trips to the nearby Cheyenne Mountain Zoo. The program runs most days from 9 A.M. to 4 P.M. (plus 6 to 10 P.M. during the summer and holiday periods). *1 Lake Ave., Colorado Springs; (800) 634-7711; (719) 634-7711;* www.broadmoor.com

Colorado Springs South KOA ★★★/$

Located on the banks of Fountain Creek near the base of Pikes Peak, this campground offers family activities throughout the year, including movies, hayrides, ice cream socials, and pancake breakfasts. There's an outdoor pool, place to check E-mail, and an ATM so you won't feel all that removed from modern civilization. *8100 Bandley Dr., Fountain; (800) 562-8609 or (719) 382-7575;* www.koakampgrounds.com

Embassy Suites ★★★/$$–$$$

This all-suite hotel, one of the chain's best locations, has an atrium lobby with a koi-fish-stocked pond. There's a complimentary breakfast and a pool with a deck, which has a great view of Pikes Peak. *7290 E. Commerce Center Dr., Colorado Springs; (800) 362-2779; (719) 599-9100;* www.embassysuites.com

Lost Valley Ranch ★★★★/$$$$

Set in the tall pines of 40,000-acre Pike National Forest, Lost Valley has been in the ranching business for more than 100 years. The 24 cabin suites all have living rooms, fireplaces, refrigerators, and covered porch swings. Be advised that there are no televisions or telephones. The children's program includes horseback riding (ages 6 and older), swimming, crafts, hiking, and fishing. *29555 Goose Creek Rd., Sedalia; (303) 647-2311;* www.lostvalleyranch.com

GOOD EATS

Conway's Red Top ★★/$

With locations throughout Colorado Springs, this fast-food restaurant serves up world-class burgers. Kids can choose the Half Hot Dog or Half Hamburger (kid-size versions of the massive adult servings) or a grilled cheese sandwich. Milk shakes are old-fashioned thick and frosty. *1520 S. Nevada Ave, (719) 633-2444; 390 N. Circle Dr., (719) 630-1566; 3589 N. Carefree Circle, (719) 596-6444.*

Flying W Ranch Chuckwagon Suppers ★★★/$$

You won't have to saddle up at this working cattle ranch that's been rustling up barbecue suppers since 1953. In the summer, the ranch can draw 1,400 or so city slickers a night. Get there at least an hour before the

7:15 P.M. mealtime so your kids can wander the grounds and check out the restored Western building, the blacksmith shop, and the miniature-train ride. When the dinner bell rings, make your way through the buffet line for barbecue beef or chicken, potatoes, beans, applesauce, and spice cake. After the meal, singing cowboys put on a show, which winds down by 9:30 P.M. *3330 Chuckwagon Rd., Colorado Springs; (719) 598-4000; www.flyingw.com*

The Golden Bee
★★★★/$$$

Even if you aren't staying at the Broadmoor, you can enjoy the upscale atmosphere with a meal at the Golden Bee. There's no kids' menu, but youngsters can get a grilled cheese sandwich or half an adult-size sandwich. The famous bar features a piano player who leads sing-alongs. *International Center at Broadmoor; (719) 634-7711.*

Michelle Chocolatier and Ice Cream ★★★/$-$$

Longtime a local favorite, this family-run café serves up great burgers and sandwiches, but the real treat is the ice cream. Try one of the huge specialty ice-cream creations; our favorite is the Pikes Peak Surprise, a 14-inch-high concoction of ice cream and cake topped with whipped cream. Be sure to sample the hand-made chocolates. *122 N. Tejon St., Colorado Springs; (719) 633-5089.*

Souvenir Hunting

Garden of the Gods Trading Post

This adobe building was crafted in 1900 and has been a major retail force ever since. It is billed as Colorado's largest trading post, selling the usual T-shirts and trinkets as well as Native American wares. Be sure to keep a tight rein on the kids; they can get lost in the store's aisles for days. *Located by Garden of the Gods; (800) 874-4515; (719) 685-9045; www.co-trading-post.com*

Myers Gourmet Popcorn

This family-run company serves up popcorn in almost every flavor imaginable, including cherry crunch, mountain raspberry, and almond-pecan. Free samples are available (and addictive). *Pikes Peak Hwy. and Hwy. 24, Cascade; (800) 684-1155; (719) 684-9174; http://members.aol.com/ptqpop*

Patsy's Candies

This shop is famous for its chocolates and saltwater taffy. *1540 S. 21st St., Colorado Springs; (719) 633-7215; www.patsyscandies.com*

Rocky Mountain Chocolates

Chocolate fudge in traditional flavors, including pecan and walnut, are here to tempt your sweet tooth. *2431 W. Colorado Ave., Colorado Springs; (719) 635-4131.*

There is so much for families to do in southwest Colorado that you'll want to schedule some take-a-breather time, too.

Durango and the San Juan Mountains

I F YOU ARE LOOKING for a place that feels remote, but where there still is plenty to do, consider coming to Durango and southwest Colorado, home to Mesa Verde and the hip ski town of Telluride. Nestled in the rugged San Juan range of the Rockies, Durango is a laid-back ranching and rail-roading town where getting dressed up means pressing your blue jeans. The city's promoters like to call Durango "the official speed bump of the rat race" and maybe your family will agree after enjoying a breakfast trail ride around Lake Vallecito or watching the sunset turn the rocky peaks of the San Juan Mountains pink, purple, and blue.

Getting here is the hard part. Durango is located about seven hours from Denver, eight from Salt Lake City, and nine hours from

THE FamilyFun LIST
MUST-SEE · MUST-SEE

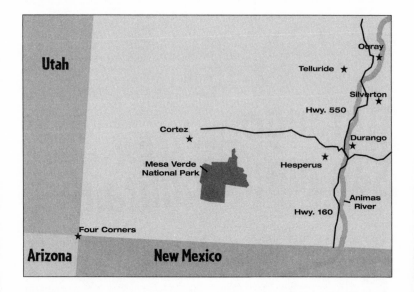

Phoenix. Once you arrive, it's time to let everyone recuperate from the long journey. Start off with a soak in one of the area's hot springs. In Ouray, located north of Silverton, you and your kids can frolic year-round at the Ouray Hot Springs pool. Bring some cash to rent floats and chow down on corn dogs while enjoying the view.

Sit back and enjoy the canyon views of the Animas River as you ride the Durango and Silverton Narrow Gauge Railroad, one of the most popular train excursions in the world. Be sure to stop by the coffee shop in the station, where your child can chat official railroad business with the line's conductors and engineers. And Mesa Verde is a must-see despite the devastating damage done by fires in the summer of 2000 (for more, see page 370).

Like most of Colorado, the Durango area is an outdoor lover's mecca. Your family can take on the moderate white-water rapids of the lower Animas River, ski on the peaks of Telluride, or hike a trail in San Juan National Forest. But don't worry if that's not your thing; there is plenty to do indoors, too. Be sure to visit the Durango Children's Museum, which has interactive arts-and-crafts projects and tackles natural-science topics like how trees grow. The cost is cheap, a mere $4, and grandparents get in free.

It's easy to have a great family vacation in Durango, but we'll make it even easier with tips on kid-friendly hiking trails, accommodations—and restaurants that hand out cookies with kids' meals.

CULTURAL ADVENTURES

Anasazi Heritage Center ★★★/$

Unlike most historical museums that have "look but don't touch" rules, this center actually encourages youngsters to handle stuff in its innovative "touch me" drawers. Kids can use a floor loom and grind corn (which is hard work). They can also watch an informative film detailing Anasazi history and culture, which makes for a great prelude to Mesa Verde. The center contains one of the world's largest collections of Anasazi artifacts and is set in a hillside near the 12th-century Dominguez and Escalante ruins. The steep but paved trail up to the ruins features signs identifying native plants. Shaded picnic tables are also available. *Hwy. 184, ten miles north of Cortez; (970) 882-4811; www.co.blm.gov/ahc/hmepge.htm*

Animas Museum ★★/$

Housed in an old school, this small historical museum lets kids step back in time to a circa 1910 classroom. Upstairs is a decent collection of Native American artifacts and assorted relics from the city's past, including a 1940s-era firefighter's uniform. The best part is outside, where a replica of a small cabin from the 1870s shows kids just how rough

the pioneers had it. There's only one bed, a small table, and—guess what?—no video games. Adult admission is $2; kids 11 and under get in free. *Corner of 31st St. and W. 2nd Ave., Durango; (970) 259-2402; www.fronteir.net/~animasmuseum*

Durango Children's Museum ★★★★/$

Located upstairs from the Durango Arts Center, this small museum does more with its limited space than any other kids' museum we've ever seen. The intimate setting seems to make kids feel comfortable and even settles them down a bit. There's a small table where they can work on arts-and-crafts projects, including making necklaces, printing with rubber stamps, and painting on an easel. Next door, youngsters will find a bed filled with storybooks and a television with videos. The books, videos, and other activities are all tied to a certain theme, which rotates during the year. During our visit, the theme was trees, and our small band made leaf stamps and read books about the life of trees. In another room, there was a tree house and a game kids could play that tested their knowledge of trees. The museum also had a scavenger-hunt-inspired quiz that forced kids to read the displays in order to fill out their work sheets; there's a prize upon completion. One museum staff member spent 20 minutes counting tree rings with a 7-year-old visitor. Open

Wednesdays through Saturdays from 9 A.M. to 6 P.M., Sundays from 10 A.M. to 2 P.M. *802 E. 2nd Ave., Durango; (970) 259-9234*; www.childsmus eum.org

JUST FOR FUN

Animas River
FamilyFun ★★★/$$$-$$$$
Mild to Wild Rafting offers a two-hour river trip that goes through Class II and III rapids, which are suitable for kids ages 4 and up. Longer trips are offered. *53 Rio Vista Circle, Durango; (800) 567-6745; (970) 247-4789*; www.mild2wildrafting.com

Bar D Chuckwagon Suppers ★★★/$$$
With singing cowboys, a miniature-train ride, and a chocolate factory, this place has all three major kid magnets and more. Come around 6 P.M. and make a night of it at this cowboy theme park complete with a Western-themed variety show and dinner—barbecued beef or chicken and applesauce cake. (Sorry, no hot dogs or other kid fare is available.) Dinner is at 7:30 P.M. sharp, but before the show, you can amble the grounds, check out the train ride that chugs around a small track, and take a tour of the chocolate factory. There's also a blacksmith shop, as well as shops selling T-shirts, singing-cowboy compact discs, and other souvenirs. *8080 County Rd. 250 (north of Durango); (888) 800-5753; (970) 247-5753*; www.bardchuckwagon.com

Durango Ski Mountain Resort ★★★/$$-$$$$
This resort, formerly known as Purgatory, offers ski programs for youngsters ages 11 and under. In the

RIDING THE RAILS

A hundred years ago, the coal-fired, steam-operated Durango and Silverton narrow-gauge railroad hauled "silver by the ton," hence the name Silverton. Now the trains haul passengers by the thousands. The route takes you through breathtaking vistas—you'll see waterfalls, fields of wildflowers, and the occasional deer, elk, or mountain goat. If the weather is good, you can enjoy the open gondola cars, but be sure to pack sunglasses or other protective eyewear to shield you from the engine's cinders. To be safe, choose the coach cars, where you have the option of opening and closing the windows, a handy feature if your kids want to stick their heads or hands out too much. You should also carry a light coat, because temperatures in Silverton's higher elevations (up to 9,318 feet above sea level) can be quite chilly even in summer. Each train has a summer, the resort's ski lifts are used for scenic rides to the mountaintop, where you can go mountain biking (older kids only) or take a trip down the Alpine Slide, a concrete sled run. Kids also enjoy Adventure Park, with its miners' cabin and maze. Summer activities include horseback rides, miniature golf, trout fishing, volleyball, and horseshoes. There is also a music festival, which brings in famous classical musicians and orchestras, a definite plus for Mom, Dad, and possibly older kids who have a love of music. The resort's extensive ski program includes child care for kids ages 2 to 12 and ski lessons for those ages 3 and older. While there are some easy runs here, the area is famous for its steep runs, best left to expert skiers. *20 miles north of Durango on Hwy. 550; (970) 247-9000;* www.durangomountainresort.com

 **Four Corners**
★★★/Free

This is the only place in the United States where four states come together—a major photo opportunity if nothing else. Youngsters (Moms and Dads, too) can stand on the small point where Colorado, Utah, Arizona, and New Mexico touch; the optimal pose is standing on one leg with the other leg lifted up behind and arms out like a ballerina. There are rows of booths where vendors sell Native American wares, including jewelry and sand paintings, and often kids can watch crafts demonstrations. You'll also find typical roadside-stand fare like hot dogs and potato chips as well as T-shirts and postcards for sale. Open year-round from 7 A.M. to 8 P.M. in summer; slightly shorter hours in winter. *Located off U.S. 160, 40 miles southwest of Cortez.*

snack bar onboard that sells popcorn, soda, and candy.

Trains depart daily, with as many as four at a time operating daily during peak tourist seasons. You have many options when booking a trip, but we suggest getting a one-way ticket: it's a three-and-a-half-hour ride, long enough to get the experience of rocking to the rhythm of the rails, but not so long that everyone falls asleep or gets hopelessly bored.

Catch the train in Durango in the morning and head up to Silverton through the gorgeous Animas River Canyon. You'll arrive in time for lunch. The **Pickle Barrel** (page 374) offers great burgers and sandwiches, and (usually) there is little or no wait for a table. Afterward you can take a bus back, or have one parent opt out of the train trip and drive on up to Silverton to meet the family there. The latter option gives you more freedom either to travel on to Ouray or head back to Durango.

Honeyville ★★★/Free

If you're ready to have that talk about the birds and the bees—well, the bees, anyway—head to this working bee farm and honey factory. Kids love looking into the glassed beehive and trying to spot the queen. They can also look inside the honey-bottling operation and get a free sample. It's a sweet way to spend a half hour. *Located 10 miles north of Durango on Hwy. 550; (800) 676-7690; (970) 247-1474;* www.honeyvillecolorado.com

Lake Vallecito
FamilyFun ★★★★/Free

Twenty-five miles northeast of Durango, Lake Vallecito is a tranquil spot with ample hiking, horseback riding, and camping opportunities. Deer are plentiful, so walk (and drive) carefully. You can also rent a pontoon boat at one of the marinas, but be sure to check the lake levels, which can be very low in the summer. The San Juan National Forest (use the entrance at the end of Highway 501) has great camping spots by the Pine River, and there's a hiking trail that heads into the Wavasupi Wilderness. The Pine River is a great spot for relaxing after a hike. Be on the lookout for deer and brown bears, which can come into the campground area in search of food during long summer dry spells. *From Durango, take County Road 240 east to County Road 501 north;* www.coloradovacation.com/vallecto

Mesa Verde National Park
FamilyFun ★★★★/$$

One of the most magical areas in the Southwest, this park is home to the world's largest and best preserved cliff dwellings, once home to the ancient Anasazi. The park suffered devastating fires in the summer of 2000, but the major dwellings and the park's main structures were unscathed. While the fires burnt much of the forests and brush, rangers say the cycle of life will start anew and visitors can enjoy the rebirth of nature. (The scarred areas can prompt a discussion of how

---

DAY TRIP
Anasazi Site-seeing

7 A.M. Breakfast at M&M Family Restaurant and Truckstop *(7006 U.S. 160 South; 970/ 565-3414)*.

8 A.M. Mesa Verde National Park (this page).

Noon Lunch at The Pickle Barrel (see page 374).

1 P.M. Explore the Anasazi Heritage Center (see page 367).

lightning-ignited fires are part of nature's cycle and the ways the National Park Service deals with them.) As you enter the park, stop at the Far View visitors' center to pick up your tickets to the ruins; you can also get a map to guide your explorations. From the visitors' center, you can board a tram (operated in the summer, it runs every half hour from the Wetherhill parking lot) that takes you on a four-mile loop to view the ruins from a distance.

If you want an up-close look, take Ruins Road to the park's museum, where displays detailing Anasazi culture prepare school-age kids for what they are about to experience. Cliff Palace, the world's largest cliff dwelling, is reached by taking a somewhat strenuous half-mile hike that is easy enough for most families, but be sure everyone wears comfortable, closed-toe shoes. Reaching Balcony House is more difficult and requires climbing a 20-foot ladder and crawling through a tunnel to get inside.

If you are traveling with preschoolers or are on a tight schedule, take the short trail from the museum at Chapin Mesa Cliff Dwellings and the park headquarters to Spruce Tree House in the canyon below. You can enter an excavated kiva and imagine the religious ceremonies once held here. Younger kids are content to simply play house for the better part of an hour. If you are coming in the summer, be aware that lots of others are too, so get there as soon as the

park opens (at 8 A.M.) to beat the heat and the crowds. *The park is located about 10 miles outside Cortez on Hwy. 160; (970) 529-4461;* www. nops.gov/meve

The Million Dollar Highway
★★★/Free
This is the nickname for Highway 550 between Silverton and Ouray. We're not sure how it got its name (some say it's because the ore buried underneath is worth millions), but we do know it's not for the faint of heart. The speed limit slows to 10 miles per hour in winding, crooked corners that snake around the massive mountains. There are few, if any, guardrails, making it a treacherous road even under ideal driving conditions. Be sure to give Dramamine to anyone susceptible to car sickness before attempting this drive. The incredible views of rocky mountaintops and ponderosa pines will make you glad you made the trip— you just may not want to do it again anytime soon.

Ouray Hot Springs
FamilyFun ★★★★/$-$$
The view from these mineral waters is one of the best in the state, and the water's warmth (93 to 104 degrees) makes it comfortable year-round. Kids can swim or rent floats shaped like kayaks and paddle around the pool area. Be advised that although there are plenty of lifeguards at the pool, there are strict

Dogsledding

Forget skis or snowmobiles—the best way to see the San Juans in the snow is wrapped in a sleeping bag, behind some Siberian huskies. Instead of the roar of motors or the whoosh of skis, the mountain air is filled with the yipping and yapping of the dogs enjoying their romp. Durango Dog Ranch offers half-day and full-day trips, which include snacks and hot drinks. You also get hot dogs to feed to the dogs as a treat for their hard work.

Owners Gregg and Gretchen Dubit don't mind explaining the finer points of "mushing" to youngsters. If your children are good pupils, they may even get to take control of the sled for a while. Durango uses small, curved ash sleds with eight to ten dogs. Kids can snuggle in sleeping bags with faux fur wrapped around them, or stand on the sled like true mushers do.

Be ready for adventure. The Dubits say they never know what's going to happen on any given ride. Sometimes the sled turns over, heaving passengers into the snow. Most don't seem to mind as long as they can keep mushing. At press time, half-day trips cost $110 per person and full-day trips with lunch were $175 per person. Reservations are required. *2525 County Rd. 124, Hesperus; (970) 259-0694;* www.durangodogranch.com

requirements that any child younger than age 7 has to be "within reach" of a parent or other supervising adult; lifeguards are authorized to make unsupervised tots leave the water. Towels and lockers are available for rent, but during our visit we had a hard time getting any of the lockers to work, so we just stashed our stuff poolside. If your kids aren't into swimming in the springs, there's a nice playground in front of the entrance with slides, monkey bars, and forts. *1200 Main St., Ouray; (970) 325-4638.*

Telluride
FamilyFun ★★★/Free

This rugged mountain town has survived mining booms and busts, mud slides, avalanches, and fires without too much complaining, earning its nickname "The town without a belly ache." It remains to be seen whether Telluride can survive its status as one of the world's hippest ski resorts. In recent years megastars from Oprah Winfrey to Tom Cruise have moved in and real-estate prices have skyrocketed, forcing out longtime locals. Restaurants and retail stores have gone upscale too, making it more challenging for families in search of good deals. You may pay a premium to spend time here, but it's worth it given the spectacular setting of the town—surrounded by 14,000-foot peaks—and the world-class skiing offered here. The mountains can make anyone accustomed to more open spaces (like Texans) feel a bit claustrophobic.

In the winter (December 1 through early March), the town has a ski rink in Town Park; in the summer, there's an annual bluegrass festival, held the third week in June, which includes a creative program for kids where they can learn to pick the banjo and write songs. Telluride Academy—a unique school for those ages 4 to 18—offers a wide range of summer programs and camps from four days to four weeks long. Activities include drama (as a member of the Mudd Butt Mystery Theater), photography, backpacking, kayaking, llama trekking, robotics, and mountaineering. *725 W. Colorado Ave., Telluride; (970) 728-5311;* www.tellurideacademy.com

Trimble Hot Springs ★★/$$

Open year-round, this Olympic-size pool warmed by hot springs has water temperatures of 83 degrees, while smaller pools closer to the springs are between 100 and 110 degrees. The springs contain more than 15 minerals, including zinc, iron, calcium, and boron. At press time, admission for adults was $8.50; 12 and under, $6. The landscaped grounds also have a snack bar. *The springs are located six miles north of Durango off Hwy. 550 at 6475 County Rd. 203, Durango; (970) 247-0111;* www.trimblehotsprings.com

BUNKING DOWN

Far View Lodge ★★/$$

This place has the old "location, location, location" thing going for it: It offers the only accommodations inside Mesa Verde. The rooms are pretty basic (but that means your kids can't break much). *Mesa Verde is located on Highway 160 between Durango and Cortez; (800) 449-2288; (970) 529-4421;* www.visitmesaverde.com

Hampton Inn ★★★/$$

Yes, it has a pool (which is indoors). Families also appreciate the large suites, which come with pull-out sofa, microwave, and refrigerator. Kids stay free and breakfast is included. This location adds extra touches such as fresh-baked chocolate-chip and oatmeal-raisin cookies at night. *3777 Main Ave., Durango; (800) 247-6885; (970) 247-2600;* www.hamptoninn.com

Wilderness Trails Dude Ranch ★★★★/$$$-$$$$

Located on the edge of the Piedra Wilderness, this place offers comfortable two- and three-bedroom cabins with porches. The ranch raises its own horses and offers a first-rate equestrian program. Special activities are offered for kids and teens. Swim in the pool, soak in the hot tub, catch a trout, hike forest trails, take a 4x4 trip, water-ski,

FamilyFun TIP

Keep a Trip Journal

On a kayak trip to a new spot, pretend that your family is recording a great expedition, in the spirit of Lewis and Clark, and imagine that you've discovered the place. Have people take turns recording their feelings, plus the weather and wildlife sightings.

go rafting, ride the Durango and Silverton Narrow Gauge Railroad, or visit Mesa Verde National Park. When the stars come out, there may be a country-and-western dance, campfire, hayride, or show. *1766 County Rd. 302, Durango; (970) 247-0722; www.wildernesstrails.com/*

GOOD EATS

Burger King ★/$

We've included this fast-food restaurant not because they were offering Pokémon cards during our visit, but because they had a picnic table that overlooks the Animas River. It's not often you can get a view with your fries. *1415 Main Ave., Durango; (970) 247-9095; www.burgerking.com*

Christina's Grill ★★/$$-$$$

This glass-topped-table spot may not look that child-friendly at first, but ask and they'll bring your kids plenty of crayons and even coloring books. The kids' menu has the stan-

dards such as hamburgers (be aware—they are the same size as the adult burgers) and chicken fingers; there's also a large salad bar, which features fresh fruits and soups. This is also a great breakfast stop to fuel up before a day of hiking or biking. *3416 N. Main Ave., Durango; (970) 382-3844.*

Gazpacho
★★★/$$-$$$

This is the place for traditional New Mexican fare—kids can chomp on chips while they wait for the meal; meanwhile, Mom and Dad can enjoy top-notch margaritas. The kids' menu includes tacos and enchiladas, plus quesadillas, Mexico's version of grilled cheese sandwiches. *431 E. 2nd Ave., Durango; (970) 259-9494.*

The Pickle Barrel
★★/$$

A pleasant option if you've taken the train up to Silverton and are looking for lunch (for more about the train, see "Riding the Rails" on page 368). The burgers are first-rate, and the children's menu includes hot dogs, corn dogs, peanut-butter-and-jelly sandwiches, and grilled cheese with a choice of chips or fries. *1304 Greene St., Silverton; (970) 387-5713.*

Steamworks Brewing Company
★★★/$-$$$

Okay, so the kids won't be able to taste the great microbrews made here—Rockhopper Ale and Steam Engine Steam beer—but they'll like the lemonade fine, and the kids' menu includes pizza and corn dogs that are so good adults will want to eat them, too. It's located right across the street from the Durango Children's Museum, making it a nice stop for lunch after the museum. *801 E. 2nd Ave., Durango; (970) 259-9200;* www.steamworksbrew ing.com

Souvenir Hunting

Gardenswartz
This sporting-goods store carries plenty of kids' gear, including pint-size fishing poles, hiking boots, and Teva sandals. Youngsters don't seem

to mind trying on shoes as long as they can play with the mounted bass that sings "Please Release Me." *780 Main Ave., Durango; (970) 247-2660.*

Ouray Toys
Filled with toys that are educational and just plain fun—including dolls, games, puzzles, and arts-and-crafts kits—this is a great stop if you need to grab a few new diversions for the drive to Durango or Montrose. *242 7th Ave., Ouray; (970) 325-4000;* www.ouraytoys.com

Out of the Blue
Kids are greeted by a huge stuffed bear dubbed Grand Paw Grizzly at this T-shirt and toy shop that's Beanie Baby Central. *645 Main Ave., Durango; (970) 247-0185.*

Digging the Scene
AT THE CROW COUNTY ARCHAEOLOGICAL CENTER
Families with children over 10 looking for a hands-on Mesa Verde experience may consider taking the Archaeology Day Tour program offered at this non-profit center. Your family can sign up for an all-day workshop where you will learn about the ancient Anasazi and actually help unearth artifacts on an archaeological dig. You'll spend half the day at an active excavation, walking around the site and talking with archaeologists. Lunch is then served back at the center. In the afternoon, you'll be taught how to think like an archaeologist (after all, maybe years from now, your home will be excavated; what will they think of the Coke cans your dog buried in the backyard?) and you can tour the lab to see what else has been uncovered here. **NOTE:** The program requires advance registration. The center also offers weeklong programs for families with teens and leads other family adventures in the region. *Crow Canyon is located four miles northwest of Cortez off Hwy. 666; (970) 565-8975;* www.crowcanyon.org

Index

Also from FamilyFun

FAMILYFUN MAGAZINE: a creative guide to all the great things families can do together. Call 800-289-4849 for a subscription.

FAMILYFUN.COM: visit us at www.familyfun.com and search our extensive archives for games, crafts, recipes, and holiday projects.

FAMILYFUN COOKBOOK: a collection of more than 250 irresistible recipes for you and your kids, from healthy snacks to birthday cakes to dinners everyone in the family can enjoy (Disney Editions, 256 pages; $24.95).

FAMILYFUN CRAFTS: a step-by-step guide to more than 500 of the best crafts and activities to do with your kids (Disney Editions, 256 pages; $24.95).

FAMILYFUN PARTIES: a complete party planner featuring 100 celebrations for birthdays, holidays, and every day (Disney Editions, 224 pages; $24.95).

FAMILYFUN COOKIES FOR CHRISTMAS: a batch of 50 recipes for creative holiday treats (Disney Editions, 64 pages; $9.95).

FAMILYFUN TRICKS AND TREATS: a collection of wickedly easy crafts, costumes, party plans, and recipes for Halloween (Disney Editions, 98 pages; $14.95).

FAMILYFUN BOREDOM BUSTERS: a collection of 365 activities, from instant fun and after-school crafts to kitchen projects and learning games (Disney Editions, 224 pages; $24.95).

FAMILYFUN HOMEMADE HOLIDAYS: A collection of 150 holiday activities, from festive decorations and family traditions to holiday recipes and gifts kids can make. (Disney Editions, 96 pages; $14.95).